JANE ADDAMS

Photograph by Campbell

JANE ADDAMS AT SEVENTY

JANE ADDAMS
A BIOGRAPHY

By

JAMES WEBER LINN

Introduction by
Anne Firor Scott

UNIVERSITY OF ILLINOIS PRESS
Urbana and Chicago

Publication of this work was supported by the
Illinois Center for the Book.

Library of Congress Cataloging-in-Publication Data
Linn, James Weber, 1876–1939.
Jane Adams : a biography / James Weber Linn ;
introduction by Anne Firor Scott.
    p.   cm.
ISBN 0-252-06904-8 (pbk.)
1. Addams, Jane, 1860–1935.
2. Women social workers—United States—Biography.
3. Women social reformers—United States—Biography.
4. Hull House (Chicago, Ill.)—History. I. Title.
HV 28.A35 L5 2000
361.92—dc21
[B]
99-088394

P 5 4 3 2 1

To the memory of

MY MOTHER

MARY CATHERINE ADDAMS LINN

this book is dedicated

CONTENTS

Introduction by Anne Firor Scott   ix

PREFACE   XXV

CHAPTER

    I. JANE ADDAMS'S FATHER   1

    II. A "DIFFERENT" CHILD   22

    III. ROCKFORD COLLEGE   40

    IV. WHAT SHALL SHE DO?   65

    V. SHE FINDS A WAY   91

    VI. HULL HOUSE BEGINS   110

    VII. SIX WOMEN   129

    VIII. ETHICS IN POLITICS   151

    IX. WORK FOR CHILDREN   178

    X. GROWTH   190

    XI. WIDENING INFLUENCES   209

    XII. A DECADE OF WRITING   242

    XIII. SUFFRAGE AND PROGRESSIVISM . . .   262

    XIV. PACIFISM   284

    XV. "CONTINUOUS MEDIATION"   300

    XVI. STANDING ALONE   312

    XVII. THE CONGRESS OF WOMEN   335

    XVIII. POST-WAR REFLECTIONS   352

    XIX. THEY COME TO PRAISE   369

    XX. QUIET YEARS   395

    XXI. SHE GOES IN PEACE   410

    XXII. IN RETROSPECT   429

INDEX   441

ILLUSTRATIONS

Jane Addams at seventy . . . . *Frontispiece*

FACING PAGE

The Addams home at Cedarville, Illinois 16
The Addams mills at Cedarville, Illinois 16
Jane Addams at four 24
Jane Addams at six 24
John H. Addams 32
Jane Addams at sixteen 32
Jane Addams as an undergraduate at Rockford College,
   1880 48
Jane Addams in London, 1888 48
The original Charles Hull homestead 94
Hull House as it is to-day 94
Hull House founders: Ellen Gates Starr, Jane Addams,
   Julia Lathrop, Florence Kelley 116
Hull House friends: Dr. Alice Hamilton, Mary Rozet
   Smith, Mrs. Joseph T. Bowen, Jane Addams . . 148
Jane Addams with her little friends at Hull House . . 182
Jane Addams at fifty 238
Music Cottage at the Bowen "Country Club," Waukegan,
   Illinois 252
The dining-room at Hull House 252
Jane Addams in Honolulu 322
Jane Addams in the Philippines 322
Jane Addams at sixty 360
Reunion at Hull House 376
Jane Addams's summer home at Hadlyme, Connecticut 408
Jane Addams's summer home at Bar Harbor, Maine . . 408
The funeral service for Jane Addams in the court at Hull
   House 422

INTRODUCTION

Anne Firor Scott

J ANE ADDAMS died in 1935, but judging from the steady stream of interpretive and biographical books and essays, interest in her life remains high. In spite of all this work, the first and so-called authorized biography published in the year of her death is still an important resource. This engaging story offers scholars and general readers alike an intimate portrait because the author, Addams's nephew James Weber Linn, had known his aunt for more than sixty years. He recalled himself at age seven, "listening entranced while she presented never-varying repetitions of the tale of the Princess and the Frog. 'What thou hast promised thou must perform!'—the King's words to his daughter have echoed in his ears ever since" (69). Growing up, Linn spent a great deal of time at Hull House; he knew all Addams's intimate friends and co-workers as well as many of her more distant admirers and detractors. He was able to interview many of these friends and associates, including some Addams had known in childhood and several Rockford Female Seminary classmates.

If one could say nothing else about it, the book is beautifully written and an excellent beginning for readers who have just discovered Jane Addams. It is, of course, much more than that. Like any other primary source, however, this one is most valuable when used with care. Readers need to know Linn's qualifications for writing this biography and to understand his emotional relationship to his subject. It is useful as well to have some familiarity with subsequent scholarship, especially the careful study published by Allen F. Davis in 1973, and current opinions of Addams's work and personality.[1] For one thus prepared, whether scholar or interested layperson, the Linn volume provides a unique resource.

∽

James Weber Linn was the son of Jane Addams's much-loved older sister, Mary Addams Linn, who had married an impecunious minister and struggled to bring up her four surviving children. Mary Linn died young and Jane Addams became guardian of the three younger children.

Weber, as he was called, was seventeen and in no need of a guardian. He enrolled in the new University of Chicago, which kept him close to Hull House. In an autobiographical novel published when he was sixty he painted himself as a naive, inexperienced, and self-centered seventeen year old trying to cope with the (for him) sophisticated world of the university. Naive or not, he did well and graduated in 1897. After a brief stint as a newspaper reporter he returned to his alma mater, first for graduate study and then to begin what would be a long career of teaching English. At his death it was estimated that he had taught fifteen thousand students and could call five thousand of them by name.[2]

Linn was known to be an extremely demanding teacher who also had a reputation for keeping a class spellbound even in so technical a subject as composition. His interest in and concern for students was legendary, and anecdotes abounded about the lengths to which he would go to be helpful to them. A typical one had him roused from sleep at midnight by a student who had absentmindedly tossed beer bottles from his dorm window and was about to be expelled in consequence. Fulminating in colorful language, Linn nevertheless woke the sleeping president to plead on behalf of the student for a second chance.

He was not content, however, simply to be a highly regarded professor and author of textbooks, one of which sold two hundred thousand copies. He also wrote four novels, another biography, numerous essays for various journals, including the *University of Chicago Magazine,* and a famous column for the *Chicago Herald* (later renamed the *Chicago Herald-Examiner*) that eventually appeared in the *Chicago Times.* Perhaps inspired by Jane Addams's untiring work in the legislature, he ran for office after her death and was elected to the Illinois House of Representatives, where he served until his own untimely death. This biography and his life experience testify to Addams's profound influence upon his values. He translated her concern for all kinds of people into a willingness to be empathetic and helpful to all kinds of students. He adopted her political positions and thought she understood the basic issues of life as well as anyone had.

At first glance or if one believes Linn's opening sentence, this book would appear to be a straightforward narrative of Jane Addams's life. It is much more than that. Though he would not have used the term, Linn had a clear interpretive framework. He argues that as a very young person his aunt developed the basic philosophy she first publicly articulated in 1892 in "The Subjective Necessity for Social Settlements" and that it became the bedrock for her thought through the rest of her life. Addams believed that democracy required a social dimension and that people must learn to act collectively for the public good if they hope to survive as a society. She did not believe a society could function well when its resources were concentrated in the hands of a few. Beyond that she thought the test of any idea was the action it inspired. From this fundamental set of values all her work for what came to be called "progressivism" could be said to have stemmed.

The book begins with a description of Addams's upbringing. Linn's narrative makes the culture of her early life concrete with his vivid depiction of her father, John Addams, and his new wife, Sarah, pioneering in Illinois in 1844 and helping to build a new community. John Addams was a builder, not a speculator, but he was ambitious and very able. He became not only the town's leading citizen but also one of its most prosperous. Reading that Jane's mother died at forty-six after the birth of her ninth child and that only four of these children would grow to adulthood, today's readers can perhaps begin to understand one of the many ways in which life in the nineteenth century differs so profoundly from that in our own time.

Linn's description of Addams's experience at the Rockford Female Seminary reveals a good bit about the way women's higher education began and changed over time. He understood better than most Addams scholars that feminism could be part of such a determinedly evangelical environment. More perceptive than many of his male contemporaries and many later historians, he recognized the significance of the fact that two of her favorite teachers became active in the women's club movement.[3]

Linn's early chapters follow the general outline Addams

had laid down in *Twenty Years at Hull House,* while expanding some things that are mentioned there only in passing and correcting a few with gentle humor. He is not sure, for example, that John Addams was always, especially in his early years, the paragon of virtue and lofty rectitude that his daughter described or even that he was—as she had so often asserted—the chief influence on her life. Although he corrected some of his aunt's romantic versions of events, he adds a few romantic notions of his own.

He paints a vivid picture of Chicago as it was when Hull House began—a city with a majority of foreign-born inhabitants but in which power was concentrated in the hands of a native-born minority. It was that minority, he wrote, "who had 'made' Chicago, and they believed it to be their own" (100). His close association with Hull House had taught him a great deal about the majority, but that did not mean he could not appreciate the perspective of the minority. He was a Chicago patriot curious about every aspect of the city. This prepared him to understand and situate Jane Addams's long career in the context of the politics, the economics, and the public opinion of her time.

When Linn agreed to write her biography Jane Addams turned over to him a vast accumulation of papers and documents. From them he learned a great deal, but—particularly after her death when he could no longer ask questions—he also discovered some notable gaps. For one thing, though there were plenty of letters written to her, there were few copies of her own correspondence. Although he did not undertake the formidable task of collecting her letters from her numerous correspondents, he did make other significant efforts, particularly in consulting people who had known Addams in various contexts.[4] He had excellent advice from perceptive observers, especially Ellen Starr, Alice Hamilton, and Catherine Waugh McCulloch, all of whom had been very close to Jane Addams at different stages of her life. He implored Dorothy Detzer to take time from her busy life to tell him her view of his aunt's role in the peace movement. He persuaded her to send him papers relating to that movement, especially those of the Women's International League for Peace and Freedom, which Addams had helped to found. He wrote Nicholas Kelley, whom he had known at Hull House, for information about his mother, Florence Kelley, a key figure in the close-knit group of Hull House women. He consulted friends from Cedarville and Freeport who remembered Jane Addams from her early youth. He sought records from Rockford Female Seminary and dug out copies of the *Seminary Magazine* for which she had written as a student. And he relied heavily on his own memory of events and of many, many conversations with his aunt.

Though a scholar in his own field, Linn was not a trained historian. While he diligently collected indispensable data, to the dismay of later historians he made no effort to document his findings or to provide a record that would permit later scholars to retrace his research. There is no reason to doubt the care with which he reported what he learned from his informants and from written records, but he apparently relied too much on memory for dates and other details.

Before Jane Addams died in May 1935 she had read and commented on the first eight chapters of Linn's manuscript and discussed his plans for the next three. We do not know what changes she suggested, although Linn recorded that she thought perhaps the pages exhibited a bit too much of the admiring nephew. She did let certain things stand that give some insight into her self-image, but like her nephew, she was too close to the subject to be objective. "I realize now," he wrote in the summer after her death, "that as we talked things over, neither she nor I saw her in perspective. Neither of us had any just conception of the view the world seems to have had of her importance to it" (xxvi).

When they talked he had not yet witnessed the extraordinary response to her death, which may have come as a surprise to a person for whom she had been, above all, "Aunt Jane." By the time he wrote the preface to the book he had, perhaps, a better grasp of his shortcomings as a biographer: "It is to be hoped that some day some scholar, completely acquainted with the history of the development of sociology and of American civilization in the last half-century, will offer a picture of it as illuminated by her life, for I think she threw more light into its dark places than any one else" (xxv).

Even if he could not fully recognize her role in history he was well aware of the importance of his biography. While it was in progress he commented to Dorothy Detzer, "You see, people like Alice Hamilton and Mrs. Bowen and Mrs. Blaine are saying to me fiercely, 'You must do your aunt justice in your book,' and how can I do her justice? I don't know as much, think as straight, or feel as deeply as she did. So naturally I am worried. She would forgive a poor life of her, think nothing of it, but they won't."[5]

A great deal of what Linn wrote reflected his firsthand observation and interpretation of events. Much of what he records, things he witnessed, things she told him, the judgments of many of her contemporaries can be found in no other source. Because he knew and admired most of Addams's friends, he was able to elicit private information, such as Ellen Starr's worry that his aunt would have objected to the mass Starr planned for her memorial service. He responded that he might not have fully understood his aunt, but was certain she would be pleased indeed to have such a mass said for her.[6]

Linn is also able to give insight into one aspect of Addams that has not always struck other biographers: her sense of humor. Attentive readers of her papers will remember many clever quips, such as her response when the Daughters of the American Revolution expelled her during the hysteria of World War I. "I thought I was a member for life," she said, "but I discovered it was only for good behavior."[7]

Unlike later scholars, Linn did not have to imagine Jane Addams's life or the context in which she lived it since he had shared so much of it. A close reading of this volume must thus call into question the conventional wisdom about her that has been created by later researchers. Scholars who have not succeeded in fully imagining the world in which she lived and instead reflect their own twentieth-century values often seek complex psychological explanations for behavior and ideas they do not understand. In his otherwise excellent scholarly biography, Allen F. Davis suggests that the motivating force of Addams's adult life was a need for approval and that this drove her to manipulate people and events to create her saintly image. This view is adopted and carried even further by Gioia Diliberto in her popular biography.[8]

Linn's book offers overwhelming contrary evidence. He

shows that from 1892 on, though she was feared and even hated by many Chicago businessmen, who saw her as a dangerous radical, she did not swerve from her own notion of what was right. Invited to be one of only three speakers at the funeral of another "dangerous radical"—Governor John Peter Altgeld—she was told that if she accepted the invitation, support for Hull House would evaporate. She spoke nevertheless. In the furor that followed McKinley's assassination an innocent man was thrown into prison as a suspected anarchist. Addams first went to see the mayor on the man's behalf and then visited him in prison to offer reassurance and make sure that he had a lawyer. For this she was roundly criticized. It would not be the last time popular opinion was stirred up against her. The most violent opposition came during World War I when she took an unswerving stand for peace in the midst of war. Though suddenly among the most unpopular people in the country, she held fast. Linn notes that this position not only subjected her to harsh criticism, some of it from old friends, but also dramatically reduced the lecture fees that had been her principal source of income for years. That, too, did not deter her.

In 1953 Alice Hamilton, the longtime friend and companion with whom Addams had toured the European capitals in 1915 in an attempt to persuade the warring powers to go to the conference table, summed up Addams's personality as well as it has ever been done:

She had two conflicting traits which sometimes brought her great unhappiness: she was very dependent on a sense of warm comradeship and harmony with the mass of her fellow men, but at the same time her clear sighted integrity made it impossible for her to keep in step with the crowd in many a crisis. Most reformers I have known have enjoyed, more or less, the sense of being in advance of their times, of belonging to a persecuted minority. That was never true of Jane Addams. The famous Pullman strike, the rise of the radical Industrial Workers of the World, the war fever of 1914–1918, the suddenly panicky persecution of suspected disloyalty after the war, to mention only a few instances, were for her most painful experiences because then she was forced by conviction to work against the stream, to separate herself from the great mass of her fellow countrymen. Nor did she ever fall into the mire of self-pity or take refuge in the comfort of self righteousness. She simply suffered from the spiritual loneliness which her far sighted vision imposed on her.[9]

This statement, made nearly twenty years after Addams's death by a woman who knew her well and who was known for her plain speaking, strikes me as more persuasive than the inferences of scholars based on their reading of the record. Hamilton's words support Linn's view and are confirmed by those of Ellen Gates Starr, another intimate, who said at Addams's memorial service, "All, even the great, naturally enjoy the sunshine of approbation and work more easily in its congenial warmth. Jane Addams knew it well and parted with it under no misconceptions, and what was more remarkable, no bitterness. She could not foresee that it would return."[10] The overwhelming public reaction to her death, the testimony of her closest associates—strong-minded women in their own right—and much else in the record undermines the view of her as manipulative and completely dependent on approval.

Less damaging but still inaccurate is Diliberto's assertion, without offering any evidence, that the poor health Addams experienced in the 1920s stemmed from the castigation of her peace work in the previous decade.[11] By the 1920s, however, she was already in her sixties and throughout her life had never been without some physical ailments. During this period she had her first brush with the cancer that ultimately took her life.

Some biographers doubt that Jane Addams was capable of close emotional ties beyond her family. Linn, as if to refute this view, supplies plenty of evidence to the contrary though, alas, without adequate citation. This quotation from a Greek newspaper in Chicago is a good example: "Her death had stirred in us memories that go back . . . to those days when in the buoyancy of our youth we would walk into Hull House as though we walked into our own house. . . . There sound in our ears the soft words and sentences of the women of the House, the only soft and kind words we immigrant boys heard in those days. . . . For we of foreign birth have lost our best friend and the only one who understood us" (111). It is impossible to believe that a person who could inspire such a tribute or whose seminary classmates would endow a professorship in her name fifty years later was incapable of far-reaching emotional ties.

The warmest and most visible of such ties was Addams's long friendship with Mary Rozet Smith. Linn describes Mary Smith when she first came to Hull House to volunteer:

She was barely twenty; tall, shy, fair, and eager. From that day until she died, forty-three years later, the interests of the House remained the center of her own interests, and the friendship of Mary Smith soon became and always remained the highest and clearest note in the music that was Jane Addams's personal life. . . . No little child and no timidest of aliens or gawkiest of adolescents, ever knew Mary Smith without falling in love with her. It was not only that she delighted in children, but that she treated them, even babies, with manners and respect. They found her spirit—so did their elders for that matter—a Cave of Adullam, in which however oppressed they might have been by misunderstanding, they could rest in peace. . . . Her talk was a bubbling fount of amusement. . . . No better story-teller every delighted her friends, no more coöperative listener ever carried a conversation. (147–50)

Present-day writers, for whom the idea of same-sex erotic relationships is commonplace, speculate about the nature of that friendship. Linn could not have foreseen such questions. When Alice Hamilton was in her nineties Davis asked her about lesbianism at Hull House. Her answer was that if there had been an erotic component in some relationships it was unconscious and therefore unimportant. "Then," Davis writes, "she added with a smile that the very fact that I would bring up the subject was an indication of the separation between my generation and hers."[12]

Then there is the question of Jane Addams as a thinker. Davis asserted, and others have echoed him, that she was not an "original thinker." Opinions on the meaning of that phrase may vary, but consider the facts. Who else in her time had already grasped the coming interdependence of the whole of human society? Who else was writing, as she did in 1929:

Whether we like it or not, our own experiences are more and more influenced by the experiences of widely scattered people; the modern world is developing an almost mystic sense of the continuity and interdependence of mankind.

We are obtaining a new sense of unexpected but yet inevitable action and reaction between ourselves and all the others who happen to be living upon the planet at the same moment. It lies with us who are here now to make this consciousness—as yet so fleeting and uncertain—the unique contribution of our time to that small handful of incentives which really motivates human conduct.[13]

The question is still before us. Who else in her generation had realized that only collective action could address the problems of the twentieth century? Probably observers were misled about her originality because she presented her ideas so skillfully. She used language that anyone could understand and say, "Oh, yes I already knew that," when in fact her formulations were far ahead of her time.

∽

Linn's biography was published in the fall of 1935 and was widely reviewed in the United States and in Europe.[14] The reviews, whether perceptive or not, were generally favorable, but perhaps the most telling of them came from Carrie Chapman Catt, a person not given to hyperbole who had known Jane Addams for many years. Catt had differed with Addams during World War I but had also worked closely with her in the peace movement in the 1920s:

> History, certainly, will grant her a seat among the immortals.
> Jane Addams gave her long life for others, but men and women have done that in many times and places. At her death, Governor Horner, of Illinois, said: "Her life was dedicated to a selfless service which has few parallels." True, but even this did not inspire so many people to call her greatest. Her immortality rests upon the more unusual ground that she was an intellectual among the best educated, *who had more often thought through the problems of life than had they.* Among the poor and lowly, and especially those of foreign birth, she was a sincere democrat, inspiring them with her faith in equal rights for all. Said a Greek at the time of her death: "Her no just one people; her no just one religion. Her all peoples; all religion." No one has pronounced a more perfect interpretation of her character and life.[15]

Catt went on to say that the greatest contribution any man or woman could make to humanity was a new idea and that Jane Addams had contributed several. She also asserted, "Every reform or progressive law passed by the Illinois legislature was helped along the way by the sponsorship of Miss Addams and often by much tedious work on its behalf. Again, the gains met hostility and left behind much resentment." She wrote, too, about the peace movement and concluded that Jane Addams left her mark upon her city, her state, her nation, and the world: "Her spirit is still marching on."[16]

The spirit Catt described was never more needed than it is today. If Linn's biography can arouse even a little of the idealism that motivated Addams and her contemporaries to work so hard to remake democracy, the book will deserve this reprinting.

NOTES

1. Allen F. Davis, *American Heroine: The Life and Legend of Jane Addams* (New York: Oxford, 1973).

2. Frank P. Breckinridge, "James Weber Linn: An Appreciation by an 'Ole Grad,'" *University of Chicago Magazine*, Oct. 1939, 8.

3. The Jane Addams clipping file for 1896 (Jane Addams Papers, Swarthmore College Peace Collection, Swarthmore College Library, Swarthmore, Pa.) contains a laudatory article about her role in the convention of the General Federation of Women's Clubs and how the women's club movement had played a role in bringing out the talents of women such as Addams.

4. Linn wrote to Emily Balch, "I did not seek to secure by advertisement or in any other way her own letters to anybody; all I have in the collection are those she wrote many years ago to Mary Smith. . . . Probably in many private files (such as yours) there must be a great deal of material that is of tremendous importance that I have not seen. For one thing, there must be a record of her work with negroes, in and

out of the Urban League. I have found none. Her work as a suffrage advocate I have no record of at all. Of her lectures all over the country on behalf of the Hoover food-conservation work in 1918, there is no record in my files" (Apr. 4, 1947, Jane Addams Papers, Swarthmore College Peace Collection). The letters would remain uncollected until the 1960s when Mary Lynn McCree Bryan undertook the vast Jane Addams Papers Project, which now includes microfilms of all the extant papers, a guide to the microfilm, and a letterpress volume of selected letters.

5. James Weber Linn to Dorothy Detzer, June 11, 1935, Dorothy Detzer Papers, Swarthmore College Peace Collection.

6. James Weber Linn to Ellen Gates Starr, May 30, 1935, Sophia Smith Collection, Smith College, Northampton, Mass.

7. Jane Addams, *The Second Twenty Years at Hull House* (New York: Macmillan, 1930), 180. For other examples of her gentle humor, see pages 349, 378, and 412 of Linn's biography.

8. Davis, *American Heroine*, 85, 91, 94, 104–5, 114, 125, 148, 159, 182, 193, 198, 209–11; Gioia Diliberto, *Useful Woman: The Early Years of Jane Addams* (New York: Scribner, 1999).

9. Alice Hamilton, "Jane Addams of Hull House," *Social Service: A Quarterly Survey* (June–Aug. 1953): 15.

10. Ellen Gates Starr, tribute prepared for the memorial service organized by the National Federation of Settlements, June 1935, Sophia Smith Collection.

11. Diliberto, *Useful Woman*, 262.

12. Davis, *American Heroine*, 306n.45.

13. Jane Addams, "After Sixty-Five," *Survey* 62 (June 1, 1929): 303.

14. Among the reviews are those in the *Chicago Daily Tribune*, Sept. 28, 1935, 16; *Christian Century*, Nov. 6, 1935; *New Statesman and Nation*, Dec. 14, 1935; *New York Times*, Dec. 1, 1935, 16; *Saturday Review of Literature*, Dec. 21, 1935; and *Times Literary Supplement*, Jan. 4, 1936, 3.

15. Carrie Chapman Catt, "A Great American: Jane Addams by James Weber Linn, D. Appleton-Century Co.," *Yale Review* 25.2 (Winter 1936): 401–2, emphasis added.

16. Ibid., 403.

PREFACE

THIS book is intended to be not so much an interpretation of Jane Addams as the story of her life. She has interpreted herself not only throughout her books but particularly in a single sentence written only a few years ago, in 1929: "The modern world is developing an almost mystic sense of the continuity and interdependence of mankind—how can we make this consciousness the unique contribution of our time to the small handful of incentives which really motivate human conduct?"

As the story of Jane Addams's life, this book is "authoritative" to this extent: Before my aunt died, she turned over to me all files of her own manuscripts, published and unpublished; all letters, records, and clippings which she had preserved, from her first valentine to her last round-the-world speech in Washington on May 1, 1935. "Do what you like with them," she said. "I have left them to you in my will." My own personal acquaintance with her, or hers with me, perhaps I should say, lasted almost sixty years. It is to be hoped that some day some scholar, completely acquainted with the history of the development of sociology and of American civilization in the last half-century, will offer a picture of it as illuminated by her life, for I think she threw more light into its dark places than any one else. But for her personal history I had all available information. My aunt read over and annotated the first draft of the first eight chapters of this book, talked over the next three, and agreed upon the proportion of the remainder. I realize now that as we talked things over, neither she nor I saw her in perspective. Neither of us had any just conception of the view the world seems to have had of her importance to it.

In the preparation of the book I have specifically to thank my daughter Elizabeth Allen for her help in examining the great mass of personal records; the Macmillan Company for permission to use many extracts from Miss Addams's published works; and many old friends of hers, in particular Mrs. Catherine Waugh McCulloch, Doctor Alice Hamilton, and Miss Ellen Gates Starr, for facts, suggestions, and comments that have proved invaluable.

JAMES WEBER LINN

JANE ADDAMS

JANE ADDAMS

Some workmen, who in boyhood knew
    The glory of the sunset's beams
Upon the great Acropolis,
    Watched by her coffin. "It is true,
The only one who knew our dreams,"
    They mourned, "is dead!" Did she hear this?

Do you suppose that she could hear
    Within God's high, enclosing wall,
Some echo of the cry of praise
    That rose above her quiet bier
In the brief interval of days
    Between her death and burial?

Do you suppose that she can know
    How still so many find the earth
Since that one great heart ceased to move?
    How wonderingly on they go
Listening in the huge implacable dearth
    Of sound, for that one sound of love?

Ah, many love their fellowmen,
    Thank God, as she did. It was hers,
Uniquely hers, by radiant gleams
    Of pure imagination, then
And now, where'er her spirit stirs,
    To understand their highest dreams!

Among us whom she understood,
    Statesmen or children in the street,
Who doubts that she is yearning yet,
    Fearing no evil, for the Good?
Bold herald to the Court Divine
    For us, whom she cannot forget!

CHAPTER I

JANE ADDAMS'S FATHER

THE dominant influence on the life of Jane Addams, she has always declared, was that of her father. Whether she is right in this conviction is arguable; whether, that is to say, any influence except that of her own genius was *dominant* in her. Certainly however it was her father who was the "supreme affection" of her youth, and no clear understanding of her can be secured without a knowledge of him.

He was born in Pennsylvania, of English stock, but American ancestry for four generations. On December 22, 1681, by a deed recorded in Philadelphia, William Penn the Quaker granted to Robert Adams of Ledwell, Oxfordshire, England, five hundred acres of land to be surveyed in Pennsylvania. The next year, 1682, Penn and various other Quakers voyaged to America in the ship *Welcome*, a ship and a trip almost as famous in American genealogical history as the *Mayflower* and her passage to Plymouth sixty-two years before. There is no record of Robert Adams's arrival. It seems certain he did not accompany Penn. He seems, at some later time, to have settled in Oxford Township, Philadelphia County, now the city. He is said to have died there in 1719. There is no record either that his brother, Walter Adams, came on the *Welcome;* but he at least was certainly living in Oxford Township before the end of the seventeenth century.

1

Walter's son, Richard, was married to an Elsie Withers, of Providence Township, Philadelphia County, in 1726. Richard's son, William (grandnephew of the original grantee of the Pennsylvania land) moved to Cacalico Township, in Lancaster County, and there in 1761 laid out the borough of Adamstown. Another of Walter's sons, Isaac, born in 1746, is said by family tradition to have been the one who first adopted the "double d," to avoid confusion with a cousin (or perhaps a nephew) Isaac, who was a year younger. This first American "Addams," a captain in the Revolutionary war, lived until 1809, and died in Reading, Pennsylvania. The youngest of his six sons, Abraham, married a Reading damsel, and in 1811 removed to Millerstown, Pennsylvania; his oldest daughter married James Beaver, and became the mother of, among other children, James Addams Beaver, subsequently Governor of Pennsylvania. An older son of Isaac, Samuel by name, married Catherine Huy. They had six daughters and four sons. The seventh child and third son, born July 12, 1822, at Sinking Springs, Pennsylvania, was named John Huy Addams. This was Jane Addams's father.

One of Jane's early recollections is of demanding from her father a statement of "what he was," that is to say, what were his religious beliefs. The little girl was not unnaturally puzzled, for she knew him to be a good Christian, and yet an attendant on alternate Sundays at two of the four different denominational meeting-houses of the village in which they lived, Methodist, German Lutheran, Evangelical, and Presbyterian. She may even have known that he was accustomed to give $100 a year to each church, more than anybody else in the village gave to any one. Also, he had been for all her life teaching a class in the "union Sunday-school" of the village. She had to know where in all this theological and denominational confusion he aligned himself: "His eyes twinkled as he soberly replied, 'I am a Quaker.' 'But that isn't enough to say,' I urged. 'Very well,' he added. 'To people who insist upon details, as some one is doing now, I add that I am a Hicksite Quaker'; and not another word on the weighty subject could I induce him to utter."

In fact he was not even a Quaker by inheritance; unless the grant of land from Penn may be thought to have carried Quaker responsibilities along with it. For the original Robert was not a Quaker, and neither was Isaac, John Huy Addams's grandfather. Nor was John Addams inclined either to profess Christianity, or to interfere with the religious professions of others. His articles of belief were integrity and self-respect. As a young man, at a time he thought critical in his affairs, he wrote in his neat firm hand, in his neat leather-bound diary, "What would a man Proffit by gaining the whole world and lose his soul? Am firmly impressed that 'Honesty is the best Policy,' and hope that I may by all means and through all hazards stick to the above Proverb. Let come what may, let me stick to the above." Through all hazards he stuck to it. It seems to have been his creed in business, in politics, and in matters of personal salvation. Integrity was his "inner light." When he was a member of the Illinois Legislature, Abraham Lincoln wrote to him on one occasion, to inquire how Addams meant to vote on a certain measure. "You will of course vote," Lincoln commented, "according to your conscience, only it is a matter of considerable importance to me to know how that conscience is pointing." John Addams always knew how his conscience pointed; "doctrine" concerned him little. He was a shrewd man of business. When he died, he left an estate, mostly of land, valued at the time at more than $350,000—a fortune for his section of Illinois in his day. But none of it was what subsequently came to be called "tainted" money. He had been uniquely incorruptible. When he died, the worldly wise editor of the *Chicago Times* wrote that although there were doubtless many members of the state legislature even during the days of war-time contracts and the demoralization of reconstruction who had never *accepted* a bribe, John Addams was the only man he had ever known to whom nobody had ever dared offer one; there had never been any one so bad as not to realize Addams's unapproachable honesty.

In late July, 1844, John H. Addams, then twenty-two, and his bride Sarah Weber Addams, five years older, left Kreidersville, Pennsylvania, on the practical honeymoon of a journey to northern Illinois to begin a new life together in what was then still a new country.

Four years earlier John Addams, a tall, dark, silent young man, had gone from a brief experience of country-school teaching near Millersville, to become a miller's apprentice under Enos Reiff, who had a flourmill at Ambler on the Wissahickon not far from Philadelphia. Reiff had married the daughter of George Weber (then and still pronounced by the family Weeber, not Webber). George Weber was a flourishing citizen who owned land and a flourmill near Kreidersville. The Webers' American residence was not quite as long as that of the Addamses, but nearly so. Christian Weber and his wife Appolonia, emigrating from Germany, landed in Philadelphia in the *Goodwill* in 1727. Their son Christian was born in 1743, and died in 1803; his son John was born in 1768 and died in 1815. George Weber, son of this John, was born in 1786. He became a vigorous, enterprising, humorous, and social-minded man. A miller in Kreidersville, in 1812, he began to take a certain interest in military affairs locally. In 1828 he was made Colonel of the 26th Pennsylvania militia. But he was still more concerned with church and school. He helped to organize the first Sunday-school in that region. In 1826, he was one of the founders of Lafayette College, and served on its board of trustees from the beginning until 1847. In the year 1850, he was made an Associate Judge of Northampton County. But in all old letters he is referred to as Colonel.

John Addams had worked assiduously for four years according to the fashion of the trade, getting up at three in the morning to take his turn in the mill. He had learned the business, and acquired the flattened "miller's thumb" which comes from feeling the flour between the thumb and forefinger to determine its quality. In his leisure time he had "read all the books in the village library," and developed an interest in history, European as well as American, which he was never to lose. Also he had made the acquaintance of his employer's sister-in-law, Sarah Weber. He was a thin youth, but strong and in a serious sort of way handsome, ambitious and able to turn his hand, then and afterwards, to any sort of labor. He records in his diary, a month or so after he reached Illinois, and while he is waiting for prospects to clear, "Helped this day all day in threshing, had never done this before but found it Pleasant." He was not a church-member, but he was inclined to godliness, and already, though he had not had a chance to vote in any presidential election, a determined Whig. To Sarah Weber he proposed marriage, and he was accepted. On her side it was a love-match; doubtless also on his, though his youthful diary does not refer to her very frequently, and there were soundly practical considerations also in the marriage. He was the more solidly educated of the two; but she was the older, and the better off, and also an intelligent and devoted young woman, who had attended a "boarding-school" in Philadelphia, and was "accomplished in music and drawing." They were married July 18, 1844, at Kreidersville.

For some time before the wedding, there had been much family discussion about "going west." The Webers had various acquaintances and two relatives who had already gone out to Illinois, and Colonel George Weber, the bride's father, still vigorous and energetic though more than fifty years of age, was of the opinion that a mill in that section would be extremely profitable. Finally agreement was reached that not only John and Sarah, but George Weber himself, should make the trip to Illinois and look the country over. John's father, Samuel Addams, wished to sell his place and retire, and proposed to finance his son, if he should decide to buy or build a mill in Illinois, to the extent of (ultimately) four thousand dollars, which was no small backing for those days, and shows the confidence in his abilities and judgment which the young man had already engendered in his elders. So on the morning of July 29, 1844—it is the first entry in the diary—"Myself and Wife left Kreidersville at four A.M. in a two-wheeled conveyance," first for Somerville, New Jersey, and thence "by Railroad," and "arrived at the

Great City of New York at 11 o'clock P.M., traveling 47 Miles in three hours."

Thence, after two days of sight-seeing, by boat to Albany—"the Knickerbocker, a splendid Boat"; a night trip, 160 miles in nine hours, "Freight $5 for both, with pleasant state-room." Colonel Weber, joining them in New York, was now along. By train to Buffalo, a city "destined in my humble opinion to become one of the most Noted Places along the lakes." From Attica on, John Addams notes, "the country is covered with heavy timber, Beech and Hemlock principally, in fact the wood extends to within 1 mile of Buffalo." To Niagara Falls the next day —it must be remembered that this was in part a honeymoon journey—which while John Addams remained on the American side filled him with suitable emotions elaborated at some length, but "upon Canada shore a feeling of derision crosses one's mind thinking that all this country is subject to the government of a *Woman,* for republicans this will not do"—the only remark in the diary, incidentally, which conveys the faintest shadow of scorn for anybody or anything. That afternoon they boarded the "St. Louis, a splendid Steamer, her first trip to Chicago," where, after a somewhat sea-sick passage, they arrived on the 8th of August; ten days from Pennsylvania by way of New York City, a quick trip for ninety years ago.

Chicago did not very favorably impress the youthful John Addams. That in social thinking Chicago was one day after a fashion, and reluctantly, to "become subject to the government of a Woman," and that woman his own daughter, did not occur to him, naturally. He noted only that the town "was commenced ten years ago and now has a population of about 8 thousand—nearly every person is engaged in some mercantile business, in my opinion too many for the place." The business district was, he thought, "Located entirely too Low." That evening he "attended a Whig meeting which was addressed by a Mr. Allen of Ohio who did not do the Tariff subject much justice." The next day after a considerable search he bought a "Bay Mare for $41, had her shod for which I paid $1.75, bought a buggy and Harness for $28, tolerably good"; and at half-past one in the afternoon he had arranged to have the heavy baggage stored "till we could find a home to take it to," and "Father-in-Law, Sarah and Myself got on and left Chicago for Freeport," a small town in Stephenson County, one of the northern tier of counties in Illinois, near which his cousins were settled. There they arrived with little misadventure, after three days of driving over the prairie, frequently through "sloughs." And six miles from Freeport, after some three months of further exploration of northern Illinois, including a horseback journey down the Rock River to the Mississippi, and much careful consideration of soils, waterpowers, and neighbors, they settled for the remainder of their lives.

The diary of this journey from Pennsylvania to Illinois, which John Addams kept for six months without the break of a day, many of the entries being made at considerable length, is of a certain historical interest. Illinois was still something of a "pioneer" state in 1844. The young Pennsylvanian was a shrewd observer of material things. But the personal interest of the diary is much more considerable than the historical. The record was intended for his own eyes only; indeed, until the little leather-bound volumes turned up in a "secret drawer" of an old desk in the attic of the Addams homestead, full eighty-five years after they had been written, that record was probably seen by no other eye than his. And it is with himself, his own ambitions, uncertainties, exaltations and depressions of spirit, that he is principally and properly concerned.

He reveals his eagerness for exact information, his caution as a bargainer, his determination not to be "over-reached" as he determined never to over-reach; his industry, his endurance, his physical equability. But he reveals also the fact that he was by no means equable in temperament. It is curious to note how many of the entries conclude with an estimate of the day's feelings. Here are successive final lines from one week's entries in September, while he was waiting, as he was to wait for three months longer, in the hope that the owners of the mill he desired to buy might come to terms. "So ended this day in tolerable spirits." "My spirits were however good to-day." "Upon the whole I was very much discouraged to-day." "This day spirits good." "I will endeavor to pray for better spirits." "Spirits to-day good while at work (he was helping to pick potatoes that day) but otherwise discouraged." There is nothing precocious, or even mature, in such entries. Indeed when Jane Addams read them, for the first time, in her own old age, she was amazed. She had had no conception of her quiet father as qualmish in youth. The simplicity of the father's self-analyses is the more striking when they are compared to the similar diarial "searchings after self-understandings" of the daughter at the same time of life—twenty-two. In a "common-place book" dated 1882, the year after

John Addams's death, and a gloomy year for Jane, she writes: "The difficulty is not in bearing our ills, but in knowing what ills are necessary, not in doing what is right but in knowing what is right to do. I suppose to say that I do not know just what I believe is a form of cowardice, just going on trying to think things out instead of making up my mind, but then why am I happier when I am learning than when I am trying to decide? For I do not think there could be any happiness in being a coward."

The longing for self-understanding is the same, the souls of father and daughter dwelt in intimacy, but how different the approaches to self-knowledge! The difference is partly in the forms of their education, partly in the generations; the daughter was spiritually an inquirer, the father in many ways conventional; their wish however was the same, to possess and recognize the "inner light."

"My mind was very much perplexed again and the future at times looks very dark," John Addams writes after three months in Illinois. "I hope and pray God some permanent light may very soon appear—and settle down in life, to do honour to God and selves." What at the moment darkened the future was a difference of two hundred dollars between what the young man could afford to pay for the mill property he sought, and the price the owner set upon it. Two weeks later, "Think if I can get the Winslow property I will take that—but as to getting it I think the prospects poor. But Pray God all may yet go aright—as human beings must know that Providence ways are not our ways." Just before Christmas however the bargain he had been considering so long was concluded. He bought of two pioneer settlers, Conrad

Epley and John Shuey, a sawmill and a grist-mill "with one run of stone," which had been erected by Doctor Thomas Van Valzah six years before, the first mill in Stephenson County; also 80 acres of woodland adjoining. There was no house anywhere near the place, which was on the banks of "Cedar River," six miles north of Freeport.

Cedar River was not really a river at all, but what is called throughout most of the United States a "crick"— the smallest stream, in the least inhabited spot, and the smallest mill on it, anywhere around. Had John Addams gone to Rockford instead, twenty miles or so east, and planted a mill on the Rock River, it is likely with his business acumen in that wider field that he would have become a very rich man indeed. But he chose the tiniest opportunity of all, planted a hill beyond the creek with the seeds of Norway pines, of which he had brought a bagful from Pennsylvania, and, as he had hoped, "settled down" for all that remained to him of life—thirty-seven years of unbroken and rising prosperity.

It was lovely country; the most beautiful spot near Freeport. Just a little further west, toward the Mississippi, is "the land the glaciers forgot," wonderful rolling hills and magnificent valleys, the most charming scenery to be found anywhere in the state—"the Alps of Illinois," it has been called. Round Cedar Creek the prospect is not quite so noble, but it is stirring enough; thrilling to the young Jane Addams who was to grow up amidst its beauty. John Addams loved it. The pines he planted are dying or dead now, but not the least interesting thing about the young man is that his first act after purchasing the place should have been to plant them.

The section, first settled nine years earlier, was already flourishing. But the problem of trade, John Addams saw at once, was that of a market. In fact the great problem of the three central counties of the northern tier of Illinois, Stephenson, Winnebago, and Boone, was the market problem. The labor was there, and the products were there—lumber, flour, and agricultural produce of all sorts. But how to get it either to the Mississippi, or to the Great Lakes? At once John Addams turned to the consideration of this matter. His own future, the future of his neighbors, depended on the solution of this problem.

The efforts to find markets, either by a waterway down the Rock River, or by a railroad outlet to Chicago, were practically simultaneous. The improvement of navigation on the Rock River was mooted at a ship convention held in Sterling, Illinois, in November of 1844, at which one amateur expert reported that all obstacles to navigation for a hundred miles, from the Wisconsin line southwest, could be removed at an average cost of $45 a mile. There was great enthusiasm over this report, and in February, 1845, the state legislature passed an act permitting this improvement. But nothing came of this act, naturally; for the cost would probably have been at least twenty times the estimate. On New Year's Day, 1846, a "ship Canal" convention at Rockford urged a still more grandiose conception—provision for slack-water navigation of the Rock River from some point in lower Wisconsin, and from the same point a canal eastward 80 miles to Lake Michigan. But nothing came of this either; nor of the casual incorporation, while the navigation of the Rock River was still under consideration, of the Chicago and Rock River Plank Road Company, which was to construct 100 miles of plank road at $3,000 a mile, from Rockford southeast to Chicago.

Young John Addams was little interested in the proposed waterway, and not at all in the proposed plank road. He pinned his faith to a railway. In January of 1846, when he had been in Stephenson County less than a year and a half, he became, according to the county history, the "leading figure" in assembling a convention at Rockford, to organize the building of a railroad, to be called the Galena and Chicago Union, across the northern part of the state from Chicago on Lake Michigan to Galena on the Galena River (a navigable stream) just east of the Mississippi. More than three hundred delegates attended this convention, which met on January 7, 1846, one week after the ship canal convention, already referred to.

At this railroad convention, sensible resolutions were presented and unanimously adopted, urging the start of the project. "It is indispensably necessary," ran one clause of these resolutions, "that the owners of property between Galena and Chicago should subscribe to the stock according to their means." Farm values, it was asserted, would double at once when the railroad reached the central counties, and each farmer was exhorted by resolution to take at least one half-share at $50; preferably a whole share at $100; if possible, more. John Addams, not yet twenty-four, undertook the job of securing Stephenson County subscriptions. By April 1, 1848, two years later, $351,800 had been subscribed along the line. Only $20,000 was raised in Chicago, although some remarkable Chicago business men, including William B. Ogden, Stephen Gale, Walter L. Newberry, John Y. Scammon, Mark Skinner and others—were delegates at the Rockford convention, and Ogden was president of the proposed company. On April 1, 1848, the first grading-peg was driven, at the corner of Halsted Street and Kinzie in Chicago—just west of the Chicago River, and exactly one mile north of the site of the future Hull House. John Addams raised more than twenty thousand dollars in Stephenson County for the new road. He was also largely responsible for the defeat of a plan to run it south to Savanna. Nevertheless it was ten years before the road was actually built into Freeport. From the first, however, it was profitable. The subscribers all made money. And when in 1864 the Galena and Chicago Union was consolidated with the Chicago and Northwestern, John Addams went into the banking business in part to see that every subscriber received Northwestern stock share for share of his holdings on the old road.

It was his experiences in collecting subscriptions for the Galena and Chicago Union in 1846 and 1847 that made him what the old newspapers call "the best-known man in the district." He drove all over the county, visiting every settler. Many of the Pennsylvania German farmers doubted the value of "the whole newfangled business," having little use for any railroad, and none for one in which they were asked to risk their savings. But John Addams persevered. In *Twenty Years at Hull House,* Jane Addams tells of the occasion when at the annual meeting of "Old Settlers," always held in the grove beside the Addams mills, her father related some of his experiences of this time, thirty years before:

He told of his despair in one farmer's community dominated by such prejudice, which did not in the least give way under his argument, but finally melted under the enthusiasm of a high-spirited German matron who took a share to be paid for "out of butter and egg money." As he related his admiration of her, an old woman's piping voice in the audience called out, "I'm here to-day, Mr. Addams, and I'd do it again if you asked me." The old woman, bent and broken by her seventy years of toilsome life, was brought to the platform, and I was much impressed by his grave presentation of her as "one of the public-spirited pioneers to whose heroic fortitude we are indebted for the development of this country."

In 1846 John Addams rebuilt the grist-mill he had bought. There was still no settlement round it; the land was merely "an eighty in Buckeye Township." Not till 1849 was a town "laid out" by a pioneer speculator. By that time John Addams was on the highroad to prosperity. In 1854 he built for his increasing family a wide, two-story and attic gray-brick house, in the simple oblong architecture of the day. It is still after eighty years "the best house in the village," standing across the road from the mills and on the top of a slope from the creek to the east. That was the main road from Freeport north into Wisconsin in those days. Now a highway has been constructed a quarter of a mile still further east, along a ridge on the edge of the village, and the Addams's homestead is left solitary. Visitors to the spot to-day are more likely to call it "quaint" or "interesting" than beautiful, but it has strength and peace. It is very little changed, except in furniture, from what it was eighty years ago. Its blank front and sloping roof give it a somewhat high-shouldered appearance, and the "front yard," one part of it level with the road and the other well above the road-level, looks one-sided; but from the side both the proportions of the house and the slope of the roof are most attractive. Enter the fan-lighted front door and you find yourself in a hall from which a room which was of old John Addams's office opens off to the left, and the living-room to the right. Beyond is the dining-room and the huge kitchen, in which is the "Dutch oven" from which John Addams used to feed twenty mill employees at times. There are brick fireplaces. Behind the house, but not conspicuous, is the stone-banked barn, the first building on the place, built in 1848, six years before the house was; the original wooden beams in it seem as sound as ever after almost ninety years. Beyond the barn lie wooded cliffs, the foot of which the dammed reaches of Cedar Creek used to lave. Those reaches are as fine farming-land now as there is in the county. In this house Jane Addams was born. According to Cedarville legend, it was for several years a station on the Negro "underground railroad" to Canada. The house and the old home farm of four hundred and fifty acres are now owned by Jane Addams's niece, Marcet Haldeman-Julius.

In the progress of the district John Addams continued to pull the laboring oar. When he was thirty-two, in the same year that he built his house, he was elected to the State Senate, as a Whig. The next year, however, he was one of the "committee on resolutions" at the meeting at Ripon, Wisconsin (fifty miles to the north; John Addams drove up there) at which the Republican Party was launched, and thereafter he was reëlected Senator seven successive times as a Republican. And when he declined a ninth term, in 1870, an editor of the day said that "the district might as well go into mourning politically." He refused the nomination for Governor, when the Republican nomination was equivalent to an election; and he repeatedly declined to run for Congress when to refuse

THE ADDAMS HOME AT CEDARVILLE, ILLINOIS

Jane Addams was born in this house.

THE ADDAMS MILLS AT CEDARVILLE, ILLINOIS

From a somewhat imaginative drawing made in 1871.

took determination, for his ambitious second wife—whom he married in 1868—was very desirous of going to Washington. Many a night she argued the matter with him till well into the morning, with an unsleeping guest in the room above who still remembers wishing that either Mr. or Mrs. Addams were less determined. The fact is that John Addams had no political ambition. He knew Lincoln well for the ten years before the great man's death, knew him and loved him; Jane has recorded in her autobiography the fact that when Lincoln died she saw her father cry for the first time in her life, and discovered that "grown-ups" could shed tears. But John Addams had little of the pliability of Lincoln, the ablest politician of his day. John Addams did not so much care to know what the people wanted, as what would be good for them. He took advice only from his own conscience. When he died the editor of the Democratic paper of Freeport, which had opposed John Addams bitterly, nevertheless asserted that there had never been a funeral in Stephenson County to which so many had gone, and "gone with tears in their hearts." And yet John Addams had few really intimate acquaintances. To almost all but his daughter he seemed a very reserved man. Even she wrote of him most frequently as "grave." This gravity undoubtedly added to his influence. A Freeport legend is of a farmer who stood on the street one winter morning with the flaps of his cap turned up, and when he was told by a friend to pull them down or he would freeze his ears, replied, "No, I won't; I just saw John Addams and he says 'tain't cold." His gentleness is still traditional, too, but he had little of the approachability of the man who seeks office in a democracy. Nor, except in business affairs, did he ever offer advice to anybody. Accustomed to walk himself by the "inner light" of the Quaker, fully convinced that the great duty of a man or a woman was the preservation of mental and moral integrity, "Honorable John Addams" refused to interfere in the spiritual affairs of others. One of the vivid recollections of Jane's childhood is of an occasion when during the day she had told a lie, and after she had gone to bed, could not sleep for thinking of this dark deed. She slipped out of bed and, fearfully facing the darkness of the stairs and the risk of passing the front door, which as a Quaker John Addams never locked, she finally reached her father's bedside and standing there barefooted panted out her confession. Solemnly he responded only that "if he had a little girl who told lies, he was very glad she felt too bad to go to sleep afterward."

John Addams was a member of the Illinois legislature throughout the Civil War. On all measures of supply of men and arms he voted with his party. Moreover, he was instrumental in 1861 in raising and helping to equip a company called, after him, the "Addams Guards." The roster of that company, engraved, decorated with the American eagle clutching battle-flags, and framed, still hangs on the wall of the family living-room. General Smith Atkins, second in command to the notorious Kilpatrick on Sherman's march to the sea, used to tell in later life, when he was a Freeport newspaper proprietor, of a time when he returned from camp in September of 1861 to raise sixty volunteers in Stephenson County in four days. He went first to John Addams, whom he found in the harvest-field driving a reaper. Addams unhitched the team, leaving the reaper in the field, and drove off with Atkins to a recruiting meeting, where mainly by his influence twenty volunteers were secured. In this there is no evidence of any Quaker blood, no touch of the philosophy of non-resistance. Addams seems to have stood by the Lincolnian insistence that even should the war continue until every drop of blood drawn by the lash should be paid by a drop drawn by the sword, yet were the judgments of the Lord true and righteous altogether. Jane Addams always believed that she came by her theories of non-resistance from her father, but he has left no record indicating any such point of view. She said herself not long before she died, when her attention was called to her father's zeal during the Civil War, and she was asked, "What *did* your father think about the war?," "I don't know what he thought." In his patriotism he was probably as conventional as he was sincere. His zeal was in no way inconsistent with any other expression of his philosophy in action, that one is able to discover. In some respects, he never outgrew the simplicity of his early thinking, as it is revealed in his diary.

But in one great respect, he changed altogether. Reading and reflection combined with his essential kindliness of spirit to make him a pillar of tolerance. He was perhaps the only man of his community who was as much interested in European as in American liberation. He was no mere abolitionist, centering all his efforts on getting rid of Negro slavery. What he objected to was tyranny in any form, anywhere. Jane never forgot the moment, when she was not yet twelve, when she came into her father's room

to find him sitting beside the fire with a newspaper in his hand, looking very solemn; and upon my eager inquiry what had happened, he told me Joseph Mazzini was dead. I had never even heard Mazzini's name, and after being told about him I was inclined to grow argumentative, asserting that my father did not know him, that he was not an American, and that I could not understand why we should be expected to feel badly about him.... In the end I obtained that which I have ever regarded as a valuable possession, a sense of the genuine relationship which may exist between men who share large hopes and like desires, even though they differ in language, nationality and creed; that those things count for absolutely nothing between groups of men who are trying to abolish slavery in America, or to throw off Hapsburg oppression in Italy.

There is something superb in the picture of the small-town banker, a town in which there was not one person of Italian birth, the statesman of the American Middle West, utterly removed at the time from any possibility of "foreign entanglements" with Italy, the Hicksite Quaker a world away in religious thinking from the Catholic Mazzini, sitting grieved by his fire at the news of Mazzini's passing. The neighborliness of his youth had become a higher fellowship. In this respect at least the shrewd hardworking young man had turned into a philosopher. Touched by time, the rods of his dogma blossomed into social understanding; the crude blacks and whites of his honesty and his efficiency were transformed into the glowing colors of comprehension and sympathy. The "rugged individualism" of the boy of twenty-two who began the diary of his honeymoon journey with the word "Myself," the youthful narrowness that found expression in derision of a country "subject to the government of a *Woman*," which "would not do for republicans," perhaps never disappeared altogether. Never a dreamer, John Addams never became utterly trustful of humanity;

though as a follower of Quaker tradition he left his front door always unlocked in quiet Cedarville, he would have locked it in Freeport. He was not quite, perhaps, as his daughter remembered him. But in his integrity, his incorruptibility of spirit, his grave courtesy to the least as to the ablest, his invariable recognition of the rights of the weak, his constant silent generosity, he was the great man of his day and place—"the king gentleman of the district," as one of his sorrowing neighbors quaintly described him when he died.

CHAPTER II

A "DIFFERENT" CHILD

IN January of 1863 Sarah Addams, then forty-six years
old but carrying her ninth baby, was called over to
help in the delivery of the wagon-maker's wife. The doctor
was somewhere out in the country on another case. Sarah
Addams worked over the wagon-maker's wife until the
doctor came, when she collapsed and had to be carried
home. The exertion brought her own baby prematurely.
It was born dead, and a week later Sarah Addams died.

Jane herself was only two years and four months old
at the time. Yet she believed that she remembered the
occasion. She remembered being aware that her mother
was in the ground-floor bedroom of the house; pounding
on the door with her fist, and hearing her mother say,
"Let her in, she is only a baby herself." As she declared,
"No one ever told me this, and it is impossible that I
could have invented it." At any rate the memory of it as a
memory corresponds to the facts of her mother's last
illness, and Jane was an extraordinarily precocious child
in many ways.

Sarah Addams had become a woman of real force of
character. She was devoted to her family, yet "with a
heart ever alive to the wants of the poor," as one of the
numerous "obituary notices" of the time says in its old-
fashioned phraseology. "Mrs. Addams," the writer adds,
"will be missed everywhere, at home, in society, in the

church, in all places *where good is to be done and suffer-ing relieved*." She is still remembered in the village, where the child she helped bring into the world that gloomy winter day of 1863 is still living. She came of prosperous Pennsylvania people. Her father, Colonel George Weber, had, like John Addams, purchased land in Illinois and built a mill. Colonel Weber's mill was at Como, on the Rock River not far from what is now called Grand Detour. The mill he built was an elaborate affair for those days, with six stones. It was meant to supply the needs not only of the Como district, but of distant markets. Unfortunately for Colonel George the Rock was never made navigable to the Mississippi, and Colonel George's investment floated off with it, along with the bran and "shorts" he threw into it disgustedly because there was no other way of disposing of them. The Galena and Chicago Union might have made him rich, if it had been diverted to the southward, but this diversion John Addams prevented. Old letters indicate a slight feeling between the Addamses and the Webers in consequence, though long before Colonel Weber had built at Como, John Addams urged him not to do so. In spite of the complete failure of the big Como mill, however, Colonel Weber left a considerable estate when he died in 1851. His wife, Sarah, had died in 1846; indeed, it was her death which finally determined him to emigrate to Illinois. Of George Weber's children, five besides Sarah, the youngest, lived to maturity. George, the second son, and Harry, the third, came with their father to Illinois. Harry became a merchant, in Chicago, was "burnt out" in the Chicago fire, and returned to New York, where he prospered; two of his sons married daughters of Senator Stamford of

Connecticut. George became a minister and "missionary," first in Illinois and later, following the frontier, in Iowa. George was bitterly opposed to the war; in a letter written at the time of his sister Sarah's death it is interesting to read the statement of this opposition and, between the lines but clearly enough, his feeling that her death was part of the "chastisement" which according to his views was bound to fall upon those who entered into the support of what he regarded as an "Unchristian" conflict. George was not a Quaker, but he evidently felt that John Addams's activities in support of the war were unsuitable to his beliefs.

Jane was the eighth child, of whom only four lived to maturity and three died in infancy; Martha, traditionally "the beauty of the family," died at sixteen. Jane herself in her autobiography insists that she was "ugly." Nobody now living who remembers her as a child agreed with her. She was small, frail, and pigeon-toed, and carried her head to one side, as the result of a slight spinal curvature due apparently to abscesses; but this seems to have given her only a sort of bird-like look, so at any rate described by her childhood acquaintances. She carried her head in the same way when she went to boarding-school at seventeen, but nobody there seems to have thought her plain. The emphasis of others' memories is laid on her "different" appearance in childhood; "spiritual" is the word usually chosen to characterize it, sometimes "dreamy." The truth seems to be that she was not only a child of strong feelings, but that she began thinking very early. She was precocious, highly introspective, and full of strong feelings she wanted to express but was at first unable and a little later afraid to voice. She not only

JANE ADDAMS AT SIX

JANE ADDAMS AT FOUR

inherited her father's reserve, but was as a child much in his company. She adored him, there is no other word for it, accepted his word as gospel, and even tried to imitate his ways of speech.

While he was in Springfield, conscientiously legislating, she fell back upon the equally conscientious bringing-up of her oldest sister Mary (mother of this biographer), who was seventeen when Mrs. Addams died. Mary too was not robust; according to family tradition, she had weighed only forty-nine pounds when she was nine years old. However, at seventeen she assumed the general direction of the complicated household affairs, and particularly of the little Jennie. Mary was her mother's replica, "so far forgetting herself in others that by them she became unforgettable," thoughtful, affectionate, and competent. She married the Presbyterian minister of the village when Jane was ten years old, and when she died in 1894 left her own youngest child, a boy of ten, to Jane Addams's guardianship. That boy and his older brothers and sisters remained Jane Addams's special "family" responsibility ever afterward.

She spoke of her feeling for her father, when she was a little child, as a "doglike affection," but it was not quite that; it was fuller of quaint reasoning than that. She followed him adoringly about in private, but on occasions she carefully refrained from being seen with him in public, on the streets on Sunday for instance, because she could not bear the thought that "strange people should know my handsome father owned such a homely little girl." That feeling would have interested Freud. Because her father had the flattened "miller's thumb," she spent hours rubbing between her own tiny thumb and fore-

finger the ground wheat as it fell from between the millstones; because her father's hands were still, when she
knew him, faintly marked with the purple and red spots
which are always found on the hands of one who has
often dressed millstones, she used to run to the mill whenever she knew the stones were being dressed, and spread
out her own hands near the stones in the hope that the
bits of flint flying from the dresser's chisel would speckle
them; but it seldom or never did, as Edward Lear remarked of the young couple who churned salt-water violently in the hope that it would turn into butter. Later on
because she knew that her father still woke punctually at
three A.M., having for years had to take his turn in the
mill at that hour, she "curiously enough," as she says,
often woke at that hour and lay awake thinking of her
father. It was not curious; it was merely characteristic of
her affection for him, which amounted to a possession.
Because she knew that he had read "right through the
village library" of Ambler back in Pennsylvania, beginning with the lives of the signers of the Declaration of
Independence, she too undertook a "course of reading"
at the same unearthly hour, a course which included
Pope's translation of the *Iliad*, Dryden's translation of
Virgil, and a *History of the World*, all of which seems
stiff food for the digestion of a ten-year-old before dawn.

Her dreaminess and her precocity combined to make
her a mystical child. In her autobiography she says:

When I was six years old I dreamed night after night that
every one in the world was dead except myself, and that upon
me rested the responsibility of making a wagon-wheel....I
always stood in the same spot in the deserted blacksmith shop,
darkly pondering how to begin, and never once did I know how,

although I fully realized that the affairs of the world could not be resumed until at least one wheel should be made and something started. ... The next morning would often find me standing in the doorway of the village blacksmith shop, anxiously watching the blacksmith at work. I would store my mind with such details of the process as I could observe ... then sigh heavily and walk away, bearing my responsibility as best I could, and of course, confiding it to no one.

Note the phrase "of course"! To confide such a dream would be much more a matter of course for any normal child than to hide it. Not one child in a thousand would even dream of having to make a wheel alone, not one in a million would realize that until *somebody* made a wheel the affairs of the world could not be resumed. The whole philosophy of individual social service is instinct in that realization. She was only six, too, when upon her first glimpse of "the poverty which implies squalor" in the back streets of Freeport, she insisted that when she grew up she would have a big house like the one she herself lived in, but it would not be built among other big houses, "but right in the midst of horrid little houses like these." She was only eight when, her father having suggested that she should wear her old coat on Sunday, instead of her new and pretty one, she found her mind "busy with the old question eternally suggested by the inequalities of the human lot," and at the church door ventured "to ask what could be done about it."

It is a strange thing that in her autobiography she records this kind of speculation as "natural to all children." As a matter of fact, nobody she knew when she was a little girl had any similar ideas. Not even many adults, not even her father, had them in those days. Jane was indeed "different"; more different in her spirit and capacity than even in her wistful and visionary look. She was no more like other children than when she grew up she came to be like other people.

To be sure her concern with the problems of social advancement even before the dawn of adolescence was not her only concern. She could lose her temper and stamp her feet on occasion; she told lies, even if she repented of them afterward; and she was not to be distracted from doing anything she wanted to do. "Every child," to use her own phrase, has found chips or stones in the road and kicked them ahead for hundreds of yards on the way to or from school. But if Jane started such an object on its way, she kept it going, whether it made her late to school or not; and when she got there, she always left it in a safe spot, and kicked it home again to the precise place where she had found it. "If she began doing it," an old playmate declares, "you couldn't make her quit." Nobody ever was able to "make her quit." She never permitted ill-health much of her life and half a dozen major operations to interfere with what she wanted to do. In this respect indeed her life was one long illustration of the truth of Robert Louis Stevenson's philosophic comment that "most of the good work of the world has been done, probably, by those who were 'not feeling very well' at the time."

Jennie Addams was seven years old when her father began to consider the advisability of marrying again. The oldest daughter, Mary, was being overworked with the household responsibilities, and was besides getting to the age when she ought to marry. The second daughter, Alice, always the strong one—indeed, the only one of the eight children who was really vigorous—was an adventurous, domineering girl, frequently in trouble. Alice got on to the back of her father's prize bull on one occasion, and rode it about until she was thrown off—a feat dangerous enough so that she remained proud of it until the day of her death.

Besides, prosperous, distinguished John Addams needed a wife. One day in 1867, as he was driving in to Freeport to the bank, as he did every day, the thought came into his mind, "What a good wife for me Mrs. William Haldeman would make!" Now William Haldeman was a citizen of Freeport, with whom John Addams was well acquainted, and his wife was a handsome, able woman. Suddenly John Addams realized that he was considering marriage with another man's wife. He was amazed and displeased with himself. But when he reached town, he was informed at the bank that "William Haldeman had died in the night." What if the thought of Mrs. Haldeman had been sent him for guidance? A year later he offered her marriage, and his offer was promptly accepted.

The second Mrs. John Addams was beyond any doubt a remarkable person. She lived to be ninety-three years of age, and was still handsome, in a terrifying sort of way, when she died. She awed her neighbors, though she never allured them. Strange stories of her determination, and even of her cruelty of purpose, are still in circulation; the sort of legends that grow up only round a strong character. She was a skilled musician, giving lessons to Freeport aspirants. She was a constant reader, even of novels, which in her day and neighborhood were thought by most good people to be dangerous. But she did not confine her reading to novels; she was fond of reading plays aloud to her family, and as her son George and her stepdaughter

Jane grew a little older she would gather them both round the living-room table on many an evening, and read Shakespeare, taking the characters turn about. Once in a while even John Addams was induced to join in this reading-circle, but usually it was confined to Mrs. Addams, Jane and George. Later at Hull House it was the memory of these many evenings of reading aloud that led Jane Addams to put such emphasis on similar "reading-clubs" for the neighbors. The stepmother played the guitar too, and sang endless songs from Tom Moore, whose lyrics she knew by heart, as well as many others. She was what in those days was called "accomplished."

Mrs. Addams was fond of society; even at ninety an amusing talker when she chose to be; and in the early days after her second marriage she was determined to have more society than Cedarville afforded. She was not only as Mrs. John H. Addams a personage in that section of Illinois, but she knew herself to be a personage in her own right; well educated, witty, high-spirited, and rich. She meant not to remain in Cedarville. But she encountered a quiet will even stronger than her own. Not only did the family remain in Cedarville, but in 1870, two years after his second marriage, John H. Addams declined further renomination to the state Senate. In the preceding session his new wife had gone with him to Springfield as a matter of course, and there had been social wars and rumors of wars, of course in a mild way, but disturbing to the Senator's mind. He never gave this as his reason for refusing further renomination, but his wife never had any doubt that it was his reason, and nagged him about it in consequence for years.

In all minor matters Mrs. Addams had her own way.

Mary, the oldest sister, who had managed the household since she was seventeen, quietly withdrew to Rockford Seminary, where she took lessons on the piano and in china-painting for a while, and then married the Presbyterian minister of Cedarville and set up a home of her own. Alice too, after a year or so, was sent to Rockford to school. Jane only remained at home, under her stepmother's domination.

It was not a harsh domination, in itself. The little girl and her stepmother were fond of one another, and allowing for their difference in ages, had many of the same tastes. And moreover, the years at Cedarville from 1868 to 1877, when Jane went away to boarding-school, were enriched by a new companionship—with George Haldeman.

The second Mrs. Addams brought with her to Cedarville her two sons, Harry and George Haldeman. Harry was eighteen, but George was only seven, six months younger than Jane. Eight years later Harry Haldeman married Alice Addams, after a tempestuous season in which the stepbrother and stepsister, violently in love, were vigorously opposed by the parents of both. Strong-willed Alice carried it through, though not until the very last moment was she sure that her father would attend the wedding. Harry Haldeman became a clever and daring surgeon, asserting in later days that he was the first man west of the Alleghenies to "set a broken neck and have the patient recover." He was also a brilliant musician; an extraordinarily skilful chess-player, competing with masters in his student days in Germany; and grimly witty. Subsequently he became a keen man of business. It was Harry Haldeman who when Jane Addams was twenty-five boldly operated on the spine from which she had suffered so much, and was supposed to have remedied the curvature. At length he abandoned the medical profession, both his temperament and the habits which had led John Addams to oppose the marriage interfering with his practice, and turned to banking in Kansas. When he died, it may be remarked, his vigorous and able wife took over the bank and ran it so successfully that she became known far and wide as one of the most successful business women in the country. Harry Haldeman did not much affect Jane Addams's life. He was as cynical as she was always the reverse, as coldly definite as she was doubtful, and sympathetic; and the sword of his bitterness, sharp as it was, seldom penetrated her armor of aspiration.

But the younger brother, George, was after her father the devotion of Jane's girlhood, as they grew up together. Later he wished to marry her, although he resented her social ideals, which he regarded as very vague, and he laughed at her sociological inquiries. In time, from concentration on study, particularly biological research at Johns Hopkins, he had a nervous breakdown from which he never fully recovered. But for nine years, from the time they were eight years old until they were seventeen, when she went away to Rockford Seminary and he to Beloit College, they were inseparable companions. He was a brilliant lad. Which was the leader, in play or study, it is impossible to say. Whenever Jane Addams wrote or spoke of those nine years, she used always the pronoun "we," and it meant always "Jennie and George." And what she wrote of those years when "George and I were together" had a sort of unique loveliness about it, as here:

JANE ADDAMS AT SIXTEEN

With her are her step-mother, Anna H. Haldeman
Addams, and her step-brother George.

JOHN H. ADDAMS

The dominant influence on the life of Jane
Addams was that of her father.

We had of course our favorite places and trees and birds and flowers. It is hard to reproduce the companionship which children establish with nature, but certainly it is much too unconscious and intimate to come under the head of esthetic appreciation, or anything of the sort. When we said that the purple wind-flowers—the anemone patens, "Looked as if the winds had made them," we thought much more of the fact that they were windborn than that they were beautiful; we clapped our hands in sudden joy over the soft radiance of the rainbow, but its enchantment lay in our half-belief that a pot of gold was to be found at its farther end; we yielded to a soft melancholy when we heard the whippoorwill in the early twilight, but while he aroused in us vague longings of which we spoke solemnly, we felt no beauty in his call.

Few American poets have written stanzas more beautiful and thoughtful than that; and to miss the emotional underbeat of that "we" is to lose part of the understanding of Jane Addams's early life.

Many years afterward, when both George and his mother were dead, one summer on the coast of Maine, Jane Addams used to sit occasionally in those circles which, with their hands resting on a table, await the rappings that follow, if any of the company are "psychic," and a believer in the "spirits" once informed Jane Addams that she was psychic to a high degree. At any rate, after a moment or two of silence the table would begin to rap; invariably the first raps would indicate that Jane Addams was being addressed; and she would remark, half whimsically and half in boredom, "Oh, it's my stepmother, of course, it always is. Now she will be reproaching me again for not having married George." And the table would inquire with some petulance, "How long are you going to keep on with that philanthropic nonsense?"

Jennie and George went to school together in the village, just a little walk down the hill and across the creek. The teacher for part of the time was Samuel Parr, later a professor of Latin at the University of Illinois. Latin and "English" were always Jane's favorite studies. George very early developed an interest in "nature study," and Jane devotedly worked with him—or under him, rather, in this subject. Biology became a primary matter with him, and he was keen in it; she could only struggle along behind. Nevertheless she was sufficiently interested, or sufficiently admiring of her stepbrother's concentration, to make up her mind to study medicine; kept that idea in her mind all through the years at Rockford Seminary; and only abandoned it after a year in the Women's Medical College at Philadelphia, which ended in a long illness. She would not have made a good doctor, any more than she would have made a good poet; neither the purely scientific nor the purely esthetic were ever her basic interests. She "liked" biology, and so she liked the sunsets of Cedarville, and its sheer stony tree-clad cliffs, and music and pictures, all God-created or man-created beauty, but her real eagerness was always for understanding. The association with George Haldeman was the very best thing that could have happened to her. It was not only that her young stepbrother's keenness of mind combined with her father's serene reflectiveness to mature her own intellectual ability; it was after George's coming that she ceased to be solitary-minded. Her earlier years were in some respects morbid. She looked inward too much. George, almost from the beginning, was a practical inquirer into facts, and the interest she got from him in bugs and worms and snakes tended to withdraw her from the coils of her childish introversion. Until George came, a "sense of solitude" had been too much with her. George's presence drove it away. Except her father, he was the best influence in her life, in those years of adolescence.

George and Jane carried on the same games week after week, even summer after summer. Their play gave her, the thought, a feeling of the continuity of things, of life as going on in a sort of pattern, instead of being a series of fragments. Their sports were a sort of constructed performance, rather than an unconnected group of acts. Remembrance of this was later to move her heart to sympathy for "youth in the city streets," so constantly interrupted in their play, so unable to follow out the dictates of their imaginations, often even brought into actual conflict with "the law" for doing the very same sort of things which had been the delight of her own heart and the education of her spirit. She was so eager to give them a chance to play in peace, that the development of the present splendid Chicago system of playgrounds may be said without exaggeration to have been started by her.

She and George were particularly great at "crusades." George was "The Knight of the Green Plume," always with a green feather in his hat, and a wooden sword painted green. He carried the sword season after season, and fought snakes with it. Once he seized a muskrat under water; it fixed its teeth in his hand, and Jane and a small boy who happened to be with them had to cut off its head and pry its jaw open before they could free him.

But it was unusual for some one else to be with them, they were usually alone together. "Free-ranging country children," but they ranged alone. The country round Cedarville was then—in spots still is—delectable. There were hills and cliffs, and even caves in the cliffs, to be explored with lighted candles; woods everywhere, mostly their father's woods, and streams; there were splendid places to visit near at hand when Jane's back was too bad for far wandering, and equally splendid places they found miles distant, when she was up to whole-day excursions. One is reminded almost as much by the countryside as by the association and interests of the two, of Dorothy and William Wordsworth in the north of England, ninety years earlier. Jane Addams and William Wordsworth both developed into very practical adults, but there was a touch of the mystic in both as children. One year Jane and George built an altar beside the creek, on which they placed thereafter all the snakes they killed, not only that summer but for several summers, sometimes carrying the limp bodies on sticks for miles to the sacrificial spot. One year they laid upon the altar one out of every hundred of the black walnuts they had gathered, most delicious of the fruits of the forest, and poured a pitcher of fresh cider over them, "for tribute." Tribute to what, Jane did not say. The general goodness of life, probably. Even in her early days, with a "religious" up-bringing, she was more interested in what was to be done in this life, than in how to reach another somewhere else. It was before she was eighteen that she wrote of one of her teachers, "She does everything for people from love of God alone, and *that I do not like.*"

Her father's mills were as fascinating as was the

countryside itself. The sawmill was melodramatic; one might sit on a log until just before the saw seized it—the "nigger" was not used then—and anticipate with splendid horror the catastrophe that must follow if one did not jump off in time. But the flourmill was purer drama. There was the realism of playing house in the bins, or building up the wet bran and shorts into piles, and there was the romance of the floury dusky storerooms and the basement full of the mystery thrown off by the water-wheel and carried up into usefulness by the endless bands. Mills have always been the favorite play-places of children lucky enough to possess them. It is a pity there are so few children so fortunate any more.

So with George for years she played as hard as her back would let her, and studied hard too, and read all her father's books—induced thereto on some occasions by a reward of five cents a volume, to be paid only after she had stood up to a cross-questioning on what she had read; and grew up certainly not an "ugly" little girl, but good-looking. Perhaps too "good"-looking, for much pain had already made her eyes a little sad. She was slender, and rather quaint, seeming older than she really was; as if she had already begun to wonder at the persistence of social confusion and inertia, which for fifty years she was to seek single-heartedly to overcome. There was rebellion in her eyes as well as the touch of sadness. She meant to know what she thought, and to think it without submission. When she once confessed to her father that she was not sure what she believed, he told her in whatever she did she "must put mental integrity above everything," and she agreed with him.

Occasionally even as a child she caught glimpses of the

"great world" outside Cedarville. That world was not close enough to satisfy the second Mrs. Addams. It interested Jane. She often looked over with a thrill the little packet marked "Mr. Lincoln's Letters" which her father kept in his desk. There were three framed pictures of Lincoln in the house, one with "Tad." In the great world, her father's friend Lincoln had been the greatest man; she was sure of that. But there were others who had been heroic, who lived in the neighborhood, returned from fighting for their country and helping to free the slaves; or those, equally heroic, whose sons had *not* returned from that service, and they carried her childish imagination out and far. Notable men too came to Cedarville to consult her father, on problems of politics, state and national; the great Representative Lyman Trumbull, and Richard Oglesby, "Uncle Dick" as Illinois called him, governor of the state—as John Addams might have been, had he not declined to be a candidate. Once John Addams drove his wife and the two children, Jennie and George Haldeman, up to Madison, Wisconsin, sixty-five miles away, to see "Old Abe," the war-eagle of the Eighth Wisconsin, who lived in the state capitol building. "Through all my vivid sensations there persisted the image of the eagle in the corridor, and Lincoln himself, as an epitome of all that was great and good. I dimly caught the notion of the martyred President as the standard-bearer to the conscience of his countrymen, as the eagle had been the ensign of courage to the soldiers of the Wisconsin regiment." Conscience—to be followed and upheld with courage. That was the lesson she learned from these glimpses of the great world; or was it the lesson she brought to it, when later she tracked her own way through its astonishing maze? Thirty-five years later, on the occasion of the fiftieth anniversary of the University of Wisconsin at Madison, she went there again to receive a doctor's degree, the first the institution had bestowed upon a woman. "Old Abe," who had gone through thirty-six battles and skirmishes unhurt, was dead of old age then, but the great bird's brooding courage lived on in America, and not least vitally in one who by that time had gone through as many social "battles and skirmishes" as the eagle had gone through in the South.

When did Jane Addams's childhood end? One is inclined to think she first stepped over the threshold of maturity when she was fifteen; when she was sent, because no one else was available, to go and see her old nurse, who was reported to be dying:

I left the lamp-lit, warm house to be driven four miles through a blinding storm which every minute added more snow to the already high drifts, with a sense of starting upon a fateful errand. An hour after my arrival ... I was left alone to watch with Polly. The square, old-fashioned chamber in the lonely farm-house was very cold and still, with nothing to be heard but the storm outside. Suddenly the great change came. I heard a feeble call of "Sarah," my mother's name, as the dying eyes were turned upon me, followed by a curious breathing, and in place of the face familiar from my earliest childhood and associated with homely household cares, there lay upon the pillow strange, august features, stern and withdrawn from all the small affairs of life. That sense of solitude, of being unsheltered in a wide world of relentless and elemental forces, seized me. . . . As I was driven home in the winter storm, the wind through the trees seemed laden with a passing soul, and the riddle of life and death pressed hard; once to be young, to grow old and to die, everything came to that!

Not long afterward she went away to college.

CHAPTER III

ROCKFORD COLLEGE

IN June of 1877, Jane, not yet quite seventeen, went to Northampton, Massachusetts, to be examined for entrance to Smith College. The examination was oral, and though she was "nervous," she passed satisfactorily; but her father, a trustee of Rockford, thought she should attend that institution. Two of her older sisters, Mary and Alice, had studied there, Alice with distinction; indeed after her graduation she had returned for another year of work, including the tutoring of some of the younger students. Jane went to Rockford, it must be confessed, with great reluctance. There were various reasons for this reluctance. She was not a church member; had never in fact even been "baptized"; and she knew that Rockford stressed "profession." Besides, Rockford though chartered as a college had never given degrees, as Mount Holyoke and Smith gave them, and Jane wanted a degree. However, John Addams's word was law with his daughter, and she made no fuss about the matter.

Though she had been notified of her admission to Smith, she had nevertheless to take examinations again at Rockford, and written examinations at that. Eleanor Frothingham Haworth, her classmate, says:

On Saturday, September 23, 1877, on my way to a third-story recitation-room in Middle Hall, I met a little girl with very pretty light-brown hair, pushed back, and particularly direct, earnest eyes; but she looked as I know I was feeling, very trembly inside. She said her name was Laura Jane Addams and she had just come from Cedarville, but she had found the office closed and could get none of the paper given out for the examination. I gave her some of mine and we went to try our fate together. The examiner was a Mrs. Carpenter, County Superintendent of Schools, and she had no mercy on us. She gave us a regular "teachers' examination," full of very difficult problems. But we pulled through. I have always wondered if I looked as young and worried as Jane did that day.

She had formed in the solitude of Cedarville and from her own precocious introspection, a talent for sympathy; now she was, to use her own magniloquent phrase, "to mingle in the stream of life," though it was but a rivulet at first. She was to encounter among others the redoubtable Miss Sill.

Miss Sill's portrait hangs on one side of the entrance hall of Middle, the oldest of the Rockford College buildings. She was the founder of Rockford Seminary, and its principal for more than thirty years. On the other side of the hall hangs the portrait of Jane Addams, best known of Rockford alumnæ. Their eyes gaze in different directions. In the long history of the institution, however, they are the two outstanding figures. And Rockford College played a large part in the history of Jane Addams. It must never be forgotten that she had determined to be a "college woman," and that it was as a "college woman" that she planned particularly to interest other college women in the humanization of democracy and their own social salvation.

A charter for an educational institution for young women at Rockford, Illinois, *with permission to confer degrees,* was granted as early as 1847. No advantage was taken of the charter at first; but in 1849, Miss Anna P. Sill came on from New York to spy out the land. She was then thirty-three, well educated for a woman, and well trained as a teacher. And in particular she was possessed of a most passionate earnestness for Christianity in general, and for the development of Christian missionaries in particular. From childhood she had longed to be a missionary herself; but finally, when an opportunity came, decided that she could do more for missions by preparing others to go. It was in that spirit that she came to Rockford, and in that yearning conviction that she remained there. For thirty-two years she made, or tried to make, the "missionary spirit" pervasive of the institution, and when Jane Addams was at Rockford Miss Sill could boast that thirty-seven Rockford girls were active foreign missionaries themselves, besides many who were the wives of "home missionaries."

Miss Sill established a preparatory school for children in Rockford on June 11, 1849, holding classes in what was already the "old" courthouse, though the town itself had been first settled fifteen years before. In the autumn of 1851, $1,000 having been secured from the women of Rockford for the purchase of land, and $3,500 from the men of the community toward a building, fifteen girls were admitted to the first "collegiate class" of Rockford Female Seminary. This has often been said to be the first "collegiate class" in a women's institution in Illinois. The Illinois Conference Female Academy at Jacksonville, chartered in 1846, is reported by the registrar of Mac-Murray College, successor to Illinois Woman's College, successor to the "Female Academy," to have graduated its first class in 1852. The problem seems to be one of definition of terms. In 1852 Miss Sill was formally elected Principal, and the cornerstone of Middle Hall was laid with elaborate exercises. The chief speech was a sermon, from the text "That our daughters may be as cornerstones, polished after the similitude of a palace." The founders supposed that the only similar woman's educational institution then in existence anywhere was Mount Holyoke in Massachusetts.

The first "graduating class" of Rockford Seminary, seven in number, received their certificates in 1854. Fifty years later, in 1904, all seven were present at their half-century reunion—a record unique in the history of American colleges. The valedictorian of that class of '54 was Miss Adeline Potter of Rockford; afterward the mother of Julia Lathrop, who became head of the Children's Bureau of the United States. In the first ten years of the Seminary, there were 206 girls in the college classes, of whom 102 received their certificates of graduation.

The growth of the Seminary was slow. The catalogue of 1855 shows, in the three-year collegiate course, ten seniors, twenty-two "middles," and thirty juniors. Twenty-five years later, Jane Addams was one of only seventeen seniors, and that was the largest senior class up to that time. The four original "collegiate" departments, Mental and Moral Philosophy, Mathematics and Natural Sciences, History and English Literature, and Ancient Languages, had added only one, and that optional— Modern Languages, though the study of Civil Government had been added to the Natural Sciences. The departments of Music and Drawing and Painting had considerably increased; indeed, under the well-known and

able Daniel N. Hood, the Department of Music was
famous throughout the state. But year after year the
catalogues state, in unchanged phrases, the purpose of the
institution, "especially to develop moral and religious
character in accordance with right principles, that it may
send out cultivated Christian women in the various fields
of usefulness." It was Miss Sill's phrasing, it was Miss
Sill's school, and Miss Sill knew "no variableness nor
shadow of turning." By "various fields of usefulness" she
meant usefulness to God, and particularly the field of
missions. Remember the phrase in Jane's notebook,
already quoted: "She does everything from love of God
alone, and I do not like that." At seventeen Jane
was in entire accord with the idea of educating women for
usefulness, but she was presently to define new "fields of
usefulness" for herself, and at twenty-nine to define a
new field for the college women of the whole United
States. Her instinctive conflict, both in theory and spirit,
with Miss Sill, is a matter of importance in her life. For
the consciousness of this conflict tangled and confused
her not only while she was at Rockford, but for years
afterward. Until she satisfied herself that, for her at any
rate, she was right and Miss Sill was wrong, Jane Addams
was never spiritually at ease. Miss Sill was not a person
to be opposed in conviction lightly; she was too fine, too
passionate and too grimly sure that *she* was right for any
young girl, however precocious and determined to preserve
her "mental integrity," to differ with comfortably.

In 1877 there were fifty students in the collage. In all
the departments of Rockford Seminary there were 180
girls. The "tuition," which included board, plus a few

extras such as five dollars for the rent of a carpet for your room, came altogether, plus the maximum of fifty cents a week spending money if parents insisted on this plutocracy (it was discouraged), to about $275 for nine months; this did not however include music lessons, which Jane Addams took throughout her first year, but discontinued thereafter.

Also entering Rockford Seminary in 1877 was Ellen Gates Starr from Durand, Illinois, a little country town near by. Ellen Starr's father was a village businessman, a quiet conforming man of no special force; but her aunt, Miss Eliza Allen Starr, was already well-known in high Catholic church circles, and was later to be decorated for church service by the Pope himself. Ellen remained at Rockford only one year, going thence at nineteen to teach in a country school at Mount Morris, Illinois, and at twenty to Chicago. In that single year, however, Ellen Starr made a distinct impression on Rockford Seminary. She was "spiritually concerned" as deeply as any girl in the school, already seeking another denominational faith than the casual Presbyterianism of her father, and already seeking also to tie up her faith with beauty of form. It was Ellen who wrote in the school magazine on "Poetry" and on "Art in Florence." Both Art and Florence seemed to Miss Sill a long way from Rockford and its ideals. But Jane greatly admired Ellen Starr, admired her almost passionate eagerness to understand both divinity and beauty, admired her wit, admired her intelligence. She was to write to Ellen Starr oftener in the next few years than to any one else except her own family, bring her frequently to Cedarville to visit, and assert more than once that "you are wiser and better than I am." And in

1889 it was to be Ellen Gates Starr whom Jane Addams was to persuade to take up residence as a "co-founder" of Hull House.

When Jane entered Rockford, she was no longer 'homely," if indeed she ever had been except in her own eyes. She was small, five feet three inches tall, and weighing ninety-five pounds—but she no longer "carried her head on one side," only a little forward, which with her seeking eyes gave her an appearance of unusual earnestness even at that abode of earnestness, Rockford Female Seminary. And throughout her years at the institution, her health remained better than it had ever been. She sparkled with enthusiasm. In the little town of Winnebago, eight miles from Rockford, they still tell stories of the lively young girl who used to come from the college to visit her sister, the wife of the Winnebago Presbyterian minister. There was a wedding at a farmhouse some miles from Winnebago one snowy winter evening, at which her brother-in-law was to officiate. Jane insisted on driving out with him in the "swell-bodied cutter," which tipped over twice in the drifts. At the farmhouse Jane burst into the kitchen, shook the snow from her skirts, and cried, "I can't wait to tell the girls I've been to a wedding and turned over twice to get there"! Many years afterwards, the bride of that occasion applied to a Judge of the circuit to certify her application for a pension following her husband's death. The judge asked her for proof of the marriage. "Miss Jane Addams was there and will tell you all about it," said the woman.

"In this district," the judge commented, "that's the best evidence you could offer."

In 1909 Corinne Williams Douglas, a graduate first of

Rockford and then of the law school of the University of Michigan, and founder of a girls' technical school in Atlanta, Georgia, wrote:

My first memory of Jane Addams brings back to me a Sunday evening in Rockford Female Seminary, where we had both just matriculated and entered upon that wonderful time of deep impressions, our freshman year. It was then the custom on Sunday evenings, after a supper of Puritan austerity, for all those who were sitting at table with their backs towards the center of the room, to rise solemnly and replace their chairs, facing inward. When this evolution had been completed on this particular September night, I found myself on the inner line of the quadrangle, and just opposite me, Jane Addams. Of course, I already knew her name, and had begun to feel the charm of her personality, but this is my first distinct remembrance. I see her as plainly now as though it were but yesterday. The brown hair drawn plainly back, with a decided inclination, never encouraged, to fall apart on the side, the chin raised, the head slightly bent to one side, the face turned at an angle to me as she gave her attention to the speaker. . . . School girls are not psychologists, and we never speculated as to why we liked to go to her room so that it was always crowded when the sacred "engaged" sign was not hung out. We just knew there was always something "doing" where she was, and that however mopey it might be elsewhere there was intellectual ozone in her vicinity. But now looking back over the last thirty years, one sees that then in her little world, as now in the great world, she had the same intellectual vitality, the same cosmopolitan sympathies, the same strong self-poised character.

Jane was the daughter of the leading citizen of his neighborhood, the largest land-owner in Stephenson County, perhaps the only man in the state who had refused the Republican nomination for Governor, and a trustee of the institution. Her dresses were the best the regulations and traditions of the Seminary permitted; her socially ambitious stepmother insisted on that. And besides the girls quickly perceived in her the touch of rebellion which was to flavor her conscientiousness all her life. Mrs. Haworth writes:

As soon as we became aware of the "missionary atmosphere" of Rockford we passed about a paper with the promise that none of us would go as missionaries. Miss Sill would have been saddened. But the paper never got to her, and two of us did go later, one to Japan and one to Korea. Whether Jane signed that paper I do not remember. But I do remember that whenever difficulties with Miss Sill came up for settlement, most of us "let Jane do it" in presenting them. Miss Sill, stately and dignified, tried regimentation, and there was opposition to it. We were quite willing to work hard, but we were sometimes on tiptoe with the desire to work in our own way. In our class in Moral Philosophy, Jane insisted on giving the name "Don Quixote" the Spanish pronunciation. We backed her up with laughter at Miss Sill's "Don Quix-ott." Miss Sill suspended the whole class for two days, then took us back without comment. At chapel exercises that day Jane took my hymnal and wrote on the fly-leaf,

> Life's a burden, bear it.
> Life's a duty, dare it.
> Life's a thorn-crown? Wear it
> And spurn to be a coward!

She was a rebel but she "spurned to be a coward."

She was literally unable to accept conventions of thought, at Rockford or later. The wind of her spirit blew through the old house of Rockford Seminary, stirring up the dust of intellectual tradition.

The life at the Seminary in the late 1870's was industrious, idealistic, and yet lively. The food was plain and some of the girls thought it was bad, though most of them

JANE ADDAMS AS AN UNDER-
GRADUATE AT ROCKFORD
COLLEGE, 1880

JANE ADDAMS IN LONDON, 1888

came from unluxurious homes. And the rooms in the dormitory, heated by wood-stoves, were either too hot or too cold in winter, depending on the amount of interest possessed by the occupants in fresh air. Every girl had to bring all her own equipment, even her "teaspoon," and the girls had to take care of their own rooms. In 1877 the smelly laundry was next to the class-rooms, though in the following year it was moved into the basement. And the emphasis of the whole routine was on study and religious discipline—Miss Sill's religion. Even the prescribed physical exercise was very dreary—every day each girl must walk for one hour on the wooden walk about the grounds, making the same narrow circuit twenty or thirty times in damp weather. Jane preferred even that to her stepmother's prescribed Saturday morning horse-back riding, which hurt her spine.

But the spirit of youth was not to be suppressed. The relaxations were both social and intellectual. Monday morning to Friday night, one worked and studied, but Saturday and Sunday were different. On Saturdays the boys from Beloit College, twenty miles away, and chartered for young men by the same group and at the same time that Rockford was chartered for young women, came to call; now and then in the winter to take some of the girls on properly chaperoned sleigh-rides; and to seek wives. Sixteen Beloit theological students, it is said, married "missionarily inclined" girls from Rockford Seminary. George Haldeman came, he was a Beloit boy now, and Rollin Salisbury. Salisbury was an orphan from Lake Geneva way (there is a tablet commemorating him now on the old farmhouse where he spent his sad, resentful boyhood). Salisbury, already interested in geology, accustomed to labor fourteen hours a day, debater, orator, president of his class, the ablest of his group, was at the end of his senior year to propose marriage to the class president of Rockford, Jane Addams, and to be refused. Salisbury remained a bachelor all his days. From 1892 until he died, he was the distinguished professor of geography at the University of Chicago, and Jane Addams was the head resident of Hull House only six miles away, but Salisbury never entered its door. A romantic story, often whispered, probably true.

Then on Sundays Jane, first giving her room a thorough cleaning, could go into "Miss Blaisdell's room" and read the Greek Testament with her—"blessed Sunday morning readings," she calls them, with a blessed lack of emphasis either on meticulous translation or meticulous interpretation of doctrine. Or she could go to Winnebago and listen to her brother-in-law's exposition of an unferocious version of Presbyterian doctrine (the Reverend John M. Linn could never bring himself to accept infant damnation), and play with her small nephews, in whose company she delighted. Or she could take a friend or two to Cedarville, two hours away by train and the family carriage, and proudly present them to her tall, gentle-mannered father and her magnificent and somewhat terrifying stepmother, whose piercing eye noted their school-girlishness in every detail, but who would play on her guitar and sing to them nevertheless on Saturday evenings, though not on Sunday. On Sunday afternoons John Addams used always to retire to his own room for private devotions. Sometimes Jane Addams's young visitors heard odd sounds coming from the room, almost like groans. When they inquired the cause of these groans, Jane explained,

"Father is getting heavy and rheumatic, but he insists on kneeling to pray, and it hurts him."

Most of the Rockford relaxations however were literary. To quote again Mrs. Douglas:

In those days sororities were not, at least in our western colleges, and the literary society flourished like the green bay tree. At Rockford we had two such societies, the Castalian, which held itself proudly aloft as the repository of intellect, with an Emersonian motto and real programs, and which rather looked down with a condescending tolerance upon the more frivolous and worldly-minded Vesperians. The first few weeks of each school year were given over to a maddeningly exciting game of politics to see which society should capture the most and the most desirable new girls. The very storm centers of these campaigns were the public entertainments, to which neophytes and enemies were alike invited. . . . A little band of us were much impressed with the evils of studying for teachers' grade or percentages, instead of being actuated by the pure love of learning without regard to any reward from without. That one should study, that one went to college for that purpose, was to our unsophisticated minds a simple self-evident fact, not debatable. *Tempora mutantur.* Our only problem was study to what end? Also we felt laid upon us that obligation to reform the world now, immediately, which is a part of youth. So that night we presented an allegory of which Jane was the author. . . . It represented a girl fresh from home entering her academic career and eager to drink deep from the Pierian spring. As she enters the classic portals, on the one hand love of learning, study for its own sake, the seeking for the highest in order to attain the highest, beckons beseechingly in the guise of a stately Minerva, clad all in white, and mounted on a pedestal to look more statuesque. On the other hand, clad all in red like Morrison's Faust, is Marks, tempting by divers arts to study for the world's, that is, the teacher's, approval. . . . So the struggle went on between the higher motive and the lower until after much hesitation the decision went against Minerva, who retired weeping to her pedestal. "Right Front!" and the misguided devotee of Marks entered into servitude to her diabolical master. The last end of that girl was something quite too dreadful to contemplate, but a mixture, no doubt, of the end of Ben Greet's *Everyman* and the damnation of *Faust*, spectacularly limited to the resources of a chapel platform.

In the spring of Jane's first year she became a member too of a newly formed scientific association, which listened to lectures from outside talent on botany, and on the structure and diseases of the eye. Ellen Starr was also a member of this association—one would like to have seen Ellen Starr listening to such recreational disquisitions! Jane placed glasses of water containing corn and wheat grains on the floor under the stove in her room, and watched their germination, already suspecting that the study of science was to become important in woman's education. Bronson Alcott, ponderous, vague, but after all "a friend of Emerson," also came to lecture, and in "a state of ecstatic energy" Jane cleaned the clay of the miry Rockford streets from his heavy cloth undershoes, and the next night secured permission to go down town and hear him lecture once more—to what, alas, the newspaper report seems to consider a somewhat bored "city" audience. Later there was a "birthday fête" in honor of Mark Hopkins, author of *Evidences of Christianity*, and the same of whom it was said that Mark Hopkins at one end of a log, and a boy at the other end, constituted a university. At this fête, it may be noted, although the first toast was of course to Mark Hopkins, the second was to Jane Addams, the "best evidence of Christianity."

She was more or less constantly a "debater." On one occasion she advocated no less unpatriotic a thesis than that "the English form of government tends to produce better statesmen than the American," and won the convictions of her audience. And in her last year she was chosen to represent Rockford on the first occasion when that institution was permitted to send delegates to the Interstate Oratorical Contest. This was in June of 1881. Among the nine contestants were Rollin Salisbury of Beloit, and a young man from Illinois College named William Jennings Bryan. Neither of them won, but both were ranked ahead of Jane, who stood, as she says, "exactly in the dreary middle." By her account, she was felt on this occasion to represent "not only one school but college women in general," to stand as it were for "the progress of Women's Cause," and when she returned to the Seminary she found "the ardent group not only exhausted by the premature preparations for the return of a successful orator, but naturally irritated as they contemplated their drooping garlands. They did not fail to make me realize that I had dealt the cause of woman's advancement a staggering blow." She herself however had "so heartily concurred with the decision of the judges that it was with a carefree mind I induced my colleague (Annie Sidwell) to remain long enough in Jacksonville to visit the state institutions, one for the blind and one for the deaf and dumb."

One wonders if any others among the defeated oratorical warriors could so light-heartedly hang up their shields and turn to the problems of institutional research. That colleague subsequently became a teacher of the blind for many years. Perhaps the trip had a positive as well as a negative effect upon the "progress of women."

The most exciting, the most arduous and the most continuous literary relaxation, however, Jane Addams found in the *Rockford Seminary Magazine.* She began writing for it in her freshman year; in her next year became editor of the "Home Department," and presented jokes and anecdotes which have not entirely lost iridescence, though it must be granted that she had not at that time the "light touch." In her senior year, the "quarterly" having already become a "monthly," she was editor-in-chief, and was able to say that the *Magazine* "for the first time has money in the bank."

Until Jane Addams went to Rockford, the *Magazine* had been frankly, if idealistically, propagandist. For a time it remained chiefly so. In October of 1878 Miss Sill could still declare that "we publish the quarterly in the interest of the Seminary and the cause of Christian education in general," and on that basis solicit its support. The occasional "stories" were determinedly moral, as for example "How Shall She Be Made to See?" which discusses the fatality of a hostess's offering of punch to a young gentleman caller on New Year's afternoon. The essays were sternly moral also—"An Hour With My Herbarium" considering the lessons to be drawn from struggling plants and vines, "The Brightness of a Rainy Day" developing no fresher a thesis than that into each life some rain must fall, and "The Progress of Foreign Missions and the Reflex Influence Upon Women" laying a somewhat heavy hand upon education. Incidentally it may here be noted that there were three Missionary Societies in Rockford Seminary during Jane Addams's stay there, and they were the only societies in which she never held office.

But the tone of the *Magazine* changes. It becomes both philosophical and critical. In Ellen Starr's "Poems" in 1878, in her "Soul-Culture" (in spite of its title) and in her "Florence and Edinburgh," there is far less of the moral than of the eagerly esthetic; in the last, indeed, an enthusiastic description of the beautiful in the Catholic religion may have made Miss Sill not unregretful that one sensitive to such beauty had already left Rockford, and may perhaps have foreshadowed the decision that later turned Miss Starr to acceptance of the Catholic faith. Jane Addams's own contributions to the magazine are from the first purely critical, and they seem to this writer to become, as time goes on, brilliantly critical; remarkable in various passages, and in one entire article, demanding preservation.

The earliest, "Plated Ware," published in April 1878 when she was still seventeen, is high-sounding enough. Yet the idea may be noted—that as articles placed in molten metal are plated by the introduction of an electric current, so the negative minds of the human majority are plated with convention by strong currents of contemporary thought. Fantastic? Perhaps, but it is just possible that such a conception, uniting an interest in scientific mechanics with an interest in individual thinking, had not occurred to any other woman in America in the Victorian 'seventies, and highly probable that if it had, she was not a young girl of seventeen.

In the next year Jane improves in clarity while maintaining originality of idea. "The Element of Hopefulness in Human Nature," with its optimistic certainty that in the inevitable hopefulness of children is indicated the inevitable persistence of hope in the human race;

"Marks," the little morality play which half-humorously, half-regretfully, points out the fate of him who works for reward, not for the "joy of the working"; and "One Office of Nature," repeating in prose the poetical Wordsworthian conviction of the possibility that the study of Nature may teach us understanding of the Divine—these are typical. From the last one may quote:

Probably no man ever came into the pure presence of Nature who was more unworthy to know her secrets than Wolfgang Von Goethe, yet he came in a moment of repentance and kindly Nature received him. In his era all Germany was overcivilized, entangled in a morbid feeling of oppression; she was weighed down under a load of books and modern philosophies, surrounded by a rolling miscellany of facts and sciences, and German life had a narrowness and hardness. Goethe bore the curse of his time; he was filled full of its skepticism, hollowness and a thousandfold contradictions, till his heart was like to break; yet it was given to him to change the chaos into creation, and to dispose with ease of the distracting variety of claims. He turned away from all the confusion and studied with human eyes the unity and simplicity of Nature. It was he who suggested the leading idea of modern botany, that the leaf is the unit of growth, and that every plant is only a transformed leaf. In optics again he rejected the artificial theory of seven colors and considered that every color was the miniature of light and darkness in new proportions. He did away with a great deal of the sham learning and cant of the age by teaching to modern scientists the high simplicity of Nature. Many of the theories he formed from his discoveries were false, yet even these theories unlocked the narrow ties of the old order, and human nature breathed freer. Goethe was the deliverer of his time; he studied nature throughout his long life, and his last words, while waiting for his eighty-second birthday, were a welcome to the returning spring.

But one article, on "The Macbeth of Shakespeare,"

may be given in full. Jane Addams at nineteen was flying high, in the pathway of light radiated by Coleridge and De Quincey (of whose works she was for some reason particularly fond). Judge for yourself whether her young wings blaze into a fall:

The Macbeth of Shakespeare

In the Eleventh Century Duncan and Macbeth were two grandsons of the reigning king of Scotland. In course of time the old king peacefully died and Duncan ascended the throne. He had but the shadow of a claim over his cousin, he was not as gifted a man, he probably made no greater effort toward the crown and yet he gained it. The divine right of kings was bestowed upon him while Macbeth was merely one of his subjects. We should take Duncan to be one of those men who in some way have the material universe on their side, a "great vague backing" in all they do and undertake, the word "luck" somewhat expresses their success, things turn out just to suit them, and honors are easily granted them. Macbeth had no doubt observed this ever since he could remember, it seemed perfectly natural for Duncan to be king and gain that which he desires. Macbeth is not envious, but he continually thinks of these things, he is a nervous man and cannot think calmly.

Shakespeare leaves us to imagine all this. He does not present Macbeth until these thoughts have begun to pursue and control him; until his mind has gained that sort of exasperation which comes from using living muscle against some lifeless insurmountable resistance.

All the scenes of the play are laid at night, and we are hurried on with feverish rapidity—we do not know the Macbeth of the day time, how he appears in council or battle—we meet only the nervous high strung man at night, pursued by phantoms and ghosts, and ever poetically designing a murder.

Shakespeare presents the man's thoughts ere he presents the man himself, and in the very first scene the three witches frighten us before we know what they are to represent. As Macbeth enters they hail him with the three titles his heart most desires; he starts, who wouldn't? The thoughts he has been thinking and thinking, have suddenly embodied themselves, and stand before him on the bold bare heath; they have all at once grown into definite purposes, have spoken out before a third person, Banquo, and he knows that ever afterwards he must acknowledge them, that they will pursue and harass him. We have all had the experience—how we prepare ourselves for sudden deeds by the intuitive choice of good and evil, or, as our thoughts go forth never to be recalled, how they increase and gain enormous proportions until we lose all control of them. But Macbeth had this experience in a way that was simply frightful; his thought grew so powerful as to assume form and shape, as to be endowed with life and a distinct physical existence to baffle and confront him. His first impulse is one of fear and terror at the metaphysical confusion in which he is entangled. He is lost in a maze of his own thoughts, he knows not what is real and what is fantastical, he is filled with horrible imaginings and doubts; but slowly from all this confusion there arises a phantom distinctly before him, it seems afar off, he detaches it from himself, and yet he knows it is his own creation. He says:

"Why do I yield to that suggestion,
Whose horrid image doth unfix my hair"—

That image is murder, it takes a poetical man to call it an image, but Macbeth tries to deceive himself and keep his heart of hearts pure. Here he yields to that impulse of a sort of self-preservation, that shielding of his inner character, he wishes not to harm or shock himself, he would gain a deadly end, but without the illness that should attend it; with this purpose he reorganizes the witches and phantoms, and shifts upon them the entire moral responsibility of his future actions, he follows them mechanically and saves himself—it is a phantom that murders Duncan.

He discloses his purpose to Lady Macbeth, and thus gives to her the physical or material responsibility, she plans and contrives, does all coolly and calmly, for she is but murdering a man—avenging her father; Macbeth meanwhile is struggling throughout with murder itself, invisible yet clinging and horrible the phantom pursues him until the last moment. Just before the final deed he soliloquizes:

"Now o'er the one half world
Nature seems dead, and withered murder
Alarmed by his sentinel the wolf
Moves like a ghost"—

'Tis "withered murder" that leads him on to his destruction, and he follows it as something inevitable. Macbeth has slowly prepared a splendid defense for himself, it is utterly impossible for him, murdering Duncan, to receive any conscious harm or any violent shock to his inner self, and yet he is thwarted by his own ends. He kills Duncan and comes back to his wife horror-struck and frightened, not because of the bloody deed, but because he has murdered sleep, because he has heard a voice cry "Sleep no more! Macbeth does murder sleep!" No matter how often we read it, it always produces the same thrilling effect; the idea of a man murdering sleep; think of being pursued by withered murder and a sleepless sleep.

This then is the result, by getting rid of his will and following merely the poetical idea, he kills not a man, but an imaginary, an invisible horrible being; it is frightful.

After the death of Duncan, the rest of the play is virtually but a repetition. Macbeth is driven from murder to murder, ghosts and phantoms pursue him, he consults again the weird sisters, gains courage and is lost through his own daring—a poetical man doing the worst deeds in a poetical sense—the philosophy of murder.

In the course of her four years at Rockford Seminary, Jane Addams studied Latin, Greek, Natural Science, Ancient History and Literature, Mental and Moral Philosophy, and French, which was "optional." She concentrated on the Greek and Natural Science, and on her own private exercises in English composition, which were very dear to her. After her first year she dropped music, for which she had no talent whatever, and added mathematics through differential calculus, which she found "exceedingly interesting," though her interest may have lain in the fact that she and Catherine Waugh were the only girls in Rockford who were studying it. They had their special reason for doing so, of which more later. She stood high in all her classes, usually the highest, and she fulfilled every detail of the stern disciplinary code. One of the college jokes was her punctuality. In her second year Miss Sill advised the young women to guard against tardiness by seeing to it "that at least one other girl beside yourself is on time," and to save bother, the *Magazine* remarks, most of the girls decided "to be responsible for Jane Addams." Her interest in George Haldeman's field of "natural science" was constant. She read Darwin's *Origin of Species* and *The Descent of Man,* and accepted the doctrine of "evolution," though even then she could not see that "the struggle of the fittest for survival" in the physical world had any direct connection with the ethical and moral struggle. It is recorded in February 1880 that "Jane Addams and May Southworth have been taking lessons of a taxidermist, and the results of their labors are most astonishing." Tradition reports that a live hawk was sent them to kill and stuff. A caller from Beloit was consulted on how to kill the hawk, and advised putting salt on its tail, but was finally persuaded to take it somewhere and shoot it.

The teachers at Rockford College in the late 1870's were of the sort to appreciate the strenuosity of their pupils. There was for instance Charlotte Emerson in Modern Languages, who after her retirement to marry, became the organizer and first President, reëlected three times, of that astonishing organization the General Federation of Women's Clubs of the United States. There was Caroline Potter in History and Literature, who also later withdrew into matrimony, and as Mrs. Brazee became second only to Charlotte Emerson Brown as an organizer of women's clubs. There was Sarah Blaisdell—"a teacher whose ideal was perfection." Sister of the distinguished Blaisdell of Beloit College, she was determined that scholarship among women should maintain a standard men might admire. "Not an a or a the could be dropped or changed in place in the long lessons to be committed to memory, and Latin translations must be made with the same exactness. . . . She was most feared, but by those who knew her intimately, greatly beloved." And above all there was Miss Sill.

Miss Sill perhaps more than other teacher appreciated strenuosity and earnestness. And she appreciated Jane Addams. But they differed not only on the matter of professed Christianity, but also on the matter of Seminary versus College. The charter had provided permission for the granting of college degrees to women. But in all the years since 1853, Rockford had never given one woman a college degree, B.A., by Jane Addams so eagerly desired. Smith would have given it to her, but her father would not let her go to Smith. She determined that Rockford should give it to her. Some of the teachers, two or three of the girls, agreed to agitate and work for it. To secure it, they must have not only a reasonably scholarly acquaintance with Greek, but also higher mathematics. It was for this reason that Jane Addams and Catherine Waugh fought for and obtained permission to study calculus; for this reason that Jane determined to deliver her own graduation oration in Greek which should be worthy of the intelligence of women. In her Junior Exhibition speech, given in April, 1880, when she was still only nineteen, Jane declared: "The change which has taken place in the last fifty years in the ambitions and aspirations of women, we see most markedly in education. It has passed from the accomplishments and the arts of pleasing, to the development of her intellectual forces and her capabilities for direct labor." That was a nailing of her thesis to the door of Miss Sill's religious training-school cathedral. The times had changed, and Miss Sill could not change. In her first year Jane had set down in her notebook more legibly than any other entry the quotation, "Always do what you are afraid to do." But three years later she remarks in an editorial article in the *Magazine*, "To do what you are afraid to do is to guide your life by fear. How much better not to be afraid to do what you believe in doing! Keep one main idea, and you will never be lost. 'For the end of man is an action and not a thought, were that of the noblest.'" More than any other Rockford person of her time, Jane Addams, by sticking to her main idea and "ending it in action," forced Rockford Seminary to become Rockford College. The college idea won the battle. Though Jane was not given the precious A.B. degree when she finished her course in 1881, it was agreed that she should receive it the next year, without further study, and that from then on all young women who chose might study for the degree and receive it in regular course. Rockford "Female Seminary," had at last become what it had been chartered to be, Rockford College for Women.

Seventeen young women were graduated in 1881. Jane,

the class president, was the "valedictorian." She declared
to the "salutatorian," second highest in rank, "Nora, when
we speak, we must *say* something." She did say words
that, according to the salutatorian, "some of us have remembered and kept as a heritage all through the years":

We have expressed to each other higher and nobler things
than we have probably ever said to any one else, and these
years of young life being past, better perhaps than we shall
say again. We stand united to-day in a belief in beauty, genius,
and courage, and that these expressed through truest womanhood can yet transform the world.

"As she stood up to speak," says one who was a Beloit
undergraduate and came over to the Rockford commencement exercises, "she was slight and pale, spirited and
charming. I have to confess that I fell in love with Jane
Addams that day, and never got over it."

Miss Sill listened with a slight severity of look. She
was a woman of nobility, but her elasticity was gone. The
change to a college did not wholly please her, the change
in the ideals (there was no change in the principles) of the
institution did not please her at all. Jane turned and
addressed her directly: "By the mysterious laws of culture which come from giving, each year you have had
more to give.... If in future years any of us stand firm
where it would be easier to fall, if we are moved by principle while those around us are swayed by impulse—to
you will redound the glory."

It was a noble tribute to a great woman from one who
was to become great. But it was a tribute to a woman
whose eyes are turned one way, as in the Middle Hall
portrait, from a woman whose eyes are turned the other.

The following year Jane returned to take her degree

formally. First to receive the A.B. were the two "regular" graduates of 1882, Julia Gardiner and Harriet Wells; then Jane Addams of 1881, the first college woman to finish the course at Rockford. She was shaky with the fatigue of a long illness that spring; she had had to force herself to be present. But she stepped out proudly. She was to be honored with fourteen "honorary degrees" before she died, more by far than any other woman in the world has ever been the recipient of, but none of them meant to her what that A.B. meant, for which she had fought as a girl in behalf of other girls as well as herself. Her "certificate" the year before had been made out to Laura Jane Addams. Her degree was in the name of Jane Addams. She never used any other name thenceforward.

Her connection with Rockford remained close till she died. In 1886 she made the largest single gift to Rockford Library funds ever made by a graduate up to that time— $1,000 for books on scientific subjects. Next year the college made her a trustee, the youngest trustee in its history. In 1888 she contributed to the little volume of memorial addresses to Miss Sill, who had just died, the most beautiful words Jane had written up to that time. From 1891, and for ten years thereafter, Rockford Colleged allowed her the use of its buildings for a "Hull House Summer School" in July and August. The Jane Addams Professorship of Social Science was established at Rockford in 1930, endowed by contributions from or secured by her own classmates. She was the speaker at all commencements for which she could be secured. In the love and honor of Rockford College she stands with many a glorious woman, but she stands foremost; perhaps always will.

CHAPTER IV

WHAT SHALL SHE DO?

FROM the time she left Rockford, in June of 1881, until she went to Hull House in September of 1889, Jane Addams says that she was "absolutely at sea so far as any moral purpose was concerned, clinging only to the desire to live in a really living world and refusing to be content with a shadowy intellectual or esthetic reflection of it." That she drifted along is true. But that desire of hers to live in a really living world was a safe spar to cling to.

A summer of pleasant anticipations of a "career" in medicine, of visiting friends at Mount Carroll and entertaining other friends at Cedarville, ended in August, just before her twenty-first birthday, with the terrible shock of her father's death. Mr. and Mrs. Addams, with Jane and her stepbrother George Haldeman, had gone on a trip to the Lake Superior copper country, where John Addams was thinking of investing. He did some rather thorough investigation of mining properties, which required considerable physical exertion. It is possible that climbing about had some connection with his fatal illness. At any rate, he was suddenly stricken. They got him back to Green Bay, Wisconsin, and there within thirty-six hours he died. It was a burst appendix—what was then called "inflammation of the bowels"—and John Addams never had a chance. The family brought the body back to Cedarville and laid it in the cemetery on the slope a quarter of a mile from his house, just beyond the crest which was then crowned by the umbrella-shaped tufted pines he had planted thirty-seven years before. He was fifty-nine years of age when he died.

"The greatest sorrow that can ever come to me," Jane wrote to Ellen Starr three days later, "has passed, and I hope it is only a question of time until I get my moral purposes straightened." But it is characteristic that most of this short and broken letter should be practical. "I am so sorry you are tired out and wish with all my heart I could do something for you. I solemnly charge you, drink a bottle of malt every day and use for your chief food *desiccated blood*, the first called Hoff's Extract and the second manufactured in Detroit. I know they will help build you up for I have wilted, tried them and revived. I wish you could come to Cedarville before you return to Chicago if only for a day or two . . . only prepare yourself so you won't be too disappointed in me when you come."

John Addams's habit of thought is illustrated by the fact that though he had been a banker he left no will. As a State Senator he had helped to formulate the laws of inheritance in Illinois, and he told his family they were sound laws and he intended to take advantage of them. A third of the estate went to his wife, a sixth to each of four surviving children, all of whom were of age. A large part of the inheritance of each child was a farm of 160 acres, a quarter-section either in Buckeye or one of the adjoining townships. Three of those farms are still in the possession of the family after fifty-five years.

The sorrow of that summer was increased for Jane

by the fact that in July Julius Guiteau, the half-brother of Jane's best friend in Freeport, had in a fit of insanity shot President Garfield. The senior Guiteau was the cashier of John Addams's bank in Freeport, and his two younger children, by a second wife, were constant visitors at Cedarville. Even one who was only five years old at that time remembers the storm of fury that swept over the country at the assassination of Garfield, and the center of that cyclone of feeling was Freeport, where Julius Guiteau had lived. The day that the insane man was hanged, Jane herself was hidden away with a member of the Guiteau family on the shore of Nantucket Island, trying by reading aloud to her to keep her friend's thoughts from the horror of the murder and the execution. Of the insanity of Julius Guiteau there can be no doubt. To Nantucket in a day or two came a letter from Julius's brother, who had been with him on the scaffold, telling how Julius had died. "Don't be frightened," Julius had persisted. "I am not to be hanged. I have had a message from God the father over and over again, and he says he is sending a band of angels to carry me away to heaven. You will see, brother, it will all be all right."

Twenty years later Czolgolz assassinated President McKinley. In the midst of similar storms of public feeling, a harmless and innocent old man who lived near Hull House in Chicago was arrested on suspicion of having conspired with Czolgolz. The old man's house was searched from top to bottom by the police, his wife and daughter were taken to the police-station and kept there, and the old man himself and his son were flung into some long-disused cells in the basement of the city hall, and denied the right even to see a lawyer. Jane Addams and a young man named Raymond Robins went to see the mayor at his house to urge that every citizen had rights under the law. The mayor refused to permit a lawyer to see the old man, but told Jane Addams that "in the interests of fair play" he would permit *her* to talk to the prisoner. As soon as she left, whether or not still in the interests of fair play, he informed the newspapers of his decision. Surrounded by sixteen policemen, Jane Addams talked to the old man, told him his wife and daughter were safe, and advised him that if he was innocent public feeling would soon die down enough to allow of the resumption of legal procedure. From the city hall she went back to Hull House, to find it swarming with reporters, friendly enough, but sent by violently hostile city editors. The papers proceeded for days to assert that she was "abetting anarchy." Her mail for weeks was a horror of accusation, reproach, and even threat. At that time she was constantly in the expectation of having her relation to the Guiteau family in 1881 brought up, but it never was. This is the first statement of her connection with *both* the hysterias which followed those presidential assassinations. The immured old man was presently released, without a stain on his character, but shattered to the breaking-point by the treatment bred of panic.

Before her father's death, Jane had made her plan to register at the Woman's Medical College in Philadelphia in October of 1881, and his death made her all the more determined to go. She not only wanted, or thought she wanted, to study medicine, but she also wanted to get away from Cedarville. She went therefore to Philadelphia, where for seven months she worked hard, and passed with high credit her examinations in the subjects then required in the first year. But though she had long thought the matter over her heart was not wholly in the job. She had no such passionate interest in anatomy as her stepbrother George had in biology. And besides, her health broke down completely in the spring of 1882. She spent some time in Weir Mitchell's hospital in Philadelphia, and when she was able to travel came back to Cedarville, only to break down again. She went to Rockford, to receive with one classmate and two other girls the A.B. degree from the college, but her back was very bad, and her nervous system was shaken by her father's death and her endeavor to forget it by concentrated study. The following winter she was completely invalided, "bound to a bed," as she says, for six months, the longest consecutive period she ever spent in a sick-room. The bed she was bound to was in the home of her sister Alice in Mitchellville, Iowa, not far from Des Moines. It was here that Doctor Haldeman, her stepbrother and her sister's husband, operated on her spine. As she recovered she passed the time reading Carlyle to herself, and telling fairy stories and "Stories from Homer" to this biographer, whose earliest recollection of Jane Addams is of listening entranced while she presented never-varying repetitions of the tale of the Princess and the Frog. "What thou hast promised thou must perform!"—the King's words to his daughter have echoed in his ears ever since, but with no moral implication. His "poor auntie" as he called her, was an entertainer in those days, not a moralist. Indeed, she never confused the two functions.

Doctor Haldeman devised a sort of strait-jacket for the support of her spine. It was constructed of steel ribs with whalebone between them, was so high in front that it pressed constantly on her lungs, and so uncomfortable that fifty years later she declared she could still remember the feeling of it. She wore it first on a train-ride from Chicago to Albany. "It pounded and rubbed all the way," she wrote her sister, "but I did not have a backache and although I feel sore to-night I have not the regulation pain, so I guess we can call it a success, although I do hope it will grow more comfortable in time than it is to-day." She continued to wear it for more than a year, but never once refers to it again in all her voluminous letters to her family.

She spent the early summer of 1883 planning a trip to Europe, which Dr. Haldeman had also prescribed "for relaxation of the nerves." Her stepmother, who was to accompany her, was in Annisquam, Massachusetts. Jane left Cedarville late in July; visited in Waukesha, and in DeKalb, Illinois, where she found herself entertained in a house "the most elegant I ever was in or saw. The manifest evidence of unbounded wealth is perhaps somewhat shoddy, but withal there is something historic and impressive in grand staircases, a gardener's house in the grounds, and stables filled with horses and dogs." Thence to Philadelphia and New York, where she enjoyed herself with her many uncles, aunts and cousins, the Webers, Reiffs and Worralls "who were so cordial and affectionate it seems like a blessing just to have seen them"; though in Philadelphia she had her pocketbook stolen, containing twenty-five dollars and her letter of credit. With her stepmother and six friends in the party, she sailed on the *Servia* August 22nd. "They all seemed well and happy," wrote "Uncle Harry" Weber, who saw them off. "Jane's mother shed a tear which I promptly dried up with my 'kerchief and with all due respect bade her 'dry up' also. Kissed her and Jane and left them standing on the deck."

Theodore Thomas was on board. "I saw him sitting to-day on the same bench with a small boy who was playing a jews'-harp, he was watching him with a mixture of good-natured contempt and kindly amusement which made his face very pleasant to remember. Celebrity number two is Henry James the novelist, whom I look at most of the time between courses at table; he is very English in appearance, but not especially keen or intellectual." There was also an Englishman who viewed with pleasure the phosphorescent sea which rolled away from the stern, and declared "it was almost as fine as the American lightning-bugs"; he had made the tour of the United States, and declared that the fireflies were the finest thing he had seen. After much discussion, the party of ladies decided to land at Queenstown, which they reached on August 29th.

Jane began at once to keep a notebook account of her experiences. Such a journal was inevitable in the case of a well-educated young woman of twenty-three on her first journey to Europe in those aspiring days. But the first entries are somewhat singular for the times. For instance Blarney Castle the next day inspires the following observation: "Owner said to have an income of thirteen thousand pounds a year; ordinary man six shillings a week; could not kiss the Blarney stone, though the castle is very beautiful." The following day they drove through Dunloe Pass, "a black valley where the sun does not shine for three months in the year. The poor people have only land enough to raise hay and potatoes. Some of the houses have no windows, and I was told they 'don't need to see in the winters, ma'am, they can sit in the dark.' But the Earl of Kennan has built 170 beautiful workmen's cottages on his estate, and the workmen earn nine shillings a week beside their homes. Even the Dunloe Gap is said to be so healthy that people live in it to be 115." Life, it may be perceived, and no "shadowy or intellectual reflection of it," was what interested her, chiefly.

It was not until two months later, however, in London, after they had "done" Scotland and the English Midlands—including Stratford-on-Avon, where she notes "a drunken man at the gates reciting 'all the world's a stage' " —that she got that one ineradicable glimpse of "how the other half lives" which may be said to have first opened to her the vista of her own future. Her notebook says little of it, to be sure. "We took the Underground to Aldersgate Street, then a street-car, (on top) down to Bethnal Green. Came back the Mile End Road to Aldgate Station near the old debtors' prison. The thousands of poor people who were marketing at the booths and stalls along the streets." What had happened along the way that was to influence, if not to direct, her whole life? It was a Saturday night, and Jane Addams and other tourists were taken by a city missionary to see the weekly "auctions" of decaying food —vegetables and fruit which by law could not be sold on Sunday, and would not keep till Monday morning. On Mile End Road, from the top of their omnibus, they looked down a dingy street lighted by gas-flares, and saw masses of people

clamoring around two huckster's carts. They were bidding their farthings and ha'pennies for a vegetable held up by the auctioneer. . . . Only one man detached himself from the group. He had bidden in a cabbage, and when it struck his hand, he instantly sat down on the curb, tore it with his teeth, and hastily devoured it, unwashed and uncooked as it was. . . . But the impression of the whole was of myriads of hands, empty, pathetic, nerveless and workworn, showing white in the uncertain light, and clutching forward for food which was already unfit to eat. . . . I have never since been able to see a number of hands held upward, even when they are moving rhythmically in an exercise, even when they belong to children who wave them in response to a teacher's query, without a certain revival of this memory . . . of the despair and resentment which seized me then.

Thus she wrote, forgetful that she supposed herself to have been at a time much later than this absolutely at sea as far as any "moral purpose" was concerned. And "for the following weeks," she says, "I went about London furtively, afraid to look down narrow streets and alleys lest they disclose again this hideous human need . . . bewildered that the world should be going on as usual."

Bewildered, too, by the assumption that she herself had nothing to do toward satisfying this human need; mocked not only by a sense of her own uselessness, but by the realization that *she was not expected to do anything*. The opportunity to develop in herself the power of acquiring knowledge had been freely offered her, and she had acquired a good deal; the opportunity for further self-cultivation was now hers, and she was expected conscientiously to take advantage of it. But with all her education and her cultivation, she was not held to any responsibility. Both education and cultivation were dear to her, but as stimulants, not as sweetmeats. And not being held responsible, would she ultimately, she brooded, become indifferent? "I gradually reached a conviction that the first generation of college women had developed too exclusively the power of acquiring knowledge and of merely receiving impressions; that somewhere in the process of 'being educated' they had lost that simple and almost automatic response to the human appeal, that old healthful reaction resulting in *activity* from the mere presence of suffering or of helplessness."

In this conviction she was probably in error. Certainly she herself had lost nothing of this response. Eager recipient of impressions as she was for the two years in Europe that followed, impressions of art, of architecture, of music, she remained burdened by a sense of the futility of her study, a belief that "the pursuit of cultivation would not in the end bring either solace or relief." And now and again her "response" broke out into open rebellion:

One snowy morning in Saxe-Coburg, looking from the window of our little hotel upon the town square, we saw crossing and recrossing it a single file of women with semi-circular heavy wooden tanks fastened upon their backs. They were carrying in this primitive fashion to a remote cooling-room these tanks filled with a hot brew incident to one stage of beer making. The women were bent forward, not only under the weight which they were bearing, but because the tanks were so high that it would have been impossible for them to have lifted their heads. Their faces and hands, reddened in the cold morning air, showed clearly the white scars where they had previously been scalded by the hot stuff which splashed if they stumbled ever so little on their way. Stung into action . . . I found myself across the square, in company with mine host, interviewing the phlegmatic owner of the brewery, who received us with exasperating indifference. . . . I went back to a breakfast for which I had lost my appetite.

The indifference of the brewery owner is not remarkable. It was probably touched with a sort of dull amazement. In all his life, certainly, no other woman or man had ever thus interfered with what he regarded as the natural and inevitable course of his business. One is tickled at the thought of the ponderous chuckle with which he must have sometimes to the day of his death recalled the incident—a fräulein incredible! So later, in the very early Hull House days, did the solid business men of Chicago chuckle over Jane Addams, until her insistence upon factory legislation, which really did to some slight degree lessen their profits, changed their amusement to irritation and dislike. As for the sight by which Jane Addams was at Saxe-Coburg "stung into action," it is illustrative of the wide difference between the practical modern young woman, and the idealistic Victorian social philosopher John Ruskin, with whom she shared so many sympathies. She saw the women, heavy-laden; Ruskin would have seen only the continuation of the medieval tradition of the worker on an individual job, without the intrusion of machinery, and would have been delighted no doubt by the picturesqueness of the procession. Did he not found the ill-fated Guild of St. George on precisely the basis of this system of personal transport? But it was neither principle nor picturesqueness that concerned Jane Addams; it was oppression.

Constantly disturbed as she was however by this automatic response to suffering and helplessness, by this belief that "culture" was in and of itself futile, however acquired, she continued to seek it. It was in these years of the middle 'eighties, abroad and at home, that she developed through both instinct and association those deep esthetic interests which later were to show so plainly in the working out of the plans for Hull House. As we shall see, the first new building of the "settlement" was a picture-gallery. The Hull House Music School was started soon afterward. The oldest and most celebrated group of amateur actors in Chicago is the Hull House Dramatic Association. Manual arts of all sorts, from the most primitive to the current, have been elaborately encouraged at Hull House. All these things will be considered subsequently in more detail, as "activities" resulting from the reaction to the mere presence of helplessness. Here one merely points out how Jane Addams got the information and interest in such things which permitted her to understand their overwhelming significance to the immigrants and aliens of Chicago; how she steeped herself in the traditions of the arts of brain and hand, which are the most important of the traditions of the European immigrant, and possibly the immigrant's most important contribution to American spiritual life. He came here to find liberty and a job; these we had in more abundance than the older world. But he brought with him a longing for beauty, a longing individually to create beauty, indeed in many cases an individual power to produce it, which the descendants of the American pioneers did not have in any such measure. The advantage of this potential contribution of the immigrant to a finer national culture, Jane Addams was the first person, if not to comprehend, then at any rate insistently to express. It is hardly too much to say that she went to live at Hull House more to make opportunities for this potentiality to fulfil itself, than for any other reason. Certainly that was why Ellen Starr went there.

In this first stay in Europe, Jane was definitely the student. She "pursued culture." From the British Isles she went to Holland, thence to Berlin, Dresden, where they spent Christmas, thence round about Germany and Austria, to Italy, to Greece, back to Italy again, to Switzerland, to England and Wales, to Berlin for two months, finally to Paris—a "tour" lasting twenty-one months. Jane studied the architecture of fifty cathedrals and was keenly interested in the historical development of Gothic; looked over paintings in dozens of galleries, evolving a scheme of "not more than two or three pictures a day" when time permitted; lost no opportunity to attend concerts or the opera, and in Paris even undertook (one of her old friends asserts, though Jane Addams denied it) to learn to dance. "I would have been glad to learn to dance," she said, "but it hurt my back as much as the horseback riding did that my stepmother made me do at Rockford." She studied German, Italian, and French; and continued her Rockford reading in history and philosophy. Positivism, the outgrowth of the speculation of August Comte, had begun to interest her; she saw in it a connection between the Democracy she already loved, and the Christianity she longed to understand. She was supposed to be "resting," but she was no casual tourist. She wrote and wrote in her notebooks, half the night sometimes, in a fever of esthetic and devotional interest, and with an interest also in self-expression. She was deliberately setting down at this time almost the "million words" which all of us have been enjoined to write in practice before we attempt publication.

On almost every page of these notebooks there are the notes both of aspiration and of dissatisfaction. These were perhaps the two most restless years of Jane Addams's life. She was looking for something she could not find. She had promised her classmates at Rockford not to lose their precious ideals, not to fail to follow the way of high purpose they had marked out for themselves, but whither did this way of high purpose lead? In everything she did was mingled "a sense of futility," of misdirected energy, the

fear amounting to a belief that the pursuit of culture
would not in the end bring either solace or relief. She could
not forget that when she had seen the pitiful hands raised
in the Whitechapel auction,

> at the very moment of looking down the East London Street,
> from the top of the omnibus, I had been suddenly reminded
> of the Vision of Sudden Death which had confronted De Quincey
> one summer's night ... when he tried to shout a warning but
> found himself unable to make a sound because his mind was
> hopelessly entangled in an endeavor to recall the exact lines
> from the *Iliad* which describe the great cry of Achilles. ...
> Suddenly called upon for a quick decision in the world of life
> and death, he had been able to act only through a literary
> suggestion. ... It seemed to me too preposterous that in my
> first view of the horror of East London, I should have recalled
> a literary description of a literary suggestion.

Was she in fact pursuing not an ideal, but "the shadow
of a shade"? Not the poverty of the East Londoners, but
her own poverty of accomplishment became the symbol of
the world's sorrow. And so everywhere she found herself
visiting not only galleries but the slums of cities, not only
cathedrals but salt-mines, to see how lived what had not
yet been described as "the other half" of humanity. She
found nothing quite so terrible as that first glimpse of
misery and squalor in London, but she found in many
places misery and squalor and lack of opportunity, and
she was unhappy because she seemed to be getting no
nearer to an understanding of what if anything she could
do about it. To study medicine had seemed simple and
genuine; but that avenue of approach to understanding
had been closed to her, and now all her increasing knowledge brought her nothing but growing-pains. She kept this
feeling sedulously out of her letters, she had no intention

of distressing her sisters and her brother in this country with her own spiritual irritations, but after almost two years she returned to Cedarville spiritually more confused than when she had left it.

She did not stay long in Cedarville. George was by this time working for his doctor's degree in the new Johns Hopkins University in Baltimore, and Mrs. Addams thought it a good plan to spend the winter there. She could look after George, she could enter upon a wider social life than Cedarville or even Freeport afforded, and she could keep Jane in George's company, in furtherance of the plan of getting them married which had long been in her mind. So to Baltimore they went, and "social" they became. Jane had brought back some Paris clothes, one "blue dress" in particular which seems to have particularly impressed her, and her mother launched her upon the gentle waves of Johns Hopkins University society. The voyage was apparently rather a dreary one. Jane was still far from strong, and she was still rather obviously in earnest. A depressed young woman who wished to devote herself to the archeological lectures of an Italian professor (Lanciani) which she found "fascinating," and to careful study of the United Italy movement, and who had at this time little command of "small-talk," was not likely to appeal to the social interests of a group of budding scientists. She did not like them much. "I was certainly much disillusioned at this time," she has written, "as to the effect of intellectual pursuits upon moral development." She meant in herself, of course, but she also meant in the young Johns Hopkins men. She thought they too were "misdirecting their energies." At Baltimore she "reached the nadir of ... nervous depression and sense of maladjustment." She assisted her stepmother in giving parties, even card-parties, having developed an acquaintance with whist; but on one occasion such a card-party produced a slight difficulty between them, Jane refusing to provide fresh cards for the company on the ground that "the old ones were clean enough." Those who knew Jane Addams only after she had gone to live at Hull House, after she had "found herself" as one might say, delighted in her humor, but that was an acquisition, really, from Julia Lathrop and Florence Kelley and Mary Smith, a sort of borrowed refuge from fatigue. There is hardly a touch of it in these early days. In Baltimore she was as nearly unhappy as it was in the power of an individual "born for others" to be.

The summers of 1885 and 1886 she spent in Cedarville, and in 1885, when she was twenty-five, after long searchings of her heart, she decided to be baptized and "join the church." She says:

I was conscious of no change from my childish acceptance of the teachings of the Gospels, but at this moment something persuasive within made me long for an outward symbol of fellowship, some bond of peace, some blessed spot where unity of spirit might claim right of way over all differences. There was also growing within me an almost passionate devotion to the ideals of democracy, and when in all history had these ideals been so thrillingly expressed as when the faith of the fisherman and the slave had been boldly opposed to the accepted moral belief that the well-being of a privileged few might justly be built upon the ignorance and sacrifice of the many?

So though she never accepted Presbyterian doctrine in its theological rigidity, she became a member of the Presbyterian church. It was a considerable, though it did not prove to be a particularly momentous, step. It must be remembered that her idolized father had never definitely "professed" Christianity, had never been a member of any Cedarville church, and had assured his daughter that she must above all things preserve her "mental integrity" in every decision. It must be remembered too that Jane had steadfastly resisted at Rockford the proselytizing zeal that characterized the Seminary in her day; had indeed been practically at odds with the tremendous Miss Sill about any profession of faith. Her desire for an outward symbol, an acknowledged bond of peace, must therefore have been very great in 1885 to induce her to accept baptism. Indeed, she may be said not so much to have accepted it as to have undergone it.

It has been said that the step did not prove momentous. The fact is that her humanitarianism was too pervasive of her to permit the entrance of any large interest in dogma. Later in the early years at Hull House she transferred her membership in the Presbyterian church to membership in the Congregational church, a struggling home of that denomination being just around the corner; but it is probable that she affiliated with that particular church less because it was doctrinally agreeable to her, than because it was convenient and struggling. She joined it, in other words, as she might have joined a labor-union, because she thought her membership would help out. In the end neither her Presbyterian nor her Congregational affiliation availed much with many churchmen, who continued in some cases to persist in the belief that Hull House would have been more admirable if it had been less tolerant, and Jane Addams herself more Christian if she had been more steadily denominational. Fortunately, perhaps, the world has not agreed with the more rigid churchmen in this mat-

ter. Of course many clergymen were her warmest friends
and approvers; of the few letters she preserved, it is curious too to note what a large proportion were from ministers of this gospel or that, who have written in a kindly
spirit of her and her work.

It was in her second summer after she returned from
Europe that she first faced the confusion of practical economics. Her father's estate having been administered, she
had placed some of her money in "chattel mortgages" with
her stepbrother Harry Haldeman's bank in Kansas.
(Doctor Haldeman had become a banker by this time.)
She visited Girard, where the Haldemans lived, and there
saw some of the "chattels" which were the security for one
such mortgage—a pen full of half-starved hogs, which
were devouring the weakest of their number:

The farmer's wife looked on indifferently, a picture of despair as she stood in the door of the bare crude house, and the
two children behind her thrust forward their faces almost
covered by masses of coarse, sunburned hair, and their little
bare feet so black, so hard, the great cracks so filled with
dust they looked like flattened hoofs. The children could not
be compared to anything so joyous as satyrs, though they
appeared but half-human. It seemed to me quite impossible
to receive interest from mortgages placed upon farms which
might at any season be reduced to such conditions, and with great
inconvenience to my agent and doubtless with hardship to the
farmers, I withdrew all my investment.

This was bad enough; but having the money, she went
into partnership with a young college man who knew little
of farming, and bought a farm near Cedarville and stocked
it with sheep. To this day those hilly pastures of northern
Illinois are sheep-country, and the enterprise looked both
sound and, in a way, rather esthetic. But the partner

bedded the sheepfold with straw, and the sight of two hundred sheep with four rotting hooves each, was not reassuring to one whose conscience craved economic peace.

From this experience she extricated herself without much loss of money, but still further confused in spirit. Was there no way of squaring even economic ideals with the practical facts of life? She concluded that if she and her partner had known how to handle sheep, the investment would have been a proper one and the result agreeable even to the sheep. Idealism meant service; but service that was worth anything must come out of knowledge, not out of impulse only.

She had now been out of college for six years, she was twenty-seven, and yet she had done nothing which she considered of importance for herself or the world. She had traveled, studied, written, even submitted articles to magazines, which the editors had declined. She had learned to manage her own business affairs adequately, except for her inveterate habit of giving away more than she could afford ("I am a little weak-minded about giving away money," she writes in one letter). She had presented Rockford College with $1,000 for books, the largest gift the college had ever had from a woman, and had been made a trustee of the institution, as her father had been before her; helped two young men through college; and been a ministering angel to her oldest sister, with whom and with whose growing family she spent a good deal of her time. ("I am sorry not to write oftener," she confides to Ellen Starr, "but I am busy with the children. Esther [a niece] has been driving me crazy with questions about John the Baptist, and Weber [a nephew] has had his sled stolen, and is railing at the world with a power of invective that I have never heard equaled.") She had an income of almost three thousand dollars a year. Her health was as good as it had ever been, or ever was to be for that matter. Ellen Starr, on whose friendship she had come to rely, had gone abroad. Jane decided to join her, and see if through direct association with her in centers of historical development, she could get back that sense of continuity, of pattern, which she had somehow lost. She had been gradually approaching a sort of conclusion, which was best summed up perhaps twenty years later by her friend Mrs. Elia Peattie:

A curious, large, unformulated idea was growing in her mind. It was not a personal idea. It had a philosophic source, perhaps, for Miss Addams was a student, and a grave, wholesome, deliberate and logical thinker. She had begun to ask herself of what use she was to her time; how she justified her life; to what employment she put her education; how the commonwealth was being benefited by her existence; and how, having no family of her own, she was to utilize the energy of which she was conscious. And out of vagueness and dreams, as out of a summer night of cloud and mist, one idea came, starbright. . . . She wished to live as a true member of a republic. Her patriotism took to itself an exquisite feminine and spiritual form. Not to destroy the actual enemies of the republic, but to build up friends for it, to assist in the making of independent, free-thinking, loyal and happy citizens, was her idea. . . . She entered upon her work with a sort of divine inquisitiveness. She wanted, perhaps, to know why men were sad. I think she thought it was because they were lonely. They were bitter, she opined, because the democratic principle was not applied— because there was a lack of unity in society.

It is true that not even yet had what she calls "the very simple plan that afterward developed into the Settlement" shaped itself into any definiteness in her mind—the plan "to rent a house in a part of Chicago where many primitive and actual needs are found in which young women who had been given over too exclusively to study, might ... learn of life from life itself." She was just thinking over possibilities.

With her friend Sarah Anderson she sailed on December 14, 1887, from Hoboken, landing in Southampton nine days later. The first two days of the trip were delightful, the rest of it was a horror; Jane did not leave her stateroom for seven days. "I dressed several times, but could never make the deck." From Southampton they went to Paris; thence Jane traveled alone to Munich. "I am impressed," she wrote, "with the difference in my age and dignity between this trip and the one before. Then I was Mademoiselle and Fräulein; now everywhere it is 'Madame' with the utmost respect, and I felt perfectly at my ease all the time." At Ulm, on the way to Munich, she began to find what she had come to Europe to seek— a conception of humanity supreme through morality and theology. "The religious history carved on the choir stalls in the Ulm cathedral contained Greek philosophers as well as Hebrew prophets, and among the disciples and saints stood the discoverer of music and the builder of pagan temples ... and I was startled to catch sight of a window showing Luther as he affixed his decrees on the door of Worms, the picture shining clear in the midst of the older glass of saint and symbol." The saints, she decided, "but embodied fine action," and she wrote half the night that night setting forth her hope for a "cathedral of humanity," which should be "capacious enough to house a fellowship of common purpose," and beautiful enough "to persuade men to hold fast to the vision of human solidarity." It was in the sense of her own embodiment of fine action that John Burns of England and the neighbors around Hull House were to call her a "saint" later, and in the understanding of this fellowship of purpose and vision of human solidarity that Walter Lippmann was when she died to describe Hull House itself as a "cathedral of compassion." This visit to Ulm was one of the great moments of Jane Addams's development.

At Munich she joined Ellen Starr, and thence they went to Rome to spend the winter; Ellen to study paintings, Jane to continue her long inquiry into the history of Christianity and its relation to humanity. In Rome, however, Jane acquired a new illness, sciatic rheumatism, which kept her suffering for weeks. When she improved, though she could not leave her rooms, she insisted nevertheless that Ellen and Sarah Anderson, who had by this time joined them, should carry out their plan of going to Naples and South Italy. "I've seen it," she said, "and you two must." Jane was paying half the expense of the trip for both of them, and so they did as she commanded. "I never felt so utterly selfish in my life," Miss Starr wrote, "but what is our selfishness compared to her unselfishness?" As soon as she could travel, Jane herself went to the Riviera to recuperate; thence, joined once more by her friends, to Spain. And in Madrid, at Easter-time, the "curious large idea" which Mrs. Peattie has described, finally formulated itself in her mind. It was an idea which was to revolutionize social thinking, in America at least; to first develop and then redeem "social service"; to go far toward the realization of the meaning of democracy.

And this remarkable idea was crystallized, though not inspired, by a bull-fight! One wonders if the arena of that bull-fight is still in use at Madrid; and if so, whether some day Spain will not put up a tablet in it somewhere, with the date, Easter-day 1888, when the blood of slaughter became the milk of human kindness.

In her autobiography she speaks of herself on this journey as if she were talking of a lazy child. She had been making "a dreamer's scheme an excuse for going on indefinitely with study and travel"; she had "fallen into the meanest type of self-deception in making myself believe that all this was in preparation for great things to come. ...So far from following in the wake of a chariot of philanthropic fire, I had been tied to the tail of the veriest ox-cart of self-seeking." Mrs. Peattie's version is perhaps more accurate. Jane Addams herself in the first place fails to take into consideration the fact that she had got back her physical strength very slowly, had very gradually overcome the nervous weakness that her "bad back" had brought upon her. And she further fails to take into consideration the still more important truth that she had been developing in herself the instinct for culture which lay, a seed of splendid growth, in many of the "poor people" she loved. Without the full development of that instinct, Jane Addams would have succeeded as a "social worker," but she could not have succeeded as she did as a sympathizer, as an influence for the spiritual civilization of America. She had not been, it is true, preparing herself to help the American immigrant. She learned how to do that only on Halsted Street. But she had been preparing herself to understand his deepest needs, and without that understanding she must have remained to the end with a consciousness of the futility of good deeds, of "works without faith."

At any rate, in Madrid the party, now five friends in all, went to see a bull-fight. The other four left early, but Jane stayed until she had seen five bulls killed. As she watched the pageant of the performance, she found herself in memory back in the days when she and the Knight of the Green Plume had fought dragons together round Cedarville, and in imagination still further back, in the days when the Christian gladiators in the Roman arenas had faced martyrdom. She felt the thrill of her recollections without perception of the horror of the actual spectacle. When she finally went out, she found her friends in the entrance, waiting to reproach her for her endurance. Suddenly she felt herself "tried and condemned," not only for callousness to the torture of the bull-ring, but for failure to end her thoughts of years in action. Not "the fruit of experience, but experience itself," as Pater had expressed it, had been, she concluded, what she had been seeking. She would seek it no longer. The very next morning she broached to Ellen Starr her childhood plan to have "a big house right in the middle of horrid little houses," and found Miss Starr enthusiastic. In the next month they talked it out. Then from Granada Jane hurried back to London, to get advice.

In London she looked into the matter of trades-unionism for women, reflected on the "socialism" which was at that particular time stirring older Englishmen like William Morris, and younger ones like Bernard Shaw and the Webbs, sat under Frederick Harrison and reconsidered the religion of the Positivists, of whom she says that she "imagined their philosophical conception of man's religious development might include all expressions of that for which so many ages of man have struggled and aspired." But in particular she studied Toynbee Hall.

Toynbee Hall had been established in the Whitechapel district of London four years before, with the Reverend Samuel Barnett as its first warden, or "head resident." Jane's interest in it was partly that it was the sort of home for the prosperous among the poor that she hoped to make, but more because it had a "university" origin. As Oxford University men had been inspired to live in Whitechapel, so might American college women live happily and usefully in the Chicago slums. Young women who had been "smothered and sickened with advantages," without responsibilities or expectation of being able to use what they knew or respond fully to the demands their own instinctive womanly sympathies made on them—it was to such that she wanted to give an opportunity. Toynbee himself, and other educated, cultivated young university men had found a way to use their advantages and satisfy their sympathies, and she wanted to look over the house of dreams they had built.

Twenty years earlier, in the 1860's, John Ruskin had said to his Oxford University students: "I have not yet abandoned all expectation of a better world than this. . . . I know there are many who think the atmosphere of rebellion and misery which wraps the lower orders of Europe every day is as natural as a hot summer. But God forbid!"

And so first Edward Denison, and then later Arnold Toynbee and his group, had gone to do what they could to dissipate this atmosphere of misery, to make dreams into activities. After a short examination of Toynbee Hall, with a glance also at Walter Besant's People's Palace, though this was not quite in her line, Jane Addams came back to the United States in the late summer to set her own finances in order for the new venture, and to rejoice that she "had at last finished with the everlasting 'preparation for life.' "

The seven years covered in this chapter are the years of what she calls in her autobiography "the snare of preparation." They were also years of investment in understanding, of which Hull House was to be the sizable dividend.

CHAPTER V

SHE FINDS A WAY

RETURNING to the United States in June of 1888, Jane Addams proceeded to set her business affairs in order in preparation for the "big house down among the little houses" that she was to live in for the rest of her days. She knew she would need all she had in the way of money, and more, and she tried to draw in the horns of her generosity. She writes lamenting to Ellen Starr in September, "I have given something to Beloit, though I knew I shouldn't. I must save all I can for our project"—which as yet had not even a name. She arranged a new lease for her farm, sought some financial backing from her step-mother—which she did not get—and even studied book-keeping. She was a practical idealist. She found herself fully occupied. At Thanksgiving time she went to visit her sister Mary, who was now living at Geneseo, Illinois, and talked the plan over with her brother-in-law, whom she found a little doubtful. While at Geneseo she took general charge of her four-year-old nephew Stanley, whose legal guardian she was to be after her sister died a few years later. "Stanley makes me say all his prayers for him," she wrote, "and unless I include a prayer for Charles Hodge (a baby brother who had died) Stanley makes a terrible fuss; and if I do, Mr. Linn does not like it, as of course it is not Presbyterian to pray for the dead." In January of 1889 she went to Chicago and began looking about for the "big house."

She knew more or less what she wanted in the way of
a house, and she knew exactly what she wanted in the way
of neighbors. The problem was to find both together. She
was in no hurry. Hurry had never been her failing. She
spent five months in the solution of her problem. In company with a young architect, Allen Pond, she went about
everywhere. Newspapermen were a great help to her also,
reporters showing her all the "queer" neighborhoods, and
informing her of the efforts—chiefly the Sunday-school
efforts—to inspire the poor to a happier and better life.
One day she saw an old house on Halsted Street, just off
Polk. She liked it, but for a long time she never could find
it again, for whenever she was on Halsted Street she
turned off always on the diagonal of Blue Island Avenue
two blocks north of Polk, and so missed it. In May, however, still in company with Pond, she ran across it once
more, and then and there made up her mind to rent it if
she could. It was number 335 South Halsted; the number
was long afterward changed to 800. Halsted Street is
exactly one mile west of State Street, one mile east of Ashland Avenue; all three were originally township lines. In
1889 State was the great business street, Ashland Avenue
the fashionable street of residence. Halsted was then
nearer Lake Michigan than it is now, the shoreline having
been shoved a quarter of a mile out east in the last half-
century.

The house was of brick, two-storied, beautifully propor-
tioned, set well back from the street, with a great front
entrance under a piazza and framed by wooden pillars of
nice Corinthian design; this piazza ran all round the house.
The rooms were large and high-ceilinged, covered with
good molded decorations. Charles J. Hull, an early citizen

of Chicago, had built it for his suburban residence in 1856, when Chicago's population of 85,000 was very thin west of the river. A painting of the house as it was in the 1850's hangs in the reception-room; it seems to stand in open country, and is surrounded by large oaks. Hull himself had been the most successful dealer in real estate, in a city of remarkable dealers of that sort. Hull was born in Manchester, Connecticut, in 1820. A poor boy and presently an orphan, he went to live with his grandfather on a farm in New York state. He had a common school education, taught a district school for a while and came to Chicago in 1846. There he studied law, made his way to Harvard law school, lived on oatmeal mostly, graduated, returned to Chicago, and instead of practising law turned to real estate. He is said to have been the first man in Chicago to have begun the practice of buying outlying property, subdividing it and selling lots on the instalment plan. Later he invested in real estate in Baltimore, Maryland, and in Lincoln, Nebraska, and Houston, Texas; he is said to have been at one time the largest landowner in Lincoln. "I had to work too long getting a start," he said many years later to a young lawyer of his acquaintance. "If I could live to be a hundred, I could be one of the richest men in the country." In Chicago he thought out a scheme of putting up three sixteen-foot front buildings on each fifty-foot lot along a street, and renting them to small shopkeepers. In the panic of 1857 he lost everything, but soon paid his debts and accumulated another fortune. After the Civil War he developed the plan of providing working-people, both whites and Negroes, with houses on the instalment plan; this idea worked in Savannah, Georgia; Baltimore, Maryland; Jacksonville, Florida;

and Cairo, Illinois. He was cautious with his own personal expenditures, but socially high-minded; he wrote to a friend from Savannah, "Our enterprise is not a land-speculation. We are endeavoring to distribute the lands adjoining certain large cities, among the poor. If I succeed in my enterprise, the question what is to be done with the pioneer, the outcast and the criminal will be solved." The tradition is that he was extremely fond of little children, who used to surround him to be kissed and given pennies as he walked along the streets. He was a trustee of the first Chicago University, but on Sundays he always visited the Bridewell and chatted with the inmates there. He died in Houston, Texas, in February, 1889, just a month after Jane Addams went to Chicago. His wife had died in 1870 and his three children also were dead. He left his money, more than four million dollars, to his cousin and for many years his secretary or "woman of business," Miss Helen Culver. She gave a quarter of it to his surviving relatives, withdrew as rapidly as she could from the real-estate business, and settled down to spend the money for Chicago. It was at this very time that Jane Addams, knowing nothing of Charles Hull or of Helen Culver, picked out the old house to live in. After watching her there for a year or more, Miss Culver fell into the spirit of the enterprise. Presently she turned over the House itself, and the very valuable land it stood upon, together with other lots in the block, to Jane Addams. A little later she gave the still new University of Chicago more than a million dollars for the development of the biological sciences and the erection of buildings around what is now known as Hull Court of the University.

But for the interests of Charles J. Hull, passed on to

THE ORIGINAL CHARLES HULL HOMESTEAD
The painting hangs in the Hull House reception room.

HULL HOUSE AS IT IS TO-DAY

Helen Culver, and for Miss Culver's own remarkable understanding of the new "social settlement," Jane Addams's experiment could never have grown as it was to grow. The hand of Providence was in this coincidence of time. Jane Addams always felt, too, that the hand of Providence was in the escape by a miracle of the old house from the Great Fire in 1871. It stood on the very edge of the neighborhood where the fire started, within a stone's throw northwestward of the stable of Mrs. O'Leary's cow, which according to legend kicked over the lantern and destroyed a city. The house was rented then, and a man who still lives in Chicago watched, as a boy, the flames rise, from the window of a bedroom which was to become Jane Addams's office—the well-known "Octagon." On the day Jane Addams's funeral service was held in Hull House court, that boy, old and deaf, came to look about him curiously. "I've never been here since I lived here," he said, "but about all I've got to leave my family is the memory that I once lived where she did."

In 1875 the house was taken over for a short time by the Little Sisters of the Poor. Then it became a habitation of small shops on the first floor and tenement-rooms on the second. When Jane Addams saw it in 1889, it had become half saloon and half office and storage-room of a furniture factory, with lodgings still on the second floor, and an authentic ghost on the staircase. This second floor, and that part of the first floor which lay to the south of the main hall, Jane Addams was able to secure. For some months the part of the first floor to the north of the hall, that part which is now the main reception-room, continued to be used as a repository for school desks. In the Spring of 1890, however, Miss Culver granted Jane Addams a free lease of the whole house, and the land immediately adjacent to it, for five years. The house, or that part of it of which the new residents took possession, they furnished with some old family mahogany and new things bought with an eye to character as well as permanence— "perhaps no young matron," Jane Addams says, "ever placed her own things in her own house with more pleasure than we did"—and on September 14, 1889, the first members of the new "family" moved in. They were three, Jane Addams, Ellen Gates Starr, and a housekeeper, Mary Keyser, who had been a friend of Jane Addams's older sister, and whose brother Frank, it may be mentioned in passing, is still at Hull House, the "oldest inhabitant."

The Chicago of 1889 was a city of very slightly less than one million people. That year and the next, seven "towns" were annexed, adding thus 200,000 more in time for the census of 1890, which thus showed Chicago to be the "second city," only 400,000 behind New York. Of the million in 1889, almost three-quarters were foreign-born. In 1890 only 292,000 Americans were listed; and that included 15,000 Negroes. There were 400,000 Germans, and 215,000 Irish. Of the 54,000 Bohemians, 42,000 lived along Blue Island Avenue, a little south and west of Hull House; this settlement, called "Pilsen," was said to be the third largest Bohemian city. Hull House cornered other foreign colonies. Ten thousand Italians were said to live between Halsted Street and the river eastward—more than half of all then in the city. Just south were many Germans, including German Jews; alongside them, the side streets were given over almost entirely to Polish and Russian Jews. Just North of Hull House were thousands upon thousands of Irish:

Halsted Street is thirty-two miles long. ... Polk Street crosses it midway between the stockyards to the south and the ship-building yards on the north branch of the Chicago River. For the six miles between these industries the street is lined with shops of butchers and grocers, with dingy and gorgeous saloons, and pretentious establishments for the sale of ready-made clothing. Polk Street, west from Halsted, grows rapidly more prosperous; running a mile east to State Street it grows steadily worse, and crosses a network of vice on the corners of Clark Street and Fifth Avenue. ... The streets are inexpressibly dirty, the number of schools inadequate, sanitary legislation unenforced, the street lighting bad, the paving miserable and altogether lacking in the alleys and smaller streets, and the stables foul beyond description. Hundreds of houses are unconnected with the street sewer. ... The houses, for the most part wooden, were originally built for one family and are now occupied by several. They are after the type of the inconvenient frame cottages found in the poorer suburbs before the Fire. Many of them were built where they now stand; others were brought there on rollers, because their previous sites had been taken for factories. ... The little wooden houses have a temporary aspect, and for this reason, perhaps, the tenement-house legislation in Chicago is totally inadequate. Rear tenements flourish; many houses have no water supply save the faucet in the back yard, there are no fire-escapes, the garbage and ashes are placed in wooden boxes which are fastened to the street pavements.

So Jane Addams described it in 1890. Twenty years later she declared, "This description still stands in my mind as correct." And so it was; although few of the present day remember the region as it was, and not many more believe it was so bad. With the change for the better in the physical characteristics of that section of the city the efforts of Jane Addams were to have as much to do, perhaps, as those of any other one citizen. She was put on the executive committee of the Chicago Housing Commission when it was organized in 1934, and the day after her death the Director of Housing at Washington wrote: "Her work will stand long as her monument, but it is my hope that somewhere in the housing projects in which she was so interested there may be developed a form of useful institution in her memory... my hope that the Chicago Commission will create something which will specifically record her well-spent life, will meet new needs as she met old ones."

The physical characteristics of any community are just a reflection of its spirit, and it was on the spirit of Chicago that Jane Addams helped to work a sort of slow miracle. What was the spirit of Chicago in 1889 when she went there to live? What was this "second city of the United States"?

One Ridpath, author of a popular "History of the World," climbed to the tower of the new Auditorium Building in 1890, looked out over the neighborhood described by Jane Addams—as much of it as he could see for the smoke of the factories—and over the adjacent and more prosperous neighborhoods, and declared that "even from the dome of St. Peter's the landscape is by no means so fine, so extended, so full of life and progress and enthusiasm." Nor was Mr. Ridpath altogether mistaken in the choice of his final nouns. Take "life," for instance. The report of a Hull House investigator of the period says:

... little idea can be given of the filthy and rotten tenements, the foul stables and dilapidated outhouses, the piles of garbage fairly alive with diseased odors, and the numbers of children filling every nook, working and playing in every room, eating and sleeping on every window-sill, pouring in and out of every door, and seeming literally to pave every scrap of yard. In one block the writer numbered over seventy-five children in the open street; but the effort proved futile when she tried to keep the count of little people surging in and out of passageways and up and down outside staircases, like a veritable stream of life.

Life enough. As for enthusiasm, that was quite as striking. The most vivid and one of the most accurate historians of its development, Henry Justin Smith, says of the Chicago of 1889, "It was a city which had accomplished Herculean feats, and was continually facing new ones. . . . It had money and power. Both of these it wasted as it chose. It pulsed with complex human energies; it was quick to adopt new inventions and apply new ideas." True of most northern American cities in the 'eighties and the 'nineties, but truest of Chicago. It had just built the largest opera-house in the United States, the Auditorium, at the dedication of which the westerner who was President of the United States is reported to have whispered to the easterner who was Vice-President, "New York surrenders, eh, sir?" It was about to build the tallest office building in the country; to erect a noble Public Library building, and to organize the splendid Newberry Library for scholars in the humanities and the Crerar Library for scholars in science, both to be eagerly affirmed by Chicagoans as "the best in the world." Already it was getting ready to seize the chance of building and, with the assistance of the Federal Government, was to build the greatest "Exposition" the world had known; an exposition to commemorate the four hundredth anniversary of the discovery of America, presented by a city incorporated for only

sixty years! John D. Rockefeller was about to decide that
Chicago was the proper place for the development of
a university for research on a scale as yet unprecedented.
With unsurpassable eagerness too, Chicago was thrusting
under the somewhat reluctant nose of the whole world,
its incomparable but odorous stockyards. Chicago businessmen, many of them already millionaires, were said
everywhere to work harder and plan more daringly than
businessmen anywhere else. Yes, observer Ridpath was
right about Chicago's enthusiasm.

In this populous, lively, industrious city, there was
however as definite and even dramatic a clash of social
interests as could be found anywhere. To understand it,
it is only necessary to recall the figures which have just
been given regarding the population. In 1889, more than
70 per cent of the inhabitants of Chicago were literally
foreign-born. About 30 per cent were classed as "American," but even of this 30 per cent many were second-
generation Europeans. But, the business, the money, the
prosperity, the power, were chiefly in the hands of the
30 per cent. Only one of the great meat-packers, Nelson
Morris, had come from Europe; the rest, Armours, Swifts,
Libbys, were all native. The merchant princes were all
native, the bankers, the real-estate dealers, the big manufacturers—the Bartletts, Cranes, Fairbanks, Fields, Keiths,
Kimballs, Kirks, Hutchinsons, Leiters, Lyons, McCormicks, McNallys, Medills, Ogdens, Pullmans, Wards,
Wentworths, even the Mandels and the Rosenwalds (not
yet considerable figures) and their prosperous and powerful
associates, were all native. It was they who had "made"
Chicago, and they believed it to be their own. To be sure,
in 1887 Mayor Carter Harrison had told Marshall Field

to his face, when Field asserted himself to be "the representative of the interests of Chicago," that "any poor man owning a single small cottage as his sole possession has the same interest in Chicago as its richest citizen," but in the first place Field did not agree with him, and in the second place comparatively few of the 70 per cent of immigrants owned even a "single small cottage." The population had been classified by birth and prosperity into a confident and compact minority, and a sprawling, neglected and frequently miserable majority. Work for this majority was plentiful, but wages were low. For ten and twelve-hour days, skilled labor was paid from $2.50 to $4.00 a day; "common labor," including teamsters, from $9.00 to $12.00 a week. Children in the sewing trades could make about four cents an hour.

And particularly the scores of thousands who not only did not own a small cottage, but who lived in the vast "slums" already described, were not considered by the business rulers of the city to possess any interests comparable to their own. Indeed the interests of the immigrant majority were thought by the leaders of Chicago to be inimical to their own, and their ideas to be dangerous. Labor unions, already agitating for an eight-hour day, were fought on principle. An eight-hour day was connected in the minds of many employers not only with laziness but directly with anarchy, the blackest word in the vocabulary of the governing minority. This minority had not forgotten the Haymarket Riot of 1886, and the conviction of the "anarchists" for conspiracy six months later. What were these conspirators but immigrants, with un-American names—Spies, Lingg, Schwab, Fischer, Engel, Fielden, Neebe? Only Parsons had been American, and Parsons had been run out of Texas as a "nigger-lover." Judge Joseph E. Gary, who by his conduct of the anarchist trial practically assured the conviction of such "aliens" and "labor agitators," probably regarded himself, and was certainly regarded by most prominent citizens, as having saved society. At a meeting of the Chicago Bar Association held during the Christmas holidays in 1887, Wirt Dexter, a famous citizen of those days, declared: "When men armed with destructive theories seek their enforcement, which would speedily make for us an earthly hell, the law—I say it with Judge Gary sitting in the midst of us—will *hang*."

The Judge sat unsmiling, the applause of the assembled lawyers "amounted to an ovation." Lyman J. Gage, banker but humanitarian, in 1889, the year Jane Addams came to Chicago, organized a forum for the discussion of social problems, and presided over Sunday afternoon meetings in the Auditorium addressed by radicals as well as by conservatives. But he was regarded by most of his associates as eccentric. And when Governor Altgeld, himself an immigrant, pardoned four years later the "anarchists" who still remained alive in prison, he was thought to have signed his own political death-warrant. Had the germ theory of disease been known at that time, Altgeld would have been supposed to carry in his own immigrant blood the infection of American Society. In 1889 Chicago was eminently class-conscious and blood-conscious. It was a house divided. The small governing American minority was profoundly suspicious of the vast governed immigrant majority.

Yet it was this immigrant majority that particularly interested Jane Addams; not because it was immigrant but, at first, because it was unprivileged. It was in one of their neighborhoods that she had chosen to make her home. From the very beginning, therefore, among those of the governing minority who were aware of her settlement, Jane Addams herself was an object of considerable suspicion. Few who knew of her, none who knew her, doubted the honesty of her intentions. But exactly what were those odd intentions? And in any case, what could come of them but trouble?

Twenty years later she could write, "From the very first our plan received courteous attention, and the discussion, while often skeptical, was always friendly.... Our early speeches were reported quite out of proportion to their worth." The courteous attention was however from the group, small in Chicago in that day, of what subsequently came to be called the intelligentsia, and it was even by them that her plan was received with skepticism. The renowned philosopher Thomas Davidson, on a visit to Chicago, could say no more for it than that "it was one of those unnatural attempts to understand life through coöperative living." Doctor David Swing, eloquent above even the other eloquent pulpit orators of the day in Chicago, wrote a commendatory column about the plan in the *Evening Journal,* but he understood it and Jane Addams very slightly; when soon afterwards he met her on State Street as she was carrying a bundle wrapped in a newspaper, he remonstrated with her amiably, pointing out that by indulgence in such social unconventionalities she was likely to impair her influence with the best people. Such of the "best people" as came into the Hull House group at first came mostly through their acquaintance with Miss Starr—she had taught at a fashionable girls' school on the north side—and with the young architect Allen Pond, who introduced Jane Addams to Mrs. Coonley and Mrs. Wilmarth, both of whom were to be long her support and stay. She formulated her philosophy in "talks" wherever she got a chance to talk. In 1892, at a summer school of Ethical Culture societies, held at Plymouth, Massachusetts, she organized these formulations into a remarkable paper. It will have to be summarized here at some length, for it signalized the beginning of a new era of social service in the United States:

This paper is an attempt to analyze the motives which underlie a movement based not only on conviction, but upon genuine emotion, wherever educated young people are seeking an outlet for that sentiment of universal brotherhood, which the best spirit of our times is forcing from an emotion into a motive. These young people ... feel *a fatal want of harmony between their theory and their lives,* a lack of coördination between thought and action. These young men and women, longing to socialize their democracy, are animated by certain hopes which may be loosely formulated thus: If in a democratic country nothing can be permanently achieved save through the masses of the people, it will be *impossible to establish a higher political* life than the people themselves crave; it is difficult to see how the notion of a higher civic life can be fostered save through common intercourse; *the blessings which we associate with a life of refinement and cultivation can be made universal,* and must be made universal if they are to be permanent; the good we secure for ourselves is precarious and uncertain ... until it is secured for all of us and incorporated into our common life. ... Nothing so deadens the sympathies and shrivels the powers of enjoyment, as the persistent keeping away from the great opportunities for helpfulness and a continual ignoring of the starvation struggle which makes up the life of at least half of the race. To shut one's self away from that half of the race is to shut one's self away from the most vital part of life; it is to live out but half the humanity to which we have been born heir and to use but half our faculties. . . . In our attempt to give a girl pleasure and freedom from care we succeed for the most part in making her pitifully miserable. . . . There is a heritage of noble obligation which young people accept and long to perpetuate. The desire for action, the wish to right wrong and alleviate suffering haunts them daily. Society smiles at it indulgently instead of making it of value to itself. . . . We have in America a fast growing number of cultivated young people who have no recognized outlet for their active faculties. They hear constantly of great social maladjustment, but no way is provided for them to change it, *and their uselessness hangs about them heavily.* Huxley declares that the sense of uselessness is the severest shock which the human system can sustain, and that if persistently sustained it results in atrophy of function. These young people . . . are sustaining this shock of inaction. They tell their elders with all the bitterness of youth that if they expect success from them in business or politics in whatever lines the ambitions of the elders for youth has run, they must let the young people consult all humanity, find out what the people want and how they want it. It is only the stronger young people, however, who formulate this. Many of them dissipate their energies in so-called enjoyment. Others not content with that go on studying; not that they are especially fond of study, but because they want something definite to do. . . . This young life, so sincere in its emotion and yet so undirected, *seems to me as pitiful as the other great mass of destitute lives.* One is supplementary to the other, *and some method of communication can surely be devised.*"

It is perhaps permissible to believe that no such clear and eloquent summons to the idealism of a group as this had been offered in America since Emerson challenged education with his famous address on "The American Scholar" sixty-five years before. He spoke to a limited audience; she spoke to the vast audience of the young people of

America. In England, Ruskin and Walter Besant and Arnold Toynbee and Canon Barnett had said something of the sort, but Jane Addams clarified their philosophy. Those who listened to her, almost in the shadow of the great rock near which the Pilgrims landed, and which has come after a fashion to symbolize "Puritanism" in America, were filled with a most "un-Puritan" sense of understanding of social interests and social values, a conception of the essentiality of human unity, if social progress was to persist, that in some at least amounted to awe. This young woman of thirty-one was inevitably to become a force. The sensitiveness of her perceptions, the solidity of her reasoning from what she perceived, and the emotional eagerness of the philosophy she had evolved, were equally obvious. Here was a new voice in the American chorus, striking with precision and color a higher note than had been reached before.

The essence of her message, the purport of her intentions may be perceived at once by reading the brief phrases which to that end have been italicized in the foregoing summary. It was the necessity, for progress *in a democracy,* of the achievement of a life which shall be both *good* and *common.* Jane Addams went to Hull House to live, no more to help than to be helped; no more to provide opportunities for others, than to provide herself with an opportunity; no more to satisfy the longings of others than to satisfy her own longing; no more to "save" than to "be saved." This is the point on which she, and all others who have lived in "settlements" from that time forward, have continued to insist. The medieval Christians returned to monasteries to save their own souls, and thence issued to save the souls and relieve the miseries of others. The modern missionaries go forth to save the souls and relieve the miseries of the heathen, confident in their own preliminary salvation. But a "settlement," as conceived by Toynbee, and adapted by Jane Addams and her successors in America, is not a refuge; the neighborhoods in which settlements become homes are not of "heathen." Belief in *mutuality* of interests, spirit and even affection is the foundation of them.

In that same talk at Plymouth, Jane Addams stressed at considerable length another "subjective necessity" of settlements, the impulse in Christianity toward social service. "The early Christians," she said, "added a new treasure to the sum of all treasures, a joy hitherto unknown to the world—the joy of finding the Christ which lies in each man, but which no man can unfold save in fellowship. . . . I believe there is a distinct turning among many young men and women to-day toward this simple acceptance of Christ's message. . . . The Settlement movement is only one manifestation of that wider humanitarian movement which throughout Christendom . . . is endeavoring to embody itself not in a sect but in society itself." She touched upon even a further complexity of minor motives toward "settlement living," including "a love of approbation so vast that it is not content with the treble clapping of delicate hands, but wishes also to hear the bass notes from toughened palms." But her major insistence was upon her conviction that "the good we secure for ourselves is precarious and uncertain until it is secured for all of us and incorporated into our common life." It is this conviction, from which she was never to waver, that forced her comprehension that "from its very nature a settlement can stand for no political or social propaganda. It must, in a sense, give the warm welcome of an inn to all such propaganda, if perchance one be found an angel. It must have . . . a deep and abiding sense of tolerance. . . . . It must be grounded in a philosophy which will not waver when the race happens to be represented by a drunken woman or an idiot boy. . . . Residents are bound to regard the entire life of their city as organic, to make an effort to unify it, and to protest against its over-differentiation." Life at Hull House was often to be hard. Drunken women and idiot boys are not in themselves agreeable. Neither are burglars, or murderers, or what politicians call "double-crossers," or wife-beaters, or "fallen women" of a certain type, and all of these were to come to Hull House from time to time. Neither, at times, are ferocious "radicals" of various schools of thought particularly charming visitors or companions. But what made life most difficult on Halsted Street, and in the world, was perhaps not the fundamental necessity of persistent tolerance within doors, so much as the frequent inability of many more distant "neighbors" to comprehend the philosophy of Jane Addams, even as thus simply stated and reiterated. Few in Chicago comprehended it in 1889; perhaps she did not fully comprehend it herself. Not all came to comprehend it even by 1915, when she turned her major efforts from the social service of settlements to the wider social service of the promotion of world peace. Between 1889 and 1915 there were many businessmen in Chicago who at times "would have paid almost any sum to get that person out of the way." The conviction that "the entire life of the city is organic," the protest against its "over-differentiation," and the virtue of a burning tolerance, even when understood, are not always by "rugged individualism" easy to forgive.

With such motives, however, and with such hopes, Jane Addams settled down in her comfortable rooms in the stately if battered old house on Halsted Street, to find out what she could do for herself, her neighbors, and Chicago.

CHAPTER VI

HULL HOUSE BEGINS

WHEN some time later the neighborhood venture of the Misses Addams and Starr was incorporated, the charter gave the objects of incorporation as follows: "To provide a center for a higher civic and social life; to institute and maintain educational and philanthropic enterprises, and to investigate and improve the conditions in the industrial districts of Chicago." Those "objects" are put, whether by accident or design, in the chronological order in which they had appeared. It was first to provide a center for social life that the young women rented the old mansion and moved in their belongings. When within two weeks a dozen young women of the neighborhood were invited to a "reading party" in the evening, two being asked to come to dinner first, to help clear away the dishes and get the dining-room ready for the readers, and when soon afterward a kindergarten was started in the drawing-room, the first "educational and philanthropic enterprises" were instituted. And before the end of the year, the residents had begun "to investigate and improve the conditions" in their own neighborhood. Hull House has grown enormously since then, but the growth has all been a simple extension of the life of those first few weeks. As a snowball may be rolled into something huge but never changes its quality, so accomplishments were to roll into something like vastness around two eager young spirits, but the quality of those accomplishments has never changed.

Because the original purpose never changed, it seems important to point out exactly what that purpose was. It was not to provide a higher civic and social life for anybody; it was to provide *a center for the development* of such a life. The difference is essential, but it has often been misunderstood, and will probably always be misunderstood by some people. Jane Addams and Ellen Starr were not reformers. They did not begin or go on with the insistence either of reformers or providers. They wished to make a place, if they could, in and around which a fuller life might grow, for others and for themselves, a happier life, a life richer in interest. A columnist in a Greek newspaper published in Chicago, wrote when Jane Addams died:

Her death has stirred in us memories that go back ... to those days when in the buoyancy of our youth we would walk into Hull House as though we walked into our own house, there in absolute freedom to enjoy the House, not in its physical aspects but in that nurturing warmth that animated everything and all ... there sound in our ears the soft words and sentences of the women of the House, the only soft and kind words we immigrant boys heard in those days ... for we of foreign birth have lost our best friend and the only one who understood us.

She would have liked that more than the praise of a statesman. The Greek who wrote that comprehended the meaning of the social philosophy of Hull House.

There were no "social workers" in 1889. There are hundreds of thousands of them now, educated and trained to a profession, just as teachers are educated and trained.

There was not even a department of "sociology" in an American University; the first such department was established in the new University of Chicago in 1892. Jane Addams, as she lived on, learned by experience the profession of social work, and so to-day much of what she has written is "source material" for research by students in the departments of sociology everywhere. But she did not go to live on Halsted Street either as a "social worker" or as a student; nor have the purposes of either ever been her primary aspiration since that time. So she can neither be given the credit for developing the profession of social service, nor be held responsible for the growth of scholastic interest in sociology. She blazed no trail for others to follow; she only climbed a high mountain to look across for herself into the Promised Land. Others, many others, have climbed after her—none, maybe, quite so high—but by their own paths, not following her but only seeking the vision of which her life has been the report.

Daily life at Hull House immediately became busy. Jane Addams's engagement books, for the first months of residence, show hard work on her part. She was going out a good deal, meeting new people of all sorts and trying to interest them in settlement living and settlement help; she was making speeches about the needs of the neighborhood, always taking one or another of her new neighbors along with her to check any tendency to hasty generalizations by forcing on her "the consciousness that I had at least one auditor who knew the conditions more intimately than I could hope to do"; and she was studying those conditions as carefully as any man ever studied the conditions of an industry in which he was determined to survive. Those things would seem to have been plenty in themselves to occupy the time of one person, yet they filled only the smaller portion of her day. The really major portion of it she spent in getting acquainted with the people among whom she had come to live.

Among these neighbors was of course at first some suspicion. Most of them lived where they did because they had to live there, not because they wanted to. Miss Addams and Miss Starr could afford to live elsewhere. Why then had they settled on Halsted Street? They were sometimes cross-examined with care; one old Irishman, shaking his head, declared, "It was the strangest thing he had come across in his experience." But as time went on, this suspicion died away. It was obvious that if you went to the House you were welcome; if you called, you were called upon; and if you let the young women know there was anything they could do for you, they did it if they could. Miss Addams herself washed new-born babies, and "minded" children, and nursed the sick, and prepared the dead for burial, as naturally as any other woman of the neighborhood did for her friends. She had more friends, that was all. And some things she would do that other women would not do—as when she and Julia Lathrop officiated alone at the birth of an illegitimate child, because the doctor was late in arriving, and the neighboring matrons who knew the circumstances "would not touch the likes of her." According to the police, the house was in a "bad" section. But Jane Addams even in those earliest days would go anywhere, quite alone, if she was summoned, at three o'clock in the morning, "just as if she was a doctor." She had all her life many doubts, but no fears. On two occasions, it is recorded, she woke to find a burglar in her room. The first time her small nephew was asleep in the next room, and she thought only of not awakening him. "Don't make a noise," she said to the burglar. Startled, he leaped for the window by which he had entered. "You'll be hurt if you go that way," she said. "Go down by the stairs and let yourself out." He did. On the second occasion, addressing the house-breaker, without embarrassment, she succeeded in removing his own. Discovering that he was not a professional, but an amateur out of employment, she told him to go away and come back at nine the next morning, when she would see what she could do about getting him a job. He came, and she got him work.

The first suspicions of the neighbors were soon allayed, their doubt replaced by what she calls "uniform kindness and courtesy"; and outside the neighborhood, the plan and methods of Hull House were much praised. Jane Addams herself was young, good-looking, earnest, and good-humored; if her life was an odd one, it seemed from the outside nevertheless to be picturesque. David Swing, the most popular preacher of the day, and himself a picturesque figure, had written with patronizing kindness of her scheme "to make the desert blossom as the rose," as he put it. "It is not claimed that this renting and opening of a house will equal in significance the affair of 1492 or of 1776, but it is hoped that it will demonstrate that there are new and good ways of benefiting the less fortunate thousands of the large cities." The *Advance* had carried a long article, which ended, "The plan should carry with it the earnest sympathy and hearty god-speed of every heart which rejoices in the old Christmas prophecy of 'peace on earth, good-will to men.'" And in 1890, 1891, 1892 the newspapers of Chicago said a number of kind words; sentimental, but well-meant. Bitter opposition was to come in 1892, when the residents began to investigate the "sweat-shops" and urge factory and child-labor legislation, and the department-store advertisers were to order "thumbs down on those damned women." But the city was approving enough until then. There were more roses thrown than stones at first. Young women of the "best families," Jenny Dow, who took the kindergarten, Mary Rozet Smith who took the boys' clubs, Maude Warner, Anita McCormick, many others, were permitted by their parents to go over to Halsted Street and help out; and the number of actual residents soon increased to six, then to fifteen, then to twenty, as rapidly as they could be accommodated.

But the work was terribly hard for all. In the first year 50,000 people (not 50,000 individuals, of course) came to the House, and it is no exaggeration to say that Jane Addams talked to most of them. The second year the number increased to 2,000 a week. Jane was doing whatever part of the housework Mary Keyser left over, calling on hundreds of people in the neighborhood to interest them if she could, keeping the books as she raised the money to supplement what she and the other residents paid in, studying conditions with the care of the modern sociological scholar—ten hours a day including a hundred conferences with child, woman, man, were nothing unusual to her—and in addition speaking whenever she got a chance.

In power as a speaker she had advanced greatly since the days of her college competition with William Jennings Bryan and other budding orators; advanced chiefly of course in her power of thought and phrase, but to some degree in technic. Her voice was clear and agreeable. She never raised it, but she modulated it pleasantly in the lower registers, and she could be heard easily by large audiences. She was accustomed to stand with her head thrown a little forward, sometimes fingering a string of beads, often with her hands clasped behind her back, looking, even in the early days, a little weary. She was; she was not physically strong and she worked long hours. There was nothing dramatic about her appearance on the platform then or later, there was little appeal, as such, to the emotions of her audiences; but she interested them.

She prepared her speeches with the greatest care. Of many passages the notebooks of those days, in which she wrote out in full what she meant to say, show four or five preliminary versions. It was her habit, then and later, to plan her talks with the idea of subsequently publishing them as magazine articles; later she might collect these articles into a book. So from the beginning her talks read well. Charles James Fox said that a good speech never reads well, by which he undoubtedly meant that a real oration has a freshness and glow which are lacking in an essay; and in a sense he was right. In Jane Addams's talks, however, there was so much freshness and glow of information and reflection that they seemed good speeches. Her material, much of it gathered at first hand, soon came to be large in amount, her arrangement of it was clear and competent, and her inferences were logical. Yet, and in this lay much of the attraction of what she had to say, her conclusions were never conventional. Her reasoning was too subtle, her illustrations were too enlightening, for that. The validity

HULL HOUSE FOUNDERS

Upper left, ELLEN GATES STARR; upper right, JANE ADDAMS at the
opening of Hull House in 1889; lower left, JULIA LATHROP; lower
right, FLORENCE KELLEY—all residents of Hull House in 1890's.

(Photograph of Miss Lathrop by Moffett.)

of the convictions at which she arrived (though she put them always as views, never as dogma) was difficult to deny. "I do not know," William James wrote her, "why you should always be right, but you always are. You inhabit reality." Yet those convictions were hardly ever obvious, and they were now and then startling; vivid in themselves, however they might be phrased. And as everything she said proceeded from her daily experience, she did not require, as most statesmen and indeed most "orators" of any type require, a "great occasion" for the stimulation of her powers. Life was her occasion, and the possibility for progress that lies in mutual understanding and common opportunity was invariably her text. She was as much at her best in the 1890's before small neighborhood organizations and women's clubs, as later when she was presiding over national or international organizations, or seconding the nomination of the best-known man in America as a candidate for the presidency at a new party convention.

One who heard her often, remarked:

She seemed to me from the first a really great orator, and yet her most striking characteristic was her extreme simplicity. Her preparation seemed to consist in laying out a line of thought, and her oratory in giving that thought to her hearers, or hearer, for she has always had the effect of speaking to but one, and that one is each one. The message itself is all that concerns her, the manner of giving it and what you are going to think about her as a speaker do not seem to enter her consciousness at all. When you heard her speak, you felt that she knew *thoroughly* what she was talking about, knew her subject on every side and not just the side of it she was presenting to you. Often she concluded her prepared talk by asking for questions, and her answers to even the most abstruse or apparently unexpected queries were always exact and full. If her interest in every shade of opinion upon every issue had not interfered, she would I think have made a great debater; perhaps even greater than she was as a public speaker.

Often when she was speaking she would pick out one person in the audience, and concentrate upon him, or her. If the audience in general was friendly, she would select some one who seemed puzzled, or not particularly interested, and try to make herself clear or interesting to him; if the audience was at the beginning apparently hostile she would select some one whose look was encouraging, and as it were confide her views to him alone. Talking to such an audience in New York on one occasion, she selected in this fashion a benign elderly gentleman, whose appearance gave her not only courage but a haunting sense of familiarity. After the speech had ended in something of an ovation, the elderly gentleman came up on the platform and shook her hand warmly. "Miss Addams," he said, "that was a wonderful speech; and do you know, I had a curious and delightful feeling all through, that you were talking personally with me."

"In a way," she confessed, "I was. And you helped me out so splendidly that I shall be very much obliged to you if you will tell me who you are." He smiled more benignly than before.

"My name," he said, "is William Dean Howells."

But the daily routine of Hull House in those first years was an exhausting business. Kindergarten children in the morning, clubs of older children in the afternoon, and more clubs and classes for adults in the evening, which filled every room in the old house, including the bedrooms, put privacy out of the question. Curious visitors, too, overran the place in those early days. In time as the size of the place increased regular "tours" were arranged, with individual residents taking the duty, during specified hours, of "toting" people about (the word was Mrs. Florence Kelley's, and has persisted; visitors to Hull House to-day are always called "totees"). But in the first years they simply poked their inquisitive noses in everywhere, as if the settlement were a sort of museum, and the residents and neighbors alike were specimens of one sort or another. This biographer, who happened one day to be reading a "Henty book" in a corner of the dining-room, still remembers after forty-five years the amiable old lady who startled him from his wanderings with Magellan round Cape Horn by putting her hand on his shoulder and demanding, "Are you one of the dear boys who have been saved here?"; his own resentful reply, "No, ma'am, I am just visiting my aunt"; and his aunt's brief comment, "You see he is not saved *yet.*"

In the rush and the crowd housekeeping had to be carried on as it could. Every resident did what came to hand in the House as out of it—cooked and cleaned and washed windows and replaced the furniture that was constantly shoved here and there and everywhere. It was in those days that Jane Addams acquired the habit, persistent till the end, of moving about while she conversed, shutting drawers, adjusting pictures, even shifting desks; acquired the habit also of making requests that had the force of orders. It no more occurred to her to spare others than to spare herself. A fine but quick impatience with anything dilatory or inefficient in the service of others marked her for many years. She was past sixty when on one occasion she rose suddenly, remarking, "I like pictures to hang

straight," got up on a chair to adjust a framed etching
which was not placed to her liking, fell off and broke her
arm. Next day in the hospital, after the bone had been set,
when she was being mildly reproached for her impulsive-
ness, she said defensively: "If that picture had been hung
right in the first place, this needn't have happened."

The worry over money was also fatiguing. The residents
who kept coming—fifteen "permanents" in the first five
years—paid their own way, of course; they were not pro-
fessionals, either, merely young women or young men who
would rather live at the corner of Halsted and Polk Streets
than anywhere else. But none of them was rich, and for
what the House was doing the bills were heavy. Many
things they wanted to do, they could not afford at all.
Sometimes Jane Addams worried over the "essential difference between the neighbors and ourselves," in that she
had a "sense of security in regard to illness and old age,
and the lack of these two securities is the specter which
most persistently haunts the poor"; but sometimes that
sense of security faded into the background. And Hull
House was not the sort of institution that could afford
deficits. Down on the South Side of Chicago William
Rainey Harper was about to depend largely on deficits to
urge the new University of Chicago forward to greater and
greater things in education, but Hull House was different.
It was personal, and it was an experiment contrary to the
business attitude of the city; therefore it had very definitely to prove itself practical in finance. A statesman like
Daniel Webster might be careless in matters of money,
but an "idealist" had to be extremely careful in this material thing. The books simply *had* to balance; whatever
she might want to spend, Jane Addams simply *had* to live,

and to run her household, within her income. She talked
for pay, when she had the opportunity and the time; there
were financial contributions, now and then, to the work of
the House; but it was a tough and constant struggle to
make ends meet. She did it, however, as Hull House has
continued to do it to this day. Through good and evil report, through depressions and wars, Hull House has never
had a deficit.

Some offers of contributions were refused. One of $20,-
000 to build a boarding-club-house for young women; another of $50,000 if the residents of Hull House would stop
their agitation for a factory law for Illinois. This latter
being a bribe Jane Addams wrote afterward of the injury
it did to her pride, as she remembered her father, "the one
man in the Senate of Illinois who had never been offered a
bribe because bad men were instinctively afraid of him.
... What had befallen the daughter of my father, that
such a thing could happen to her? The salutary reflection
that it could not have occurred unless a weakness in myself had permitted it, at least withheld me from any heroic
display of indignation." Ah, those salutary reflections!
Who but Abraham Lincoln and Jane Addams, of the
"workers in the burden of the heat of the day," ever had
such? Fancy the savagery with which Theodore Roosevelt,
or Woodrow Wilson, would have turned on anybody who
dared offer them bribes! To understand evil in others is
not difficult; to perceive weakness in one's self is easy in
the weak; but among the strong it is not usual. But the
$20,000 was offered in all good faith; by a man who subse-
quently gave that, and more, to the University of Chicago.
He was well-known, however, as one who paid his girl
employees a wage so low that they were wretchedly poor

in consequence, and it did not seem logical to Jane Addams to accept illgotten money for the promotion of salvation. Perhaps it is not logical to-day, though it was logical enough in the Middle Ages; it was the system that financed the Christian church then.

It was more characteristic of Miss Starr, perhaps, than of Jane Addams, that art should have been the first Hull House activity to have a building of its own for development. Edward Butler, a Chicago merchant, gave $5,000 in 1891 for the erection and maintenance of an Art Gallery—the first large gift Hull House had received. Mr. Butler, diligent in business, had already begun to stand before the kings of painting. He was a trustee of the Chicago Art Institute, which had been one of the prides of the city since the Great Fire, and which was just completing a fine new building on the lake front; he was a collector; and he was himself to become a painter of considerable skill and charm, frequently exhibiting, though for a long time anonymously. Miss Starr found him easy to persuade of the civilizing value of good pictures in an immigrant section. The free lease of the land on which the "Butler Gallery" was to stand would expire in four years, and there was no certainty that it would be renewed, but Mr. Butler magnificently took the chance. Pond and Pond, the architect-brothers who had put the old Hull House into shape, and whose hearts as well as hands were concerned in the enterprise, built it, flush with Halsted Street, on the southeast corner of the Hull House lot, with a passage-way running from the House itself into the Gallery. There was a reading-room on the first floor, an exhibition-hall which was the last word in design and lighting for those days, and a studio above. The Butler

Gallery, since much enlarged, has stood for two generations as a monument to the early interest of Chicago in
art, an interest which has never flagged, and to the daring
of its donor.

If it was somewhat surprising to Chicagoans that the
first brick-and-mortar expansion of Hull House should be
into the field of pure esthetics, it must have seemed more
reasonable that the second should have been into the field
of dietetics. Not everybody could see what good a chance
to look at fine pictures and to study painting would do the
poor, but anybody could understand that a chance to buy
good food cheap would be welcome to them. When the
starting of the Hull House Public Kitchen was announced,
there was general approval. This at any rate was something practical, a kind of "doing good to people" that any
one could comprehend. But the comparative lack of
neighborhood interest in the Public Kitchen, in contrast
to the eagerness with which the people of the neighborhood greeted the Butler Gallery, was one of the innumerable things that made life interesting to the residents in
those early years. Not that the Public Kitchen was a
failure; but it had little of the popularity that followed
the art exhibits. The idea behind it was that cheaper cuts
of meat, and simpler vegetables, skilfully and scientifically
cooked, could be distributed to the households everywhere
in the neighborhood, thus not only relieving the hard-
worked women of much of the labor of getting the family
meals, but supplying real nourishment to the workingmen
and the children who were not getting it from canned
goods and candy-store lunches. It was a sound idea, and
it was carefully studied out. First the neighborhood
dietaries were thoroughly investigated, to see whether the

need for better food and less sketchy preparation actually existed, and what the people were paying for what they ate. Then one of the residents went down to Boston, and took a training-course in public kitchen management and supervision. When she returned, she worked out all details carefully, simple shining ovens, glittering copper tanks, and ingenious, convenient containers for distribution of her wares. How those utensils gleam in memory down through the years, like a good deed in a naughty world! Publicity was secured through the newspapers, as well as by an alluring sign; the first soups and stews were carefully made ready, tasty and inexpensive, and Hull House Public Kitchen sat back and waited for trade. It came, but in disappointing volume. The chief patrons were the nearby factory workers. The housewives looked in occasionally, but purchased seldom. Alas, like the rest of the world, they preferred what they were used to eating, and what "they'd ruther," to the nutritious. It is easier to get people to form new interests in their leisure time, than to change old habits of their routine. The Public Kitchen continues, but it has never to this day affected the lives of the Hull House neighbors as has the Butler Gallery. In the endless game of matching services, human nature always remains one up.

Another accomplishment of the early 'nineties was the establishment of the "Jane Club," a coöperative boarding-club for working girls. It grew out of the discovery, soon made, that women workers were the weak spot in the efforts that were even then being made toward the establishment of what has come to be called "collective bargaining" in labor matters. If they struck they could not pay for their room and board, and the fear of being put out on the streets made them easy capitulators in any dispute with their employers. At a meeting at Hull House during a strike in a shoe-factory, one girl exclaimed, "Wouldn't it be fine if we had a boarding-club of our own, and then we could stand by each other in a time like this?" At once the idea was taken up; the problem was studied both theoretically and practically, and on the first of May 1891 two apartments near Hull House were secured and fifteen young women moved in. In three years all of the six apartments in the building had been taken over, and the "club" had fifty members. Hull House paid one month's rent on the first two apartments, and furnished them; after that the club was self-sustaining; the first coöperative association of the sort, founded and managed by women, that had ever succeeded in the United States, according to a statement made by the head of the Department of Labor. In 1898 a friend gave $15,000 to build a club-house, which has since been maintained with entire success. It was in connection with the effort to secure money to build this club-house, that the $20,000 previously mentioned was refused, because it seemed to Jane Addams to be "tainted" at its source. Her refusal, like many other of the decisions she was forced to make in those days, was long a source of painful consideration to her. She did not distrust her own moral logic; she was quite sure she was right to decline the money; but just *why* was she right? Long afterward she summed up her convictions in a typical sentence: "Social changes can be inaugurated only by those who feel that contemporary conditions are wrong, and the expression of their scruples may be the one opportunity for pushing forward moral tests into that dubious area wherein wealth is accumulated." The pushing forward of moral tests into dubious areas has been the substance of her social ethics all her life; flash-lighting passages that have long been dark, to find where they lead.

Of these three more or less successful early efforts to "improve conditions" in the neighborhood, the Butler Gallery, the Public Kitchen and Coffee-House, and the Jane Club, the first two were inspired by the residents, the Jane Club was the suggestion of the "neighbors"; therefore the Jane Club was the nearest to Jane Addams's heart. To her at that time the "subjective necessity" of living in a settlement was greater than the objective necessity of helping others. One might say she read the Golden Rule backwards in those days.

"Inasmuch as our philosophy at Hull House has always been one of coöperation," Jane Addams wrote in 1909, "we have always tried to turn over to properly organized bodies the work we were able to begin but were not equipped to carry on." Among others, such as the Rockford Summer School and the Public School Art Society, two illustrations of this method of procedure may be cited here.

The first was the provision of playgrounds for the children. It was as early as 1892 that a rich, hard-bitten young man named William Kent heard Jane Addams make a speech on sharing opportunity. Kent was far from being a sentimentalist. He had spent most of the summers, and many of the winters, of his young manhood on a ranch, where he had learned to ride hard, to shoot straight, and to tell the truth, like the young Persians of old. He was a fighter by instinct and training. "She was the first person who ever forced me to try to think things out," he wrote long afterward. "You might say she converted me; civilized me, any way, to some extent." He went to see her to find out "what to do," as she herself was to go to Tolstoy later. She called his attention to the fact that on certain lots he had just inherited not far from the House the buildings were not only ramshackle, but were being occupied as houses of prostitution. "You might begin there," she suggested. He went away annoyed, not to say indignant. He did not know what advice he had wanted, but it was not this. In two weeks he was back. "I have decided," he told her grimly, "to turn over that property to you to use as you please."

"You might tear the buildings down and make the lots a place for the children to play on," she said. "They have nothing but the streets now."

"Do as you please about that," he answered

"Will you pay for tearing them down?"

"I don't see why I should."

"And will you pay the taxes?"

"You ask too much," he said, still more annoyed, and went away again. This time he was back in a week. "I'll do whatever you say," he consented. The first public playground in Chicago was opened on May 1, 1892, on the Kent lots.

Time went on. The playground proved its value. The alderman of the ward, in spite of the fact that Hull House was consistently opposing him in his campaigns for reelection, coöperated to the extent of arranging to have other vacant lots flooded for a skating-pond in winter. The day came years later when William Kent gave his land to the city for a municipally owned and operated "small park" for playground purposes. From that came others. To-day no other city in the United States has as wide or a better-managed system of playgrounds. The second illustration is of Chicago's milk supply. In 1898, in spite of the drop in the neighborhood death rate that resulted from the Hull House campaigns to clean up the ward, Jane Addams was much dissatisfied with the quality of the milk the neighborhood, and the residents, for that matter, were getting. She personally undertook an investigation. She discovered not only that the milk in many places was dirtily kept, but that it came dirty to the houses and the small shops of the district. Immediately she wrote to the head of the College of Agriculture of the University of Illinois to enlist scientific coöperation. He turned the problem over to the Experiment Station of the University, and Professor H. S. Grindley took it up in detail. In December, 1898, he and Jane Addams jointly reported their findings in a circular, with the title "A Study of the Milk Supply of Chicago." From that bulletin led further investigations and publications, which have played the most prominent part in establishing higher standards in Chicago, and have indirectly benefited milk consumers in many other cities.

CHAPTER VII

SIX WOMEN

NO more remarkable group of women was ever gathered together in a "settlement" anywhere than lived and worked at Hull House in the early years. Besides Jane Addams and Ellen Starr, the residents in the 1890's included Florence Kelley, Julia Lathrop, and Alice Hamilton; and among the Chicago women who came constantly to the House and steadily supported it with gifts for current needs and for new buildings, were Mrs. Joseph T. Bowen and Mary Rozet Smith. Against a background of usefulness and charm provided by a score of other residents and regular workers—Rose Giles, Ella Waite, Enella Benedict, to name a few only—the personalities and powers of this half-dozen still stand out vividly after forty years of acquaintance. They all lived long; Miss Starr, Mrs. Bowen, and Alice Hamilton are still living, and Mrs. Kelley, Miss Lathrop and Miss Smith have but recently died. Jane Addams when she died had just completed a biography of Miss Lathrop, and was planning one of Mrs. Kelley. In 1930, pressed by the newspapers to make a list of the twelve greatest American women, Jane Addams included Mrs. Kelley, Miss Lathrop and Alice Hamilton. Miss Starr and Miss Lathrop had been friends of Jane Addams for more than fifty years then, the others for forty years. Together or apart, they were all intimate in spirit and accomplishment, and did more than any other group of women in American history to improve the position of women in general, and social legislation and administration in particular. A biography of Jane Addams that did not include special mention of this group would be absurd.

Ellen Gates Starr and Jane Addams were freshmen together in Rockford in 1877. Ellen Starr flashed brilliantly through her first year, then left college to teach, first for a year at the little town of Mount Morris, Illinois, then in Chicago, at the famous old Kirkland School for Girls, fashionable but strenuously educational too. The reputation of Miss Kirkland as a teacher and director of the daughters of "old Chicago families" has never had a rival in that city. Ellen Starr taught English and "art" —not drawing and painting, but appreciation. Her preparation for such teaching was not remarkably extensive, but her delight in it was keen. She thrilled to beauty, then and all her life thereafter. For ten years she and Jane Addams maintained their girlhood acquaintance, until in 1887 they were abroad together. Ellen had gone to continue her study of "appreciation." When however in Madrid, on Easter day 1888, Jane confided to Ellen Starr her scheme for a house among the poor people somewhere in Chicago, Ellen embraced it at once, with that vivacity, sincerity and confidence which had been always characteristic of her. She would live there too. Together they would live and work. And so they did, for forty years.

A strange thing about Ellen Starr was that as she grew older she grew more, not less, intense. Her major interests at Hull House at first were what they had been at the Kirkland School—in teaching. She organized reading-classes and clubs; drew the young people by scores into

the studio of the Butler Gallery for the study of painting;
began at the grammar-school nearest to Hull House that
scheme for giving the public school-children of Chicago a
chance to see good pictures every day, which has since
developed so splendidly into the Public School Art Society;
and finally studied and taught bookbinding as a fine art
in a way that made it literally fashionable. It was partly
through Ellen Starr's connection with the Kirkland School
too that in the early 'nineties so many young women of
social prominence came to Hull House to direct "clubs"
of young people and to help with the "classes." In these
earliest years she lived a life of merely continuing interests. She was aspirational, shining, and serene. But as
time went on, the serenity soon changed to something no
more purposeful, perhaps, but more vividly purposeful.
Her interest in the unionization of women became intense.
She concerned herself directly with strikes and women-
strikers. She picketed. She harangued on occasion. She
became a member in good standing of the Socialist Party,
and argued for its tenets with a sort of charming fierce-
ness. Her quest for beauty, her dream of bringing beauty
into even the ugliest and most miserable of the lives about
her, did not cease, but it was accompanied by a more
passionate quest, a more partisan longing, for social
justice. She remained an artist, but she became a combatant. Her development paralleled that of William
Morris; only Ellen Starr was closer to the people than
William Morris ever became. He believed in Utopias, and
brought back news from Nowhere. She crusaded down
dirty streets, and frail and gentle as she was in appearance, was no more daunted by policemen than she would
have been by Saracens or dragons.

This alteration of the direction of her interests did not decrease her influence at Hull House, but to some extent it changed that influence. She had begun, and she remained, at the head of the institution of Hull House, so far as it was an institution. No one ever forgot that she was a co-founder of Hull House. On the other hand, in so far as the House was institutional, it stood for tolerance, for opportunity, not for combat. So far as it was an institution, it was a City of Refuge, to whom might come all who were oppressed; those who were oppressed by riches and responsibilities, as well as those who were oppressed by misery and by social theory. The only word upon the mat was "Welcome," the only motto over the entrance, "May you find hope who enter here." Miss Starr never doubted that tolerance was good, but was it not a good that interfered with the Best? There arose a militancy in her that found tolerance difficult, and welcome to certain ideas almost distasteful. In the end she satisfied that militancy, that desire for self-discipline, in the Church. She became a Roman Catholic. And with that submission of herself to authority, her old serenity returned. In her old age, her health shattered, her spirit is as young as ever, but she is willing, she is even eager, to do what she is advised to do by others. She who was the passionate advocate first of culture, then of rebellion, has become the advocate of discipline. But she is still eager, uncontemplative; as passionate for divinity and salvation, as she ever was for beauty or for justice.

Julia Lathrop, like Jane Addams and Ellen Starr, was a pupil of the Rockford Seminary. Miss Lathrop, born and brought up in Rockford, went to the Seminary however for only one year, 1876-77; the September of 1877 that found Jane Addams a freshman at Rockford, found Julia Lathrop at Vassar. She graduated there in 1880. A tablet there in her honor, erected while she was head of the Children's Bureau, first recorded her as "A.B., M.A., PH.D." On hearing of this inscription, Miss Lathrop remarked that she would have to discover which was the less expensive, to secure a PH.D. at her age, or to have the inscription changed. It was changed, and reads "LL.D.," now, in accordance with the facts.

Returning to Rockford, Julia Lathrop was promptly impressed for service by the Seminary girls in helping to stage a show, and in this connection met Jane Addams. She came to Hull House as a resident in its first year, ten years after that first acquaintance. Meanwhile Julia Lathrop had pleased her father and somewhat scandalized her older brother by studying law. She had had to go on studying something; her easy energy and her keen mind made stagnation and "waiting for something to turn up" impossible for her. Blackhaired, witty, and determined, descendant of the Puritans and inheritor of their devotion to causes but utterly un-Puritanic in her humor and in her culture, daughter of a rich man who had made himself one of the best-known lawyers in Illinois outside of Chicago, and of a high-spirited great lady determined to achieve suffrage for women, Julia Lathrop found herself at thirty educated, cultivated, trained, and without the opportunity of responsibility. Naturally she accepted what Hull House had to offer, and at and through the House she became a great figure.

It is difficult to conceive of any attribute of Julia Lathrop that might be wished changed. She sparkled, as did Florence Kelley; their talk was a firework. Yet her wit was never mordant. Florence Kelley could be terrifying, and when she chose to be, was so; but Julia Lathrop, who could have been quite as terrifying, never chose to be. She was not so much detached as restrained. However full her information, and however eager her sympathies, she always kept her head and her temper. Her very humor was informational; her quizzical smile was evidence of the stupidities at which she smiled, and her laughter was as good as an argument. It was undoubtedly her humor which made her virtue seem what Jane Addams calls it, "disinterested virtue." In its light, she could not see her own preoccupations as of any more importance than those of any one else; nor yet the preoccupations of others as inevitably of the last importance. She did what her hand found to do, and so did others; but more than any one else, she was contented to wait awhile for results. Perhaps she was foolish, she reflected; but then, so perhaps were those to whom she found herself in opposition. Wait and see; but meanwhile, whatsoever your hand found to do, do it with your might. Cry if you must; laugh when you could; work and wait.

Only women like that first group of Hull House residents could begin by organizing a "Plato Club" for the discussion of Greek philosophy with the old men of the neighborhood, and pass directly from such organization to amateur midwifery. Jane Addams recalled Julia Lathrop's interest in both, and in connection with the latter, when the two of them had gone to the help of an unmarried girl in a tenement "who was having a baby all by herself, and hollering something fierce; disgracing the place, she was!" their conversation after the child had been brought safely into the world and the young mother quieted:

I said, "This doing things that we don't know how to do is going too far. Why did we let ourselves be rushed into midwifery?" To which she replied, "If we have to begin to hew down to the line of our ignorance, for goodness' sake don't let us begin at the humanitarian end! If Hull House doesn't have its roots in human kindness, it is no good at all."

A trained investigator, Julia Lathrop was the great inspiration of *Hull House Maps and Papers,* the first direct contribution to sociological scholarship which came from the place. A vigorous executive, she was the first resident to be given a "state job," as a member of the first state board of charities in Illinois. Thereafter she was what Jane Addams calls "a great servant of the state" for eight years, when she resigned; only to be reappointed later. Meanwhile she was also a regularly appointed "County Visitor" for Cook County; she was directly concerned in the long battle for the organization of the Cook County Juvenile Court, first of its kind in any American city; and at the same time, she was the executive staff and stay of Hull House itself, never "hewing down to her ignorance" of anything that had to be done, and that only she apparently was on the spot to do. A marvelous emollient she was for disputatiousness. With a house packed with strong characters, equally full of ideals and energy, seldom any three residents seeing anything in precisely the same way, and only Jane Addams, perhaps, seeing everything from everybody's point of view, there was plenty of disputatiousness about the place to practise emolliation if your taste and powers ran that way. Julia Lathrop's did. She could argue with the keenest until argument ceased to be fruitful, and then laugh temper out of court; lighten the ponderous, deflate pomposity, and praise the sensitive with so light a touch that it was impossible to suspect either patronage or irony.

When she was made head of the Children's Bureau she spent most of her time in Washington. Even in the earlier years, she was often with her father and mother in Rockford, or on her visits down state. So one of the clearest and fondest recollections of every resident of Hull House, from the first years on till the end of her life, is of coming in at the end of some day's work, and being met in the hallway with the cry, "J. Lathrop's here!" It was as if their weariness fell from them at the news.

One chapter of Miss Addams's biography of Julia Lathrop is headed "Friendship with Florence Kelley." And seldom do old residents of Hull House think of the one without thinking of the other; so like they were in many things, so opposite in others; as like, as opposite, as an electric current and a trail of sparks. Mrs. Kelley was an old Philadelphian, the descendant of Quakers (John Bartram, the botanist and friend of Franklin, was one of her ancestors). Her father, William D. Kelley, was one of the founders of the Republican Party in Pennsylvania, Congressman for almost all of the thirty years subsequent to 1860, at one time Chairman of the Committee on Ways and Means; his grandfather captain in the Revolutionary War of a company he had himself raised. Florence Kelley studied at Cornell University in the days when no other eastern university admitted women; then went abroad and studied at Heidelberg and Zurich, becoming fluent in French and German and acquiring a good reading knowledge of Italian and Swedish. Her interest was always more in facts than theories. Her studies impressed on her the necessity of applying the power of the *state* to prevent the modern industrial system from destroying its own workers, particularly women and children. She married in Europe; after a stormy marital experience, brought back her three children to America, divorced her husband, and resumed her maiden name. She took a fixed fierce resolution: she would make the salvation of women and children from blind industrial greed the work of her life.

She became a resident of Hull House in the winter of 1891, and was from the first day a power. "She galvanized us all into more intelligent interest in the industrial conditions about us," Jane Addams said. It was Mrs. Kelley who pestered the state legislature into sending a Commission to investigate the Chicago sweat-shops; who forced a conviction of sin upon the big department-stores, best customers of the sweaters; who urged on Governor Altgeld the maintenance of that pressure on the legislature which resulted in the passage of the first factory-act in Illinois. Altgeld at once made her Chief Factory Inspector, on July 1, 1895. Presently she saw the section of the law providing an eight-hour day for women declared unconstitutional by the state Supreme Court. Later she was to see other similar acts declared unconstitutional by the United States Supreme Court. She was not discouraged, but she was furious. She added the study of law to her other labors, was admitted to the bar, and fought the old battle on a new field—in the courts. She insisted that "intelligent experimentation to prevent an admitted social evil was preferable to the use of outworn methods of production made obsolete by changed conditions"; and though she was beaten in those early battles, she had the glory later of finding her views supported by such Justices as Holmes and Brandeis, and of seeing the Court as a whole come round to the conclusion that the only way to preserve the Constitution, is to keep it adjusted to current facts of life. Is this Constitution of ours, she demanded, a river of life, to be kept within new banks as it flows on, or is it a stagnant pool?

Driven from factory inspection, she turned to the business of organizing a Consumers' League, which should by indirection force decency into the business of manufacturing. For thirty years she was the executive head of the National Consumers' League, and for thirty years in speech and writing her trumpets challenged the Jerichos of indifference and cruelty to the weak. One by one they fell, before onslaughts she as much as any other woman in the United States inspired. She died before the passage of the Child Labor Amendment; but she died a happy warrior, for the fight to which she had devoted herself for almost half a century was almost won.

Her oldest son (incidentally a member of the national Automobile Labor Board) says: "I believe that from the time my mother first went to Hull House until her death, more than forty years later, she looked upon Miss Addams as her dearest and most intimate friend. She loved Miss Addams and admired her and approved of her unreservedly. The last afternoon I spent with my mother, when she was well enough to talk at all, we spent talking of Miss Addams and the early days at Hull House."

Yet Florence Kelley, full of love as she was, still seems to this biographer the toughest customer in the reform riot, the finest rough-and-tumble fighter for the good life for others, that Hull House ever knew. Any weapon was a good weapon in her hand—evidence, argument, irony or invective. She was perhaps the only resident of Hull House who ever habitually made fun of "Sister Jane." "Do you know what I would do," she said to her once, "if that woman calls you a saint again? I'd show her my teeth, and if that didn't convince her, I would bite her." A few months before she died, when she was in great pain, she remarked to Jane Addams one day, with a smile for this biographer, "I don't know why I have always been fond of your nephew; he's never been anything but a cumberer of the ground!" And she meant it too—both the fondness and the objurgation. She had no use for loiterers on the edge of the social struggle, but she could spare from her enormous store of sympathy a liking for them, if they amused her.

Her bursting vitality in the early days was a little frightening; she hurled the spears of her thought with such apparent carelessness of what breasts they pierced. She drove through her duties as factory inspector with a dismaying energy, and issued her orders with the same negligence of appearance that she showed in throwing her clothes on in the morning and like some daughter of Minerva and Mars sallying forth to war. And among all the associations of Hull House one suspects it was that with Julia Lathrop that Florence Kelley enjoyed most, though she was far from "approving of her unreservedly." Mrs. Kelley was a fighter; Miss Lathrop was a diplomat. Both were brilliant, imaginative, humorous, and troubled by injustice; both had great powers of persistence in daily routine; both had studied law, and been admitted to the bar. But Miss Lathrop had endless patience; Mrs.

Kelley a kind of fiercely joyous impatience. Miss Lathrop glowed with determination, Mrs. Kelley burnt with eagerness. Miss Lathrop could bide her time, Mrs. Kelley must on. The logical disciplined minds of both were accompanied by gentleness in Miss Lathrop, and high-spiritedness in Mrs. Kelley. Even their wit was different; one flashed, the other scorched. When both were at Hull House together, arguing some problem of correcting a social injustice, and disagreeing as they often did on the best method of procedure, it is doubtful if any better talk was to be heard anywhere. Prime ministers of Europe, philosophers of all doctrines, labor leaders and great capitalists and unpopular poets and popular novelists and shabby exiles from half the kingdoms of the world visited Hull House and dined there, and listened willingly to the odd half-reluctant meandering sentences of Miss Lathrop, with their often marvelous Mark Twain-like twists into high philosophy or sudden nonsense at the close, and to the interrupting thrusts or the quick, close and yet sweeping logic of Mrs. Kelley, and were glad to be there; and if they had only known it, in the "house meetings" afterward, which only residents attended, they would have heard more vivid discussions still, sternly practical, yet still enlivened by the same patient or impatient humor, as the case might be. Not *horas serenas,* those; not where Florence Kelley was; the shadows on her dial were oftener thrown by lightning. But her straightforwardness was pure gold.

Mrs. Bowen was, and is, an "old Chicagoan." She has called her brief autobiography *Growing Up With a City,* and she could have found no better title. Her grandfather's house, in which she spent her childhood, stood

on the corner of what are now Wabash Avenue and
Monroe Street, and they kept their cow in a pasture at
the corner of Wabash and Adams street, where $50,000
now would not buy as much ground as the cow needed
to lie down on. Her family was so fashionable in her youth
that she was not permitted to take part in the graduating
exercises of her "finishing school," her father considering
it "unwomanly" for a girl of sixteen to appear upon a
platform in public; and she was the first young woman
in the city to drive behind her own coachman in livery.
But she was of a social sympathy amazing in her day;
the essay she was not permitted to read, was on the
problems of the workingman! And in the following winter,
having taken over a Sunday-school class of "big, bad
boys," of her own age, she began by telling them that she
would not tolerate any disorder, and when one boy
promptly kicked another next him, she seized him by the
collar, pulled him off the bench and down the aisle, and
when she had dragged him to the door, opened it and cast
him forth. "From that time on I never had one bit of
trouble with the boys, and I held this class for eleven
years. The boys grew into young men, but stayed with
me, and brought in others until I had a class of one
hundred."

It was inevitable that such a young woman, when Hull
House was founded, should go there to see what it was
like. She did not go, however, until the autumn of 1893.
She joined the Hull House Woman's Club, and having
prepared herself by an intensive study of parliamentary
rules, taught them to the other club-members; was soon
made secretary, and not long afterward president, an
office she filled for almost seventeen years. To accommo-

date the Club as it increased in size she built Bowen Hall for it; then later, after careful study of boys' clubs in other cities, she built the Hull House Boys' Club, the largest building in the present group of nineteen. Still later, to the Hull House Association, she gave seventy-two acres of ground at Waukegan, which, with the ten buildings that stand upon it, is called the "Country Club." Mrs. Bowen has been for many years a trustee and treasurer of the Hull House Association, and has been the largest contributor to it over the years.

But neither as a worker nor as a donor has Mrs. Bowen been most exciting at Hull House, but as a personality. Though she was never an actual resident, her spirit has nevertheless pervaded the place. Of all the large-minded women who have been associated with Jane Addams at Hull House, only Florence Kelley ever equaled Mrs. Bowen in directness. From young girlhood she has been accustomed to command, and to be obeyed. It was typical, and not incidental, that first dismissal of the big bad boy from the Sunday-school class, by the ear. Equally typical, that she kept the class for eleven years, for with her habit of command she has always associated habits of sympathy and tolerance. Her militance like her aristocracy is of the heart. When she became a member of the advisory committee of the Chicago Bureau of Charities she discovered an old Englishwoman who lived in a rat-infested room, with no fire:

> She had some stomach trouble and she subsisted entirely on beer, which she had to take through a rubber tube. There was a temperance parson on the Committee who didn't feel that the United Charities money should be spent on beer. I represented to him that the poor woman could not get much

enjoyment out of it, since she had to take it through a rubber tube, but he was adamant, and said it was wicked. I finally told him that I didn't care what he thought—this woman was going to be supplied with beer just as long as I was chairman of the committee.

It was Mrs. Bowen, with her imagination, her energy, and her wealth who drove through the project of the Juvenile Court in Chicago, and only Mrs. Bowen who could have done it. Julia Lathrop was the first president of the Juvenile Court Committee, organized to carry out the provisions of a law which had provided for the establishment of the court and for the services of probation officers, but made no provision whatever either for the salaries of such officers nor for a place of detention of children found guilty of misdemeanors. Mrs. Bowen succeeded Miss Lathrop as president in 1900, and promptly "made the wheel" that set the law in motion. She raised the money for salaries, selected the officers of enforcement, and instructed them in their duties on the basis of "a complete lack of proper information, our own knowledge of human nature, and our best guesses." Presently she got the city of Chicago to furnish the land, and the county to furnish the money, for the erection of a Juvenile Court Building and a Detention Home. In effect, as the years went on, Mrs. Bowen selected the judges for the Court; Tuthill, Mack, Pinckney, Arnold, Mary Bartelme, a splendid succession. Still later she organized the Juvenile Protective Association; and this will stand as the finest monument to her ability, her intelligence, and her persistence.

Rooted in conservatism, a patriot of the old school, proud of her long record of "Black Republicanism," Mrs.

Bowen surveyed some of the activities, a few of the residents, and many of the visitors to Hull House with a severe though humorous eye. She liked things the way she liked them, and eccentric manifestations of radicalism she never liked; nor did she ever join the Women's International League for Peace. But she no more dreamed of forcible interference with the opinions of other people than she dreamed of the possibility that any one might successfully interfere with her own opinions, and took the same pride in the hospitality of Hull House to every shade of political expression that she took in her own hospitality to every sort of guest. To oddity of all sorts she opposed merely a kind of queenly acceptance. Jane Addams herself, in Mrs. Bowen's view, might think strangely, but she could never do wrong, any more than Mrs. Bowen herself could be mean; both conceptions were impossible. For four decades Mrs. Bowen has retained a sense of feudality in connection with Hull House, a consciousness that noblesse oblige. She has laughed at herself, laughed at what she has regarded as centrifugal, laughed at everything except service and fineness; those two are the articles of her creed.

Alice Hamilton came to Hull House later than any of the other women in this group. She went from a "finishing school" at Farmington to the University of Michigan, where she was given the M.D. degree. "Years afterward," as she once remarked, "I became a doctor." After Michigan, she studied medicine abroad and at Johns Hopkins, and in 1898 came to Chicago to work at Rush. Hull House had been established for nine years when she became a resident; Florence Kelley, having done what she could in Chicago, was just leaving for New York and the headship of the Consumers' League. Doctor Hamilton may be said, in a way, to have taken her place.

But the saying would be misleading. Except in the startling keenness of their intelligence, the two were quite unlike. Mrs. Kelley was a propagandist, Alice Hamilton a scientist; the one relied for reform on action, the other on investigation. Yet when the one went and the other came, the social life of Hull House lost little of its old color or fun. In table-talk a rapier was merely substituted for a sword. Though Doctor Hamilton spent at first many hours of every day in the Rush laboratories, a mile west of Hull House, and a little later still longer hours as professor of pathology in the Women's Medical College of Northwestern University, she found time for elaborate medical investigations of the Hull House neighborhood, and in the evenings to be "woman-of-all-work" in the House activities, doing everything from showing round the constant sight-seers, "toting," as Mrs. Kelley had always called it, to convincing worried mothers that babies with a high fever had better be kept at home and not brought round for inspection. Slender, bright-haired, charming, with that finish of manner which a "finishing school" is still supposed to give, she "toted" tirelessly; the most brutal ignorance of Hull House life, motives and methods never distressed or seemed to weary her. "Are any bathing facilities provided for those who reside here?" she was once asked somewhat sternly by a lady from Boston who had somehow got west of the Alleghenies, and Dr. Hamilton replied with enthusiasm,

"Yes, indeed. You must come round some Saturday morning and help me with the Italian babies in the basement."

From the first her major interest as an investigator was in occupational diseases, and this interest after a while took her away from Chicago; she was from 1911 until 1921 engaged in investigating "industrial poisoning" for the Government, and in 1919 she was appointed professor of industrial medicine at the Harvard Medical School, a position she retained until she resigned in 1934. But like Miss Lathrop, she continued to come back to Hull House, sparkling, amusing, lovely and tireless as before. Her research, however, or rather the grim conclusions it forced her to regarding industrial indifference, the horrible risks of disease, indeed the inevitable deaths, that she came to know women in industry were casually paid to take and face, made her a little less gentle in spirit as the years went on; her own flair for absurdity turned toward the ironical. There were times when in discussion Alice Hamilton could be as "hard-boiled" as Florence Kelley. But she never lost the light touch, or neglected the most delicate of argumentative amenities. Fierce she could be, but harsh never.

And more perhaps than any of the others of the group, except Mary Rozet Smith, Dr. Hamilton made Miss Addams her special charge. Of course, as a physician, she understood more clearly how far Jane Addams constantly went beyond her strength, and could do more to hold her back and save her from the consequences of overwork. Alice Hamilton could issue orders, when the others could only advise. To be sure, Jane Addams seldom obeyed orders, even Dr. Hamilton's; but she did obey those occasionally. Without the care of Alice Hamilton and Mary Smith, it is unlikely that Jane Addams would still have been able to do a good day's work at seventy-four.

Mary Rozet Smith, though the youngest of the group, was early at Hull House. Like Mrs. Bowen, Mary Smith was of an "old Chicago family." She was born and died in a house on Walton Place, Chicago, which her father had built "before the fire." Few indeed of such houses are left now in Chicago. Her mother was a Philadelphia woman of "position," her father the best-known manufacturer in his field in the Chicago of the 'sixties, the 'seventies, the 'eighties, and the 'nineties. Mary went to the Kirkland School, traveled abroad with her father and mother extensively in her 'teens, and in 1890 found herself precisely in the situation that Jane Addams so gloomily analyzed as that of many young women in the 'eighties: "She appreciated only too well that her opportunities had been fine and unusual, but she also knew that in spite of some facility and much good teaching she had no special talent. . . . She looked with positive envy upon those girlhoods which had been filled with happy industry and extenuating obstacles." A friend of the fascinating Jennie Dow's, the first kindergarten teacher at Hull House, Mary Smith drifted to the House in the course of its first year, to see whether there was anything she could do there. She was barely twenty; tall, shy, fair, and eager. From that day until she died, forty-three years later, the interests of the House remained the center of her own interests, and the friendship of Mary Smith soon became and always remained the highest and clearest note in the music of Jane Addams's personal life.

In the early years of the House, which were of course the most difficult years financially, Mary Smith was the most unfailing helper-out. She enlisted the interest of her father in gifts for buildings; later, when she was made a trustee of the Hull House Association, she herself gave largely. But it was her constant overcoming of deficits here and there, small but apparently unsurmountable, that literally kept the work going, or at any rate kept Jane Addams from black discouragement. Scores of letters to her from Jane Addams, written in the earliest days, beginning at first "Dear Miss Smith," presently changing through all degrees of salutation to the simple "Dearest," carry on every page the acknowledgment of Mary's unfailing generosity. Some of them gratefully refuse offers; many of them reluctantly accept. When Mary Smith died, every letter that she had ever received from Jane Addams was found in her desk. The earliest are the most revealing; revealing of a devotion on both sides to a constant purpose, and of a ripening trust, that was never for a moment to be interrupted for more than forty years. If those letters are ever published, in their entirety and chronologically, they will give a reflection of a woman unsurpassable in Matthew Arnold's characteristics of "sweetness and light." The illumination of Jane Addams's spirit dimmed when Mary Smith died; she walked as steadily as ever, but in the twilight.

It cannot have escaped notice that Julia Lathrop, Florence Kelley, Mrs. Bowen, Dr. Hamilton, were all women of distinctive accomplishment, women who made for themselves careers, women who "became famous." Ellen Starr was less a woman of this sort of distinction, Mary Rozet Smith not so in the least. She was a member of many national and civic organizations for service, she was particularly useful in plans for making life better and fairer for the colored people of the United States, she gave lavishly though intelligently to many things, but she

HULL HOUSE FRIENDS

Upper left, DR. ALICE HAMILTON, one of the founders; upper right, MARY ROZET SMITH; lower left, MRS. JOSEPH T. BOWEN—both early supporters of Hull House; lower right, JANE ADDAMS at thirty-five.

(Photograph of Dr. Hamilton by Bachrach; Mrs. Bowen by Koshiba.)

never wanted a career and never even permitted publicity
for herself. She knew she lacked the rigorous disciplinary
education the others of the group had had, education in
philosophy, in law, in medicine, in business even; she was
not even a "college woman," and that realization may
have influenced her. Her mother was an invalid, her
father went blind toward the end of his life, her brothers
and their families demanded her care as well as her affection—she was the gladly responsive center for decades of
domestic demands, and that realization may have influenced her. But one suspects that the real influence was
from the very beginning her decision to be primarily concerned in making life easier for Jane Addams. That was
her career, that was her philosophy. Even at Hull House
itself, she did not work outward, by investigation and
study, as did the others of this group; she worked only
within. She had her clubs, and she "just looked after
things"; looked after the music school, looked after the
studios, looked after the Dramatic Association, looked
after the boys, looked after the girls. In any case people
interested her more than causes or schemes, and children
perhaps more than any other sort of people. Whether they
were her own nieces or nephews, or the children of her
friends, or the children of the neighborhood, she was nothing less than amazing in her understanding of them. No
little child and no timidest of aliens or gawkiest of adolescents, ever knew Mary Smith without falling in love with
her. It was not only that she delighted in children, but
that she treated them, even babies, with manners and respect. They found her spirit—so did their elders for that
matter—a Cave of Adullam, in which however oppressed
they might have been by misunderstanding, they could

rest in peace. It is possible to believe that she was as tolerant as Jane Addams herself, and she was unquestionably gentler. She lived and died serene.

She sympathized divinely; she worked with a wistful intelligence that was poignant in itself; she cried on occasion; but she was never sad. Her talk was a bubbling fount of amusement. She could be witty, but she preferred to be entertaining. No better story-teller ever delighted her friends, no more coöperative listener ever carried a conversation. Yet to the end of her days she remained shy at heart. Her inner life was all her own, her shrine was secret, her instinct was for reserve; she shepherded to the end her own white thoughts; in the field of her feelings she walked alone. But it is improbable that any other woman or man who ever shared in the life of Hull House, ever quite so fully understood the almost incomprehensible truth, that it is more blessed to give than to receive.

Such were, or so at least they seemed to Jane Addams, the six women who through Hull House associations, early and late, most influenced her life. A group which in its civilizing and socializing influence, seems unlikely soon to be surpassed.

CHAPTER VIII

ETHICS IN POLITICS

IN legislation for the regulating of conditions and hours of labor, Illinois was a backward state in the early Hull House days. There was a group of laws in connection with coal-mining, which by 1890 had developed into what might be called a civilized code for the time. But of "factory" legislation, there was none at all until 1891. In that year a law was passed forbidding the employment of children under thirteen in stores and shops, as well as in "factories and manufacturing establishments." No method of enforcement being provided, however, this law had little or no effect. The Hull House residents had eagerly supported it. Some of the little girls who came to the first Christmas party at the House in 1889 refused candy, because they had been working fourteen hours a day for six weeks in a candy factory, and were sick of it. Children of four and five worked all day long pulling out basting-threads from the garments on which their mothers sewed—piecework, with a *family* profit of perhaps ten cents an hour. Three boys were hurt, one of them dying of his injuries, working at the same machine in a factory almost next door to the House, for lack of a machine-guard that would have cost only a few dollars to install. Such incidents as these, constantly recurring in one fashion or another, led the residents to urge the law. But when it did not work, they wondered. What sort of law,

151

then, was needed? "To our general impression of neighborhood conditions," Jane Addams wrote, "it becomes evident that we must add more widely and more carefully collected information." Mrs. Kelley, a new-comer to the House, suggested to the Illinois State Bureau of Labor, a fact-collecting not an executive body, that she should be engaged to investigate the sweating system of garment-making in Chicago. The Bureau agreed, and turned her loose on the industry, in the autumn of 1891.

Mrs. Kelley investigated, embodied her findings in a report presented to the legislature, and as a result had the satisfaction of seeing a legislative commission appointed to look further into labor conditions in Chicago. Mrs. Kelley's report was statistical, careful, and unprovocative; but behind it was fury. Once she said in a talk to a group of businessmen:

I spent seven hours yesterday in a district where smallpox is epidemic. I found clothing manufactured in houses where there were smallpox patients, and I saw children flocking round an open candy-shop with the sign "Smallpox" on the window of the floor above it. I spent three hours looking for a coat which had been made in a room with a smallpox patient and at last found it hidden in a house where four cases of smallpox had developed since the coat had been secreted there. I found in one block four large sweat-shops in operation with smallpox cases in the center house of the block; these four shops were making clothes for our largest and finest downtown store.

The committee of the legislature recommended provisions which in the following year, 1893, were enacted into a law which Henry D. Lloyd called "the best anti-sweat-shop law on the statute books of any civilized community." From nothing in the way of protective legislation in

1889, to the "best," in less than four years—that was quick and effective work. Too quick, indeed, as we shall see.

The law was passed by union-labor influence plus a conjunction of two forces—Hull House residents, and Governor John P. Altgeld. Mrs. Kelley, chiefly, had provided the information on the basis of which the law was planned; and now Mrs. Kelley, Julia Lathrop, and Jane Addams proceeded to speak and lobby for it. "We addressed the open meetings of trades-unions and of benefit societies, church organizations, and social clubs, literally every evening for three months . . . and with the trade-unionists moved upon the state capitol in behalf of factory legislation." It was a great campaign; one which Mrs. Kelley delighted in, and Julia Lathrop and Jane Addams shrank from but kept steadily on with. But the Legislature would never have passed the law, in spite of trade-union and social-worker effort, had it not been for Altgeld.

Altgeld had said in an address on Washington's birthday, in 1890, that in the United States "most laborers are in a condition where they are absolutely helpless, absolutely in the power of a stronger class, where they are the slaves of adverse circumstances, and where individual action can accomplish absolutely nothing." He urged organization. "All classes are organizing on the theory that in unity there is strength, and in order to be better equipped to hold their own and to secure justice in the fierce struggle that is going on in the world. The only hope of the laboring man in this country lies in organization." The organization was to secure justice; and justice was the product of law. Therefore, having himself been elected Governor, in 1892, Altgeld devoted an enormous amount of energy to seeing that this first proposed factory-inspection law should pass. He had the pleasure of signing it on June 17, 1893, with its "radical" provisions thick upon it: Minimum age raised to fourteen, with affidavits from parents, and further affidavits from physicians certifying to physical fitness for all under sixteen; and the employment of women limited to eight hours a day. He appointed Mrs. Kelley chief inspector, with an assistant and ten deputies wholly under her control; and nine days later, on June 26, 1893, he pardoned the three "anarchists," Fielden, Neebe, and Schwab, who still remained alive.

It was partly the juxtaposition of the passage of the factory-inspection law and the anarchist pardons, partly the inclusion in the factory-inspection law of the provision that women might be employed only eight hours a day, which presently led to the nullification of the law. Mrs. Kelley did a splendid work as inspector, but in 1895 the Illinois Supreme Court declared the eight-hour provision unconstitutional, being unable to see any "fair, just and reasonable connection" between the limitation of working hours for women "and the public health, safety, or welfare proposed to be secured by it." Two years later Governor Tanner finished the job of pulling the teeth from the act by removing Mrs. Kelley from the chief inspectorship and appointing in her place a factory superintendent who had just previously been arrested and fined for open violation of the act. For six years Illinois became once more a "backward" state, as far as labor legislation was concerned. The community had not been ready for the reform.

This first venture into the field of direct propaganda for

legislation left Jane Addams with a divided mind, "a distrust of all legislation which is not preceded by full discussion and understanding. A premature measure may be carried through a legislature by perfectly legitimate means and still fail to possess vitality and a sense of maturity." Such tolerance in connection with matters so near her heart as giving children and working-women a chance, deserved better of her community than it got. For it was the activity of Hull House residents, particularly of course Jane Addams who took the responsibility, for this factory-inspection law that more than anything else fixed the reputation of Hull House and of Jane Addams as "radical."

The act ran counter to the deepest instincts of the "self-made" manufacturers of Illinois, men who had grown to power by exploitation of American resources, foreign labor, and their own titanic energy. Their opportunities had long been limited only by fortune, never by law. Then presently, though legislation remained aloof, organization began to interfere with them; Populism and Farmers' Alliances threw a shadow across the state, trades-unionism developed in the cities. In Chicago, by 1885, trades-unionism had already advanced so far as to have become, in the opinion of most employers, a menace. Members of unions which were led by men with un-American names, were demanding the right to extend their membership without employer-interference; the right to be protected from accident, and to be compensated in case of employers' negligence; above all, commonest demand of all, the right to have eight hours regarded as a full day's work. There was hardly an employer in Chicago who did not fully believe that the "eight-hour day," if adopted in his business, would ruin him, and if adopted generally, would mean that the workmen became in fact the employers, that labor controlled capital, that the tail wagged the dog. The stockyards strike of 1880, the street-car strike of 1885, were regarded as pointing to revolution; and the International Harvester Strike of 1886 had actually produced what Chicago believed to be and called revolution—namely, the Haymarket Riot of May 4, 1886, with its bomb-throwing incited (as some Chicagoans believe even to this day), by anarchists. Judge Gary hanged the anarchists, and the police clubbed and arrested "labor agitators." But now the state had an act which legalized (to be sure, for women only, but the principle was the same) an eight-hour day; which in so doing, it was declared, definitely violated the old principle of "freedom of contract"; and which went further in interference with the rights of employers to establish and maintain precisely what hours and conditions of labor they chose, than any other state law in the whole country outside of New England. Nothing could be expected of the employers of the state except a certain conviction that this act was in itself revolutionary.

And further, this act was signed, as it had been urged on, by a Governor who had been elected as a "union-labor supporter"; and this union-labor Governor, nine days after signing the factory-inspection law, had pardoned the anarchists who had urged workingmen on to "revolution," a revolution which had for sole immediate object the establishment of the eight-hour day. That pardon of the anarchists it was thought would destroy Altgeld; he thought so, saying at the time, to Brand Whitlock, "If I do it, I will be a dead man politically." But it would be three years before his enemies could get him out of the governorship, and what might he not do to destroy and damn industry in the state in those three years? The hatred and fear of Altgeld inspired among prominent citizens by his message pardoning the anarchists has never been equaled in any similar case in this country, in time of peace. That such a conspirator against industry should promulgate such an act as the factory-inspection law, was evidence enough that the very throne of industry was being torn down in its own palace. And who had conspired with Altgeld? The women at Hull House. The Chief Inspector, the first assistant inspector (Mrs. Alzina P. Stevens) both lived at Hull House. Alexander Bruce, the young lawyer who prosecuted the cases Mrs. Kelley brought against violators of the law, lived at Hull House. The most vigorous of the five women deputies under the law, Mary Kenny, was president of the Jane Club of Hull House. And the office of the Chief Inspector was directly opposite Hull House, on Polk Street. The newspapers published these things far, wide, and constantly. What inference was possible to earnest employers, but that Hull House, like the Governor, was a menace to industry? It was "a nest of radicals." And yet, the amazing thing, when the spirit of Chicago in general at this time is taken into account, is not that it should have been suggested at private dinner-tables, as it was on at least one occasion for which this biographer can personally vouch, that "Jane Addams ought to be hanged to the nearest lamp-post"; but that she should have retained almost all the friends she had already made among the employing-classes, and made more. It was at this very time, for example, that Mrs. Joseph Bowen, rich, conservative, and individualist to the backbone, first came to Hull House and quietly, without defiance but without hesitation, identified herself with its interests; at this time that Charles Mather Smith, manufacturer and aristocrat, contributed the largest gift to buildings and endowment of Hull House that had yet been made; at this time that Mrs. Charles Henrotin, president of the National Federation of Women's Clubs, took a stand for ameliorative labor legislation that practically dragged the Women's Clubs all over the country to her position.

To the day of her death, however, there were, in proportion, more intelligent men and women in Chicago than anywhere else in the United States who believed Jane Addams to be a "radical." Outside of Chicago she has been viewed as if in perspective. In Chicago she stood for some years as if in the shadow of Altgeld, "Viper Altgeld," as the *Chicago Tribune* was accustomed to call him in its editorial captions. When he died in 1902, Jane Addams, Clarence Darrow his law-partner, and the Reverend Frank Crane were the only speakers at his private funeral, and she was warned by friends that if she spoke she would "wreck the influence of Hull House." It is more likely that she would have injured that influence, and her own, if she had not spoken as she felt, on that occasion as on all others. A fanatic may yield occasionally to impulses of generosity without endangering his social value, but an apostle of tolerance who permits herself even once to be controlled by fanaticism or panic makes an almost irretrievable mistake. We shall see Jane Addams on various occasions attacked as a social peril, but we shall not see her making that mistake.

Has she, or has Hull House so far as it has been a

reflection of her views, ever been "radical"? Putting aside all such quibblings as the precise implications of the word, one may assert that in the ordinary and popular acceptance of the term, she never has been. In the obvious matters of forms of government, she began as a liberal, as a fundamentalist believer in democracy, and so remained: communism, socialism, fascism, to the study of all of which she gave much time and energy, seemed to her merely forms of class warfare, and as such neither philosophically sound nor practical in application. In this respect she was no more and no less radical than Abraham Lincoln, her first and most influential instructor in political science.

When in March, 1934, the University of California celebrated the fiftieth anniversary of its foundation by conferring honorary degrees upon Jane Addams, Herbert Hoover, and Secretary Perkins, Mr. Hoover and Miss Perkins though unwilling to be photographed together, were both quite willing to be photographed separately with Miss Addams. Each thought the other an extremist, Jane Addams as middle-of-the-road.

In matters of social reform, so far as they can be separated from political reform, her position has been much the same, and consistent. She agreed with her guide and friend in the "settlement" movement, Canon Barnett of Toynbee Hall, that higher moral standards in industrial life must be somehow attained, that as rapidly as any advance in standards can be perceived it must be embodied in legislation so that it may be as fair for one as for another, but that meanwhile an individual endeavoring to promote such advance and secure such equally burdening legislation, must forbear harsh judgment of other individuals. She declined on occasion to accept contributions to Hull House funds from men who were notoriously unfair to their employees, but on the other hand she became a member of the "university extension" staff of the new University of Chicago, an institution which the radicals declared was supported by "tainted money." Time, by the way, was to have its joke with both her and the University. In the early days of "Doctor Harper's Bazaar," as the University was often called, she was reproached by her "radical" friends for connecting herself however remotely with such a backward institution. But fifteen years later, when the professors of the University voted to confer on her an honorary degree, the conservative successor to Doctor Harper, and his cautious board of trustees, declined to confirm the action. Professors Albion W. Small and George Herbert Mead, who in the fullness of their enthusiasm had neglected formalities and notified Jane Addams of the professorial vote, were forced to go to Hull House and with tears in their eyes explain the situation and apologize for the administration. It was to be more than twenty years from that time before the administration did confirm the early action of the faculty, and offer her a degree. She took it with one regret—that Professor Small could not know of it.

Her radicalism, and the radicalism of Hull House, so far as such an institution may be said to possess a point of view, has been, however, obvious; it has been the radicalism of tolerance. Not only was Hull House "soberly opened on the theory that the dependence of classes on each other is reciprocal," but it was maintained in the belief that "if the Settlement seeks its expressions through social activity, it must learn the difference between mere social unrest, and spiritual impulse." It had been in existence only a few months when it opened its drawing-room, the largest place of assemblage available then, to "The Working People's Social Science Club." For seven years this club met weekly, on Wednesday evenings, for the discussion of social theories. A chairman for the evening was elected, a speaker was introduced who was allowed an hour in which to present his views without interruption, and when he had concluded his remarks, the meeting was thrown open to an hour of discussion. Socialists and anarchists, single-taxers and atheists, gave the speaker no quarter, and asked for none themselves. There was a never-failing earnestness, a never-lagging enthusiasm, a never wholly absent bitterness about these discussions, that undoubtedly contributed to the reputation of Hull House for radicalism. As Jane Addams says, visitors refused to distinguish between the sentiments expressed by the members of the club in the heat of discussion, and the opinions held by the residents themselves. Moreover, then as always, he who provides the opportunity for free discussion is often thought to be more dangerous to society as it is, than he who discusses. The conservative admits that society is susceptible of modification and even that all human institutions imply progressive development, but he distrusts those who seek to bring all principles and opinions out into the open. Affording such opportunity for discussion, he calls spreading anarchy, or spreading communism, or spreading socialism, or whatever term of social reprobation he may have in his vocabulary at the moment.

At any rate, the radicalism of Jane Addams and of Hull House, partly owing to her connection with the new labor legislation and through that with Governor Altgeld, and partly owing to the reputation of the Working People's Social Science Club, became more or less accepted in Chicago in the first decade of the existence of the House. About the only group who did not regard Jane Addams as radical were the radicals themselves. One evening when she was talking to a club of workmen which met at the corner of Halsted and Madison Streets, one of the roughest-looking called out:

"You won't talk like this when the millionaires begin to subsidize you."

"I don't intend," she replied, "either to be subsidized by millionaires, or bullied by labor-unionists; I expect to keep on saying what I think without consulting either of them." The audience broke into applause; to her delight as well as to her surprise, for "at many times it seemed to me that we were merely destined to alienate everybody."

As early as 1886, the broad-minded Lyman J. Gage had sought to organize a "voluntary association of citizens for the mutual counsel, support, and combined action of all the forces for good." The distress resulting from the business "panic" of 1893 brought that voluntary association into full light. It acquired a name, the Civic Federation. It had a central council of one hundred, and a branch in every ward. It had six departments, philanthropic, industrial, municipal, educational, moral, and political, each one in charge of a committee of men and women diligent either in business, in society, or in "reform." Lyman Gage rallied some prominent citizens to the banner of the Civic Federation—Harlow Higinbotham, Cyrus McCormick, Franklin McVeagh, even Marshall Field himself, among

the men of affairs; and from the ranks of the social philosophers, Graham Taylor, Albion W. Small, Emil G.
Hirsch, Sarah Hackett Stevenson. Of course Jane Addams
was in the forefront of Civic Federation efforts, or part
of them at least; some of the more dramatic, such as
"raids" staged under the direction of the Pinkertons, she
seriously mistrusted. But when after the passage of the
factory-inspection law, and its emasculation by the State
Supreme Court, Governor Altgeld called a special session
of the legislature to legislate into being some system for
"arbitration and conciliation" in labor disputes, she became the Secretary of the Civic Federation Committee on
Industrial Arbitration, and once again spoke endlessly
and endlessly agitated for a plan that might do away
with the worst of labor disputes.

The Civic Federation had advocated, and Altgeld
recommended to the Legislature, "such legislation as will
enable the parties to the dispute, alone or with the aid
of a county judge, to select their own board in each case
so that there may be no question about its impartiality,
on the one hand, and no unnecessary salary paid on the
other." But the legislature provided for a standing board
of three salaried members, one an employer, one a workingman, and a third who was neither. Massachusetts had
a board of just such constitution, which had rendered good
service. But the services of the Illinois board were seldom
asked for, and the plan failed. Jane Addams says: "Our
hopes ran high ... at the time the word 'arbitration' was
still a word to conjure with ... but even a state board cannot accomplish more than public sentiment authorizes and
sustains." The fact of the matter seems to have been that
where labor was pretty well organized, as in Chicago, the

unions saw more to be had from a fight than from arbitration, and so declined any appeal to the board; and where the employers were wholly in control, as in the coal-mining regions of the state, they in turn could see no advantage in attempting to conciliate. In any case, the second winning campaign for new legislation, like the first, turned out to have been a victory barren of results.

Such were two of the three efforts of Jane Addams in the nineties to influence state legislation directly. The other will be considered later. It seems advisable at this point to consider her relation to the great industrial disturbance in Chicago in 1894, the Pullman strike, which more than any other one thing forced on the campaign for industrial arbitration and conciliation which has just been mentioned, and which incidentally produced Jane Addams's most widely discussed contribution to the literature of labor disputes, *A Modern King Lear*. Before the Pullman strike, Jane Addams says in her autobiography, "there had been nothing in my experience to reveal that distinct cleavage of society, which a general strike at least momentarily affords. During all those dark days of the Pullman strike, the growth of class bitterness was most obvious. The fact that the Settlement maintained avenues of intercourse with both sides seemed to give it opportunity for nothing but a realization of the bitterness and division along class lines."

George M. Pullman, sleeping-car manufacturer, had with none but the best intentions founded in the early 'eighties the "model town" of Pullman for his employees, a town from which "all that is ugly, discordant and demoralizing" was to be eliminated. Situated just south of Chicago, it included some 3,500 acres of ground; in its "arcade" were concentrated stores, a bank, and the post-office; close by were a theater, a hotel, and a park for community recreation. There were schools and churches, built by Mr. Pullman; and of the houses, also Pullman-built, more than a thousand employees owned their own, so Mr. Pullman declared, though his figures were disputed. It was a flat, open, brick-built community, sanitary and well looking by the standards of the time. But it was exclusively Pullman-governed. The Pullman company bought water and gas from the city, and resold them to the householders at company-fixed prices. Even the sewage was Pullman-controlled, gathered in an underground tank and modified, thence piped to the Pullman model farm to be used as fertilizer. It was a feudal, not a democratic or American conception. The shops were of course open, unorganized; Mr. Pullman had no belief in the principle of union labor. Following the panic of '93, and the terrible winter of '93-'94, the company ordered reduction of wages and of the working force by about one-third each, but did not lower rents or prices in the company stores. The Pullman workers struck in May of 1894. Says Jane Addams:

I had known Mr. Pullman and had seen his genuine pride and pleasure in the model town he had built with so much care; and I had also an opportunity to talk to many of the Pullman employees during the strike when I was sent from a so-called "Citizens' Arbitration Committee" to the first meetings of strikers held in a hall in the neighboring village of Kensington, and when I was invited to supper in the model houses. The employees then expected a speedy settlement and no one doubted but that all the grievances connected with the "straw bosses" would be quickly remedied and that the benevolence which had built the model town would not fail them. ... The entire strike demonstrated how often the outcome of far-reaching industrial disturbances is dependent upon the personal will of the employer or the temperament of a strike leader.

The story of the Pullman strike, involving as it did strong men bitterly opposed in theories both of economics and government—Pullman and Eugene Debs, President Cleveland and Governor Altgeld—and of the dramatic violence which resulted from the American Railway Union strike that grew out of it, need not be retold here. (The best and fullest account is in W. R. Browne's *Altgeld of Illinois*.) After the complete failure of the Citizens Arbitration Committee to accomplish anything, Jane Addams took no further part in negotiations, which indeed became a matter for the National Government and the courts. Her oldest sister Mary died in a hospital in Kenosha that July, after a long illness, and Jane Addams's attention was distracted from social to family suffering. The Federal troops sent to Chicago by President Cleveland broke the railway strike; the Pullman workers or most of them ultimately drifted back to work at the lowered wages and unlowered rents; Debs and others were sent to a comfortable country jail for six months, not for conspiracy but for contempt of court; Clarence Darrow in his defense of them firmly established his reputation as a great advocate of socio-legal justice; and Jane Addams in a carefully considered paper "gathered together the social implications of the failure of this benevolent employer, and the relation of that failure to the demand for a more democratic administration of industry."

Of all the literature that grew out of the Pullman strike, and the American Railway Union strike that followed—

the manifestoes of Debs and the addresses of Darrow, the
proclamations of the General Managers' Association of
the railroads, and of Chicago's Mayor Hopkins, the long
and elaborate protests of Altgeld and the curt and contemptuous replies of Cleveland, even the careful report of the United States Strike Commission—hardly anything remains now in any general public consciousness
except this paper, *A Modern King Lear*. Neither side
approved of it; Mr. Pullman himself resented it bitterly,
Debs is said to have called it just another attempt to put
out a fire with rosewater. But it was eagerly listened to as
a lecture, and when, after being refused by nine editors, it
was finally published as a magazine article, it was greeted
with a heavy fire of newspaper comment all over the
United States. More than the appeals for mutuality of
understanding and service Jane Addams had uttered at
the Plymouth Summer School two years before, more even
than the foundation of Hull House itself, *A Modern King
Lear* began to make Jane Addams a figure of national importance in the philosophy of social progress.

Another widely discussed paper of the middle 'nineties
was the result of Jane Addams's entrance into ward politics. In 1894 politics in Chicago "smelled to heaven."
There were then 34 wards, 2 aldermen to each ward; and
according to the leaders of the Civic Federation, 57 of
the 68 aldermen were "grafters." The salary of an alderman was purely nominal, but each job was worth in graft,
it was estimated, from $15,000 to $25,000 a year. For one
big franchise it was said a small group of aldermen had
been paid $25,000 each, and a much larger group $8,000
each. Unimportant votes however might be had for as
little as $300, or $400 in case the privilege sought had to

be granted by a two-thirds vote over a mayoral veto. The city owned all the streets and alleys, and the aldermen sold them to businessmen for what could be got. Of the "grafters," one of the best known and most prosperous was Alderman John Powers of the Nineteenth Ward—the Hull House ward.

Though she was a member of the Civic Federation, it is not probable that Jane Addams would have undertaken a campaign against Powers merely because he "grafted." It was the condition of the ward, its filth, its lack of sanitation, its unhealthfulness, for which in part the alderman was directly responsible, that forced her into the effort to beat Powers. The residents of Hull House had almost from the time of its foundation continued a series of careful investigations into these conditions. *Hull House Maps and Papers,* published in 1896, showed not only that representatives of nineteen different nationalities swarmed in the ward, but that they swarmed in foulness. The streets were covered inches deep with packed and dirty refuse over broken pavements; the miry alleys smelled like sewers, and the sewers themselves were in hundreds of instances unconnected with the houses or tenements; the stables, of which there were many, were inexpressibly foul; Greeks slaughtered sheep in basements, Italian women and children sorted rags collected from the city dump, in courtyards thick with babies and vermin; bakers made bread in dirty holes under the sidewalks, and distributed it to their immigrant neighbors. Over this empire of physical wretchedness Johnny Powers ruled supreme, rich, and complacent. Jane Addams discovered, in her fifth year in the ward, that her nephew, youngest child of her sister who had just died, and of whom she had been made guardian, could not possibly stay with her at Hull House because the doctor said he would die in such surroundings. "I may well be ashamed," she wrote, "that other delicate children who were torn from their families, not into boarding-school but into eternity, had not long before driven me to effective action."

Her first move was to do something about the collection of garbage. Members of the Hull House Woman's Club, organized the year before, undertook along with Hull House residents to investigate and report on the condition of the alleys. In August and September of 1894, 1,037 substantiated reports of violations of city sanitation ordinances were sent to the city health department from Hull House. "The system of garbage collection . . . became the greatest menace in such a ward as ours," Jane Addams wrote, "where the normal amount of waste was much increased by the decayed fruit and vegetables discarded by the Italian and Greek fruit peddlers, and by the residuum left over from the piles of rags fished from the dumps and brought to the homes of the rag pickers." In the spring of 1895, after a long series of calculations, she put in a bid for the ward contract for garbage-removal. Her bid was thrown out on a technicality, but as a result of the publicity that followed, the mayor appointed her garbage inspector for the ward, at a salary of $1,000 a year; the only paid position she had ever held, and the only one she was ever to hold:

> The position was no sinecure, whether regarded from the point of view of getting up at six in the morning to see that the men were early at work; or of following the loaded wagons, uneasily dropping their contents at intervals, to their dreary destination at the dump; or of insisting that the contractor

must increase the number of his wagons from nine to thirteen and then from thirteen to seventeen, although he assured me that he lost money on every one and that the former inspector had let him off with seven; or of taking careless landlords into court because they would not provide the proper garbage receptacles; or of arresting the tenant who tried to make the garbage wagons carry away the contents of his stable.

No sinecure, truly; nor was she able to accomplish a great deal directly, though the publicity that accrued drew attention to the horrible conditions of the ward, and so did good indirectly. But that a woman, a non-voter, should have the job, annoyed the politicians. They made much of the fact that at one time she went away from Chicago on a lecturing trip, a "jaunt" they called it, "quitting her job." She replied by giving the papers comparative figures of the time she and her predecessor had spent on the work; but presently she hired a deputy, to whom she paid over her salary entire, Miss Amanda Johnson, a strong, blonde, forthright young woman who was a college graduate and had done similar inspection work in both Chicago and Pittsburgh. Miss Johnson performed the duties of inspection admirably for three years, the last two under civil service. But by that time the political difficulties with Alderman Powers had increased to such a point that he felt the necessity of getting rid of Hull House interference. So he had the garbage inspector's job eliminated by ordinance, in favor of a "ward superintendent," a position for which only men were to be eligible.

The political difficulties just referred to ran through three aldermanic campaigns. In the first, a member of the Hull House Men's Club was elected as Powers's colleague, but unfortunately after election yielded to the seductive influence of aldermanic opportunities. In the second, directed against Johnny Powers himself, not much was accomplished, although the newly formed "Municipal Voters League" fought shoulder to shoulder with Hull House, and elsewhere in Chicago managed to defeat a few of the aldermanic "gray wolves." But Powers, as it was said at the time, "paved the ward with ten-dollar bills," and increased his majority. Two years later the most determined of the three fights was made; the editor of an Italian newspaper, popular in the ward among the many Italians, and a fighter of the old Garibaldi sort, was put up as a candidate against Powers, and definitely reduced his majority. Nevertheless Powers won; and further, Jane Addams discovered that in the course of her efforts to beat him, she was in a way undermining her own influence "for the best" in the ward. To beat Powers would be undoubtedly a positive good, but would it be understood as such in principle by the people of such a ward as his and hers— the old immigrant Nineteenth? It was out of her long consideration of this situation that the paper already referred to, a paper with the academic title *Ethical Survivals in City Politics,* arose. It created a stir in Chicago. Directly in line with all the social philosophy she had already embodied in her actions as well as in her publications, it nevertheless seemed novel, and was indeed an important contribution to the discussion of municipal political thinking in the United States. She wrote:

In such a ward as the Nineteenth in Chicago all that holds together the diverse foreign populations is the few basic experiences they have in common. Ideas operate upon the popular mind only through will and character, and goodness has to be dramatized before it reaches the mass of men. Ethics and politi-

cal opinions can come to the common people only through
example—through a personality which seizes the imagination.
In such a neighborhood, the interesting thing is to find out
what ideas the people *do* have, and not what others *suppose*
them to have.

She goes on to analyze the differences in immigrant-
group ideas: the inevitable hostility to government of the
immigrant Bohemians; the desire of the Italians in coming to escape service in the army; the immigration of the
Jews to escape persecution; the notion of the Irish, Ireland having been grievously oppressed by England, that
it is only legitimate for "the people" to get as much as
possible out of "the government." "It is this Irishman
who teaches political methods to the other foreigners living in an oppressed industrial quarter, who dramatizes
for them the aims and objects of civic government."

What do such new and ignorant citizens look for in
their alderman, "in whose election the immigrant receives
his first lessons in representative government"? Most of
all, they look for simple goodness. "Abstract virtues are
too difficult for their untrained minds to apprehend. Many
of them believe that power and wealth come only to
'good' people." The successful candidate, then, is the man
whose goodness *fits the standard of his constituents.* "His
safety lies in doing on a large scale the good deeds which
his constituents can do only on a small scale. If he does
what they are all cherishing a secret ambition to do, he
will win their confidence. And there is a certain wisdom
in this course. There is a common sense in the mass of
men which cannot be neglected with impunity."

No one who lives among the poor, she points out, can
fail to be impressed with their constant kindness to each

other. This kindness is heightened by the consciousness of each that he himself may be in distress next week. So he stands by his friends. To such a man "it seems fitting that his alderman should do the same thing on a larger scale." He bails out his constituents when they are arrested, or says a word to the justice when they appear for trial; gets them off small fines, or sees what he can do to fix up matters with the state's attorney when the charge is serious. He pays rent when no rent is ready, finds jobs when work is hard to get (one in five of the voters of the Nineteenth Ward were on the city payroll under Powers in 1896, and Powers asserted that two years before, in the "bad times," 2,600 residents of the ward, more than one-third of the voters, had been on city jobs.) He is at all family festivities the simple friend; gets up "benefits" for a widow or a sick man; spends ten times as much at church bazaars as anybody else, "murmuring that it's all right as long as the church or the poor get it." Above all, he is the simple friend in periods of sorrow; quite honestly "great at funerals," and always saving the very poorest from "the awful horror of burial by the county." And at funerals, particularly, "a man who would ask 'where all this money comes from' would be thought sinister. You cannot very well run a man down when you are sitting in a carriage provided by his generosity. Many a man at such a time has formulated a lenient judgment of political corruption. 'Ah well, he has a big heart. He is good to the widows and fatherless. He knows the poor better than the big guns who are always talking about reform.' "

What headway can the abstract notion of civic purity, the conception of honesty of administration ultimately saving money for the taxpayer, or providing better surroundings for the poor, make against this stalking survival of village kindness, this constant *dramatization* of goodness and friendliness? The "bald and almost inquisitorial method" of the charity organization worker cannot hold its own for an instant in point of attractiveness with the heartiness and good-will of the other aldermanic sort of service. Even the direct purchase of votes is approved of by some of the community; a man who complains that he can get only two dollars for his vote, instead of five as in another year, seems less unethical to one who is aware that the same man's income for the previous nine months has been less than thirty dollars, and that he is in debt for more than that amount. As for the question where the money comes from, the simple answer acceptable to the ethics of the community is that the alderman "gets it from the rich," a process which tends to make John Powers as popular in the Nineteenth Ward, as the same theory made Robin Hood in Merrie England of old. With genuine pride the constituents assert that their alderman is backed by the head of the street-car company, a "swell," a man who had given a million dollars to a university, a man therefore as philanthropic, as upright, and as socially important as any "crank reformer" in Chicago.

What then is the conclusion? That if we are to hold to the theory of political democracy, we must take pains to find a common ground of ethics and human experience; that the meaning of life is after all

to search out knowledge and then to conform our activities to our new knowledge. This is the one advantage a neighborhood of simple people has, that when the dramatized truth does reach them, it excites *their disposition to follow*. Thus they balance their opinions by their living, and it is conceivable that their large and emotional ethics, just because they constantly result in activity, have in them the possibility for a higher and wider life than the ethics of those of us who are content to hold them merely as a possession. We may have to trust our huge and uncouth Democracy in our ethics, as we are slowly learning to trust it in other directions. For by slow degrees the law emerges, that conduct which opposes the ends of the *common* weal, must finally give way to conduct which furthers those ends.

This paper, though it did not attract the wide attention which was given to *A Modern King Lear,* was greeted by the newspapers of Chicago with as much attention and interest, as anything Jane Addams ever wrote. The point of view was both attacked and defended, but on the whole the opinion was that the view was "practical," that Jane Addams spoke from a closer knowledge of her material than any other "social reformer" in Chicago had yet shown. As for Jane Addams herself, with this final searching analysis she returned from the open field of political combat, to the narrower and more intimate house of acquaintance and understanding and neighborly affection which she had undertaken to dwell in, and which she had indeed left even for a short time with reluctance. Unethical, even criminal, as Powers and his like seemed to her, there were ways in which, she asserted, the "alderman understood what the people wanted, and ministered as truly to a great human need as does the musician or the artist." One episode of her experience in "attempting to substitute what may be called a later standard of ethics, if we do not care to use the expression a more civilized standard," made a particularly deep impression upon her. A new-born child had been deserted in the Hull House nursery. Investigation revealed that it had been born a week previously in the County Hospital, but afforded no trace of the mother. The frail baby, given every attention, lived for a month, then died. It was decided that it should be buried at the expense of the county. The wagon was to arrive at eleven in the morning. By nine o'clock the rumor of the arrangement reached the neighbors. A horrified deputation came to protest. They would take up a collection from their poverty to pay for burying the baby. Jane Addams told them of the care which had been given the baby while it clung to life, by a skilled doctor and a trained nurse; pointed out that Hull House had paid for this without any help from anybody; and suggested that now that it was dead, the reasonable thing was that the regular authorities should pay for its burial as they had paid for its illegitimate birth. "We did not realize that we were shocking a profound moral sentiment of the community. I do not think Hull House has ever done anything else which injured it so deeply in the mind of the community. We were forgiven, only by the most indulgent, and only on the ground that we were spinsters, and could not know a mother's heart."

As for Alderman Powers, he may be allowed to speak for himself. About a year later, apropos of an order he put through the council allowing a Hull House lot to be flooded for skating, he said:

I have the greatest respect for Miss Addams, and have had respect for her ever since I have known her in her work in my ward. There has not been any "truce patched up" between us, for the reason that there has been no enmity. If she has any ill-feeling for me I have never found it out, and I will not believe it until I have some evidence of it. If there is anything that Hull House or any other good institution

in my ward needs to have passed through the city council,
and I find out about it, they will not need to ask me for it, as
I will have it passed. If there were any favors I could do for
Hull House, and I have never been asked for any, I would
gladly perform them.

Powers remained the alderman of the ward until his
death in 1913. As the Municipal Voters' League and other
less concrete influences gradually changed the City Council, and as the standards of the voters gradually crept upward under such mayoral leaders as Carter Harrison the
younger, Edward F. Dunne, Fred A. Busse; as Chicago
grew steadily richer and steadily more conscious of its
uglinesses and meannesses and civic injustices and lack of
sanitation, physical conditions in the Nineteenth Ward
changed for the better, as they did almost everywhere in
the gigantic, wilful, young city. But Hull House never
asked any "favors" of its alderman, nor did it ever campaign against him again. Jane Addams allowed herself
to believe that more could be accomplished by the effort
to understand one another than by the effort to fight one
another, in the ward as in the world.

CHAPTER IX

WORK FOR CHILDREN

THE writings of Jane Addams are permeated with her love of children. Of all her books the nearest to her heart was *The Spirit of Youth and the City Streets*. Her memorial address on little Gordon Dewey, John Dewey's child, is the most poignant of all those in that collection of poignant memorials, "The Excellent Becomes the Permanent." And as this love of children showed in her writing, so it showed in her life and work. Her own nephews and nieces, the swarms of little folk in her ward, the forsaken and half-starved children of France and Germany during and just after the World War, she brooded over as tenderly as any mother over her own. Her brother-in-law, Harry Haldeman, had told her in 1882, when he operated on her spine, that she could never have a child of her own, and that was perhaps her greatest grief, though it may be the realization turned into an inspiration finally. The earliest activities of Hull House were clubs and classes for children, with a kindergarten and a nursery, a studio and a music-school, following at once. It was the peril of child labor that drew her first into politics, and it was child labor that engaged her attention most completely until she finally turned to the great work of her later life for peace and international understanding. Her three years on the Chicago Board of Education were one long eager yearning for the advancement of the interests of the child. Some of the relations of Hull House to the children of the neighborhood seem, therefore, to demand separate consideration.

One of her principal tasks as an interpreter was to get the parents and the children of the ward to understand each other. Thousands of the parents, by far the majority, were immigrants. As children, they had been Bohemian, Italian, Russian, Greek. But their children, born in this country, or with English as their first language, regarded themselves as Americans. Their view was obviously one to be encouraged, and yet it inevitably brought about clashes in the family life. The parents were often resentful of the different ideas of their children, the children often contemptuous of their parents, stuck in the rut of old European habits, customs, opinions. At worst, the fathers whipped their daughters for being different, and the sons sneered at their mothers' dress and ignorance, or at their fathers' maudlin babble of old days. Even at best, the pleasures of the parent and child were seldom in common, and they seldom went anywhere together:

One thing seemed clear in our associations with immigrants: we must preserve and keep whatever of value their past life contained and bring them in contact with a better type of Americans ... at the same time however we were forced to recognize that the faithful child is sometimes ruthlessly imposed upon by immigrant parents who, eager for money and accustomed to the patriarchal authority of peasant households, held their children in stern bondage. ... I meditated that perhaps the power to see life as a whole is more needed in the immigrant quarter of a large city than anywhere else, and that the lack of this power is the most fruitful source of misunderstanding between European immigrants and their children.

Out of this meditation grew first an effort to bring parents and their children together at Hull House, to give them facilities to amuse one another as families. This effort worked with some groups, like the Germans; it did not work with others, like the Italians. It was, however, persisted in. Yet there seemed more to be done, somehow. It seemed that "Hull House ought to be able to devise some sort of *educational* enterprise, which should build a bridge between European and American experiences in such wise as to give them both more meaning and a sense of relation."

And finally the idea she had longed for came to her. The sight which stirred her imagination to it may be fairly compared in influence on her life drama with that glimpse of the Whitechapel food auction in 1882, which ever afterward clutched at her heart; or with the picture of the Belgian mothers in the hall at The Hague in 1915, embracing the German women who had come as representatives of Germany to the first woman's peace conference in wartime. Only that Mile End Road vision had been horrible, the meeting of "enemies" had been dramatic, this sight in Chicago was simple and sweet:

Walking down Polk Street one early spring day I saw an old Italian woman I knew, her distaff against her homesick face, patiently spinning a thread by the stick spindle so reminiscent of all Southern Europe.... She was sitting in the sun on the steps of a tenement house. She might have served as a model for one of Michel Angelo's Fates, but her face brightened as I passed, and holding up her spindle for me to see, she called out that when she had spun a little more yarn, she would knit a pair of stockings for her granddaughter.

Jane Addams never forgot that incident either. "When you write about Hull House," she said only a little while

before she died, "don't leave out my old woman spinning."
It determined her to make a place in which the older
people could practise their known, traditional crafts, which
should parallel the studios and the music school for the
younger ones who had inherited aptitude for the arts.
What the children did in drawing and music and play-
acting drew the admiration of their parents; and so in
what their parents did, in spinning, weaving, sewing, carv-
ing, metal-working, the dramatic representation of the
abilities of the parents would rouse the admiration of the
children. Such a place was found and fitted up—one room
at first, very simply equipped. That one room has grown
into many, the equipment has become elaborate and historically interesting. Indeed, the room for old-craft practice grew into a real exhibition place of industry—the
Labor Museum, it came finally to be called. Miss Charlotte Teller described it:

Here one may find Italian women of the neighborhood
twirling the distaff, and Russian women spinning on their odd
frames, and Irish women carding wool and weaving on old-
fashioned looms, and even Syrians making rugs. Cabinet-
making and metalwork go on in another room; there is
basketry and the dyeing of raffia and straw; in one corner
a lame German potter plies wheel and thumb amid examples
of finer ceramics; there is a bindery where a pupil of Cobden-
Sanderson teaches that beautiful handicraft. An Italian woman
sometimes cooks spaghetti in a pot hanging from a crane over
an open wood fire at one end of the cooking-class, where the
walls are hung with corn, rice, barley, and other grains in their
native state. This is on the same principle that combing wool
or weaving is made to look up to the dressmaking and millinery
classes. Lectures are given, there are collections and classes,
but ... nothing is so popular as actual demonstration. It has
made Americanized children look upon the old-world accom-

plishments of their parents with something better than the eye of scorn.

Of all the individual activities of Hull House, this is perhaps the one that gave Jane Addams the most delight. It gave equal delight also to one of the Hull House trustees, Julius Rosenwald, and largely because of the interest it inspired in him he later founded with millions, the huge Rosenwald Industrial Museum in the magnificently rehabilitated Fine Arts Building of the World's Fair in Jackson Park—one of the most beautiful buildings in the country, and one of the finest illustrations of the historical development of industries. The Rosenwald Museum, however, is a place for the exhibition of industrial processes only, not for the practice of traditional crafts. The Hull House enterprise has remained faithful altogether to its original intention. The proportion of actual immigrants in the Hull House neighborhood is much less than it was in the 'nineties, but there are still plenty to practise the manual arts they once learned of necessity and now perform with pride, and to-day the Americanized children and grandchildren of the immigrants work along with them in many cases.

Jane Addams's interest in children inevitably led her, however, into careful consideration of the problems of child labor in factories. From that very first Christmas when the little girls refused the candy because they had worked for six weeks in a candy factory from seven in the morning till nine at night, and "could not bear the sight of it," on to the passage of the Illinois child-labor laws on July 1, 1903—almost fourteen years—she never stopped trying to find out what the facts of child labor were, and what could be done about it. More than any

Photograph by Wallace W. Kirkland

JANE ADDAMS WITH HER LITTLE FRIENDS AT HULL HOUSE

other citizen, even more than Florence Kelley herself, she
stirred up trouble for child labor, and organized the forces
of society against it. It was in connection with this particular activity that she was personally offered a bribe
of $50,000 to "keep quiet," and made the recipient of
her largest personal collection of insults and threats; unless she got more in 1915 in consequence of the newspaper
lie that she had accused soldiers of having to be made
drunk before they would fight. For various intercessions
on behalf of individuals illegally and unjustly treated, she
was now and then, as we shall see, to be despised; but by
the representatives of various manufacturing interests in
Illinois for her attacks on child labor, she was feared and
hated. People have said that conscious of her own good
faith, she did not mind these insults. Nothing could be
further from the fact. It is not only that she was sensitive
to misunderstanding and objurgation. It was that never
in all her life was she absolutely sure she was right. The
certainties of individuals like Charles Sumner and Theodore Roosevelt, of groups like the abolitionists and the prohibitionists, were never hers. She could not help seeing the
point of view of the manufacturers, even of the sweat-shop
proprietors, even of the owners of the glass companies, who
were as certain that a child-labor law would put them out
of business, as she was that without a child-labor law,
the infant democracy of Illinois would be put out of business. And, of course, the point of view of the children's
parents was forced upon her every day. It was these parents who were her neighbors, who came to Hull House,
whom she herself had gone to Hull House to live among.
The Italian father out of work himself who said to her
tearfully: "The kids can get work, we can't. They like it,

we don't. Then why can't they go ahead and do it?" was a personal problem to her. The other father who grieved over the death of his oldest child, a girl of twelve, saying, "She was the oldest kid I had. Now I shall have to go to work again until the next one is able to take care of me," was to her not a joke but a sorrow.

Right or wrong, however, she kept on piling up information and organizing the women's clubs and urging the unions to fight child labor. She became an authority on the subject, contributing a statistical chapter to W. J. Ghent's discussion of *Our Benevolent Feudalism*, and the recipient of innumerable inquiries on the subject of child-labor legislation from all over the country. "Laws to prevent child labor," said the Boston *Journal of Education*, "should be skilfully drawn. Get a copy of the law in your state and send it to Jane Addams. She will tell you, better than anybody else in the country, if it is wise." Her acquaintance with details became a newspaper joke. Once at a legislative-committee hearing in Springfield, she was speaking of the effects on children of acting on the regular stage.

"Have you ever seen these children at work?" a lawyer of the opposition lobby asked.

"I have seen every play in which there was a child actor in Chicago for three years," she answered.

"But you cannot judge to the effects from seeing the plays," the lawyer insisted, feebly.

"In every case I have talked with the children at their homes or the hotels where they were staying," she replied, and that line of discussion was dropped by her opponent.

At last, so far as Illinois was concerned, she and the women's clubs and the auxiliary men supporters and the unions won the fight. A bill was introduced into the legislature in March of 1903, embodying the conclusions of the Federated Women's Clubs of Illinois, the Women's Catholic League, the Chicago Federation of Labor, the Illinois Federation of Labor, and Jane Addams. It forbade the employment of children under sixteen years before seven in the morning or after seven at night, and the employment of children under fourteen after six at night. It made the maximum day's work of children under sixteen, eight hours, and the maximum week's work forty-eight hours. No child under fourteen—except newsboys—might work at all for an employer not his parent, and no child between fourteen and sixteen without an "age certificate" validated by his school authorities. It was passed and went into operation on July 1, 1903, and for the first time in thirteen years, so far as child labor in Illinois was concerned, Jane Addams rested on her oars.

A third aspect of her special interest in children during the first ten years at Hull House was her concern with delinquency. In this particular matter, in Chicago, John P. Altgeld had taken the lead. In a long-forgotten but long-important little book published in 1884, *Our Penal Machinery and Its Victims,* he had called attention statistically and otherwise to the fact that not only were a very large number of young people arrested in Chicago every year as "first offenders," but that a third of those arrested were discharged upon examination as innocent, only after having been condemned to undergo "a regular criminal experience . . . some of them shoved into cells and forced to spend a night, sometimes a week, there, forced into intimacy with criminals, before being discharged." In 1882, he showed, out of 32,800 arrested, more than 10,700 had been so treated. "Will not those who are already weak, and having a hard struggle for existence, be further weakened, and therefore more liable soon to become actual offenders than they otherwise would have been? Brutal treatment brutalizes, and thus prepares for crime." Altgeld was speaking of all "first offenders," but he emphasized the particular horror of such treatment of juvenile delinquents. After Altgeld had become Governor of Illinois, and after the Chicago Civic Federation had been organized in 1893, leadership in this particular matter was taken over by Mrs. James Flower, better known in Chicago as Lucy M. Flower, chairman of the Federation's Department of Philanthrophy. Mrs. Flower began with the problem of the care of dependent children by the county. She straightened that out. In the course of this straightening out she rediscovered how many children were confined in the cells of police stations, the city prison, and the county jail. She did what she could about that, too, raising a fund for the founding of the Glenwood Manual Training School, to which "bad boys" might be committed; and learning that truancy was directly related to delinquency, she urged on the establishment of a parental school for truants. But the original disease of juvenile delinquency remained untouched, still encouraged by the form of court procedures and commitments of children. What was to be done about that? Was not a special method of court procedure possible in the case of very young offenders? Not only a special method of procedure, but a special court, in connection with which children should not be exposed to close association with older offenders, actually criminal? Mrs. Flower thought so; Jane Addams thought so; Julia Lathrop thought so; Mrs.

Charles Henrotin thought so; a fighting Irishman named Timothy Sullivan thought so; and one or two sympathetic judges of the Criminal Court, Hurd and Carter, thought so. No such "Juvenile Court" as they visualized existed anywhere in the United States, but Illinois had been first in the field with special legislation for women workers, why should it not be first with special legislation for child delinquents?

Jane Addams did not take the lead in that struggle. But she was one of Mrs. Flower's strongest "left hands" in the organization called the Every Day Club, which carried the fight to the legislature. The bill organizing the Juvenile Court having been passed in May, the Court was legally provided for on July 1, 1899. A Juvenile Court committee was organized to see that the law worked. The head of that committee was Julia Lathrop of Hull House; she was succeeded by Mrs. Joseph Bowen of Hull House. The first probation officer provided by the law was Alzina P. Stevens, who lived at Hull House; the money to pay her was raised by the Juvenile Court committee. The committee raised funds also to provide a place to confine children before their cases could be heard; and they made it actually homelike and comfortable and healthy; with more than twenty-five hundred delinquent children passing through it yearly, it never once had to be quarantined for a contagious disease. The law *did* work. And the third of Jane Addams's child-problems was on the way to solution.

Not solved. None of her problems was ever solved. The generations in the Hull House neighborhood still clash with violence; the national child-labor amendment to the Constitution is not yet passed; juvenile delinquency runs as high, in certain sections of Chicago, as 20 and even 25 per cent to-day. But the work must be taken into consideration against the general background. In 1894 William T. Stead indicted Chicago for wickedness, foulness, and indifference as no city had ever been indicted before. "If Christ came to Chicago," Stead asked, "what would he discover? Vice, criminality, corruption, and above all neglect such as no other late nineteenth-century city would tolerate." Of Chicago, six years later, in 1900, Lincoln Steffens wrote: "It is first in violence, deepest in dirt; loud, lawless, unlovely, ill-smelling, new; an overgrown gawk of a village, the 'tough' among cities, a spectacle for the nation. Criminally it was wide open, commercially it was brazen, and socially it was thoughtless and raw... everybody was for himself and none was for Chicago."

Stead was extravagant and unscientific in his researches, Steffens was fierce in his generalities; yet both were more right than wrong. And so far as they were right, they show what sort of a situation Jane Addams faced in these first ten years at Hull House. And she was a steadily inspiring force toward better things. Her sympathies were the widest, her devotion was the most constant, her work was the most intimate. Above all, as may have been perceived in her conclusions about John Powers as a politician and George M. Pullman as a capitalist, about labor-unions and Socialism, about parents and children, about saloons and religion, she was the most tolerant of all who sought reform. The English labor leader, John Burns, was dining at Hull House on his first visit, incognito, to the city. Jane Addams asked him what he thought of Chicago.

"I think your mayor is an ass."

"But," she commented, "he is so sincere!"

"All asses are sincere."

"Perhaps. But sincerity is never asinine."

What she became in those ten years may be left to the expression of Professor Charles E. Merriam: "A great professor without a university chair, a guiding woman in a man-made world, a brooding spirit of the mother hovering with gentle sympathy over the troubled sea of poverty, of weakness, of arrogance, of pride, of hate, of force."

Later she was to be also, in Professor Merriam's phrase, "a great statesman without a portfolio," but that was still in the future in 1900. All else she was to be, except in influence, she had by the turn of the century become. Much indeed she had got from her neighbors in ten years!

CHAPTER X

GROWTH

BY 1899, when Hull House had been established for ten years, it had become large and well known. There were many "social settlements" by that time, several in Chicago, such as Graham Taylor's Chicago Commons and Mary McDowell's home "back of the Yards" at 47th street, founded and chiefly maintained by the University of Chicago. But all of them had been nurtured, so to speak, under Jane Addams's wing. Graham Taylor, for instance, who had come to the Chicago Theological Seminary in 1893, to open the first department of instruction in any church institution which was to be wholly devoted to the social interpretation of religion, says:

I had read of Toynbee Hall and had made a condition that I should have liberty to live with the masses, but I was confirmed in this purpose by the spirit and ideals of Jane Addams ... dwelling in simple natural neighborly human relations with her cosmopolitan neighbors and exerting far-flung influences over the more privileged classes ... an interpretative personality ... and most of all interpretative between the foreign-born and those to the native manner born.

And Mary McDowell, still "Mary the Magnificent" at 80, went from Hull House to head the University of Chicago settlement; which was incidentally the first to be backed by academic leaders. At the University of Chicago Albion Small had established in 1892, with the founding of the new university, the first department of sociology in any university, and the settlement near the Stockyards, two miles from the quadrangles, was an outgrowth of Small's enthusiasm. Mr. Taylor in pointing out that "no academic leaders stood by our American pioneers as, Doctor Jowett of Balliol stood by Barnett, as Ruskin and Thomas Hill Green prepared the way for Toynbee Hall, as Principal Fairbairn of Mansfield College enlisted with Percy Alden at Mansfield House" does scant justice, perhaps, to Albion Small, George Vincent, and indeed Doctor Harper himself, of the University; but he is right enough in adding that no statesmen here publicly backed our early settlement houses as Asquith and other men of public affairs indorsed and aided British settlements.

Hull House grew rapidly. In ten years there were twenty-five residents instead of two; including both men and women, Jane Addams having been the first head in the history of the movement to provide residence accommodations for both sexes, thus amalgamating the earlier "University settlement" for men only, and "college settlement" for women only, into a "social settlement" for men and women both. Not only was all of the original "Hull House" occupied, but most of the block on which it stood, by buildings all architecturally composed by the brothers Pond—Allen the "deep Pond," and Irving the "wide Pond," as they were affectionately known to all residents. Hull House had now added to the Butler Gallery, the Jane Club and the Neighborhood Kitchen, a splendid Boys' Club and Gymnasium, an assembly hall, a little theater, a big Coffee-House, and various bits to the main building itself, a suite above the Octagon Room, and the great dining-room, which Henry D. Lloyd once characterized as the most bountiful in Chicago. Miss Helen Culver, inheritor of the property from Charles J. Hull, had given a part of it to the Hull House Associates, sold them a part, and established perpetual leases on another part, so that impermanency of occupation was no longer to be feared. In ten years Hull House had become not only a "going concern," but a huge establishment.

To keep it going had been no easy task financially. Jane Addams's personal efforts to this end, alone until the incorporation of the Hull House Associates in 1894, and subsequently with the zealous assistance of the trustees, were nigh on to heroism. She was an executive, but she was no financier, and she made mistakes sometimes in her "estimates." In her many letters to Mary Rozet Smith in these years, the strain of this financial struggle constantly emerges, no less exhausting because in the end it was successful. In scores and scores of these letters Jane Addams refers to the necessity of raising money somehow, even to the struggle to pay her own personal expenses in such instances as when she had turned over her own farm rent, or sold a bond, to keep something going which had been started at the House, which was costing more than Jane had hoped, yet which nobody could bear to give up. Sometimes the references are gloomy, more often they are whimsical, but they are constant. Mary Smith's letters in reply are not preserved; but it is easy to see with what equal constancy she responded. And, of course, Mrs. Bowen was a tower of financial strength; and Mrs. Mary Wilmarth; and others, both men and women, who stood faithfully by through the foul weather of popular distrust as well as in the fair weather of popular approbation; Hull House knowing both well. "There were never such trustees as ours," Jane Addams said just before she died. "Not one was ever frightened by reproach, or made complacent by generosity."

In those ten years Jane Addams grew to full stature as a citizen. Beginning with little but the hope of somehow "socializing" a part of what Carlyle had called "this huge black Democracy of ours," she had given much, but she had got much more than she had given. She had given all her sympathy, all her time, all her energy, and most of her money; she had got an understanding which was at least as clear as that of anybody else in the field, and her "field was the world." So at least the philosophers seem to have thought, and the social workers, and the neighbors; and so the country at large apparently came to think, for on the popular conception of that understanding of hers is based her chief reputation as a great American. Her tolerance, her courage, her devotion, even her intelligence, kindly spoken of as they all have been from time to time, are incidental to this understanding that she got from living at Hull House. If her understanding was wrong, she misled hundreds of thousands; if her understanding was wrong, her influence was really unfortunate, "a menace" as some have called it.

It is interesting to compare her, in this connection, with those two famous people the Webbs, Sidney and Beatrice, who are exactly contemporary with her, who were trying to do together in London exactly what she was trying to do in Chicago in these same years of the 'nineties, namely, socialize democracy. They were, they are, embodied intelligences, students of social movements. Their joint work, published in 1894, *The History of Trades Unionism,* was a monumental performance of research, called by the

London Times "masterly" and "invaluable" when it was brought out, and still considered authoritative; and "when *Industrial Democracy* followed three years later, the same chorus of praise was repeated with emphasis. . . . The authors could almost have said, if they had been so inclined, that, like Byron, they woke up one morning to find themselves famous." The Webbs had the same eagerness to bring about a common class understanding that Jane Addams had; they possessed a somewhat larger income than hers, and possibly an even keener intelligence; but they spent every cent they had, and every ounce of their effort, on the indoor sport of scholarship, as she spent her money and effort on the outdoor game of neighborliness. The result is a curious pallidity in their reputation compared with hers, a sort of inhumane humanity that has made them famous only as Socialists, whereas her work has made her famous as a personality. They gave as much, having as much to give; but they did not get as much in return. The Webbs visited Chicago, staying at Hull House, at the time of the World's Fair in 1893, and Clarence Darrow gave a luncheon for them, with Jane Addams, and Governor Altgeld as the other guests. Beatrice Webb smoked cigarettes, and in her desire to make the visitor feel at home, Jane Addams also took and smoked one, with the most regrettable results. She never smoked again. "I felt," she said not long before she died, "as the Englishman did about spinach, I was glad I didn't like them for if I had liked them I'd have had to smoke them, and I didn't like them."

Jane Addams's own development in the 'nineties was a day-by-day business. To isolate the elements of it is difficult, and to present it chronologically would be a matter of impossibly wearying detail. The record is available, almost as full as the Congressional Record for a statesman; but the details of a statesman's career are a part of national history, whereas the details of Jane Addams's career at Hull House are purely local and domestic. Her occasional political, or half-political, concerns, have already been presented. They grew wholly out of her wish to understand herself and her neighbors. Similarly, though more briefly, two other lines of her interest may be followed, her social philosophy and her religion. One almost despairs of conveying the essential unity of all these interests, the closeness of their interweaving, their centripetality; it was as if her personality were all core, as if the garment of her liberalism were one clear color, scarcely patterned at all. But these two threads we may try to trace.

Her instinctive reaction from, rather than toward, any class conception of society is evident in her notebooks as early as 1883. In the middle 'eighties she leaned toward Positivism, the negation of the class-idea, the assumption of a "Supreme Humanity," an anthropomorphic oneness. Marxian socialism she studied carefully in London in 1888, when she went over from Spain to examine Toynbee Hall. Those were the days, just after the publication of Charles Booth's massive "Enquiry" into conditions in London—"Who are the people of England? How do they live? What are they like? What do they care for?"—when Fabian socialism, under the direction of Bernard Shaw, Sidney Webb, Graham Wallas, Sidney Olivier and others, was becoming a genuinely directive force in London. But neither the economics of Marx nor the economics of the Fabians were inspirational to Jane Addams. She attended a meeting of the London match-girls who were on the "great" strike, but she did not, she says, "understand the efforts of the London trades-unionists, concerning whom I held the vaguest notions." She adds: "I think that at this time I was still filled with the sense that Wells describes in one of his young characters, that somewhere in Church or State are a body of authoritative people who will put things to rights as soon as they really know what is wrong."

Returning to America, she took up residence at Polk and Halsted, yet of much the same mind. She merely sought to know what was wrong. But keenly conscious of her own eager desire to find some social philosophy that would "work," she very early began to welcome sociological and economic discussion, with which Chicago in the last decade of the nineteenth century was full, at Hull House. She "longed for the comfort of a definite social creed." But though she "conscientiously made her effort" once again to accept socialism, she could not agree with anything "baldly dependent on the theory of class-consciousness."

Trades-unionism, however, came to seem to her a real method of lessening the sum of human misery that added itself up all round her. She thought that the objects of trades-unionism were "immediately useful, and practically attainable" to some extent. The "Jane Club" was, as has been said, the outgrowth of a meeting of working-girls held at Hull House during a strike in a neighboring shoe-factory. The next year the Chicago Trades and Labor Assembly appointed a committee of investigation to inquire into the sweating system, and two of the five non-union members of this committee were Hull House residents. The women shirt-makers and the women cloak-makers were both organized at Hull House, as was the "Dorcas Federal Labor Union," composed of representatives from all the unions in Chicago which included women in their membership. Before long the Chicago unions, particularly of course the women's unions, became convinced not only of the sincerity of Jane Addams, but also of the ability of the House to be of service to working women even if Jane Addams herself was an "outsider." Incidentally Chicago in general came to identify her with the much-hated "unionism," and perhaps still does; twenty years ago, at any rate, she could still write that "when 'Labor' is in disgrace, we are always regarded as belonging to it and share the opprobrium."

Though after all what is "Chicago in general"? In the 'nineties, the social leader of Chicago was Mrs. Potter Palmer; wife of one of the city's richest and "hardest" business men, uniquely prominent in her own right, indeed the only actual "social leader" Chicago has ever had, and probably ever will have. Yet it was Mrs. Palmer who demanded that "artisan diplomas" should be awarded at the World's Fair in recognition of the skill of craftsmen, and who gladly accepted the coöperation of the Chicago labor-unions in enforcing her demand; Mrs. Palmer who after the veteran socialist Thomas Morgan had been howled down at a huge mass meeting held in Central Music Hall under trade-union auspices, had Morgan introduced to her afterward and shook his hand warmly, saying how glad she was of the chance to meet him; Mrs. Palmer who became a vice-president of the "federation" which was organized as a result of this mass meeting. Even in the 'nineties there was no "Chicago in general."

Jane Addams did not publicly formulate her views of unions for almost ten years. In January, 1899, however, she published an article in the University of Chicago *Journal of Sociology,* on "Trades Unions and Public Duty," which was hailed by intelligent union leaders as "a splendid explanation of a practical subject by a practical writer, and one of the best presentations of the relation of trade unionism to public duty that has ever been written":

> While trades-unions more than any other body have secured orderly legislation for the defense of the feeblest, they are persistently misunderstood and harshly criticized by many people who are working for the same ends. . . . For many years I have been impressed with the noble purposes of trades-unions, and the desirability of the ends which they seek; and at the same time I have been amazed at the harshness with which their failures are judged by the public, and the undue stress which is laid upon the violence and disorder which sometimes accompany their efforts. . . . Scenes of disorder and violence are enacted because trades-unions are not equipped to accomplish what they are undertaking. The state alone could accomplish it without disorder. The public shirks its duty, and then . . . blames the union men for the disaster which arises from the fact that the movement is a partial one. . . . There is no doubt that the employer, the man who represents vested interests, often routs and defeats labor organizations, drives them from the field, with an honest misunderstanding of what they are trying to do and of the principles which they represent.

She goes on to consider at length six measures "which trades-unions have urged, and concerning which the community has often been stirred by indignation," and yet "when the public undertakes to enforce identical or similar measures, they are regarded with great complacency. The disapproval may be merely the result of the fact that the trades-unions alone are doing that which belongs to the entire public." These six measures are: first, the treatment of the non-union laborer during a strike; second, the dictatorship of the "walking delegate"; third, the use of the boycott; fourth, the insistence upon shorter hours of labor; fifth, the limitation of apprentices; sixth, the sympathetic strike. "To find that we can parallel these six efforts of trades-unions with six others undertaken by the Government, is certainly suggestive." The careful analysis follows, factual, impartial, and brilliantly illustrated; with, in part, the following conclusion:

Probably the labor-unions come nearer to expressing moral striving in politics than any other portion of the community, for their political efforts in most instances have been stimulated by a desire to secure some degree of improvement in the material condition of working people. As a whole, they still expect legal enactment to satisfy the desire, not only for social *order,* but for social *righteousness,* and they are only slowly losing their habit of turning to the law for moral support. They are still endeavoring to secure *each advance in ethics by a step* taken in politics, and this endeavor is the one safeguard of democracy.

The "cruelty and waste of the strike as an implement for securing the most reasonable demands," however, bore heavily upon her who had to witness that cruelty and waste at the closest range among her neighbors. So did the corruption in certain types of trades-unions, a corruption which came after the turn of the century to "flourish almost as openly as it had previously flourished in the City Hall." Jane Addams was again and again appointed as an arbitrator in labor troubles; in the Pullman strike as early as 1894, in the disgraceful teamster's strike eleven years later in 1905, in the garment-worker's strike in 1910, to

name the most stormy only. She changed her views only
to the extent that she saw the Government taking over
the measures and the functions which she long ago perceived "the unions are not equipped to accomplish." Her
social philosophy indeed may be summed up in the phrases
with which the foregoing summary concludes, that each
advance in social ethics should be secured by an advance
in politics, and that this endeavor is the one safeguard
of democracy.

It is in the light of this philosophy, and this alone, that
she engaged in the long struggle for suffrage for women.
Of her personally one might say almost exactly what
Beatrice Webb said of herself:

> I never myself suffered the disabilities assumed to arise from
> my sex. Quite the contrary; if I had been born a man, family
> pressure and the public opinion of my class might have pushed
> me into a money-making profession; as a mere woman I could
> carve out a career of disinterested service. Moreover, in the
> field I chose a woman was privileged ... she aroused less sus-
> picion than a man. Further, in those days, a competent female
> writer on sociological topics had, to an enterprising editor,
> actually a scarcity value. Thus she secured immediate publi-
> cation.

This realization started Mrs. Webb off as an anti-
feminist. Jane Addams was always a feminist in spirit;
she longed emotionally for the vote even in her college
days. But her real desire for suffrage for women came as
has just been said from her growing conviction that
ethics in a democracy could only be confirmed by
legislation, and that women, freer from the dust and
blood of the arena of business competition, less burdened with the immediate economic responsibilities of

"looking after those of their own family," could see more plainly perhaps what the developments in social ethics were. What good to see, though, if you had no power to enforce your vision? For this reason, and for this reason only, she sought that power for women; merely, as it were, including herself among them.

Such may be said to have been the course of her thinking so far as any general social philosophy is concerned, apart of course from her profound individual sympathy with the misery of humanity however and wherever it was evident, and her determination to do what she could personally to relieve it in the individual case.

Now, what of her religion? From the early days in Rockford Seminary when she wrote of Miss Sill, "She however does everything from the love of God alone, and I do not like that," Jane Addams was profoundly concerned with the matter of religious conviction. Rockford Seminary itself was drenched, permeated, with religious conviction in the late 1870's. "Every sort of evangelical appeal was made to reach the comparatively few 'unconverted' girls at the school. We were made the subject of prayer at the daily chapel exercises and the weekly prayer-meeting, attendance upon which was obligatory. I was singularly unresponsive to all these forms of emotional appeal." Unresponsive to *emotional* appeal, yes; but keenly responsive to the hope of reasoning herself into the church. Her notebooks are full of self-questionings and, not infrequently, self-reproach in the matter. In a letter of August, 1879, to Ellen Starr she wrote:

What do you understand by being *saved?* I don't know, of course whether I have the right idea or not, but what I call it is this—that a people or a nation are saved just as soon as they *comprehend* their God; almost every nation has a beautiful divinity to start with, and if they would only keep right to that they would be all right, but they don't; they keep getting farther away and lowering their ideal until at last they are *lost*. Comprehending your deity and being in harmony with his plan is to be saved. . . . I am far enough away now from this. Christ doesn't help me in the least. Sometimes I can work myself into great admiration of his life and occasionally I can catch something of his philosophy, but he doesn't bring me any nearer the *Deity*. I feel a little as I do when I hear very fine music that I am incapable of understanding. This is the nearest that I get to it . . . I am not so much *un*settled as *re*-settled so often, but my creed is low, *be sincere* and *don't fuss*.

Three months later, in a totally different vein:

Studying first the reign of Uzziah and then Bacon's essays this afternoon, I was vividly reminded of you, your pity and your ideas of friendship, and so between my association of you both with a Bible lesson and moral reflections, I conclude that you must be very nearly orthodox, even if you do go to hear Swing and ride about on streetcars on Sunday, at both of which proceedings I was somewhat shocked but wished that I could do it too.

Two months later, in the course of a very long letter, written on "fast day":

I have been trying an awful experiment. I did not pray, at least formally, for almost three months, and was shocked to find that I feel no worse for it, I can think about a great many other things that are noble and beautiful. I feel happy and unconcerned and not in the least morbid. . . . Perhaps it is absurd to insist upon seeing into religion by the understanding instead of by faith, which is the highest faculty given us. There is where I think we differ. You long for a beautiful faith, an experience of this kind. I only feel that I need religion in a practical sense, that if I could fix myself with my relations to God and the universe and so be in perfect harmony with nature and deity, I could use my faculties and energy so much better and could do almost anything. *Mine* is predominantly selfish, and *yours* is a reaching for higher things.

Such passages are numerous in her letters to Ellen Starr for the next three years, a period which includes the death of Jane's father. After Jane went to medical school in Philadelphia, such epistolary analysis ceases altogether. It is however continued in her notebooks, even during her first two years abroad, from 1883 to 1885. It was on her return from this sojourn in Europe that at twenty-five Jane finally "joined the church," for reasons already given. Her church affiliation however did not make her less primarily human in her sympathies and interests. The leopard could not change its spots, even by the process of baptism. Mrs. Catherine Waugh McCulloch, who was in Rockford Seminary with Jane Addams, and who, as president for two years during that time of the college "Christian Association," was certainly in touch with the doctrinal situation, insists that Jane was regarded as heterodox only by Miss Sill, if by any one; never by the girls. But Mrs. McCulloch does admit that the little "Easter play" written by Jane for performance on the day before Easter Sunday of 1880, centered not around the resurrection of Christ, but around the constant resurrection of divine sympathy for the poor, with a theme of a very sociological millennium when there should be no more poor, but the impulse to share finding fulfilment in the hearts of peasant girls and queens alike. It was obviously this impulse to share which took Jane Addams into the little Presbyterian church of Cedarville, just as it took her later to Hull House and into the struggling little Congregational church around the corner. You could not give, unless you were in some very definite fashion one with those to whom you gave.

Dr. Graham Taylor tells a curious and interesting story in connection with Jane Addams's membership in this church. Most of the people were Ulster Irish and Scotch. They moved out of the neighborhood, and therefore attended church services rarely. A student minister from the Moody Bible Institute was put in charge of the church, and presently dropped from the rolls the names of all those who did not regularly attend; including Jane Addams, who admitted that while this particular minister was in charge she found herself unwilling to attend at all. Presently the student left; whereupon the older members of the church met and formally voted to restore Miss Addams's name, which she was glad to allow. Many years later, when she died, a note in the Congregational Church paper, the *Advance,* referred to the fact that she had been dropped from membership in the church, with the inference that she had been regarded as in some fashion heretical. The reference was unfortunate and misleading, as the authorities of the Congregational Society in Chicago thought highly of Miss Addams, and cherish the memory of her association with the Congregational denomination.

But her position did not at all please the priests, ministers, and editors of religious papers of the community. Many of them assailed Hull House frequently during the first ten years of its existence, for its lack of specific religious activity. It was not enough that Jane Addams herself should be a church member; it was not nearly enough that she should be a "good woman," as they pretty freely admitted she seemed to be. Some of them at least perceived that her religion, however honest, was merely a part of her humanitarianism, and being certain that humanitarianism should rather be a part of religion, were distressed thereby. No doubt there was good to be done; but were not the churches there to do it? It was all very well to be interested in the wretched, but were they not after all the Lord's creatures, and was not the *first* duty to "preach the gospel" to every creature? Similar attacks were made upon the Chicago Commons, although its head Graham Taylor was a minister himself, and a member of the faculty of the Chicago Theological Institute.

Another difficulty was with Jane Addams's attitude toward the saloon. When she first went to Hull House, there was said to be a saloon for every twenty-six people in the ward. There were three within fifty yards of the House. Those were the great days of the Woman's Christian Temperance Union, when the name and fame of no woman in the land was greater than that of Frances Willard. Saloons were wicked, there were no two ways about that, in the minds of religious women. Jane Addams was a church member; and yet she did not attack the saloons directly. She did attack them indirectly, to be sure. The Hull House Coffee House was undertaken largely as an indirect attack upon the saloon. But she did not damn them. To many good men and women it seemed as if she were at times almost their apologist:

> The problem of the substitute for the saloon is still unsolved. . . . The saloon is the original social center of the Hull House neighborhood, and has a valuable social element, sociability, which must be preserved. . . . I have no faith in the denunciations of saloons and of drinking; it is my conclusion that drinking is largely the indulgence not of the appetite but in the social instincts common to the human race.

Such views, which she presented again and again, even before the ladies of the W.C.T.U. themselves on occasion, were common enough even in the 'nineties among newspaper editors, but they were thought by many to be neither womanly nor religious. Like her "socialism," they were widely whispered about to Jane Addams's discredit, and particularly to the discredit of her doctrinality. And the effect of this whispering upon her was much what the effect of the religious propaganda at Rockford had been. It did not so much produce rebellion in her, as rouse in her doubts whether she really was genuinely religious. Her job was to "use her faculties and energy," as she had written to Ellen Starr years before. She still "needed religion only in a practical sense . . . to be in harmony with nature and deity." Was that harmony best assured by retiring into herself for profession, as it were? She never announced any final conclusion, perhaps never even to herself. But she went to church less and less regularly. She did not so much put aside her long questionings of her relation to "God and the universe" as overlay them with work. It was as if she had become

so disheartened with her inadequacy to marshal the moral forces capable of breaking what must be broken and of building what must be built; to reconstruct our social relationships through a regeneration of the human heart; to repair a world . . . sodden with self-seeking, that she had assumed that personal immortality is irrelevant . . . or stirred by a secret fear that such a belief might divert her secret store of moral energy, as has already occurred in other centuries, when men neglected great human tasks because they were absorbed in preparations for eternity.

Better put than in her own words, that cannot be; and yet these words do not tell the whole story of her attitude.

Life questioned her daily, hourly; and to some of its questions she could find answers. Death, God, salvation, questioned her only now and then, always the same question, and it was as if she concluded the answer had always evaded, always would evade her. In the collection of some of her many memorial addresses, *The Excellent Becomes the Permanent,* she states this realistic attitude:

I was once summoned to a Chicago hospital by a woman who twenty-four hours before had lost her children in a hideous fire. She herself had been badly burned and I could see nothing of her face but two gleaming eyes at the bottom of a well of bandages, and distorted lips through which came in husky whispers, "Do you believe in immortality? Please be sincere with me. I cannot endure any more empty words." And then even more wearily, "I beg of you, do not try to comfort me." As I visited my new-found friend through the days of her convalescence ... she seemed to me a living demonstration of the refusal to be content with a mere mechanism of escape from reality, which she suspected to have been made to the order of man's desires.

In 1899, a "congress of religions" was held in Chicago, of a sort that Doctor Hiram W. Thomas said would have been impossible twenty years before in any Christian country. It was so "liberal" that Professor Herbert Willett of the University of Chicago was applauded when he declared that "social service should come first and the church afterward"; that there was no antagonism of the masses to religion, but only to the non-essentials of religion, and that among denominations only the fatherhood of God and the brotherhood of man should be recognized as essential. It was in addressing this Congress, that Jane Addams compared the new theologians to physicians skilled in anatomy but ignorant of bone-setting. "Ethical teachings," she said, "have made their premises acceptable to society. What we desire from the church is a knowledge of what to do with these new truths; some certain fashion of connecting our conduct with our consciences."

Many years later, in a foreword to Doctor Taylor's *Religion in Social Action,* she wrote:

The reader knows that the religious synthesis, or rather that the competing religious syntheses, are constantly changing and differentiating themselves in response to special needs. . . . The church, with its chance of miracle as it were, its divine help, its faith so invincible and incalculable, offers itself as a refuge against unaided human effort and against the scientific estimate of the slow pace of social amelioration.

The two utterances, far apart in time and very different in phraseology, nevertheless express the same point of view.

And finally perhaps, in definition of the religious quality of Jane Addams, there may be quoted the remark of her physician, when a short time before she died she was convalescing from a heart attack which had seemed likely to be fatal. "She is a good patient," he said. "She is as good a patient as can be. She tries hard to do everything I tell her to do. And I am a little surprised, because such amenability generally arises from fear, and I do not suppose Jane Addams has ever known fear." Her religion, whatever it was, was fixed in her by the first ten years of experience at Hull House; and like her goodness as a patient, was the result not of personal concern, but of a genuine desire to save and strengthen her own faculties and energy for the use of others.

CHAPTER XI

WIDENING INFLUENCES

BEFORE the end of the first decade of the twentieth century, Hull House had become a great group of buildings covering a city block. Following the Butler Gallery in 1891, and the original Coffee House and gymnasium in 1893, the first story of the original building had been remodeled and a third story built above in 1895; a final remodeling to the present condition of the old House had been made in 1899. In 1895 Mary Rozet Smith built a Children's Building; the Colvins, staunch upholders of the hands of Jane Addams through the hardest years, built the Jane Club in 1898. The next year the new Coffee House and the long-desired Hull House Theater above it were erected, the old Coffee House and gymnasium being moved and developed for other purposes. Hull House Apartments, to accommodate the rapidly increasing number of new residents, and the Men's Club, were put up in 1901 to 1902; the Woman's Club (Bowen Hall) in 1904, the splendid Boys' Club in 1906 to 1907, the Mary Crane Nursery in 1907. In the course of all these changes, and the necessity of finding a place for a central heating plant, remodeling both difficult and amusing seemed to be almost constantly going on, "we used to think nothing," Jane Addams said jokingly to a visitor one day when she was talking about the Government housing projects in Chicago a little while before she died, "of moving a building twenty-seven feet west, nine feet south, and fourteen feet up." The Pond brothers did it all, harmonized everything. Allen is dead, but Irving K., at Jane Addams memorial services in the Hull House Court, when Doctor Gilkey said, "if you seek her monument look around you," looked round also with tears in his eyes but pride in his heart; the visible memorial to Jane Addams was also a visible memorial to the Ponds.

Hull House in its second decade was quite as interesting, though perhaps not so exciting, as in the early years. It had become an institution, obviously permanent like a university, but it had not become institutionalized. For all the score of buildings, for all the great increase in the numbers of the residents and the numbers of visitors, the spirit had not changed at all. Men and women still went there to live for no other earthly reason than because that was where they wanted to live. Francis Hackett, for instance, the biographer of Kings and Queens, became a resident in 1906, when he was a review, editorial and feature writer on the *Chicago Evening Post,* at $23 a week, and "totally ignorant of settlement work and devoid of missionary spirit":

> The building in which we lived on Halsted Street did not fall back from the street. It was plump in the middle of the neighborhood, and yet it had a long semi-cloistral corridor and a grave, deep, spacious reception hall which declared you were out of the world. We who came there on probation before we were accepted as residents could hardly help feeling it was a sort of withdrawn community. But in its being withdrawn it was anything but mystical or dogmatic. Its faith was humanism. It "warmed both hands before the fire of life." No newcomer could resist its ease, its tolerance, or its cordiality. . . . Our pro-

bation, I suppose, did result in a real selection. Certain thorny people were not admitted. We who were there were in harmony.

In this second decade of Hull House, the "principals" were still Jane Addams, Ellen Starr, Julia Lathrop, Alice Hamilton. Hackett records that it was even said occasionally, "without Jane Addams, the House is nothing"; which as a statement is a wild exaggeration, though as a tribute it is not unreasonable. But what might be called the second line of residents became and remained quite as varied and fascinating in personality as the first; maybe not quite so forcible, but nobody has ever charged Grace Abbott, who succeeded Julia Lathrop as head of the Children's Bureau, with any lack of force; or Gertrude Howe Britton, now executive director of the Chicago Heart Association; or Clara Landsberg, fiercely active, impatiently precise, tenderly determined. Even those who were called "the esthetes" strengthened the hash of their creative interests with the meat of industry and devotion to the neighbors. There was grand old Mrs. Pelham, who had been Laura Dainty the actress, and who built up the Hull House Dramatic Association; and Edith de Nancrede, of French ancestry, indefatigably self-effacing, who took the Association over and still maintains it as the oldest continuously performing "little theater" group in America. There were the painters, Norah Hamilton, who made the sketches for *Twenty Years at Hull House*, and Enella Benedict, one of the first group, whose "residence" has been unbroken longer than that of any one else except Miss Addams herself, and moody, sturdy, mysterious, aloof Carl Linden; there was Frank Hazenplug, who finally decided to call himself

Hazen because he did not like the sound of the last syllable of his real name, a sort of errand boy of the arts, decorator, scene-painter, dancer, doer in an inarticulate fashion of all the odd jobs that turned up to be done in connection with the Hull House theater, hopelessly the esthete but never helplessly; and Hackett himself, the Celtic *littérateur*, eccentric to the backbone, but what a backbone! Some of them were, in the slang of the House, "noble," and some were "frivolous." There was Maud Gernon, "solid worth, puzzled by life"; and Charles Yeomans, lively, conscientious, trying to make the competitive business of manufacturing pumps square with the principles of social idealism; and his brother Ned, who was to become an educational "new dealer" of distinction in California. All they wanted was to share their interests with the Halsted Streeters, and to share the interests of Halsted Street. And there was George Hooker, interested not at all in the arts, not especially interested even in the neighborhood, but with a fine feeling for social theory and what amounted to a passion for municipal ownership. Mr. Hooker was inclined to think that many of the residents, most of whom were younger than he, were amateur; and behind his back they might call him "the professor," though if there was any group that George Hooker himself regarded with scornful indifference, it was the university, the professorial, group. To almost any of these, and to many others for that matter, a chapter in the story of Hull House might well be devoted. One other must be mentioned; the memories of too many people return to him, fascinated, to permit of omitting a little picture of him—George Mortimer Rendell Twose.

Twose, in his early thirties when he came to live at
Hull House, was big bodied and bald, and long in every
feature—long head, long nose, big mouth, long chin, long
arms and extraordinarily long legs. Yet he was far from
homely. There was something about his looks supremely
natural, as there is about the look of a tree or a cliff.
When he sat, his big body and his long limbs fell into
awkward poses, but when he walked or danced he was
as light as a plume. Once in a while, at set "entertainments," he would amuse the neighbors by the performance of a Highland fling, and on such an occasion an
envious young man who with his girl-friend was looking
on, was overheard to say, "God, honey, ain't he loose!"

With an English University education behind him, he
came to Chicago to teach manual training in a high
school; why, nobody at Hull House knew. His pupils
looked upon him with awe and incredulity; he was competent, he was sympathetic, but in a Chicago high school
he seemed almost unreal. Casual visitors to Hull House,
or even probationary residents, saw him in much the
same light. His tastes were fastidious, yet his indiffer-
ences to convention were colossal. Never in all the years
did he fail to make his own tea in his own room at five
o'clock, but in hot weather he partook of it without a
stitch of clothing on him. In the same way his reserves
were complete, and yet his effervescences were constant;
he never gave anybody any information about himself,
yet he chattered like a magpie. And precisely the same
contradictions characterized his service at the House;
he was as gentle as a child; he would do anything that
needed to be done, yet before and after his kindlinesses,
he would laugh loud and long at the possibility of any real

social accomplishment—"it will be all the same in a hundred years!" He believed in Jane Addams, but in nobody else, particularly not in himself. Almost everything bored him, except doing things for people, whether they bored him or not, and painting. In the end he even grew bored with Hull House, and went away and buried himself among New England hills, with the intention of finding out whether he really had ability as a painter or not; but died before he could make up his mind. Of all the "odd" residents Hull House ever knew, the oddest; one of the most generally useful; cynical, negligent, efficient, lovable, unforgettable.

As to-day one reads in newspapers and magazines almost unqualified praise of Jane Addams, reflection upon the many occasions in the past when disapproval of her was almost equally unqualified becomes in part, at least, amusing. To be sure even to-day there are sour notes in the pæan. In a volume published in 1933, listing the activities of such "dangerous" citizens as believe in tolerance and freedom of thought, more space was given to the "un-American" affiliations and ideals of Jane Addams than to those of anybody else. And the Daughters of the American Revolution and the more grossly ignorant of the members of the American Legion cannot forgive her for her establishment of the Women's International League for Peace and Freedom in wartime. She was elected to the D.A.R. in 1895, and made an honorary member in 1900; as she remarked in 1930, she had supposed for life, but presumably only during good behavior. But in the first decade of the twentieth century, she was again and again subjected to newspaper attacks as bitter as have ever been made, perhaps, upon a woman. She was ridi-

culed, abused, threatened, and on one occasion even made
the focus of lying "evidence" presented to a grand jury.
Later, as a "pacifist," she was frequently subjected to
even more bitter newspaper insult, but that was to be
expected; militaristic storms of feeling sweep too fiercely
across the landscape of understanding to permit any
goodwill to remain rooted. The earlier attacks were almost
entirely local, personal, and calculated.

There is no reference here to the violent and frequently
obscene letters of which she had so many when she was
campaigning against Alderman Powers. That sort of thing
was inevitable. Any affront to a political "vested interest"
must be resented by the office-holders and job-holders it
supports. Her interference on behalf of the civil liberties
of unpopular individuals, and her efforts as a member of
the Chicago Board of Education to "reform the schools,"
brought down upon her the wrath, not only of correspondents but also of editors and publishers.

By far the fiercest and most long-continued assault was
made by the Chicago *Chronicle,* under the direction of
John R. Walsh. Walsh, who had been brought from Ireland to Chicago as a boy of eleven in the 1850's, had
begun as a newsboy and become famous as a financier.
His bank was a "political" bank, deriving much of its
revenue from deposits of public funds and the bonding
of public officials. In the 'nineties he established the
Chronicle, and made it the organ of the Democratic
Party in Chicago. He quarreled violently with Governor
Altgeld, however, over money matters, a bank loan for the
financing of Altgeld's "Unity Building," and later still
more violently over the Governor's veto in 1895 of the
Yerkes street-car monopoly bills; Walsh being tied up

closely with Yerkes, as a matter of political and financial course. Walsh disliked Jane Addams for her campaign against Alderman Powers, and hated her for her friendship for Altgeld. From 1896 to 1905, he was virulent in every reference to her, to Hull House, and to Chicago "settlements" in general. In 1905 his bank failed, and he was indicted for embezzlement, found guilty, and sent to the penitentiary, from which he was only released to die outside the walls. From his death-bed he sent a friend to Jane Addams with the message that he had been wrong in his attacks upon her and that he was sorry. Not many personal matters in her life have affected her more than that strange and unexpected apology from a strong and broken man.

The incidents which provoked attack were various. One was a sort of forerunner of the famous Booker T. Washington luncheon at the White House. In October of 1899, to a "congress" being held in Chicago, there came a dozen colored women delegates. Naturally, as it seemed to the residents of Hull House, Miss Addams asked them to lunch. The first resident physician at Hull House had been a colored woman; many of Jane Addams's friends were then of the Negro race, as many are now, both men and women; it may be said that it simply did not occur to her not to ask the colored women delegates to sit at her home table. But there was a good deal of stir, particularly in the South; various editors suggesting that perhaps if she came into that section again to talk as she had gone occasionally, she could hardly expect to be entertained at the tables of ladies. But that was a mild flurry. Hull House was Jane Addams's private residence; after all, even Southern editors had no real objection to the entertainment of Negroes in one's own home. The later uproar over the Roosevelt-Washington luncheon was due to the fact that the White House was a national, not a private, domicile.

A real storm broke in 1901, just after President McKinley was assassinated at Buffalo. Czolgolz, the assassin, though not sane, was not completely insane, as Guiteau had been; and he professed to be an anarchist. Requests were sent from Buffalo and presumably also orders from Washington, though this has never been confirmed, to Chicago police authorities to arrest and hold in secret all "known anarchists." The first one arrested in Chicago was Abraham Isaak, a Russian Jew, editor of an anarchist paper. Jane Addams had met him once at Hull House two years before, when Prince Kropotkin was visiting the House, and Isaak, his wife, son and daughter had come to call on Kropotkin. She had thought Isaak "a quiet, scholarly man, challenging the social order by the philosophic touchstone of Bakunin and Herbert Spencer." When he was arrested in 1901 and submerged in a dirty, long-unused cell under the City Hall, the Russian Jews of the Hull House neighborhood flooded in to complain in despair. "You see," they said, "what becomes of the *law* you boast of; the authorities will not even permit this man to see a lawyer!" Jane Addams said: "Challenged by an anarchist, one is always sensitive for the honor of legally constituted society.... As the final police authority rests with the mayor, I repaired to his house the next morning (Sunday) to appeal to him in the interest of a law and order that should not yield to panic."

The mayor declared that it was not "safe" to let Isaak see a lawyer, but that Jane Addams might see him if she liked. She did; reassured him as best she could; got permission finally to let him have a lawyer; stood by till the panic subsided, and Isaak was released, obviously innocent of any connection with Czolgolz or the murder, but crushed by mistreatment. A sample of the most high-minded of the editorial comments on this incident, much higher-minded than most, and taken from the *Central Christian Advocate* of Kansas City—the irony of the name needs no emphasis—follows:

> The visit of Miss Jane Addams to this anarchist was as un-called for as it was untimely. It may be taken for granted that the Government of the United States will not go into the business of trying to propagate anarchy by persecuting its adherents without cause. The trepidation of Miss Addams there-fore does small credit to her judgment and will do less to increase her influence for good. There is no danger of any rights being taken away from the "firebrand" Isaak. They will be safeguarded without Miss Addams's interference. She will not help the laboring classes by rushing to the aid of a fire-brand, whose torch is under the welfare of the toiler as well as of any other class.

It was hardly "gentle Jesus, meek and mild," who in-spired the central Christianity of that advocacy of injus-tice. Jane Addams had hundreds of personal letters at this time, some filthy, many abusive, a few merely reproachful; but almost none of approval. Wallace Rice wrote asking her to call on him for any service that his combined legal and newspaper experience might enable him to give, and signed his letter "yours with sincere admiration." Clarence Darrow, then at Hanover, New Hampshire, entering his son at Dartmouth, wrote at length, also offering his serv-ices, adding: "I have stood in front of mobs so long that my heart is weary, but I do not see anything else to do and shall not avoid what seems to be my duty." And William T. Stead wrote from London in mid-October: "There is always an immense danger in times of popular passion and fury that perfectly innocent philosophers may be confounded with bloody-minded assassins. The mob is undiscriminating, and lends a ready ear to those who imagine that the lawless violence of the individual can best be repressed by equally lawless violence on the part of the community."

It was at this time that Mrs. Palmer withdrew her support from Hull House. It was at this time that the Reverend John Thompson of Grace Methodist Church declared in an interview: "So far as I have observed, I have never discovered that the social settlements did much good, whether under Christian auspices or not," and the Reverend James S. Stone, rector of St. James, went still further: "I do not think there is any benefit to be derived from any alliance of a church with sociological movements." They were good men, but like a famous predecessor of theirs, they preferred to "go by on the other side."

Five years later the "Averbuch case" again produced a whirlwind of disapprobation. Averbuch, also a Russian Jew, had witnessed but escaped the Kishineff massacre of 1903. With his older sister he had got away to America, and in Chicago they lived for two years, industrious, quiet, and frugal. Then the nineteen-year-old boy lost his job. He went to the house of the Chief of Police, alone and unarmed. Admitted to the hallway, he advanced toward the Chief as that functionary came down the stairs, and said something in broken English, nobody will ever know what. The Chief drew a revolver, and somebody shot the lad four times, twice in front and twice in the back as the

boy turned to flee. Three members of the Chief's family
and the policeman-chauffeur were also on the scene. The
Chief asserted that Averbuch had come to assassinate him,
and that he had fired in self-defense. He declared that
Averbuch was an anarchist, and at once put out the old
dragnet for all anarchists, in the same sort of panic that
had followed McKinley's murder, the same panic that
for twenty long years had accompanied in Chicago the
pronunciation of the very word anarchist, since the Haymarket riot. Olga Averbuch was arrested, and her rooms
were searched. Some printed matter of "anarchistic tend-
encies," and the paraphernalia of prayer of the orthodox
Jewish faith, were found. Which of these was the better
evidence of the young man's beliefs was never determined.
Again the Russian Jews of the Hull House neighborhood,
frightened half to death, appealed to Jane Addams. They
saw another massacre about to be repeated. Miss Addams
called on the telephone a young lawyer whom she had
never met, but of whom she knew through her old and
dear friend Mrs. Wilmarth. The young lawyer, Harold
Ickes by name, now the Secretary of the Interior, and
Jane Addams fought together the battle for legal justice.
The police ransacked all the printing offices they could
find in the Jewish colony, raided a restaurant which had
been supplying food at cost to the unemployed, searched
tenements without a warrant, and carried off volumes of
Shakespeare and Herbert Spencer in triumph to the city
hall. The older Jews moaned, the younger ones preferred
to try violence in self-defense. Jane Addams quieted them;
Harold Ickes took care of the legal procedures. Between
them they composed the panic on both sides. But Miss
Addams bore the odium. The scared Chief of Police said,

"Social settlements are first cousins to the anarchists"; evidence, that Graham Taylor of the Chicago Commons had declared the police of Chicago were corrupt, and that a meeting had only a few days previously been held at Hull House, in the interests of the unemployed, which anarchists were "known to have attended." We quote a sample of local editorial comment: "Ladies and gentlemen, you who enumerate your good deeds in other respects, you who asseverate your benevolence for the poor, you who glorify your every act in behalf of the weak—you cannot escape the responsibility for this boy assassin. Raise not your hands to confirm your innocence—they drip with his blood!"

The meaning was that Jane Addams and Graham had incited Averbuch to his death.

This sort of thing, however, proved too much for respectable Chicago to stomach. The *Daily News* and the *Post* defended the settlements; public opinion in Chicago veered round presently to the belief that the Chief had been a frightened coward; and the word anarchist began to cease to terrify. Young Averbuch turned out to be an unwilling martyr in the cause of common sense.

From that time until the war, followed by the Russian Revolution, developed the bogeys of "pacifism" and "communism," Chicago was no more panicky about "conspiracies against the government" than any other large American city, and the term *anarchist* by 1917 had practically disappeared from circulation, at least as a conjuration to illegality and police interference with the civil liberties of the poor. To-day, in the various classifications of "reds" which may be found in the obscure offices of patriotic societies in Chicago, anarchist does not appear at all. When in 1908 Jane Addams and others defeated an attempt to extradite a Russian revolutionist named Rudowitz who was living in Chicago, and a series of meetings was organized to educate public opinion in the matter of political extradition, some of the papers were almost friendly; though the Russian Jewish colony itself was plunged into hysterical consternation. Every young Russian Jew in it, was in a sense a revolutionist in Russia; his whole purpose in coming to America had been to escape the horrible necessity of revolution. If he could be extradited for his opinion, we were back in political chaos. But the Department of State refused Rudowitz's extradition, and peace reigned again. Jane Addams wrote: "It was perhaps significant of our need of what Napoleon called 'a revival of civic morals' that the public appeal against such a reversal of our traditions had to be based largely upon the contributions to American progress *made from other revolutions*: the Puritans from the English, Lafayette from the French, Carl Schurz and many other able men from the German upheavals of the middle of the century."

The last burst of public obloquy against Jane Addams, before the war, though in a way the meanest of the local attacks, had also about it something humorous, which none of the rest did. Maxim Gorki came to visit America, accompanied by his common-law wife. The Russian Government, knowing that he would appeal against its tyranny, and talk of the wretchedness of the Russian peasant, which he knew well enough to portray eloquently, fomented a scandal concerning Gorki's private life. It was a successful fomentation; Gorki could not get a hearing. Again Jane Addams was appealed to by the Russians to "get justice." She went to see James Keeley, managing editor of the *Tribune,* armed with the facts in the case, to ask him if he would publish Gorki's side of it. Mr. Keeley informed her that marriage was a journalistic "sacred cow," and that he would not touch the thing unless Jane Addams herself would write and sign an article. She declined, saying that anybody who had had her opportunities to see the struggles of poor abandoned women to support their children, found it impossible to write anything which would however remotely justify the loosening of marriage bonds, whether there had really been any such "loosening" in Gorki's case or not. Exactly what happened next will never be known until James Keeley's own biography, now said to be in course of preparation, is published. Mayor Dunne presently started a libel suit against the *Tribune,* for remarks about his school-board appointees, of whom Jane Addams was one. And a few months after the interview with Mr. Keeley, a most extraordinary version of it was made the substance of evidence presented to the grand jury to show that Jane Addams was not the sort of person who could be libeled! Mr. Keeley often said, to this biographer, that he never knew how the stuff came to be so used, and that he personally had it thrown out; and there is a trace of evidence that it was fetched forth by Democratic politicians to be used as a roorback against the *Tribune.* But in any case, the publicity given to the incident again subjected her to an unpleasant correspondence.

That Jane Addams should never hesitate to move for justice to the individual was inevitable. The desire for fairness was as much a part of her nature as her blood was part of her life ; had either ceased to circulate she would have been dead. Again and again large endowments have been lost to Hull House because of the disapproval such movements for justice have engendered in individuals; but she could no more take that into consideration than she could steal. Indeed, to take it into final consideration she would regard as stealing—stealing for the House! What she did not enjoy was the tremendous effort necessary to get at the facts in these individual cases, to understand them rightly. As she has said: "If the under dog were always right, one might easily always try to defend him. The trouble is that very often he is but obscurely right, sometimes only partly right, and often quite wrong!" Quaintly she added once, when this remark was called to her attention, "like myself, for instance!"

For four years of this first decade of the century, from 1905 to 1909, she was a member of the Chicago School Board. In her autobiography she speaks of herself in this connection as "having played a most inglorious part." The extremists of both parties in the struggle that went on throughout those four years might agree with that statement. The newspaper organ of the traction companies declared that she had "sold out" to the radicals; the organ of the Teachers' Federation declared bitterly that she had gone over to the capitalists. The story is worth telling in some detail. Except her garbage-inspectorship (which by the way she never dropped from the short list of her accomplishments in *Who's Who*) this place on the School Board which she never included in *Who's Who*, was the only municipal position she ever held.

In 1905 the situation of the schools was politically, financially, and educationally very complicated. The successive Boards of Education which had been appointed by Mayor Carter Harrison, the younger, during the eight years of his four successive terms, 1897 to 1905, had stood stoutly against the graft that corroded some other municipal departments, and had stayed within the limits of their tax-appropriations. In the late 'nineties the curriculum of the public schools had been revised, partly in accordance with the suggestions of a "commission" headed by President W. R. Harper of the University of Chicago, and Chicago boasted that this curriculum was "scientifically devised" and "the best in the country." To handle the schools the Board had appointed a two-fisted, independent Superintendent, paid him $10,000 a year, a huge salary for those days, and given him dictatorial powers. But in consequence of this rigorous procedure there was trouble with the teachers. The larger number of the teachers were members of the Teachers' Federation, a union in good standing after 1902, and they fretted individually and as an organization against the rigidity of the administrative control. They objected to the low salary rates which the economical boards established, and they objected almost more strenuously to the fact that as teachers they had little or nothing to say about the curricula.

Their great fight was however made for better pay— the easiest fight for which to enlist volunteers. They insisted that many corporations and particularly the public utility groups were tax-dodgers. In 1899, they proved, $235,000,000 of value of public utility corporations paid no taxes whatever. The Teachers' Federation brought suit, and after a fierce legal battle got a State Supreme Court order that the corporations mentioned in the suit should be taxed; with a resulting increase of more than $250,000 a year in the annual income of the Board, and a still greater increase, perhaps, in the dislike of the corporations for unions and for the teachers in particular. Most of the members of the Board of Education were in sympathy with the corporation views, and to the disgust of the teachers, salaries were still not advanced, though the teachers' own efforts had provided the increase in income. Thereupon the Federation brought another suit, in 1904, this time against the Board of Education itself, to compel the advance of salaries, on the ground that it had been promised when the money for it should be available. The lower court, Judge Edward F. Dunne presiding, decided in favor of the Federation, but the Board appealed from the decision.

At this time, in the spring of 1905, after this eight-year battle, Judge Dunne, a thin-faced, quick-witted, genial, aspiring Irish-American, born in Connecticut, was elected Mayor of Chicago. He was an out-and-out advocate of municipal ownership of public utilities. Against him in the campaign the Republicans had put up a burly, wordy, self-asserting, well-meaning lawyer, John Maynard Harlan, and the campaign had been a fierce one. The city was curiously split, almost as the border states had been in the Civil War. Most of the "prominent citizens" and most of the newspapers were for Harlan; the Hearst paper, and the common people were for Dunne. Joseph Medill Patterson, twenty-six year old grandson of Joseph Medill, stumped for Dunne, although the *Tribune* which his family owned was Dunne's (and the Teachers' Federation's) most virulent opponent. Harlan called Hearst "the Daily Assassin." Dunne and Joe Patterson called Yerkes and J. Pierpont Morgan—who had recently become a large purchaser of traction stocks, and who greatly to his own surprise became a big figure in the campaign—bloodsuckers and enemies of the people, "malefactors of great wealth." Harlan said Dunne was eager to rob the rich, not to speak of the "widows and orphans." Dunne said Harlan was the champion of the absentee landlords of capitalism. It was all very spirited, sentimental, and assertive; but Dunne was sincere and Harlan was shallow, and for once sincerity triumphed; or perhaps it was only that Chicago was "naturally democratic" in those days, and Dunne headed the Democratic ticket. The Teachers' Federation backed him eagerly, led by the fiery "Maggie" Haley. What constitutions those old campaigners had! Thirty years later Dunne and Harlan, the retiring Mayor Carter Harrison, Joe Patterson and Margaret Haley, are all still alive and vigorous, with their natural forces unabated.

Dunne promptly appointed seven new members to the Board of Education, Jane Addams among them. Others were Raymond Robins, Doctor Cornelia DeBey, Mrs. Emmons Blaine, Louis F. Post, Wiley W. Mills, theorists and even radicals according to the view of the best people of the city. Judge Dunne had given a favorable decision in the teachers' suit. It seemed clear to the members of the Commercial Club and to the newspaper publishers that he had determined to put the Teachers' Federation in the educational saddle. That he *had* done so seemed equally clear, when the new Board, in spite of the fact that there were fourteen hold-over members, promptly voted to withdraw the appeal of the suit. The mayor, however, had had no such idea. Himself an idealist, he had merely proceeded upon the belief, as Jane

Addams subsequently phrased it, "that if those citizens representing social ideals and reform principles were but placed in office, public welfare must be established."

Jane Addams herself did not fully share this belief. Long before, when the first child-labor law had failed, she had concluded that nothing final in the way of "reform" could be accomplished until the time was ripe for it, that information and ethical education by shared experiences must precede action if action was to be effective, that many little things had to be done day by day and year by year till society was ready for the doing of the big thing, that agreement could only be reached after the fullest opportunity for the expression of differences of opinion: "I thought that life had taught me at least one hard-learned lesson, that existing arrangements and the hoped for improvements must be mediated and reconciled to each other, that the new must be dovetailed into the old, as it were, if it were to endure."

In deference to her civic reputation she was made chairman of the most important committee of the board, the School Management Committee. It was a distinguished committee. Mrs. Blaine was a member, and Doctor Cornelia DeBey—one of Chicago's "five maiden aunts" according to William Hard, and a fighter of the type of Mrs. Florence Kelley. Louis F. Post, "single-taxer" pre-ëminent after Henry George, and editor of that most constantly readable of propagandist magazines, *The Public,* was a member; John J. Sonsteby, now chief justice of the Chicago Municipal Court; Wiley W. Mills; and P. Shelley O'Ryan, a fighting Irish citizen to whom Jane Addams often referred in later days. "He always disapproved of me but he always liked me," she said once.

The Committee had to consider all salary increases, all problems of the voice of the teachers in school management, all selection of textbooks.

As usual she began by trying to get at the exact facts. She found that under Mayor Harrison the majority of the Board had made "economy and administrative efficiency" their watchword, and had to some extent attained it. But the capacity of the school buildings was so limited that 11,000 children could attend for half-day sessions only, and 10,000 more were taught in rented buildings. The education in the grades had been kept narrow and monotonous in the determination to keep it "cheap." And the teachers were regarded exclusively as employees, no more to be considered in curriculum policy than the motormen and conductors of the street-cars were to be considered in the policies of the traction company; "somewhat servile," however well trained.

The promotion of these teachers was dependent on, first, a percentage system based on "secret" markings made semi-annually by principals; second on examination, given also for entrance, administered by the superintendent, and third, promotional examinations given at the end of seven years' service, unless the teacher presented evidence of having taken a course of study in an academic degree-giving institution or a normal school. It was around this system of secret marking for promotions that the great fight centered. In 1906 Doctor DeBey offered a resolution demanded by the Chicago Federation of Labor for the abolition of secret marking; it was lost, but she succeeded in having a committee appointed to study the question. This committee held meetings for public discussion from July to December in 1906. These meetings were ridiculed by the Chicago press: "So anxious are the new Board members to have democracy that they are losing the advantage which they might have gained by railroading their scheme through the committee and passing it at the next Board meeting in like fashion.... Preferring consultation to action, they are to call in the general public and thus allow opposition to crystallize."

Such was the common editorial, possibly the common public, opinion. But of course "railroading" was exactly what Jane Addams did not want. As usual what she wanted was to understand all points of view. She knew that the former Harrison boards had "taken the schools out of politics," and they had taken graft out of the schools. In the "bad old days" the politicians had often not only dictated appointments of janitors, engineers, even of teachers; not only taken a rake-off on all contracts for new buildings, supplies, school-books; but had even winked at actual stealing of such supplies. Harrison's Boards had stopped that. Bernard F. Rogers, a co-grandfather of this biographer, who was in the thick of that fight, often grows dramatically reminiscential over what now and then became literally hand-to-hand encounters with the political thieves of the late 'nineties and early 1900's. All of which was a genuine fulfilment of a business ideal.

Jane Addams found on the other hand that "the teachers inside the system were unfortunately so restricted they had no space in which to move about freely, and the more adventurous of them fairly panted for light and air."

They complained with justice that Doctor Harper's

"promotional examination system" tested them not as teachers but as students, and that the time which study for these examinations required was more than the long hours of teaching and consultation permitted; and with equal justice that they were not as well paid for their heavy work as teachers in other city systems were paid. They declared that the all-powerful Superintendent was not so much efficient as dictatorial; and they protested that the "graft" had merely been transferred from the politician-contractors to the businessmen tax-dodgers, who were allowed to reap the profits of the policy of economy and tax evasion which had been established and maintained. There were no more rake-offs on coal-contracts, no more big "commissions" on school-book adoptions; but there were still larger rake-offs on leases of school property in the Loop, one splendid lot of which for example was used by the Chicago *Tribune* at a rent which according to Margaret Haley was a "steal." Finally Jane Addams found that every statement made by the members of the Harrison boards could be proved, whereas some of the statements of the Teachers' Federation and of the individual teachers could be accepted only as theories or even as charges. She found herself standing in other words between a benevolent would-be autocracy, and an indignant scrambling democracy; and though her whole sympathy, then as always, was with the democratic principle, she could then as always move forward only as she felt the ground reasonably firm under her feet.

For promotion there was presently offered what was called the "Post Plan," an elaborate and thoroughgoing program, which replaced secret marking by simple gradings of "efficient" or "inefficient" by the principals, with a description of the teacher if they chose to give it; the descriptions not to be public, but the teachers to be allowed to know their ratings. Under Jane Addams's guidance this plan became what she herself calls "emasculated," what was called by her friends at the time "practical." She was called "the Great Compromiser," the "Henry Clay of Chicago." For her clause permitting every teacher after seven years of service to attend classes of the "normal extension department" one afternoon weekly for ten weeks, in alternate years, without having pay docked, she was also called "an exemplar of futility," "an estimable but hobby-riding woman, to put whom at the head of the school system is like turning over the command of a battleship to a well-intentioned naval apprentice."

That the protagonists of both parties were unfair to one another did not of course help the situation. Both parties felt that they were fighting for a principle, but both "inevitably exaggerated the difficulties of the situation." Jane Addams says: "I at least became convinced that partizans would never tolerate the use of stepping-stones. They are much too impatient to look on while a beloved scheme is unstably balanced, and they would rather see it tumble into the stream at once than have it brought to land in a half-hearted fashion.... My efforts were looked upon as compromising and unworthy by both parties."

The appointments to the Board were attacked as illegal, and a majority of them were dismissed by Mayor Busse, who succeeded Mayor Dunne in 1907. A court decision reinstated some but not all. The salaries which had been promised years before were paid, but only to the members of the Federation which had brought the suit. The plans for educational reform which involved spending money, such as the building of smaller school-rooms to prevent overcrowding of classes automatically, the extension of the plan of "truancy rooms," the multiplication of school playgrounds, were all blocked; and on the other hand one scheme after another devised to shift the emphasis on advancement of the teachers through study of "subjects," to an emphasis on advancement through demonstration of teaching competence, was "impatiently repudiated" by the teachers as not sufficiently thoroughgoing. In the opinion of the general public, the affairs of the schools were unprecedentedly chaotic.

This particular public opinion was carefully fostered by two of the local newspapers. The *Tribune* of course was directly implicated: its lease of school property had been and remained the greatest "bone of contention" so far as the Teachers' Federation was concerned, and the Dunne board sued to cancel that lease. The *Inter-Ocean* was financially involved with the traction interests; and even the rest were violently opposed to Mayor Dunne's ideas of municipal ownership, and therefore were compelled to opposition to his Board of Education. The position of the *Tribune* was that the members of the Dunne board were "radicals," "theorists," "raw reformers" and "boodlers" and so the most effective method of attack upon them was by ridicule and misrepresentation. Looking back over the files for those years, one sees how hopeless it was for the members of the Board to get a genuine public hearing. The Board emphasized the policy of "open" meetings, but the meetings turned out to be open only to the few who actually attended and listened. The newspaper reports of what was said bore little resemblance to the facts:

> I recall the surprise and indignation of a University professor who had consented to speak at a meeting arranged in the Board rooms, when next morning his non-partisan and careful disquisition had been twisted into the most arrant uplift nonsense, and so connected with a fake newspaper report of a trial marriage address delivered not by himself but by a colleague, that a leading clergyman of the city, having read the account, felt impelled to preach a sermon calling on all decent people to rally against the doctrines which were being taught to the children by an immoral school Board.

It is fair to say that Jane Addams was less ridiculed in all this than some of her colleagues were. She indulged in no eccentricities of dress or speech, and was extraordinarily careful in "open" meetings or interviews to make no reference that could be twisted into either abuse or prophecy. It was at this time, however, rather than earlier, that she reached the conclusion about newspapers in general which she subsequently phrased: "The press, with the opportunity of determining opinion by selecting data, assumes the power once exercised by the church when it gave the people only such knowledge as it deemed fit for them to have."

Her steady effort throughout the two years of her chairmanship of the School Management Committee was to make the schools precisely what she had tried to make Hull House, "a center—indeed in the case of the schools the great center—for a higher civic and social life," among, of course, the children. Her educational theories did not center round discipline so much as round stimulation, the arousal of interests and the increasing of opportunities among the children to pursue and determine those interests. To the three Rs, "readin', 'ritin', and 'rithmetic," she would add a fourth, recreation—mental, physical, social recreation. She was not in the least afraid of what much later came to be called "fads and frills" in the schools. The John Dewey principles of education, of getting children to *want* to study and *want* to understand, had had a chance of application only to selected privileged groups of children. Jane Addams was much interested in the Dewey principles, but she was still more interested in increasing the number of privileged groups. She would have liked to see everybody in the public schools "privileged" in the same fashion. She had gone to live at Hull House with the idea of sharing what she had with those who had not the same things, and of getting them to share with her what they had— the democratic, not the socialistic sharing-system. She went on the School Management Committee, as a representative of the community, with the same idea: the community should afford the children a wider opportunity, in the expectation that the children as they grew up would be able to do more for the community. It was theoretical only in the sense that democracy is theoretical, for it was merely the application of the theory of democracy to education: "Our schools must give the children better and truer standards for judging life. Life does not ask whether a man can read and write, so much as it asks whether he can use whatever faculties have been given him."

So she had declared years before she went on the Board, and she had further insisted that the school curriculum must be adapted to both the preservation of old loyalties and the cultivation of a new understanding:

> You will not be able to substitute anything half so valuable as the child's loyalty to his parents and his home traditions, even if you succeed in making an Italian child fluent in the perusal of the Third Reader in English. You must not take away, you must add. The uneducated person is he who is bound by what he always knew. It is true that a child who goes along a country road oblivious to its beauty and unable to distinguish one bird-call from another has not been properly taught, but has he been properly taught if he never learns to recognize that the Greek peddling bananas at the corner once wakened every morning in sight of the Acropolis, and what that sight has meant to him? It is wrong everywhere, particularly wrong in a heterogeneous city like Chicago, to draw a line between the study of a pollywog in a glass, and the study of communities of human beings.

This was all no doubt theoretical, but in her efforts to permit the schools to give the children "standards for judging life," and training to "use whatever faculties have been given him," she was entirely practical. Her failure to get all she sought was due neither to any vagueness in her objectives, nor to any extravagance or eccentricity in the methods she wished employed. She lacked pugnacity, and she lacked political power. If she had been capable of permitting a single purpose to overmaster her and determine every act, she might have lined up the forces of the teachers and the parents behind her, and driven ahead to an immediate victory. If she had been a man with a vote, she might have organized some achievement which public opinion would have accepted as an effective compromise. But she could no more be a fanatic than she could be a man. She was a prophet called upon to be a general, and angels do not make good brigadiers.

It was just as well. Any sort of complete achievement would have been thrown into the discard by the extraordinary municipal administrations that were to be demanded and secured by the followers of William Hale Thompson later. And she did as much as any one to promote in Chicago the recreational principle in public school education. She went out of office finally presumed by some businessmen to be merely a visionary, and on the other hand, accused by the Federation of having in effect "sold out" to the businessmen, of "having had her opportunity and deliberately thrown it away," of having betrayed her principles like Ichabod. But to this day her influence for vitality in the school curriculum is mentioned. Schools have been named for her East and West. Until her death she was the only board-member whom people still remember as once having been a board member.

In fact, Mayor Busse's (Dunne's successor) refusal to reappoint her to the Board may even have had some slight effect on the local estimate of her as a good citizen. More than a few regarded her, to her own amusement, as having been martyred. Not long afterward the Chicago Association of Commerce elected her to honorary membership, the first woman to be so elected. She had talked to them on "social centers in schools," and ignoring their own constitution and by-laws they invited her in—which, as an envious Pittsburgh editor commented ironically, "is a high honor even for so august a body as the Chicago Association of Commerce."

Indeed, in 1910, her fiftieth year, Jane Addams may be said to have reached outside of Chicago a state almost imperial among American women. The year began inauspiciously enough with ill-health—an appendicitis operation in December of 1909, her second of the sort in twelve years, with a slow painful recovery that did not permit her to get back to work for two months. But after that the deluge of acclamation. She quoted to Mrs. Kelley with a smile the Biblical warning "Woe unto you when all men speak well of you!" to which Mrs. Kelley replied, "You'd better say 'Lawk a mercy on me, this is none of I!' "

The same Pittsburgh editor remarked, "Let the devotees of T. R., Taft, and the Hon. James J. Jeffries wrangle over who is to be called our *first* citizen; the country unanimously nominates Jane Addams of Hull House as our *second* citizen." The militant Miss Sylvia Pankhurst said, "Your American presidents come and go, and we in England often do not remember their names, but we all know Jane Addams, and can never forget her." As the first woman president of the National Conference of Charities and Corrections, she presided at the St. Louis conference, and made a speech which "stirred the nation to understanding," it was declared; indeed, it was one of her ablest, though it was a mere realinement of her previous steady thinking, with a practical foreshadowing of widows' pensions, against a half-mystical illumination of "the mysterious shortcomings on the part of life itself, the grief of things as they are." Yale offered her an honorary degree in June, the first honorary degree Yale had ever offered a woman, and almost every editor in the country applauded. "She has had a prophetic vision of what might be done and militant courage united with a high order of administrative, social

JANE ADDAMS AT FIFTY

In 1910, her fiftieth year, she may be said to have reached a state almost imperial among American women.

and political capacity in doing and getting it done," declared Professor Bernadotte Perrin at the exercises. John Burroughs and James J. Hill also received degrees, but Jane Addams got all the notice. *"Dux femina facti,"* said the learned graduates at that commencement. "Abou ben Addams's name led all the rest." She founded that continuing institution, the Chicago Woman's City Club, in the same month. Smith College—which she had wished to attend when she was seventeen—made her an LL.D. at the inauguration of its new president in October. The mayor of Northampton, Calvin Coolidge by name, walked in the procession. Julia Ward Howe, ninety-five years of age, sat together with Jane Addams and heard the crowd sing *The Battle Hymn of the Republic,* "Mine eyes have seen the glory of the coming of the Lord." "We women have not won the battle yet, for the Lord or for ourselves," the grand old author of the grand old hymn said gently afterward. The Illinois Equal Suffrage Association urged Jane Addams for United States Senator, and male editors down state remarked that "she has shown all the qualities Illinois senators should possess, but alas do not. The Senate has a lot of old women in it now; the advent among them of a live young one will have a beneficial effect." A visiting actress from Australia admitted that she had never heard of Lake Michigan or the Chicago stockyards "but there is a hospital ward in Sydney," she said, "to furnish which we all helped in a benefit, which is dedicated to Jane Addams. Is she really the only woman in America? She is the only one our papers quote." And the Chicago *Record-Herald* wound up the year by remarking editorially: "Who are the first five citizens of Chicago? Of course there can be no doubt of the first—Jane Addams leads all the rest. Next, we think, comes Julius Rosenwald. The remaining three we shall leave to be thought out by our readers."

One of her most dramatic and yet Addams-like accomplishments of the year was her intervention in the garment-workers' strike. On September 29th a sixteen-year-old girl, a "seamer," walked out of one of the shops of Hart, Schaffner and Marx because five weeks before her foreman had ordered her pay reduced a quarter of a cent per garment. She did not think of herself as a "striker," or even know there was a garment-workers' union. But nineteen other girls followed her out; the news spread; and within three weeks almost every garment-worker in the city was out, not only in the pleasant shops of Hart, Schaffner and Marx, but in the little places that almost carried on the old sweat-shop traditions. Jane Addams was asked to help arbitrate. An agreement was drawn up. When it was presently submitted to the arbitration committee of three, she found it had a new clause in it, prohibiting any form of collective bargaining. The international president of the garment-workers' union signed it; it was, he said, the best they could get. "Your own people will never agree," Jane Addams said, and refused to sign. She was right. The strikers hooted the agreement and their president down. Every worker quit; there were 90,000 out. The weeks dragged on. Jane Addams stood firm for collective bargaining; without it, she insisted, there would be only constantly recurring trouble. To her amazement public opinion was largely with her. In the end, but not by the end of the year, a collective bargaining agreement was reached. Hart, Schaffner and Marx became the leaders in unionized industry in their field. Harry Hart, president of the company, remained a devoted friend of Jane Addams. So did Sidney Hillman, the head of the garment-workers. Perhaps no more effective bit of arbitrative influence was ever shown in a labor dispute than hers in this great strike.

And yet not her doing but her thinking marked those days. For it was just at this time that she was bringing out *The Spirit of Youth in the City Streets,* and *Twenty Years at Hull House.*

CHAPTER XII

A DECADE OF WRITING

JANE ADDAMS made her reputation as a speaker in the first ten years of her Hull House life, her reputation as a writer in the second ten years. In the 'nineties she talked of social principles and social ideals before women's clubs and businessmen's associations, legislative committees and labor union assemblies, summer schools and winter congresses, in Chicago; Springfield, Illinois; San Francisco; New Orleans, Louisiana; Boston; New York; always on the basis of her own thinking and always with illustrations drawn from her daily life. Of such illustrations she had an inexhaustible source of supply. In the course of a day at Hull House she would often listen to the pitiful or defiant experiences of dozens and scores of people, and her acquaintance among the neighbors ran up into the thousands. Indeed it was even wider than the alderman's. "Nobody round here knows me any more," said an old man once, " 'cept, of course, Miss Addams." So she had an almost unlimited variety of ideas, notions, points of view to draw upon. She lightened and vivified all her generalizations with abundant anecdote, funny or tragic. In the one talk on "Ethical Survivals in City Politics," for instance, there are more than fifty such illustrations from life. Presently she began to rewrite these talks as magazine articles, for the *Forum,* the *North American Review,* the *Atlantic Monthly,* the

American Journal of Sociology, the *International Journal of Ethics.*

Then, in the second ten years at Hull House, she began collecting these articles into books, rewriting them again, amplifying or condensing them, developing them into coherent series. Four such books appeared in that second decade, *Democracy and Social Ethics* in 1902, *Newer Ideals of Peace* in 1907, *The Spirit of Youth and the City Streets* in 1909, and the best known of all, *Twenty Years at Hull House,* in 1910. It is possible that Riis and Spargo were more widely read, that Small and Ross had a higher reputation as scholars; there was not a touch in Jane Addams's work either of the sensational or of the academic. But it is no exaggeration to say that she had a greater influence on American thought and action than any of them. She in her sort of speculation, William James in his sort, stood foremost in America in those years, and side by side.

In all her books, the later as well as the earlier, there is the same eagerness to state the whole truth, the same capacity to state nothing but the truth, that indeed had characterized her self-expression from her earliest years, an eagerness and an insight that even her girlish notebooks and her earliest letters to Ellen Starr reveal. One does not know whether to regard more highly the freshness of her thought or the vigor of her imagination. She was the foremost psychologist of democracy in the world, without an equal in her social intuition; and her style was called by the critics of the day not only "masterly" but "revolutionary." In two of the books of this particular decade, *Twenty Years at Hull House* and *The Spirit of Youth,* the style as such is particularly noteworthy; so it becomes again later in *The Long Road of Woman's Memory*, and in the collection of her memorial addresses which she published in 1932 under the Platonic title of *The Excellent Becomes the Permanent*. These four are and will remain classics of American literature, as sure of immortality as anything published in this country in their time; ranking with the best decisions of Judge Oliver Wendell Holmes, the best poetry of William Vaughn Moody, and the best novelistic work of Willa Cather.

But in these, as in the others, it is most clearly the thinking that strikes home. Jane Addams read everything in her field, had a vast personal experience, wrote well, but it is the inferences she drew that are most startling, after all. She seems almost never to have written anything which is not rich with wisdom. There was an old custom, not undesirable, either, of making selections from the work of some great author and publishing them apart from their contexts as representative of the author's work as a whole. Whoever shall thus select from Jane Addams will be overwhelmed with riches. *The Excellent Becomes the Permanent* should become almost a handbook at gravesides. To select from *The Spirit of Youth* is almost to reprint the volume. The chapter on memories in Egypt, which she somewhat wistfully republished in *The Excellent Becomes the Permanent*, after first including it in *The Long Road of Woman's Memory*, is one superb jewel of thought.

Some summarization of these first books of hers must nevertheless be attempted, because they are all hooked so closely into her Hull House and Chicago experience, that they positively reflect her daily life. For instance, the chapters in *Democracy and Social Ethics* include much of the material she gathered when she was an arbitrator in the Pullman strike, when she was working for the passage of the first child-labor bill in Illinois, and when she was campaigning against Alderman John Powers. She calls the book "the substance of twelve lectures which have been delivered at various colleges and university extension centers," and she herself conceived of it as a sort of textbook on sociology, but her personality vivified it into much more than a textbook.

Her thesis throughout, that individual morality, however far it may have grown automatic, is nevertheless in a democracy not enough; "to pride one's self on the results of personal effort, when the time demands social adjustment, is utterly to fail to comprehend the situation." We meet the obligations of family life spontaneously, because of a common fund of memories and affections from which the obligation naturally develops? Very well; "we see no other way in which to prepare ourselves for the large, social duties":

By our daily experience we have discovered that we cannot mechanically hold up a moral standard, then jump at it in rare moments of exhilaration when we have the strength, but that even as the ideal itself must be a rational development of life, so the strength to attain it must be secured from an interest in life itself. We slowly learn that *life consists of processes as well as results,* and that failure may come quite as easily from ignoring the adequacy of one's method as from selfish or ignoble aims. We are thus brought to the conception of Democracy, not merely as a sentiment which desires the well-being of all men, nor yet as a creed which believes in the essential dignity and equality of all men, but as that *which affords a rule of living* as well as a test of faith.

Anybody who wants to "understand" Jane Addams would do well to read that paragraph over again. Her philosophy is founded on it. In it one can perceive her belief in the limitations of the Victorian creeds—the heroic creed of Carlyle, the feudalistic creed of Ruskin, the humanistic and paternalistic creed of Arnold, even the politically idealistic creed of Thomas Jefferson. From Democracy, since it is in Democracy we live, must come our ethics; it is the inspiration of our social righteousness, which must not only transcend, but even transform, our individual righteousness.

She applies this test to charitable effort of all sorts. We are learning to judge men by their *social* virtues, their devotion to disinterested aims, their public spirit; we have ceased to accord exclusive respect to the "money-earning capacity"; and therefore we not only "naturally resent being obliged to judge 'poor' people solely upon the industrial side, ... but at bottom distrust a little a scheme which substitutes a theory of social conduct for the natural promptings of the human heart." That distrust by 1933 had spread widely. Sociology had become a science like economics, it is true; but it is also true that the present scheme of state and Federal relief is not based on merit, but on need and need alone, and when President Roosevelt announced that nobody would be allowed to starve, he was committing the very Government to a policy of pity and kindness.

Our hunger for social righteousness, Jane Addams goes on to point out, has a tendency to transform filial relations, to advance a claim "which in a certain sense is larger than the family claim." War takes sons, husbands, even fathers of little children, for the service of society, and

if we can once see the claim of society in peace in such a light, if its misery and need can be made clear and urged as an explicit claim, as the state urges its claim in time of danger, then for the first time the daughters who leave their homes in the desire to minister to that need, will be recognized as acting conscientiously.... But the family in its entirety must be carried out into the larger life, its various members together must recognize and acknowledge the validity of the social obligation.... Doubtless, woman's education is at fault, in that it has failed to recognize certain needs, and has failed to culti-vate and guide the larger desires of which all generous young hearts are full.

Family and household relations concern her deeply. She pleads for the young women who leave their homes to minister to the larger need of society; and she urges the consideration of the social ethics of the household. What should be our attitude to "that one alien in the household, neither loved nor loving," the domestic ser-vant?:

The modern family has dropped the man who made its shoes, the woman who spun its clothes, and to a large extent the woman who washes them, but it stoutly refuses to drop the woman who cooks its food; it strangely insists that to do that would be to destroy the family life itself.... An employer in one of our suburbs built a bay at the back of her house so that her cook might have a pleasant room in which to sleep, and another in which to receive her friends. This employer naturally felt aggrieved when the cook refused to stay in her bay. Yet, viewed in a historic light, the employer might quite as well have added a bay to her house for her shoemaker, and then deemed him ungrateful when he declined to live in it.

Historically Jane Addams was right as usual. She was right again in asserting that "the enterprising girls of the community go into factories and offices, and the less enterprising into households ... the girl in the household is not in the rising movement"; and finally, right in declaring that "some employers of domestic labor grow capricious and over-exacting through sheer lack of larger interests to occupy their minds." But her conviction that "domestic service is yielding to the influence of a democratic movement, and is emerging from the narrower code of family ethics into the larger code governing social relations" does not seem to have been borne out by time. Though many more than in that period a generation ago "apprehend the tendency of our age," the conditions of this particular industry of domestic service have not yet been adapted to it, and that industry is still "out of line ethically."

The rest of *Democracy and Social Ethics* is given up to the problems of industrial amelioration and political reform, and the discussion is based chiefly on papers which have already been considered—on the Pullman strike, the labor-unions, and the aldermanic campaigns. The note of all three is struck in the following sentence: "If the need of the times demands associated effort, it may easily be true that the action which appears ineffective, and yet is carried out upon the more highly developed line of associated effort, may represent a finer social quality and have a greater social value than the more effective individual action."

This, rightly or wrongly, was her conviction. It was in this conviction that later as chairman of the School Management Committee on the Board of Education, she was constantly to call conferences for discussion, rather than force through what she individually thought best; still later, took the great Bull Moose by the horns; and finally founded the Women's International League for Peace and Freedom.

Her next book, *Newer Ideals of Peace,* will be left for consideration in connection with her forty-year struggle for a closer intimacy of nations. One turns with a lift of the spirit to her volume of purest charm, most eager sympathy, and perhaps keenest understanding, *The Spirit of Youth and the City Streets.*

The genesis of the work may be found in her own simple statement, already quoted, of her own interests and high privilege as a child:

We carried on games and crusades which lasted week after week, and even summer after summer, as only free-ranging country children can do. . . . One of the most piteous aspects in the life of city children as I have seen it in the neighborhood of Hull House, is the constant interruption to their play . . . so that it can never have any continuity; the most elaborate plan or chart, or "fragment from their dream of human life" is sure to be rudely destroyed by passing traffic. . . . Even the most vivacious become worn out at last.

Youth, says Jane Addams, demands a pattern for the organization of its eternal drama of adventure, romance, bold dreams, and high ideals. What recognition does the city give to youth's insistence? This is the thesis of *The Spirit of Youth and the City Streets.*

"Nothing is more certain," it begins, "than that each generation longs for a reassurance as to the value and charm of life, and is secretly afraid lest it lose its sense of the youth of the earth." And it ends, "We may either smother the divine fire of youth, or we may feed it. We may either stand stupidly staring as it sinks into a murky fire of crime and flares into the intermittent blaze of folly, or we may tend it into a lambent flame with power to make clean and bright our dingy city streets." Between those sentences lie, in shapes of beauty, the fruits of Jane Addams's own rich cultivation of experience and knowledge of young people; specific instances, brilliantly synthesized into a creed and a challenge.

That experience and knowledge were as specific as any sociologist in the country possessed. Children of twenty nationalities came to Hull House, and in 1909 had been coming there in greater and greater numbers for twenty years. She knew them personally by hundreds, even by thousands, and to them she was no legend of mere graciousness, no "lady of God" as some of their parents called her, but a friend, a protector, and a shelter in the time of storm. It is no exaggeration to say that many of them felt that they knew her better than they knew their own fathers and mothers. Because she was there, "we walked into Hull House more confidently than into our own houses," as a middle-aged editor of a Greek paper who had been a boy at Hull House said when she died. The boys and the girls, the young men and the young women, talked to her about themselves by hundreds, as freely as she had talked to her own father, as your children, you mother who reads this, talk to you; not because they loved her, but because they knew she loved them. If a little girl was beaten by her drunken father, she came crying to Hull House to tell Miss Addams; if a boy playing in the court broke a Hull House window, he did not run away, but stayed where he was, confident that Miss Addams would "fix it." Girls who had been arrested for picketing, girls who were in love, girls who were "in trouble," girls who had been caught in raids by the police, girls who had no "right dress" to be married in, girls who were "afraid they were going crazy," came to see her or sent for her as a matter of course. Young thieves consulted her, young vagabonds of all sorts, driven to malicious mischief or crime by their own desires or by that stress of circumstances for which we began to feel long ago that in general society is partly if not largely responsible, but in regard to the individual are hardly ever able, most of us, to feel anything but indignation, resentment, and the wish to revenge. One young man, a murderer in quick passion, in self-defense, he insisted, fled to Hull House ahead of the police, to be followed also ahead of the police by a member of the murdered man's family, who like the killer himself had run to Miss Addams to see what should be done. She shrank from no young thing, no matter what it had been or done. One man who passed her coffin when she lay in Bowen Hall, a saloon-keeper of the neighborhood, said proudly, "She tell me once when I was a bad kid, now she get me off and I be a good boy, and I am a good boy since then, you bet you, and my kids they are good kids too."

This intimate experience was not chiefly, however, with young people in trouble of any sort. It was still larger with the eager and the thwarted. Her belief was not in the cure but in the prevention of the ills of youth. From the kindergarten to the stage and the university, she knew young people for whom Hull House had provided opportunity. From the very beginning until to-day, after

school hours all the available rooms at Hull House are
occupied by children's clubs and classes. That was so in
1889, when three such rooms were available; it is so
now, when a thousand children a week find room there
to sing, to dance, to act, to draw, to read poetry, to practise the household arts, and to play games. The Boys'
Club alone affords five stories for such opportunities.
The Art School was started in the second year of Hull
House, the Music School in the fourth year, the dramatic association, oldest in America of the little-theater
groups, in the ninth year; though the children had been
giving plays at Hull House long before that. For boys
and girls, young men and women, so far as organized
play and the development of the esthetic interests are
concerned, Hull House was started in exactly the same
spirit that Cornell University was. "I want a place," said
Ezra Cornell nobly, "to which anybody in the world who
wants to study anything intelligently can come and study
it." Jane Addams wanted a place to which any child in
the neighborhood who wanted to exercise his or her
young imagination could come and exercise it. And as
they came in thousands and thousands through the years,
she got to know them at their best, as when they came
in trouble she got to know them at their worst. Only,
for her, they were all of a piece, best and worst; all seeking, rightly perhaps or wrongly perhaps, fulfilment of
their longings and desires, all working out in some fashion
the eternal spirit of youth. Of all things about Jane
Addams, this persistent belief in young humanity is the
most difficult to refrain from eulogizing. Every mother
worth the name has it for her own children; that is why
the word mother is to so many of us the dearest in the

Photograph by Wallace W. Kirkland

MUSIC COTTAGE AT THE BOWEN "COUNTRY CLUB,"
WAUKEGAN, ILLINOIS

One of the many social-service activities associated with Hull House.

Photograph by Wallace W. Kirkland

THE DINING-ROOM AT HULL HOUSE

As usual, Jane Addams dined with the residents.

language. But to have it for the children of others is less usual.

A study of youth based on personal experience alone, however, though the experience were as wide as that of Jane Addams, would be slighter in sociological value than is *The Spirit of Youth and the City Streets*. Jane Addams was a scholar and an authority. Her investigations into the conditions of children both at work and at play had been exhaustive. She had read everything, statistical reports, laws in Europe and America, magazine articles, and books, that she could lay her hands on. Her old files and notebooks are full of comments on such reading. W. J. Ghent in England recognized her as the American authority on child labor in the 1890's and so did the legislators of the state of Illinois, who may be said to have voted for years, on matters of labor-legislation, either in accordance with or in defiance of the evidence presented to them by Jane Addams. Her own collated information was largely relied upon in the effort to establish the Juvenile Court in Chicago, an effort crowned with success in 1899, when the first such court anywhere in the world began its work. Her study as much as her personal experience, as she translated both into argument, led William Kent to turn over to Hull House the lots and buildings on Polk Street which were turned into the Hull House Playground in 1894—the first public playground in Chicago; and it was her arguments based on statistics and on her acquaintance with early scientific studies of child psychology that as much as anything persuaded the city to take over and develop the playground system in Chicago. Finally, it was her scholar's knowledge of the educational theories of Colonel Parker and John

Dewey, that informed her frequent talks on public school methods and curricula. "I appointed her to the School Board in 1905," says Edward F. Dunne, then Mayor of Chicago, "first because I thought we should have a woman on the Board, and second because I believed she knew as much about education as anybody." It is impossible to read *The Spirit of Youth* without realizing that Jane Addams knew the literature as well as the actualities of her subject.

Yet the real power of the little book lies not so much in the specific character of the experience and information that give it substance, as in the imagination and beauty of phrase that give it life. To summarize its six chapters—Youth in the City, The Wrecked Foundations of Domesticity, The Quest for Adventure, The House of Dreams, Youth in Industry, The Thirst for Righteousness—as *Democracy and Social Ethics* has just been summarized, would be absurd. One might better summarize Elizabeth Barrett Browning's poem, "The Cry of the Children." The book is almost as lyric, almost as poignant, as the verses are. Not even quotation at random can quite illustrate the book's quality:

The spontaneous joy, the clamor for pleasure, the desire of the young to appear finer and better and altogether more lovely than they really are, their idealization not only of each other but of the whole earth which they regard but as a theater for noble exploits, the unworldly ambitions, the romantic hopes, the make-believe world in which they live, if properly utilized, what might they not do to make our sordid cities more beautiful, more companionable! ...

When she was at last restrained by that moral compulsion, that overwhelming of another's will which is always so ruthlessly exerted by those who are conscious that virtue is struggling with vice, her mind gave way.... A poor little Ophelia, I met her one night wandering in the hall half-dressed in the tawdry pink gown that "Pierre liked best of all," and groping on the blank wall to find a door which might permit her to escape to her lover....

As though we were deaf to the appeal of these young creatures, claiming their share of the joy of life, flinging out into the dingy city their desires and aspirations after unknown realities, their unutterable longings for companionship and pleasure. Their very demand for excitement is a protest against the dullness of life, to which we ourselves instinctively respond....

What is the function of art but to preserve in permanent and lovely form those emotions and solaces which cheer life and make it kindlier, more heroic, and easier to comprehend; which lift the mind of the worker from the harshness and loneliness of his task, and by connecting him with what has gone before, free him from a besetting sense of isolation and hardship?

The Spirit of Youth was followed in 1910 by *Twenty Years at Hull House*, Jane Addams's autobiography of her first fifty years, and her confession of faith in humanity and in democracy. This story of her life, up to the present point, is largely based on that autobiography and confession; and all other stories of her life that may be subsequently written must be similarly based. The book, both factually and philosophically, is elaborate. "Writing it nearly killed me," she said once. "Didn't George Eliot say that she began Romola a young woman and finished it an old woman? I felt a good deal that way about my *Twenty Years*. It was so hard to remember far back for the first chapters, and to get the material together and organize it for the later ones. I do hate to be wrong about facts!"

"Except dates—you hardly ever give dates."

"Well, they do not seem very important in my life.

It has just flowed on. And besides, if I don't give dates, I can't be wrong about them."

One difficulty in preparing the book was the mass of her material—the mass of her recollections, the mass of her experiences, the mass of her records and clippings. Except letters, which she had the almost consistent habit of destroying as soon as they were answered, and gifts to her, which she gave to some one else as fast as she received them, she kept everything. All her early notebooks from the time she went to Rockford Seminary; engagement books, exercises in the composition of addresses, badges and buttons reminiscent of conventions she had attended as a delegate or crusades of one sort or another upon which she had embarked; and newspaper clippings, from the time she went to Hull House, innumerable. Once the clippings were filed, anybody who wished might have access to them, and a good many of them have disappeared in consequence, but there are some hundred thousand still remaining. For her *Twenty Years* she looked over them all up to 1909, as carefully listed and filed month by month by her devoted and businesslike older sister Alice Haldeman; who also had copied carefully into three fair-sized ·volumes Jane's "European letters" to the family on her two journeys abroad in 1882 to 1883 and 1887 to 1888. But the written and printed records were the least of her troubles in writing *Twenty Years*. So far as her childhood and girlhood went, she had a remarkable memory for details, coupled with a sincere desire not to "remember anything that had not happened," as she often remarked. Of these details, what to include, what to discard, in the "autobiographical notes" of *Twenty Years?* And so with her neighborhood experiences with men, women and children of all races and of all varieties, the sort of experiences with which she had already illustrated her philosophy in many talks. This book was to be neither a textbook, such as she had conceived *Democracy and Social Ethics* to be, nor yet a gauntlet thrown down before society in behalf of youth's beauty; it was to be a "faithful record of the years" and an explication of her own personality, which she honestly believed to be typical of that of the educated woman of her time. Each of the earlier books was "an attempt to set forth a thesis supported by experience"; this book was to be a setting-forth of the experiences themselves through which her conclusions had been forced upon her. She thought that "because settlements have multiplied in the United States a simple statement of an earlier effort might be of value in their interpretation, and possibly clear them of a certain charge of superficiality." Some of it was a restatement and rearrangement of material which had already been published in magazine articles; but the possession of this material only made the job harder for her, apparently. Some of the sections ot the original manuscript were such an interweaving of clippings, and elaborations and insertions and connections written in in her own by this time almost unreadable handwriting, that the final copying was really a task for a paleographic expert.

And yet out of the difficulties of her own labor and the complications of the manuscript there emerged something so coherent, so unified, so vivid and so wise that it has taken its place unchallenged now in American lit-

erature. Of the large (octavo) edition, more than fifty
thousand copies were issued in her life-time; of a smaller-
sized edition, which has been used in high schools
and colleges throughout the country, thirty thousand
copies. In any really representative biography of the first
fifty years of Jane Addams's life, or any accurate interpretation of her thought, as much has to be quoted from
Twenty Years as from all the rest of her writing, up to
1910, put together. Her single-minded purpose was to
make it a reflection of the spirit and the practice of Hull
House; but this spirit and practice were so eminently
her own, that in spite of her the story turned out to be
her own story; as much so as the complicated drama of
Hamlet is the narrative of the single character of the
Prince of Denmark.

With the publication of *Twenty Years at Hull House,*
following so soon upon *The Spirit of Youth and the City
Streets,* Jane Addams may be said to have fixed her place
of eminence in the estimation of the American public. It is
doubtful whether she was as highly regarded by the average solid citizen of Chicago as she had been ten years
before, at the turn of the century. At that time Hull
House was still what Chicago chose to regard as a successful novelty; its connection with such "radical" movements as that for the regulation of child labor had been
forgiven, it had actually popularized the conception of a
Juvenile Court, it had introduced into state and civic life
such vitalizing influences as Julia Lathrop and Louise
DeKoven Bowen, and it was known to be more highly
regarded "abroad" than even the much-advertised stockyards themselves. Jane Addams herself, too, in 1900,
was a prophet not without honor in her own home. She

had been the recipient of honors in France; she was known to be highly regarded in England; she was looked upon with indulgence by the gentlemen of the Civic Federation and the Municipal Voters' League as a woman of real intelligence who had become, though voteless, a genuine influence for local political reform; she had been called a saint, a "lady of God," "the angel of Hull House," by her neighbors, and the names had been picked up and put in the papers as news; there was about her the definite beginning of a rosy glow. That disappeared. Kropotkin's visit, the Isaak incident following McKinley's assassination, the Averbuch case, her perennial contention for more and more child-labor legislation, her association with "fanatics" on the Board of Education (who were themselves inclined to think she had deserted the "cause") all tended to dissipate the glow and to darken her reputation with the members of the Chicago Club and the Union League. John R. Walsh of the *Chronicle* and George Hinman of the *Inter-Ocean*, both editors of considerable influence in their day, left few sneers unuttered at the menace of social settlements in general, and the bad judgment (or worse, perhaps) of Jane Addams in particular; and in connection with the question of the leasing of school property, she earned the dislike of the owners of the Chicago *Tribune*. In 1910 so far as the estimation of the local "best people" were concerned, she stood lower than she had stood ten or even fifteen years before.

But outside Chicago, in the United States generally and abroad, she stood, for a time after the publication of *Twenty Years at Hull House*, at the zenith. Her intelligent interest in peace and in progress through international understanding was already known, and because nobody was aware how firmly she meant to stand by her own guns if war came, was in general approved. Theodore Roosevelt himself always visited Hull House when he came to Chicago, and called Jane Addams Chicago's most useful citizen, with a patronizing friendliness which for a time almost amounted to affection. The humorless suffragists of Boston declared in a public meeting that she was their candidate for president in 1912. The editors of the most respectable magazines besought her for articles which she had no time to write, and the demand for lectures which she had no time to give was insistent all over the country. Distinguished reviewers asserted that her books "struck a new note in American literature, higher perhaps than has ever been sounded heretofore," and that "back of them lay illimitable sympathy, immeasurable pity, a spirit as free as that of St. Francis, a sense of social order and fitness that Marcus Aurelius might have found similar to his own." It was at this time that she began to be listed as the "greatest" woman in America, whatever that phrase may mean. Then came the war, her reassertion of the ideals of peace, the renewal of the general feeling that she was, if not mistaken in her convictions, at any rate fanatic in her insistence upon their presentation, the charge that she was unpatriotic and "un-American," and her own supposition that she "would never again be applauded in Chicago." She faced the prospect not without regret that she might have weakened her influence for social reform, but without any other regret that was perceptible. When somebody quoted to her a stanza from Robert Browning's "The Patriot"—

Alack, it was I who leaped at the sun,
To give it my loving friends to keep!
Naught man could do, have I left undone
And you see my harvest, what I reap
This very day, now a year is run—

she only commented, "That was a man, and a man's way
of looking at it. I don't think I have ever been either
very much distressed by disapproval, or surprised by
misunderstanding." She was in fact to come finally to a
more general approval, and a better understanding of
what she had meant for democracy and been to humanity
than had ever been given her before. But not, after 1914,
for many years.

CHAPTER XIII

SUFFRAGE AND PROGRESSIVISM

IN 1860, the year Jane Addams was born, the year the tenth annual "suffrage convention" was held in New York, the year Susan B. Anthony could report that "the press has changed its tone; instead of ridicule we now have grave debate," a small group of men and women toured the state of Illinois on behalf of "women's rights." Their primary interest was in securing legislation to permit married women to control their own property, but they had suffrage as a bright hope in the background. They roused the sympathy of the Hon. John H. Addams, then a state senator, and constitutionally opposed to all forms of tyranny, even the tyranny of men over women, of husbands over wives. He was already aware of Miss Anthony's arguments for suffrage, and seems to have been convinced as much by them as by the appeal of the touring group at Springfield, Illinois. In the state at large, however, there seems to have been a very mild interest in women's rights. So far as voting was concerned, the next years were "the Negro's hour," not the woman's hour. There was no form of permanent organization for suffrage in Illinois until 1866. In February of that year two conventions, rivaling for management of the cause, were called simultaneously in Chicago, and the matter of suffrage for women was spiritedly discussed by both. For various reasons, mostly personal, there was a good deal of feeling between the attendants at the two meetings, delightedly made the most of by the Chicago newspapers. One editor described the groups as "a lot of old hens cackling over the addled eggs they have laid." Nevertheless a joint organization was evolved, the Universal Suffrage Association of Illinois. Five years later the Woman's Christian Temperance Union, the grand old W. C. T. U., in all respects the most powerful woman's association the country possessed in the nineteenth century, endorsed the movement for women's suffrage as the brightest hope for "prohibition," thus giving it an ethical stamp that it never altogether lost.

Jane Addams went to Rockford only a vague believer in women's rights, but she graduated in 1881 a convinced suffragist. Her father influenced her to some extent in this. To some extent also she was no doubt influenced by that cultivated woman and ardent suffragist, Mrs. William Lathrop of Rockford, mother of Julia Lathrop—one of the first group of graduates from Rockford Seminary in 1854, witty, intelligent, a great lady, and a prominent member of the Universal Suffrage Association. But the chief influence upon Jane was Rockford Seminary itself. It was a hotbed of suffrage. In the class below Jane Addams was Catherine Waugh, one of America's "poor girls who became famous." She was to study law, practise, marry, and as Catherine Waugh McCulloch become the finest fighter for the *legality* of women's rights Illinois ever knew. It was of her that Jane Addams wrote:

My companion at Rockford in the study of higher mathematics has since accomplished more than any of us in the effort to procure the franchise for women (for even then we all took for granted the righteousness of the cause into which I at least had merely followed my father's conviction). In the old-fashioned spirit of that cause I might cite the career of that companion as an illustration of the efficacy of higher mathematics for women, for she possesses singular ability to convince even the densest legislators of their legal right to define their own electorate, even when they quote against her the dustiest of state constitutions or city charters.

By 1881, the year of Jane's graduation, suffrage in Illinois had an organ, a magazine called *Our Herald*. It seems to have been somewhat narrowly circulated; Jane Addams could not recall ever having seen a copy. It was not until 1891, ten years later, that the first suffrage newspaper in the state, the *Illinois Suffragist*, was established. In that year Mrs. McCulloch became Superintendent of Legislative Work for Women's Suffrage, and led and won the battle to establish the right of women to vote for school trustees, except in such communities as had made the organization of their schools directly dependent on the state constitution, which lawyers believed specifically denied to women the right to vote for constitutional offices.

Up to this time Jane Addams may be said to have done nothing directly for the cause of woman's suffrage, but now she followed in her old schoolmate's train. Two years later the Chicago "World's Fair" came along, and for the first time in the history of such affairs the direct contributions of women to civilization were recognized. For the first month of the Fair a "Congress of Representative Women" was called, and representative women came from all over the world. In this Jane Addams was a principal figure; though a little mild fun was poked at her because in the tremendous crowd of opening day, she not only got lost for a while but had her pocket picked. That Congress looms big in the history of the cause; in Illinois it made the city aware of women as essential to the remaking of the old rough democracy. Jane Addams's prominence in it led directly to her appointment seven years later as a member of the Jury of International Awards at the Paris Exposition in 1900. Mrs. Potter Palmer had been appointed United States Commissioner at the Paris Exposition, in recognition of her services during the World's Fair, and Mrs. Palmer used her influence to procure Jane Addams's appointment. The Jury promptly elected Jane Addams vice-president, and therefore she became ex-officio a member of the controlling Group Jury; the only woman on it, and in consequence a much advertised figure. When she returned, she was not only a convinced "internationalist" as far as her belief in the possibility and necessity of the world-coöperation of women was concerned, but a leading figure in the struggle in Illinois for women's rights.

Long before this she had passed from the stage of "conviction by emotion," through the dreary stage of abstract discussion in which in Illinois Mrs. McCulloch had shown such powers of endurance as well as such brilliant and humorous intelligence, to "conviction by experience." She had found there was a direct connection between the vote and work for social amelioration:

Because of the tendency to make the state responsible for the care of the helpless and the reform of the delinquent, to safeguard by law the food we eat and the health of the children, contemporary women who were without the franchise were as much *outside the real life of the world* as any set of disfranchised free men could have been in all history. ... We had also had practical demonstrations that if women had no votes with which to select the men upon whom her social reform had become dependent, some cherished project might be so modified by informed legislatures during process of enactment, that the law as finally passed injured the very people it was meant to protect.... A child-labor law exempts street trades, the most dangerous of all trades to a child's morale; a law releasing mothers from petty industry that they may worthily rear their children, provides so inadequate a pension that overburdened women continue to face the necessity of neglecting their young in order to feed them.

And further she had found that many women "needed the franchise bitterly for their children's sake." This was a sanction quite outside the old arguments, and even outside the arguments of most of the women in the organized movement. Pioneer women, however, had longed for the vote that they might force better schools for their growing families; immigrant women all round Hull House longed for the vote that they might force better sanitation and hospitalization. One of Jane Addams's later anecdotes, after women got the vote in Chicago in 1913, and she was acting as a judge of election in the Hull House precinct, will be sufficient illustration. A bond issue was up to provide for a contagious disease hospital:

The judge was permitted to go into the voting booth to assist illiterates to mark the ballot. When we were safely behind the little white curtain of the polling booth, one woman after another would say: "Of course I am going to vote the way my man told me to, but I won't go out of this place till I vote for that hospital for catching diseases. The visiting nurses are forever taking a child to the hospital when the disease isn't catching, but the time it is, she tells you you must keep all the children out of school to drive you plum crazy, because there isn't any hospital for what your child has got."

In the first decade of the twentieth century there were two long struggles to secure a revision of the charter of Chicago, and the women took advantage of these efforts to attempt to get municipal suffrage for women. A woman's suffrage page was started in one of the daily newspapers, and the first women quoted were Jane Addams and Catherine Waugh McCulloch—Rockford in the van as usual. In February of 1907 a tumultuous mass-meeting gathered in the Studebaker Theater to hear Jane Addams talk on "The Campaign for Municipal Suffrage." There were "storms of applause" as she first built up her solid foundation of concrete examples, and then raised her ivory tower of logic above it. She was first made vice-chairman, later chairman, of the Women's Clubs Committee for Municipal Suffrage for Women, and she took the main charge of the battle, with more than a hundred women's organizations under her generalship. It was this experience which convinced her not only that women should have the vote but that the time was ripe for the vote; because the demand for it was based on such *varied* needs:

We were joined by a church society of hundreds of Lutheran women, because Scandinavian women had exercised the municipal suffrage since the seventeenth century, and had found American cities strangely conservative; by organization of working-women who had keenly felt the need of the municipal franchise in order to secure for their workshops the most rudimentary sanitation and the consideration which the vote alone obtains for workingmen; by federations of mothers' meetings, who were interested in clean milk and the extension of kindergartens; by property-owning women, who had been powerless to protest against unjust taxation; by organizations of professional women, of university students and of collegiate alumnæ; and by women's clubs interested in municipal reforms....

Russian women waited upon me to ask whether under the new
charter they could vote for covered markets and so get rid of
the shocking Chicago grime upon all their food; and ... Italian
women sent me word that they would certainly vote for public
washhouses if they ever had the chance to vote at all. It was all
so human, so spontaneous, and so direct.

So Addams-like. As chairman of the Suffrage Committee, Jane Addams and Mrs. McCulloch organized the
"Woman's Special," famous in its day, a six-car special
train for women only which traveled down to Springfield,
the state capital, to spread along the roadside the gospel
of municipal suffrage for women; there were speeches at
eight different stops along the way, made by Miss Addams
and Mrs. McCulloch. On the legislators, however, they
concentrated the fire. Springfield knew Jane Addams well
by this time. Between 1893 and 1909 she had headed
many deputations of women, and men also, to argue for
one piece of legislation or another, for adoption or against
repeal. She had no vote, but when she went down to lobby
the members crowded into the committee chambers and
really listened. She smiled at them, with eager not sad
eyes—though in repose her eyes had grown sad by this
time, "the eyelids a little weary" with the knowledge of
so much to do and so slow the ripening of time's fulfil-
ments and the processes of accomplishment; she wore her
very best hats, generally a new one for such occasions;
and she talked to them as if she had never had a doubt
of the goodness of their intentions. She put herself in their
place, just as she had always put herself in the place of
her neighbors round Hull House, of Alderman Powers,
of parents who believed their young children should support them, of the glass-manufacturers and the garment-

manufacturers, of the labor-unionists and of George M. Pullman, of the members of the Teachers' Federation and of the members of the Commercial Club. She talked to them, in other words, as a woman of imagination—a supreme imagination which transcends perhaps even that of the dramatist. He puts himself in the place of beings he has himself created. She put herself into the place of God's other creatures. There is something even finer in that sort of re-creation, than in the creation of the dramatist. The legislators were accustomed to put it bluntly by saying "She always knows her stuff," but it was much more than that. When she had made up her mind to what was right, and had reached the conclusion that society was ripe for right action, she pleaded her case with the fervor of a spiritual demagogue.

"Life is full of hidden remedial powers which society has not yet utilized," she said, "but perhaps nowhere is the waste more flagrant than in the matured deductions and judgments of the women, who are constantly *forced to share the social injustices which they have no recognized power to alter.*"

In the spring of 1912 she published the most sustained and striking argument for woman's suffrage she ever made, the volume called *A New Conscience and an Ancient Evil.* The ancient evil is the mistreatment of girls: "In every large city throughout the world thousands of women are so set aside as outcasts from decent society that it is considered an impropriety to speak the very word which designates them. . . . This type of woman Lecky says 'remains, while creeds and civilizations rise and fall, the eternal sacrifice of humanity, blasted for the sins of the people.'"

But what is the "new conscience"? It is the change in the view of this old evil which is taken by good women. And how is the new conscience to be made effective? By securing for women more power to overcome the "moral affront" of this mistreatment.

The chapters of the book discuss recent legal enactments, amelioration of social conditions, the education and protection of children, philanthropic activities for prevention of the evil, and increased social control. It discusses them specifically, practically, even statistically now and then. But underlying every chapter is the philosophic conviction that primarily to overcome this evil, a woman must become politically a *person*. Chapter after chapter develops this argument without a break. It is illustrated by narrative so definite that a novel was made from one incident related, and a moving picture from another incident; it drips with the blood of experience. But as a whole it sums up into an assertion: women must have equal power in society. The book is the evidence for this assertion.

Its quality can be made plain only by quotation:

> However ancient a wrong may be, in each generation it must become newly embodied in living people and the social custom into which it has hardened through the years must be continued in individual lives; and unless the contemporaries of such unhappy individuals are touched to tenderness or stirred to indignation by the actual embodiments of the old wrong in their own generation, effective action cannot be secured....
>
> Every human being knows deep down in his own heart that his own moral energy ebbs and flows, that he cannot be judged fairly by his hours of defeat, and that after revealing moments of weakness, although shocked and frightened, he is the same human being, struggling as before....

If the moral fire seems at times to be dying out of certain good old words, such as charity, it is filling with new warmth such words as social justice which belong distinctively to our own time. . . .

Life is full of hidden remedial powers which society has not yet utilized, but perhaps nowhere is the waste more flagrant than in the matured deductions and judgments of the women, who are constantly forced to share the social injustices which they have no recognized power to alter. . . .

The primary difficulty of military life lies in the withdrawal of large numbers of men from normal family life, and hence from the domestic restraints and social checks which are operative upon the mass of human beings. The great peace propagandas have emphasized the unjustifiable expense involved in the maintenance of the standing armies of Europe, the social waste in the withdrawal of thousands of young men from industrial, commercial and professional pursuits into the barren negative life of the barracks. They might go further and lay stress upon the loss of moral sensibility, the destruction of romantic love, the perversion of the longing for wife and child. The very stability and refinement of the social order depend upon the preservation of these basic instincts. . . .

When a city is so large that it is extremely difficult to fix individual responsibility, that freedom from community control which for centuries was considered the luxury of the king comes within the reach of every office boy. . . .

Women may at last force men to do away with the traditional use of a public record as a cloak for a wretched private character, because society will never permit a woman to make such excuses for herself.

It was not as a leader in the woman's suffrage movement, however, but as a generally distinguished citizen, that Theodore Roosevelt sought her assistance in the Roosevelt-Progressive movement of 1912. Nor was it primarily as a suffragist that she joined that movement, but, as will presently be shown, as a sociological diplomat, an ambassador for industrial reform. She had no illusions regarding T. R. She knew him, liked him, and understood him. She had the advantage over him of the perception that goes with a mind both imaginative and logical. His reckless emotionalism, both the genuineness and the inconsiderateness of his desire to "do good," were obvious to one who had always hitched her wagon to the same star. He was kaleidoscopic in his change of views; she had kept precisely the same objective throughout, and when she altered her road to her end, knew precisely what turn she had made and why she had made it, as when, in the determination to better conditions in her ward, she turned from the fight against a crooked alderman to a scientific study of the neighborhood psychology that developed aldermanic crookedness. Roosevelt in turn had admired her for years before 1912. He had called her, enthusiastically, "the most useful citizen in Chicago." He wrote her occasional long letters. Once as late as 1915 he asked her to look up the case of a man who had written from a Chicago address, saying he had been a "Rough Rider" in Cuba, but was now sick and unemployed. Would Miss Addams use her judgment in helping the man if he deserved help? T. R. would accept full financial responsibility for anything she might decide to do for the applicant. In an earlier letter he refers to himself humorously as having been internationally recognized, by the award of the Nobel Peace Prize, as "the great American *influence* for peace," but suggests that Jane Addams remains the great American *authority* on the subject. Twice he had visited Hull House, once to review a large assemblage of Boy Scouts in Bowen Hall, and once to witness the first performance in America of John Galsworthy's

Justice. The play, as given by the Hull House Players, had much impressed him. He had never read anything of Galsworthy's, he said, but he bought all his books to be found in Chicago, to read on the train back to New York.

It had been on the occasion of the first visit, when after the review he and Jane Addams were driven together over to the Second Regiment armory to talk to a huge meeting of immigrants who had got their second papers during the year and were therefore voters, that they had had a chat about suffrage.

"How long," he wanted to know, "have you been a suffragist?"

"All my life," she said, "and my father before me."

"Well," Roosevelt remarked, "I haven't fully made up my mind. I used to be opposed to it. There are some good arguments against it. But there are some mighty good arguments in favor of it, too. Of course, you are one of the best of those arguments yourself."

"Thank you," Jane Addams murmured, and they arrived at the armory and she listened to his splendid and eager speech, in the course of which he announced with his usual platform conviction that for the best interests of the country he had always believed that women, like the naturalized aliens, should have the vote. She was not amazed. "Wherever he arrived," she said later, "he always forgot the trip." Nor was Julia Lathrop amazed. "Theodore," she commented, "always reminds me of the lines from Wesley's hymn, 'Betwixt the saddle and the ground he mercy sought and mercy found.' " That was the evening Jane Addams lost her hat in the crowd, and Roosevelt politely insisted on removing his own as they drove back to the Union League Club in an open car. Hearing of her misfortune, the Union League Club sent her a check for fifty dollars to pay for the hat. She returned the check, with the information that the hat had cost only ten dollars originally and she had had it for two years— a "human interest story" which went round the world in the newspapers. Roosevelt sent her many clippings of it, especially of the version, which delighted him, that her carelessness about her hats was one of the reasons why she had never been able to get a husband.

But if she did not become a Progressive in the hope of aiding the cause of suffrage, what was her reason? It was her interest in industrial reform.

In 1907 the Pittsburgh Survey, described as "an appraisal of how far human engineering has kept pace with the mechanical developments in the American steel districts," had concluded that an employer's business was not exclusively to produce, but also to discover the causes of and prevent if possible social waste and individual injury among his employees. The survey made clearer than ever before the danger to laborers, and the conditions of employment, in the great American industries. From that time on, there developed in the United States, Jane Addams thinks, a much more "consuming zeal" for industrial reform. Social workers tended more and more not to "charitable" effort, but "to discuss the economic conditions underlying the low standards of living, the overwork, the poverty and disease we were seeking to ameliorate." As precisely this sort of discussion was what she herself had been engaged in for almost twenty years, it was natural enough that she should be made official head of the national organization of social workers, the Conference of Charities and Correction. Both her own election, as a woman, to the presidency of this Conference, and the shift of emphasis in it from charity to correction, shocked some of the older members, particularly the businessmen members, but it did not shock Roosevelt. In the last months of his second term as President he had called a Conference of his own, to consider from the economic point of view a great social problem, the care of dependent children. That recognition by Roosevelt, Jane Addams thought, "gave to social work a dignity and a place in the national life which it had never had before." In that conference women had a prominent place. Jane Addams herself was one of the principal speakers, and

as we were waiting to file upon the platform, the young man in charge, a little overcome by his responsibilities, said, "Are we all here? Yes, here is my Catholic speaker, my Jewish speaker, the Protestant, the colored man, and the woman. Let's all go in." I remarked to Booker T. Washington, just in front of me, "You see I am last; that is because I have no vote." He replied, "I am glad to know the reason. Always before I have been the end of such a procession myself."

Following this conference, and the meeting of the Charities and Correction group, a committee was appointed to investigate Occupational Standards. After three years of investigation, a program was set up which presented, as essential in determining a standard of living among all employees, the following six factors: (1) wages; (2) hours ; (3) safety and health; (4) housing; (5) term of working life; (6) compensation or insurance. The report ended with the challenging statement, "the conservation of our human resources contributes the most substantial asset to the welfare of the future."

That report was published in June, 1912. Paragraphs from it Roosevelt was induced to put into his "keynote speech" at the Chicago convention of the new (Progressive) party in August; and the program was definitely incorporated into the party platform then adopted. Jane Addams was, at Roosevelt's request, put on the Platform Committee. She found herself more or less in the position she had been in as a member of the Chicago School Board. The radicals wanted measures endorsed which "although worthy," as she remarks, "had after all recommended themselves to only a very small group out of all the nation." The conservatives, and many of the followers of Roosevelt were conservative in 1912, wanted nothing that would really tend to alienate "capitalists" as such. What Jane Addams wanted was "to meet the fundamental obligation of adapting the legal order to the changed conditions of national life"—exactly what she had urged since her speech fifteen years before on "ethical gains through social legislation." Social ethics had altered; those alterations must be fixed in legislation, or you would have revolution. But they must be fixed *precisely;* legislation must not be in advance of democratic conviction, or you would have reversion. Her attitude toward economic slavery was exactly what that of the Republicans of the 1850's had been toward Negro slavery. She was not a twentieth century abolitionist, she was a twentieth century statesman; not a Garrison, but a Lincoln.

The platform advocated woman's suffrage, but only as it advocated direct primaries or the initiative and referendum, in the hope that the politics of the nation might be kept close to the whole of the people; not, in other words, as a matter of "justice to women," but as a matter of advantage to democratic expression.

She has written of this convention: "In spite of our belief in our leader, I was there, and I think the same was true of many others, because the platform expressed the social hopes so long ignored by the politicians; though we appreciated to the full our good fortune in securing *on their behalf* the magnetic personality of the distinguished candidate."

The words are carefully chosen, and so far as they concern Roosevelt, must be carefully read. Her good fortune was not in him, but in securing *his support for what she wanted.* She knew he had been uniquely forcible, and uniquely eloquent, loving "to put the longing of the multitude into words that they do not forget, and to banish their doubts and fears by the sheer force of his personality and the vital power of his courage." She did not greatly care that, as the cynical Henry Adams was to express it presently, "Our dear Theodore is, I very much fear, a dead cock in the pit." She was willing *at the time* to allow him to wear the plume of militarism, for the sake of those who were willing to press on to where it was shining at the moment in the van of the ranks of the social warriors. She cheerfully admits that she compromised on this occasion; even voted for a Bigger Navy platform plank—the building of two battleships a year. But the basis of her compromise is typical. It must be given in her own words, and at length:

In my long advocacy of peace I had consistently used one line of appeal, contending that peace is no longer an abstract

dogma; that a dynamic peace is found in that new internationalism promoted by the men of all nations who are determined
upon the abolition of degrading poverty, disease and ignorance,
with their resulting inefficiency and tragedy. I believed that
peace was not merely an absence of war but the nurture of
human life, and that in time this nurture would do away with
war as a natural process. ... The figures given out in 1912 were
such as these: the total number of casualties suffered by our
industrial army is sufficient to carry on perpetually two such
wars at the same time as our Civil War and the Russo-Japanese
War; the casualties in the structural iron trade, in the erection
of bridges and high buildings, bear the same relation to the
number of men engaged as did the wounded to the total number of troops in the battle of Bull Run; fifteen thousand of our
fellow-citizens are killed in industry every year—as if every
adult male in a city of seventy-five thousand were put to death;
and every year a half a million men are crippled—as if every
adult male in a state the size of Minnesota were annually
maimed. It was not sufficient for my peace of mind that a small
group of public-spirited citizens were constantly agitating in
various state legislatures for a system of industrial insurance.
Such problems belong to the nation as well as to the state.
These facts should be made public to the entire country, for it
was not a matter of abstract theory but of self-preservation. It
seemed to me that I was not being presented with a choice
between protesting against the human waste of industry or
against the havoc of war, but that I had an opportunity to
identify myself with a political party which did protest against
one of them, and advanced well-considered legislation in regard
to it. Was it pure rationalization when I persuaded myself that
the political party most surely on the road to world peace was
the one which had pledged itself to work for "effective legislation, looking to the prevention of industrial accident, occupational diseases, overwork, involuntary unemployment and other
injurious effects incident to modern industry"? I came to
believe that "the ancient kindliness which sat beside the cradle
of the race" cannot assert itself in our generation against the
waste of life in warfare, so long as we remain indifferent to the

shocking destruction of life in other areas. To protect life in industry may be a natural beginning, a response to the brother we have seen.

It was a rationalization, yes, so far as Roosevelt himself was concerned, for in spite of the fact that he had been the only American to be awarded a Nobel Peace Prize, he had already shown that he thought war "glorious," and was to show it again; he and Hearst had been perhaps the most eager proponents in America of that Spanish-American war which Jane Addams in 1903 had called baneful in effect partly because it had led to the election of Roosevelt on his war record. "There are many things I admire about President Roosevelt," she had then said, "but I object to voting for him or for any man on a 'war record.' " But it was not a rationalization so far as joining the Progressive Party was concerned; it was rather a brilliant statement of the pragmatic social philosophy she had arrived at long before. Universal suffrage, like peace, was "no longer an abstract dogma" to her, but another method of more surely nurturing human life; she had long argued that women needed the vote no more than democracy needed the women, but she now advanced beyond this "abstract argument" to the realization that "the unrepresented are always liable to be given what they do not want by legislators who merely wish to placate them," and that even legislation which the women did want could be made useless by unrepresentative direction: "We sometimes considered it of doubtful advantage that more and more women were appointed to positions in administrative government, so long as the power of general direction, of determining the trend and temper of new social experiments, was lodged altogether in the hands of men responsible only to other voting men, and politically free from the public opinion of the women originally concerned for the measures."

So although she had sat on the platform committee, and influenced its deliberations, chiefly as an advocate for the industrial reform which she believed the country to be ready for, she campaigned (through eight states) as a suffragist also.

She enjoyed the campaign chiefly as a philosopher. She did not expect the party to win, but she became "convinced that people are ready to grapple with social problems whenever a well-considered program is laid before them," and this conviction heartened her exceedingly. As usual, she distinguished sharply between the effort to "get things done" and the effort to "get things understood." What she craved was "the understanding support which results from a widespread and sincere discussion of a given subject by fellow-citizens before any attempt should be made to secure legislative action."

It was just what she had sought as chairman of the School Management Committee, and just what the newspapers had laughed at her for craving; just what she was to crave in the "war years" which were to come, and just what she was then to be decried as a "traitor" for craving. Free speech; not as an abstraction of liberty, not for its own sake, but because *without free speech the national mind could not ripen* into understanding conviction.

What happened is history. The party went down to complete defeat, defeat which would indeed have been inglorious if a fool at Milwaukee had not shot Roosevelt in the breast, and so induced a purely emotional support of him which brought hundreds of thousands of votes at the last moment. Even so Roosevelt showed himself to be what Henry Adams had called him, a dead cock in the political pit; even so it became evident to Roosevelt at least that what still determined the survival of a party was the possibility of the possession of "the loaves and fishes." But Jane Addams was no more discouraged than she had been when she had been politically defeated in her ward years earlier. "Possibly," she wrote eighteen years later, "the time was not ripe for the organization of a new political party, or *more likely we did not recognize the nation's actual needs and desires.*"

If the party had triumphed, it is probable that the course of history would have been altered. Roosevelt would beyond any reasonable doubt have led the country into the war before the end of his presidential term, for he could not have endured the thought of leaving the guidance of the nation in a military crisis to a successor; and if America had entered the war in 1915 instead of 1917, the story of European battle would have had many different turns, and perhaps a quicker ending. But meanwhile, what would have happened to Jane Addams? The thought of her personal responsibility in the election of a "happy warrior," such as Roosevelt would have been, would have overwhelmed her. It seems fortunate for her, individually, that the "nation's desires" in 1912, however blindly they have been felt, did not coincide with her own.

That was her last engagement in "party" efforts. Political parties in America, she came to believe, were and are merely "political contrivances for nominating and electing officers," not representative of social thinking.

She reviewed her past experiences. Not a party, but voluntary associations of men and women, had brought about labor legislation in Illinois; established the Juvenile Court in Chicago; reformed and to some degree democratized the Chicago public schools; won all the victories that had consolidated in legislation the advances in ethical ideals. Not a party, but the American Federation of Labor, had affected national labor legislation. Not a party, but the pressure of general public opinion in Illinois had forced through the state legislature in 1913 a bill that gave Illinois women the right to vote for president of the United States, for municipal officers and for all state officers not named in the state constitution as eligible by the votes of male electors only. Not a party, but a voluntary agency, the Anti-Saloon League, was to bring about the adoption of the prohibition amendment to the constitution, and not a party, but a general popular feeling, was to repeal that amendment. Not a party, but a group of voluntary associations, was to force through the amendment giving universal suffrage in 1920; and not a party, but the organized liquor interests of the country, were to make the fight against that amendment. Not a party but the rebellion against making internationalism a party measure, was to defeat the entrance of the United States into the League of Nations. In the next (and greatest) effort of her life, the effort to make and keep peace, Jane Addams was to rely once more altogether upon non-party associations. But her possession of the vote was nevertheless to increase her influence.

It is worth pointing out that when she finally did get the vote, she voted for men and issues, not in accordance with parties. Wilson in 1916; Debs in 1920 (this was a "protest vote"); La Follette in 1924; Hoover in 1928; Hoover in 1932. One Socialist, one Progressive, two Republicans, one Democrat—a remarkable mixture. This campaign of 1912 may be said to have finalized Jane Addams's interest in woman's suffrage. Such authorities on the subject as Mrs. Carrie Chapman Catt of the United States, and Doctor Maude Royden of England, even call her "not an active worker in the political women's movement" until that time. Doctor Royden says that she "had too much else on her hands." In 1913, however, Jane Addams went to Budapest to attend the International Conference for Women, and she was the only real world-figure there. Doctor Royden says:

She had no official position in the movement. She was not our President, or even on the International Board. She was an ordinary delegate, and although people tried very hard to get her away from her humble position on the floor of the hall and put her on the platform, and although just to avoid any kind of a fuss she once or twice allowed herself to be put there, the next morning found her sitting among the other American delegates on the floor. And yet everyone realized that among the whole of that conference of women from all over the world, she was the one that was known to the whole world. Others were known in their own nation, or perhaps in one or two others, but Jane Addams was a world-figure.... When my mind goes back to that conference, I always have a feeling that Jane Addams wherever she sat was always the heart and soul of it.

And then came the war, and all the world almost went mad; yet out of the war one good thing came that might not have come otherwise—well-nigh universal suffrage. That and the women's efforts for peace were intimately connected. But it is, so far as Jane Addams is concerned, the efforts for peace that have to be emphasized.

CHAPTER XIV

PACIFISM

WHAT first made Jane Addams a pacifist? Her conviction of the power that lay in international understanding, and the necessity of such understanding to develop civilization. Her objection was not primarily to the horror of war as such, and not to the economic folly of war. Of course she agreed heartily with Norman Angell that war was economic folly, whether a nation conquered or was conquered; and the destruction of young life that war involves was as dreadful to her as to any mother whose own son is killed in battle. But the worst thing about war, in her view, was its total prevention of the mutual understanding of peoples. She saw that in peace such mutual understanding was possible, that in war it was impossible; and she was certain that without that mutual understanding there could be no real progress. Living right among representatives of a score of nations, she saw in every individual those "universal emotions which have nothing to do with national frontiers," and she saw them confuse these emotions with "patriotism," simply because "no international devices had been provided for the expression of these universal emotions, they had no outlet into the larger life of the world." With peace, such an outlet might develop; by war, all such incipient outlets were choked.

The Nobel Peace Prize was finally awarded to her in

1931. But long before that she was known as the most effective advocate of peace among the women of the world. More than any other citizen of America, she had revealed the folly of isolation for the maintenance of good-will, and had showed how war prevented mutual understanding, and therefore prevented progress toward what *all assert* to be our national ideals.

Much of the remainder of this story of her life must be the story of her struggle to get the United States and Europe to listen to the message called down to the shepherds of Galilee by heavenly voices two thousand years ago, of peace on earth, good-will to men. It was a struggle long-continued and brave. It involved, and finally concentrated, the help of thousands of other women in many countries, finally indeed in almost all countries. It engaged the attention, admiration, and in the end the genuine conviction of many statesmen. It led her through first the patronizing commendation of millions, then through their obloquy and insult. It culminated, three weeks before she died, in a celebration personally triumphant, in which were joined not only some of the best-known men and women of her own country, but the ambassadors of England, France, Russia and Japan, praising her as no American woman had ever before been internationally praised. But it was a struggle based not on emotion, and not on economic principles, but on understanding. It was a fight for comprehension.

She never overestimated the force of this fight. She never blinked a fact. In the course of her struggle, she saw kingdoms overthrown, to be replaced not by the democracies and world-intimacies of her dream, but by fierce fascist states and a class-conscious republic. She saw the most terrible war in history take place, followed by an uncomprehending peace. She saw her own country refuse to join in a League of Nations, and even in a world-court. She saw armaments decreased only to be increased again beyond their former limits. She saw a magnificent manifesto, the Kellogg Pact, held to the futility of a gesture. She saw war threatening on as many fronts when she died in 1935, as when she inaugurated her efforts in 1897. Yet she never lost hope. For she also saw that all over the world women had become citizens, and she retained the conviction that in the end the recognition of women as citizens had at least reduced the settlement of misunderstanding by physical force to a political absurdity, had at least intellectualized the effort for peace.

Looking back upon those efforts of hers, extending over almost forty years, one cannot but be reminded of that strange dream she had "night after night," when she was a little girl; that dream that she alone remained alive in a deserted world, and that upon her rested the sole responsibility of somehow making a wheel which should start again the world's affairs; the dream that she was standing in the same spot in the blacksmith's shop, "darkly pondering as to how to begin," and never knowing how. It was because in life as in her dreams she felt her responsibility as "sole," that she could never stop pondering or trying. She tried to make wheel after wheel to start the affairs of peace. If she failed, she was at least an unforgettable inspiration to others to keep on trying; of all the women of her time, she kept at least the most glowing fire upon the forge.

She often accounted for her first disbelief in war by citing her "Quaker ancestry" and her father's influence.

This seems however to have been "wishful thinking"—
perhaps the only instance of it in her public career.
(Privately, as this biographer and all her own family
knew well, her thoughts of them were often dominated by
her wishes.) Her ancestry was very casually Quaker; her
father, the "Hicksite Quaker," was such by tradition only,
not by communion. Nor as has been pointed out, is there
any good evidence that he felt toward war as she came to
feel, or had ever thought the question out at all. As a
leader in the Illinois State Senate, he voted for every
measure from 1861 to 1865 which supported state participation in the Civil War. He personally raised a company
of volunteers, which was named for him, the "Addams
Guards." He was the first man in Stephenson County to
be consulted about enlistment by the "fire-eating" Smith
D. Atkins, later Brigadier-General Atkins, commander of
the 92nd Illinois, and second in command of Sherman's
cavalry on the "war-is-hellish" march through Georgia
and the Carolinas; and for his "splendid patriotism" he
was lauded by Atkins (then a newspaper proprietor) when
he died. Atkins was not a man to have praised a war-
hater in such terms. John Addams was a hater of slavery,
and he was a lover of freedom, and he was perhaps as
internationalist in spirit as any Middle-Western American
of his day, but no record of him has been found to indicate
that he hated all war on principle.

Indeed one finds no record in any letter, notebook, or
article of Jane herself, before 1896, when she was thirty-
five years old, of any dominating, reasoned objection to
war. In the spring of that year she did show her colors
publicly, if somewhat amusingly. Some of the young men
of the neighborhood were "drilling" for fun with wooden

guns. She tried to get them to substitute long-handled shovels, with which they might not only drill but help to clean up the filth-filled streets of the Hull House ward, and she asserts that her purpose in this was quite as much anti-militaristic as it was sanitational. They drilled with the shovels she provided, as long as she was there watching them, but promptly abandoned the implements when she went away.

The connection of Tolstoy with Jane Addams's purpose of peace is almost as tenuous as her own father's connection with it. She was a most profound admirer of the great Russian. His little book, *My Religion,* she had read when she was twenty-one, and she continued to read whatever she could lay her hands on of his throughout the years that followed. His theory of self-support, of "getting off the backs of the poor," and his theory of non-violence, had both attracted her. But however much she admired them, she could not wholly agree with them. The first seemed to her impractical, the second illogical. In one of her finest flashes of wisdom she wrote: "It seemed to me that Tolstoy made too great a distinction between the use of physical force and that moral energy which can override another's differences and scruples with equal ruthlessness." What really fascinated her in Tolstoy was not his theories, but his "sermon of the deed," his actual putting into practice, at whatever sacrifice of comfort, without the slightest fuss, of his dream of social democracy. He had made "the one supreme effort, one might almost say the one frantic personal effort, to put himself into right relations with the humblest people." Her own dream was the same as his, she had made a tremendous effort to put her dream into practice at Hull House, but she could not see her own effort as supreme, and she was certainly well aware that it had not been frantic. He had by his habit of life freed himself from the strain of "believing in a theory and acting as if he did not believe it," and for this reason she found a sort of wistful joy in contemplating him. Her essay on Tolstoy, in which she analyzes not only his conception of social responsibility, but her own attitude toward that conception, is one of the best things she ever wrote. But it is not for summarization here. This is merely an attempt to show wherein he affected her views of the necessity of peace.

One of her long illnesses prostrated her in the fall of 1895—typhoid fever this time, contracted she always declared in defense of Hull House, not in Chicago but elsewhere, and in the following May in company with Mary Rozet Smith she went abroad to recuperate. It was at this time that Miss Smith became "dearest" in her letters. There was found in her papers after she died the unfinished draft of a poem to Mary Smith, written by Jane Addams during her convalescence at this time, and apparently never completed. For the light it sheds on their relationship, a few lines of that poem are given here.

> One day I came into Hull House,
>   (No spirit whispered who was there)
> And in the kindergarten room
>   There sat upon a childish chair
> A girl, both tall and fair to see,
>   (To look at her gives one a thrill).
> But all I thought was, would she be
>   Best fitted to lead club, or drill?
> You see, I had forgotten Love,
>   And only thought of Hull House then.

That is the way with women folks
When they attempt the things of men;
They grow intense, and love the thing
Which they so tenderly do rear,
And think that nothing lies beyond
Which claims from them a smile or tear.
Like mothers, who work long and late
To rear their children fittingly,
Follow them only with their eyes,
And love them almost pityingly.
So I was blind and deaf those years
To all save one absorbing care,
And did not guess what now I know—
Delivering love was sitting there!

They went first to London, where with Ben Tillet, John
Burns, Keir Hardie, of the workingmen who had become
famous, and with Octavia Hill, the Webbs, Sir John Gorst,
John Hobson and others of the upper group of the English Labor Party, she studied municipal conditions, and
with the Barnetts of Toynbee Hall and Canon Ingram of
Oxford House she visited "settlements." She thought
England far in advance in social legislation and application of such legislation over what it had been in 1888,
and it seemed to her at the moment "as if the hopes of
democracy were more likely to come to pass on English
soil than on her own"; though in an interview at the dock
when she returned, she said unguardedly that "conditions
in London seemed in some respects no better than in
Chicago," and so traveled round the world in headlines as
declaring "London worse than Chicago." Even as early
as 1896, anything Jane Addams said about social conditions was news.

From England they went to Moscow, met Aylmer

Maude, the authorized translator of Tolstoy's works, and were escorted by him to Yasnaya Polyana to meet the Count. Tolstoy, after Mr. Maude's kindly speech of introduction, and elaborate description of Hull House, remained unimpressed. He gently took hold of the edge of Jane Addams's sleeve, full in accordance with the fashion of the year, and pulling it out to its considerable breadth, remarked that "there was enough stuff on one arm to make a frock for a little girl," and asked if she did not find such a dress a barrier between her and "the people." The girls round Hull House wore sleeves, she informed him, that were even larger. Tolstoy shifted to her means of support—who fed and sheltered her? She explained that she had a farm which she leased. He looked at her gravely. "So, you are an absentee landlord!" She summoned up for self-comfort the Hull House creed of living "with recognition of the good in every man, even the most wretched." Tolstoy, she suspected, was "more logical than life warrants"—another of her flashes of insight. But after she had left Yasnaya Polyana, and in Paris had read and re-read everything of Tolstoy's she could find in English, French or German translations, she decided that she could at least coincide in his belief that "antagonism is a foolish and unwarrantable waste of energy."

Only to this extent was Jane Addams ever a "Tolstoyan." But perhaps it was this decision that started her most definitely on the long trail of peace propaganda. It ended in her at all events any faint hope of reaching social salvation through "class-consciousness" and "class-struggle"; separated her finally in theory from Marxianism and communism; set her face like flint against social violence. From that time on she was openly a "pacifist," though the word itself had not yet been invented.

Not her father, however, and not Tolstoy, but residence in her own immigrant neighborhood, really taught her the folly of war between nations, and inspired in her her reasoned plan to get rid of it. It was borne in upon her that the association of her immigrant neighbors, nineteen races of them in the ward in 1896, tended to modify their provincialism and tame the ferocity of their nationalism:

When a South Italian Catholic is forced by the very exigencies of the situation to make friends with an Austrian Jew, representing another nationality and another religion, both of which cut into all his most cherished prejudices, he finds it harder to utilize them a second time, and gradually loses them. ...If an old enemy working by his side has turned into a friend, almost anything may happen.

Might not this forced "internationalism" developed in American cities, she wondered, be made an effective instrument in the cause of world-peace? She began to brood upon the possibilities of this idea as early as the fall of 1896, a brief entry in one of her notebooks indicates. She talked frequently about international comity in general, took a prominent part in the Chicago campaign against "imperialism" in connection with the annexation of the Philippines in 1899—a campaign that enlisted such "conservatives" as Professor J. Laurence Laughlin of the University of Chicago and such "radicals" as Henry D. Lloyd, and produced William Vaughan Moody's finest poem, "An Ode in Time of Hesitation"—but she did not publicly offer it until 1904. It has already been said that Jane Addams was never in a hurry. In 1904 there was held a convention of National Peace Societies in Boston.

Jane Addams was a principal speaker, and she talked of "newer ideals" of peace. She was heartened to find that her fellow-psychologist William James was in assent with her on the practicability of these newer ideals. What if from the melting-pot there might rise a glow of principle that should illumine the thinking of the world? Alas, ten years later she was to see the greatest war in history re-arousing the old primitive antagonisms among her neighbors! Even in 1913 she was to know a strange morning, when two hundred Greeks who had held a meeting in the Hull House gymnasium marched from there to the train on their way to fight against Bulgarians six thousand miles away; to be followed by almost as many Bulgarians, parading down Halsted Street in the pride of setting out "to defend their homeland" against Serbians and Greeks. An Irishwoman of the neighborhood looked on gloomily. "Some good mother brought every one of thim fine-looking boys up," she said, "and now there they go half across the world to fight one another. Why couldn't they pair off here in the streets and settle it with their fists, if they have anything to settle?"

In 1906 Jane Addams, already a Wisconsin LL.D., the first woman to be so honored by the university, was asked to deliver a course of lectures at the University summer school. She chose the "newer ideals of peace" as her subject. The next year her book with that title was published. It attracted considerable attention, both favorable and unfavorable. A Chicago woman, Mrs. Tiffany Blake, finding herself in Washington with an opportunity to interview Theodore Roosevelt about the protection of immigrants, identified herself by saying that Jane Addams had sent her. Roosevelt, who had been sunk down in his big green leather chair, straightened and champed his jaws.

"Jane Addams—don't talk to me about Jane Addams! I have always thought a lot of her, but she has just written a bad book, a very bad book! She is all wrong about peace." He commented in detail, showing an acquaintance with every page. Then finally he slumped down again. "But she is a fine woman in every other way. Now I've got that out of my system, she sent you here, did she? What can I do for you?"

Somewhat to her own surprise, *Newer Ideals of Peace* was enthusiastically received. The reviewers, who are generally concerned with what they regard as the "literary" value or lack of value of a book, spoke in high praise of it. But it became a best seller on the basis of its philosophy, and this philosophy in 1907 provoked no animosity. Nobody called her a traitor, or a menace, or even a radical, on account of it. Indeed a Hearst editor said of her: "On the whole the reach of this woman's sympathy and understanding is beyond all comparison wider in its span, comprehending more kinds of people, than that of any extant public man. And it is to be observed further that this comprehension is not, in Miss Addams, purchased at the price of vagueness and sentimentality. She is a thinker and a woman of action. . . . To the dust-dry counsels of materialists and statisticians she brings the lift and passion of large ideas." Among suffragists she came presently to be regarded as the intellectual leader of the movement for women's rights, her suggestions as to woman's place in the "household of government" to be called the "most sensible." Not unnaturally, such a reception of her ideas heartened her. She became genuinely hopeful of peace.

At the first National Peace Congress to be held in the United States, in 1907, Governor Charles Hughes of New York and Elihu Root made stirring addresses. Presidents Eliot of Harvard and Nicholas Murray Butler of Columbia, Felix Adler and Samuel Gompers, Archbishop Ireland and William Jennings Bryan, Edward Everett Hale and Seth Low, were among the scores of speakers. Jane Addams of course represented the women, along with Mrs. Charles Henrotin. The resolutions adopted were "strong and prophetic." The dove flew high, and brought back the green leaf of hope for the world. Conferences at Lake Mohonk enlisted the interest of the politically eminent. Presently a rich, practical Boston publisher, Edwin Ginn, established an International School of Peace, promising $50,000 a year to forward "the systematic education of the people in peace principles." Edwin D. Mead, also of Boston, asserted that: "The only trouble with the leaders of the movement for international justice both in America and Europe in the last ten years has been that they have not been able to dream daringly and fast enough to keep pace with the facts . . . if we had been told ten years ago how much would be accomplished for peace in a decade, we should none of us have believed it . . . and the achievements of the next ten years will be as great."

The next year an equally enthusiastic Peace Congress was held in Chicago. President Taft was a peace advocate, large, calm, humorous and optimistic. As time went on, Jane Addams herself became optimistic. She found that she could, for instance, oppose the fortification of the Panama Canal in good company, and without rousing the fortifiers to fury. To be sure the Canal was fortified; but at least the discussion had been carried on without charges of "treachery" such as had been made in the struggle twelve years earlier against the annexation of the Philippines. In 1912, in the Progressive campaign, she emphasized in her many speeches the statement that her candidate for the Presidency, Theodore Roosevelt, had as President made the United States first of all the nations to use the World Court of Conciliation and Arbitration at The Hague, and had secured settlement by arbitration of a long-standing dispute with Mexico. She pointed out that he had from the start urged arbitration in the Venezuela case; that he had himself settled by arbitration the Russo-Japanese war; that he, with the rest of the country, was moving away from war. At a great meeting in Carnegie Hall in New York, as late as 1913, she reaffirmed a conviction the possibilities of which had once so startled her, that, ". . . there was rising in the cosmopolitan centers of America a sturdy and unprecedented international understanding which in time would be too profound to lend itself to war."

An undramatic, intellectual remark; but the applause was "terrific." And the next year, the World War came.

Jane Addams and Mary Rozet Smith had bought a little house on the shore of Frenchman's Bay, near Bar Harbor. She was spending the summer there when she learned that Europe was all at once in arms. Then two days later right below her hill loomed up one morning a German liner, the *Kronprinzessin Cecilie*, which had put in there to escape capture. "The huge boat in her incongruous setting was the first fantastic impression of that strange summer when we were so incredibly required to adjust our minds to a changed world."

What could she do? She was not at the moment fearful that the United States would enter the war. She did not see so far as that. Already she had confidence in Wilson, a confidence which was later to be largely destroyed. Had he not said when he was inaugurated: "I summon all honest men, all patriotic, all forward-looking men to my side. God helping me, I will not fail them, if they will but counsel and sustain me."

More important, had he not instituted some of the very reforms of the social system which the Progressives had advocated? Most important of all, at the moment, did he not at once declare that the country would be neutral; that neutrality was our duty not only in action, not only in word, but even in thought? Wilson's, however, was the neutrality of indifference and irritation. Jane Addams construed "neutrality of thought" as an active thing. Neutrality meant for her, opportunity. The people of the United States, the greatest neutral country in the world, must not only remain out of war themselves, but they must do everything possible to get the participants out of it. But what?

She did not hesitate to compare warfare to human sacrifice for religious ideals. In this comparison, and in her immediate and active continuation of her long advocacy of the necessity of peace, she again had at first wide support. "Social workers" all over the country were at one in their desire to "find some channel in which the thought of America may run toward a better world order." Among the women of the country she took the lead. In January of 1915 she was elected chairman of the newly organized Women's Peace Party. She was also made chairman of the first national "peace convention," which was held in Chicago in the following March, with delegates from the Atlantic to the Rocky Mountains, and which formed a National Peace Federation over which she was chosen to preside. Said the Chicago *Daily News* of this meeting: "The petition and platform were thought by those from the east and from Europe to be worthy of the city in which Abraham Lincoln was nominated for the presidency of the United States and were expected to lead up toward emancipation from war."

The Women's Peace Party at its organization in Washington had adopted a platform of eleven "planks," some of which were subsequently embodied, with changes of form, of course, in President Wilson's famous "fourteen points." The first of these planks, however, demanded "an immediate calling of a convention of neutral nations in the interest of early peace." This plank was based on a plan for "continuous mediation," which, first suggested by Madam Rosika Schwimmer, had been drawn up by Miss Julia G. Wales, a teacher of English in the University of Wisconsin, put before the Wisconsin state legislature, and been approved by both houses and sent on to Congress with the recommendation that it be adopted by that body. The plan suggested an International Commission of Experts to sit as long as the war continued, with a purely scientific function: to explore the issues involved in the struggle, that proposal after proposal (if necessary) might be made to the belligerents, in a spirit of "constructive internationalism." Of course such a Commission must be composed of representatives of neutral nations. It was partly as influenced by this plan that the

Women's Peace Party became immediately so enthusiastic a body.

In February of 1915 a meeting of women from European countries was called at Amsterdam, to make plans for a "congress" to discuss the special problems of the existing situation. At this meeting women were present from Belgium, Germany, Great Britain and of course the Netherlands; many women from other countries, belligerent and neutral, though unable to come, sent letters of encouragement. At this meeting it was decided to hold the Congress at The Hague on April 27th, to urge representatives from the United States, the most powerful country among the neutrals, to be present, and to ask Jane Addams, president of the United States Women's Peace Party, to preside. She accepted; presided; and became thenceforth not Jane Addams of Hull House only, but Jane Addams of the W. I. L., the Women's International League for Peace and Freedom.

In *Women at the Hague* published in 1915, *Peace and Bread in Time of War,* published in 1922, and *The Second Twenty Years at Hull House,* published in 1930, she has told the story of her relations to peace and to the League, emphasizing, however, peace and the League. In retelling that story briefly, the emphasis will be shifted to Jane Addams. It has to be admitted that if she were alive, she would protest against such a shift of emphasis.

CHAPTER XV

"CONTINUOUS MEDIATION"

THE *Noordam*, with Jane Addams and forty-two other delegates to the "congress" at The Hague, sailed from New York early in April, 1915. The weather was good, the boat (loaded with grain) was steady, there were no scares, and the delegates were almost the only passengers.

There were eight club-women, six teachers, three magazine writers, three labor leaders, three settlement workers, two poets, one lawyer, one doctor, one bond saleswoman, and one painter among the party. They sailed with the curse upon them of Colonel Roosevelt, Jane Addams's former friend. "Pacifists," he had written to Mrs. George Rublee, who made the trip, "are cowards, and your scheme is both silly and base." The letter is not in the files of the Women's Peace Party, but the Colonel took care to make it an open one, and it was widely published in American newspapers at the time.

One of the few on the *Noordam* was Henry Justin Smith, then a special correspondent for, now managing editor of, the Chicago *Daily News*. Smith wrote from The Hague:

The personnel of the party, the spirit of the discussions, the motives and opinions that became crystallized, made the *Noordam's* trip a bigger thing than it seemed at Sandy Hook.

It was more like accomplishment than like preparation, more like climax than like approach.... It is difficult to put into laconic prose the meaning of this journey. To some of us as evening deepened over the sea and mist gathered around that bright spot in the west where lay America and home, it seemed as though even the striving little vessel knew its mission and as though the marching cloudbanks on either horizon kept pace with the ship, like natural convoys. These women had embarked because the cry from the women of Europe was too pitiful to be ignored, and because it is feminine nature to respond impulsively and completely.... It was a serious-minded party enough, but it was not a gloomy one. In the central group, where the women flocked round Miss Addams, there generally was laughter. But there could scarcely be hilarity, for the women bore in their memories the awful tidings they had received from their sisters abroad, tidings of sexual horrors, of naked children, of ruined generations, of racial peril.... They had left home with a purpose so lofty that merely to entertain it was in a way fulfilment. Just as the captain, weighted with a responsibility so great that he must bear it lightly or succumb, tramped the bridge and scanned the sea for an invisible goal, so the peace delegates strained their eyes toward a hope more darkly veiled than the coast of Holland—and did it serenely.

The half-dozen male passengers on board were mostly scornful at first, Smith records, but "brought into contact with some of the most intellectual women of the United States (they could not remain so." Gradually one by one they drifted in to listen to the twice-daily meetings "for instruction in international peace as a science." Finally they were all to be seen, "sitting with the delegates, imbibing the doctrines of Grotius and Norman Angell, Hamilton Holt and William Howard Taft," and ultimately imbibing nothing else. "It is doubtful," Smith remarks, "whether a dozen bottles of champagne were at the end of the voyage missing from the ship's stores." The delegates had no hope of "ending the war" speedily, little hope of even helping to end it. Their one hope was that the coming together of women from warring as well as from neutral countries might result in an influence upon statesmen, who alone could end the war. They resolved that as a delegation, their concerted effort should be to get the Congress to support the Wales plan of "continuous mediation." By April 21st they had reached the English Channel; the Congress was not to meet until the 27th. Apparently they had plenty of time. But the boat was held up near Dover for five days. The women were not allowed to land, not allowed to have any one come aboard, not allowed to indicate by any sort of messages their whereabouts. All telegrams were of course censored. They were surrounded by vessels of five nations, including many English war-vessels. Once they saw a loose mine exploded by gun-fire. Ambassador Page telegraphed that he could do nothing for them. But at last they were "released as mysteriously as they had been stopped," and were landed on the 27th at Rotterdam. They got to The Hague by six o'clock, and were on time for the first session of the Congress at eight that evening.

The English delegation of 180 had been prevented by the authorities from coming, though three of them managed to get there. No women came from France, Russia, or Servia. Germany sent twenty-eight, Belgium five. Of the neutral nations Norway, Sweden and Denmark sent delegations, and of the women of Holland there were as many present as the hall would accommodate; about 1,100 actually voted on resolutions. Twelve nations in all were represented, and resolutions of sympathy were received from women of ten other nations who had paid dues as delegates but were unable to attend. Doctor Aletta Jacobs of Holland, first woman in Holland to become a physician, welcomed the delegates. "Those of us who have convened this Congress," she said, "have never called it a *peace* congress, but an international congress of women to protest against war, and to discuss ways and means whereby war shall become an impossibility in the future." She added, "We consider that the introduction of woman suffrage in all countries is one of the most powerful means to prevent war in the future." The reader is invited to note that sentence. What those women believed, one and all, was that really to help in the prevention of war, women must have *more political power*. During and subsequent to the World War, they got more political power. Why? There can be little question that it was because men came to agree with them that political power in the hands of women does help to prevent war. Henry A. Wise Wood, speaking against suffrage in 1917, said: "Votes for women in wartime are out of place. What is needed in wartime is sternness and determination—the hand of man and the hand of man only."

It was probably the strongest argument *for* woman suffrage that he could have found.

Wednesday morning the deliberations of the Congress began, Jane Addams in the chair. Try to imagine the complications of those meetings, with twelve nations represented by women (who are notoriously unbusinesslike and emotional, or were supposed to be so at that time). All the galleries were, for the first two days, filled with police. The discussions were carried on in three languages, English, German and French, of which the chairman spoke one only. (Fortunately she understood the other two so well that often she ventured to correct the interpreters in their translations of what was said.) There were many famous women speakers present, and some of them, like Madame Rosika Schwimmer, had to speak often or burst. All sorts of resolutions were introduced, a few of them—like the demand for "an immediate truce" —almost as unfortunate as the remark later put into the mouth of Henry Ford, that the boys must be got out of the trenches by Christmas. The Congress however adopted rules of procedure so remarkably sensible that they have been maintained practically unchanged through five subsequent congresses. Throughout everything Jane Addams not only kept her head, not only kept control of the Congress, but made it a unit of feeling. In those four days she made herself a new international reputation; not so much as a parliamentarian, though she was a good parliamentarian, but as a worker in the gold of human nature. She did not so much lead as shepherd those ideas of all breeds into the fold of unity. Twenty resolutions were adopted. In the final ten minutes, Jane Addams read a cable from America. President Wilson was reported thus:

While the United States government was not consulted in connection with the International Women's Conference at The Hague, the President indicated to-day that the movement had his sympathetic support. Although the meeting has no official status, the President said he understood the delegation had not asked for official authority, because they preferred to act unofficially.

There was applause, long-continued. Jane Addams said:

There is no further resolution before the Congress. This is the first International Congress of women met in the cause of peace in the necessity brought about by the greatest war the world has ever seen. We have been able to preserve good-will and good fellowship, we have considered in perfect harmony and straight-forwardness the most difficult propositions, and we part better friends than we met. It seems to me most significant that women have been able to do this at this moment and that they have done it, in my opinion, extremely well. With these words I will, if I may, declare this Congress adjourned.

What can only be described as the most remarkable assemblage in the history up to that time of women's dealings with world affairs, ended with no more emotion than is inherent in silence.

Of the resolutions, one called for particular action. It was that based on the "American" plan:

This International Congress of Women resolves to ask the neutral countries to take immediate steps to create a conference of neutral nations which shall without delay offer continuous mediation. The Conference shall invite suggestions for settlement from each of the belligerent nations and in any case shall submit to all of them, simultaneously, reasonable proposals as a basis of peace.

A Committee of Women of All Countries was formed, to arrange for the holding of an international meeting of women at the same place (if possible) and at the same time as the Conference which no doubt would frame the terms of peace settlement after the war; and an International Committee of Women for Permanent Peace, five members from each country. Of this International Committee, Jane Addams was made chairman. And therefore she, with Doctor Aletta Jacobs, was appointed to interview the statesmen of the various countries on the subject of the wisdom and practicability of a policy of continuous mediation.

They saw the Dutch ministers first, then Asquith and Grey in London. On May 19th, accompanied by Frau Palthe of The Hague, and Doctor Alice Hamilton, as "tour managers" so to speak, they set out for Berlin. Ambassador Gerard, much against his own will, as he took pains to say later in his *My Four Years in Germany*, got them audiences with von Bethmann-Hollweg and von Jagow. Thence they went to Vienna, Budapest, Berne, Rome, Paris, Havre (where the Belgian government had headquarters) and London again. Other women were sent by the Congress to Copenhagen, Christiania (now Oslo), Stockholm, Petrograd and Washington—in the Washington instance, Madame Schwimmer, not a fortunate choice, for she was a showman by instinct, and this was no moment for showmanship. She carried the same credentials and resolutions as the other delegates; but she carried hers in "a little black bag," and surrounded them with so much mystery that many years later Mark Sullivan could call them "confidential statements." In Europe there was no showmanship. Jane Addams herself conferred with eight prime ministers or presidents, and nine foreign ministers; also with the Pope, though in this latter case not officially as a delegate from the Congress. She found them all, with one exception, (Delcassé in Paris) "ready to stop the war immediately if some honorable method of securing peace were provided," which was of course to have been expected; but she also found them ready in various cases to admit that the plan of continuous mediation was a good plan, and

found all in the neutral countries willing to undertake it
if the United States would take the lead. The most out-
spoken was Prime Minister Stuergkh of Austria. He was
a large, grizzled, formidable man. When we had finished our
presentation and he said nothing, I remarked, "It perhaps
seems to you very foolish that women should go about in this
way; but after all the world itself is so strange in this war
situation that our mission may be no more strange or foolish
than the rest." He banged his fist on the table.
"Foolish? Not at all. These are the first sensible words that
have been uttered in this room for ten months. That door opens
from time to time and people come in to say, 'Mr. Minister,
we must have more men, we must have more ammunition, we
must have more money or we cannot go on with this war.' At
last the door opens and two people walk in and say, 'Mr.
Minister, why not substitute negotiations for fighting?' They
are the sensible ones."

Later Colonel House was to tell Wilson that "Jane
Addams picked up a remarkable amount of misinforma-
tion," and that "the ministers were not quite candid with
her." There is no question of candor involved. They said
(all but Delcassé) that if neutral people commanding the
respect of the foreign offices to whom their propositions
would be presented should study the situation and make
propositions, over and over again perhaps, something
might be found upon which negotiations might begin, and
that their nation was ready to receive such service. Either
they told the truth, or they lied. It would have been easy
for the authorities of the United States to discover
whether they were lying. If they were telling the truth,
the plan of continuous mediation might have saved millions of lives, billions of dollars, and the shipwreck of
Europe.

House never wanted, never had wanted, "peace without victory." He wanted peace with the advantage inclining to the side of France and Great Britain. Lord Grey said:

> When House came to London after the outbreak of the war I found combined in him in a rare degree the qualities of wisdom and sympathy. . . . House left me in no doubt from the first that he held German militarism responsible for the war, and that he regarded the struggle as one between democracy and something that was undemocratic and antipathetic to American ideals. It was not necessary to spend much time in putting our case to him. . . . In this awful calamity of war the end to be sought for was a just, fair and reasonable peace. He was in Europe to study the situation, to investigate the means by which such a peace could be brought about.

That is to say, a peace reasonable from the point of view of Great Britain and France.

The consistency of Jane Addams's attachment to the plan of "continuous mediation" and her attachment to the "settlement idea" should be obvious. At a dinner in her honor given by twelve hundred members of the Progressive Club in Chicago in February, 1913, Bainbridge Colby had said: "Refusing to lull her conscience by any dreamer's scheme, unbeguiled by paper reforms, she set out early in life 'to make social intercourse express the growing sense of the economic unity of society.' Proceeding upon the sober theory that the dependence of classes upon each other is reciprocal, she determined to deal directly with the simplest human wants." Just so unbeguiled in wartime by any phrases, not lulled by any "dreamer's scheme," she found and lent her persistent support to a simple, practical plan of procedure. She proposed, as Miss Emily Balch put it, "the exposure of the policies of the lords of war to the pressure of the masses of the people in neutral countries whose interest was peace, not this political war aim or that." Her conviction was that the device of placing conditional proposals simultaneously before both sides would bring out into the open the real attitudes of governments, and that to place sane proposals before the nations at once would prevent that increase of misunderstanding and bitterness, which in the end made a reasonable peace unattainable. That increase of misunderstanding and bitterness she clearly foresaw: "That finely tempered sense of justice, which alone is of any service in modern civilization, is impossible of attainment without mutual understanding, and mutual understanding sinks deeper and deeper from sight as the bitter waters of war rise higher."

The House plan of sole mediation by America was entirely different. Had the plan of the women been adopted, the Scandinavian countries, Switzerland, Holland, Spain and the South American republics would have balanced the House pro-Ally bias, and been therefore acceptable to the Central Powers. The plan of sole mediation utterly failed. That failure permitted the wreckage of Europe. Perhaps the women's plan too would have failed. But not to consider it in such a crisis was dull; to sneer at it was to be callous. What House could do to sell the women down the river, he did, and his actions on this occasion are the blackest blot on his whole record.

The week by week story of that journey to European capitals has been told by Doctor Hamilton in *Women at The Hague;* there is no necessity to retell it here. They encountered a few inconveniences, no hardships—unless the necessity of listening politely to the genteel humor of

Ambassadors Gerard and Page (the latter an old friend
of Miss Addams, but of course "more English than the
English" at the moment) can be called hardships. Jane
Addams herself summed up the experience: "We do not
wish to take too seriously the kindness with which the
delegation was received, but we wish to record ourselves
as sure that at least a few citizens in these various countries, some of them officials in high places, were grateful
for the effort we made."

The horrible failure to comprehend the effects of war
which was shown by even intelligent people is well illustrated by two brief passages in Mark Sullivan's *Over
Here*, published in 1933. He points out that in the first
months of the war we had far less complaint against Germany than against England, but adds: "The average man
understood, however, a fundamental distinction between
Germany's violations of our neutrality and Britain's:
British violations injured property almost alone, never
human life; ... Germany's injuries to us on the other
hand often included bloodshed, loss of life."

And on the same page he quotes from President
Wilson's speech calling for our declaration of war:
"Property can be paid for; the lives of peaceful and innocent people cannot be. The present German submarine
warfare against commerce is a warfare against mankind."

Now, of course, the declaration of England that food
was contraband, and the blockade of foodships which
Great Britain established against Germany, caused a far
greater loss of human life than all Germany's submarines;
and not only of human life, but of child life, the life of
the future. Jane Addams and the women of the International League pointed this out over and over again, in

1915 and thereafter; but so fixed is the average mind in the feeling that there is no destruction of life except immediate destruction, by "bloodshed," that they had little effect on public opinion; how little, Sullivan's own calm passing over of the facts eighteen years later, grimly shows. To be sure, the life destroyed through starvation by England's ships was German and Austrian child life, some of the lives destroyed by the German submarines were of our own people. This may have been a fundamental difference, though it did not seem so to Jane Addams, to whom all human life was sacred. But it may have seemed so to Wilson and Mark Sullivan and the American people in general. It is not however the difference between the German and the English atrocities which Wilson and Sullivan mention.

CHAPTER XVI

STANDING ALONE

RETURNING to the United States in July of 1915, Jane Addams found herself apparently supported by public opinion in her efforts for peace. A mass-meeting in Carnegie Hall in New York agreed that "a continuous convention of neutrals would create a channel through which some opportunity might lead to peace," and accepted with applause Jane Addams's statement that "the civil leaders of Europe would welcome an opportunity to end the war and stay the carnage." Those statesmen, she told the audience, felt that if they themselves talked of terms of peace, their position would be weakened in their own country and before the world; but they had told her they would welcome action by neutrals which would make negotiations honorable, and had agreed on the United States as preëminently the country, with its mixed people and democratic prestige, to take the initiative in organizing such a convention. From New York she went to Washington, where she had a brief interview with Wilson and handed him The Hague resolutions. Thence she went to Chicago, where a delegation from the city council met her at the station to congratulate her on her service to the world and her advertisement of the quality of the citizenship of that city. She had for the moment high hopes that Wilson would take the initiative suggested in the resolutions. Had he not on October 4, 1914, urged the whole nation to pray for peace? Had he not shown in his whole diplomatic attitude both before and *after* the sinking of the *Lusitania* on May 7th, 1915, that he thought both sides in the war wrong in various ways? Had he not frequently mentioned the responsibility of the United States in this crisis, as a great and peace-loving nation? Even in October, when she saw Wilson again, "he drew out the papers I had given him, and they seemed to have been much handled and read. 'You see I have studied these resolutions,' he said. 'I consider them by far the best formulation which up to the moment has been put out by anybody.' "

But she did not know Wilson. Perhaps he did not know himself. She could not get him to commit himself to the policy of "continuous mediation."

House, who knew nothing of Jane Addams except that she had supported Roosevelt, the Wilson-hater, in 1912, had told Wilson that "Miss Addams had a totally wrong impression," and House had Wilson's ear. Another mis-representation of her had reached Wilson, as it had reached almost everybody in the United States. Within a week after she got back, the newspapers were attacking her with a quite splendid ferocity. She had said at Carnegie Hall:

The soldiers themselves call this "the old men's war." Many of the young fellows in the trenches think that war as a method of settling international difficulties is out of date. Hand to hand fighting seems to them contrary to every teaching of civiliza-tion. This detestation of violence is typical of the generation. We were told by young men everywhere who had been at the front, that men had literally to be stimulated to a willingness to perform the bloody work of bayonet charges. The English are in such cases given rum, the French, it is said, absinthe; the Germans, more scientifically perhaps, inhalations of ether.

"It did not occur to me," she said later, "that the information was either new or startling." It was not. But she would have been saved a good deal of annoyance if it had occurred to her that it was precisely the sort of remark that lent itself to misrepresentation. Richard Harding Davis, himself fifty-two and no longer up to active soldiering, naturally resented the reference to "an old man's war," and wrote a fierce letter to *The New York Times* declaring that Jane Addams in saying that English soldiers had to be made drunk before they would fight, was falsely and gratuitously insulting the youth of England. His misunderstanding, to give it a mild name, of what she had actually said, was taken up and elaborated by many others who had even less reason for resentment than he. The summer became a welter of newspaper attacks and wretched letters. To this day the belief exists in certain quarters that Jane Addams "attacked the courage of the British soldier"; various Canadian papers after she died, in editorial comment otherwise laudatory, regretted this one "grave error." It was an error—a failure to realize the emotionalism of the times. If Davis and the rest had known Jane Addams, they would have known it was impossible for her to challenge the courage of young men, if for no other reason than that she herself was fully courageous, and brave people do not suspect others of cowardice any more than truthful people suspect others of lying. But the question was after all not really whether Jane Addams had said that soldiers had to be made drunk to fight, or even that soldiers liked to drink. The question was how to make pacifism unpopular, and the swashbucklers knew that the best way was through personal attacks on pacifists. That has always been the easiest way, and always will be. These attacks on her were not important in their effect on Wilson, but they reached him. Miss Addams had hoped and expected to be able to present her case more fully to the President at Cornish, New Hampshire, where he was spending some time. But he could not be interrupted there, even by matters of state.

"He is walking humbly with God," said a friend of hers, an admirer of Wilson, in an awed fashion.

"Walking humbly with Galt," snapped Florence Kelley, and it was a fact; Mr. Wilson and Mrs. Galt were married in November.

But all these were small matters, except the caution of Colonel House. The determining factor in President Wilson's disinclination to discuss the matter of "continuous mediation" was President Wilson. The plan involved the coöperation of many neutral nations, and the President was not by nature willing to coöperate. He must not only lead; he must act alone. In December of 1915 he was to insist in a famous message on a "negotiated peace," which was in line with the women's policy; but it was to be a Wilson-negotiated peace, which was not so practical. There can be little doubt that he did not wish to see Jane Addams that summer or fall, because he did not wish to be annoyed by arguments for a line of action that must be taken, if at all, with others. He had no eagerness for work with others, and no skill in such work.

So the summer passed, and from ten to twenty thousand men were slaughtered every day, and the "hymns of hate" drowned out any faint cries for understanding that the women were able to raise. And in November began the melodrama of Ford and the "peace ship," which the newspapers so quickly managed to turn into a farce that no man can even imagine what might have been its importance in the theater of the war if it had been given a chance. Mark Sullivan, in *Our Times: Over Here,* says: "One wonders, at this distance, if the newspapers were living up to their functions in the highest way, when they made this attempt at peace an occasion for ridicule." Either Jane Addams contributed that sentence, or it is the bitterest bit of meiosis that Mark Sullivan ever penned. She, however, would have put it in just that way, gently.

In 1915 the war seemed to Henry Ford a wild and wicked business. He had no reasoned theory of it, but he had strong emotions. He wanted to "do something about it," but he had no idea what. Madame Schwimmer, in Detroit to talk on peace, discovered in the papers a statement attributed to Ford that he would be willing to spend half his fortune to shorten the war by one day. Even one day's curtailment would save, he guessed, ten thousand lives. Madame Schwimmer reached him, presented to him her version of the plan for continuous mediation, dazed him with her rapid eloquence and obvious sincerity. In a few days Ford was in New York, in a hotel suite, talking plans over with various people, Jane Addams among them. Ford sat on a bed, one foot under him, watching Madame Schwimmer gesticulate. "Earnest, well-meaning, confused," Jane Addams thought him, with the "earthy, not common" look of Lincoln. She left New York, to learn in Chicago that Ford had decided to charter a ship to take over "delegates" to a sort of private commission for continuous mediation. She was distressed. The only piece of "showmanship" in connection with the advertisement of a principle she had ever been connected with had been the "Woman's Special" in the Suffrage Campaign in 1909, and even that she had merely consented to, not advised. She distrusted the newspapers, having herself just been through a summer-long campaign of misstatement, misrepresentation and ridicule. But she could do nothing but agree to go. It was a great thing to have the fortune of Mr. Ford enlisted for peace. The chartered *Oskar II* was to sail on December 4th. On December 1st Jane Addams contracted pleuro-pneumonia in Chicago. To her in the Presbyterian Hospital President Wilson sent flowers and a letter of sympathy. The *Oskar II* sailed without her. After her partial recovery from pneumonia, in five weeks, she went to Washington to a meeting of the Women's Peace Party, and almost collapsed from weakness. She was taken to California, where her health improved; but in April, when she returned to Chicago, she suddenly showed alarming symptoms. Her friend and personal physician, Doctor James B. Herrick, diagnosed her ailment as tuberculosis of the kidneys. Surgeons removed one kidney. She was informed that when she left the hospital she must remain very quiet, spending most of the day in bed. Mr. Ford wished her to go to Stockholm as delegate to a peace conference there, of which he was paying the expenses. The doctors informed her she would die if she did. She secured Miss Emily Balch in her place, stayed in her room and spent what little strength she had on writing—producing, incidentally, one of the most interesting articles she ever wrote, the well-known "Devil-Baby at Hull House." In Bar Harbor in the summer, she tried to rest, wrote chapters of *The Long Road of*

Woman's Memory, and occasionally read the newspaper clippings that continued to pour in on her, some accusing her of having insulted the armies, all the armies, and others lamenting that a woman who had really been an influence for good should have so completely damaged her social value. In October she returned to Chicago; on November 14th she was once more able to resume her work at Hull House—one year, less two weeks, since she had been able to do anything there. She was more than half an invalid for the next two years. The newspapers said that she had pretended to be sick so that she need not accompany the Ford ship. That was natural enough. She offered the facts of the matter, but apparently nobody believed either her or her physician. Seventeen years later, in *Our Times,* Mark Sullivan wrote, of her failure to accompany Ford, that "Jane Addams pleaded illness"(!) Another example of meiosis. The truth is that disturbed as she was over the "peace ship" hysteria, she always regretted that she had been unable to sail on the *Oskar II.* She did not think her presence would have accomplished anything, but she could not help being aware of the calming effect of her spirit. It is just possible that she might have ridden the whirlwind and directed the storm of emotionalism that surrounded the expedition; it is almost certain that she would have modified its eccentricities, and to some extent clarified the purposes of Mr. Ford.

Mark Sullivan says (again seventeen years later) that the Ford expedition, "after its failure, dying down to an echo of gigantic and exhausted laughter, deprived every other peace movement in the country of force and conviction." The extraordinary inaccuracy of this comment tends to discredit Sullivan. Peace movements in the

United States were so full of force and conviction throughout 1916, that Wilson could be reëlected on the basis of the slogan "He kept us out of war." They were so full of force and conviction that the jingoes, including Theodore Roosevelt, were made furious. Such newspapers as the Chicago *Tribune* spat venom on "pacifism" day after day. If pacifism was without force or conviction, why the fear of it by the militarists?

In the summer and autumn of 1916, Jane Addams, recuperating at Bar Harbor, was a center of mild political interest. Wilson and Hughes, nominated for president, both sought her assistance: Hughes through representatives, Wilson directly. She had made, so the papers had said in 1912, a million votes for Roosevelt (a statement which she said in a speech at the Chicago City Club was like Mark Twain's comment on the rumor of his death, "greatly exaggerated"). However, there were still many people who thought her the woman of greatest political influence among women in the United States. T. R. himself had called on her in Chicago during her illness; Wilson had sent her roses, and written her several letters; Hughes supporters among the women sought comfort in the fact that her great friend and hostess at Bar Harbor, Mrs. Joseph Bowen, was eager for Hughes's election. In October, however, after her return to Chicago, Jane Addams allowed an announcement to be made that she would vote for Wilson. She followed this announcement with a detailed explanation of her reasons:

The present administration comes before the country with a social program that carries assurance because of a record of pledges fulfilled and a series of legislative achievements not equaled by any other administration. Prominent among its contributions to social and industrial justice are these:

It has been established as matter of law that labor is not to be considered a mere commodity or article of commerce.

The seamen have been made freemen and have been given the right, previously denied, to leave their employment when conditions become intolerable.

The products of child labor have been excluded from interstate commerce.

The most liberal workmen's compensation law in the world has been enacted, affecting 400,000 Federal employees.

The principle of the eight-hour day has been recognized. The rural credits bill and the Federal Reserve Act are contributions to the welfare of the entire country.

The administration has made certain distinct advances toward more rational international relations:

(a) Treaties have been signed with thirty nations which provide for a year's delay and investigation of matters at issue before diplomatic relations are severed.

(b) The repeal of the toll exemptions for American ships in the Panama Canal was a recognition of the principle of fair dealings among nations.

(c) Determination, in spite of almost insuperable difficulties and obvious blunders, to permit the Mexicans to work their way to self-government without recourse to the old imperialistic method of sending soldiers into a weaker nation, first to police property and then to become an army of occupation.

(d) During the past four years the Pan-American Union has been strengthened and made more genuine. The importance of this is not merely local, for this union has seemed to distressed and bewildered students of internationalism in Europe to offer an example of the kind of machinery for international action which is not inconsistent with a sound nationalism.

Wilson wrote:

My dear Miss Addams:

I cannot deny myself the pleasure of telling you how proud I am and how much strengthened I feel that I should have your approval and support. I know that you always act with such genuineness that no support could hearten me more than yours. . . .

                    Cordially and sincerely yours,
                                        WOODROW WILSON.

Many a newspaper carried the comment that "One of the hardest of the many hard blows dealt the campaign of Mr. Hughes among women is the announcement that Jane Addams is supporting President Wilson. The disposition of Miss Addams's first presidential vote is a matter of intense interest to every righteous American."

After the election she attended on December 12th the first "state dinner" of the winter at the White House, wearing flowers which had been sent her with a card from the President, and in that month he wrote her three times, thanking her for the encouragement of her support. The peace partisans all over the country were jubilant. "President Wilson's reëlection by the greatest popular vote ever given a Presidential candidate," they declared, "is due primarily to the fighting pacifist sentiment in the United States, which abandoned local traditions and party lines in an effort to express itself." This was a year after, according to Mark Sullivan, the Ford expedition had "deprived every other peace movement in the country of force and conviction."

It was in 1916 that Jane Addams published the book which next after *The Spirit of Youth and the City Streets* she herself "liked best"—*The Long Road of Woman's Memory*. She was fifty-six, but it was not the road of her own memory, though it was beginning to be long, that she traversed in this volume. She says:

As it would be hard for any one of us to select the summer in which he ceased to live that life so ardent in childhood and youth, when all the real happenings are in the future, so it must be difficult for old people to tell at what period they began to regard the present chiefly as a prolongation of the past.... But it is most fortunate that in some subtle fashion these old people, reviewing the long road they have traveled, are able to translate their own untoward experiences into that which seems to make even the most wretched life acceptable.

And she goes on to untangle and set forth the characteristics of the memories of women, as they have transmuted the past, interpreted the present, disturbed and denied conventions, brought the individual into relation with the impersonal aspects of life, and challenged war:

The women in every country who are under a profound imperative to preserve human life, have a right to regard this maternal impulse as important now, as was the compelling instinct evinced by primitive women long ago, when they made the first crude beginnings of society by refusing to share the vagrant life of man because they insisted upon a fixed abode in which they might cherish their children. Undoubtedly women were then told that the interests of the tribe, the diminishing food supply, the honor of the chieftain, demanded that they leave their particular cave and go out in the wind and weather without regard to the survival of their children. But at the present moment the very names of the tribes and of the honors and glories for which they sought are forgotten, while the basic fact that the mothers held the lives of their children above all else, insisted upon staying where the children had a chance to live, and cultivated the earth for their food, laid the foundations of an ordered society.

In some respects *The Long Road of Woman's Memory* is more obviously characteristic of Jane Addams's habits of thought than any other of her books. More than once

JANE ADDAMS IN HONOLULU
She was President of the Pan-
Pacific Women's Union in 1928.

JANE ADDAMS IN THE PHILIPPINES
With her is the Philippine Islands delegation to the Pan-Pacific
Conference.

in her writings she quotes Plato's phrase "the eternal pattern." Even in her childhood, as has been pointed out, she was somehow conscious of the appeal of the patterns of life. Always her heart went out to the children of the streets, piteously unable even in their play to preserve continuity in the working out of the "fragments from their dreams of life." In her philosophy she is continually going back to beginnings, tracing survivals of old impulses and emotions. In her efforts for new legislation, she ever attempted to connect it with old, persistent necessities in human experience:

> Premature reforms fail. Doctrinaire reforms fail. We must find the folkways. Reforms to be effective must be rooted in and routed through the social consciousness. . . .
> There comes to one in Switzerland more than anywhere else those glimpses of what Plato calls "the eternal pattern" . . . we are unconsciously reminded of the geologic ages with their prodigious length of time and so lose all sense of impatience.

So in this chapter on the woman's challenge to war, she went back to the first "foundations of an ordered society" to account for it and explain its implications. She could not see civilization as a series of revolutions, of transformations by violence; she could see it only as a growth, something nurtured and tended; and nurtured and tended particularly, perhaps, by women. It was a cosmic thing, this "long road of woman's memory"; symbolic in its interpretation of to-day. Though this she did not say directly. The indirection is as effective as it is unmistakable. "At the present moment the very names of the tribes and the honors and glories which they sought are forgotten"—the present moment, when Europe had been at war for two horrible years, with no change in position,

no prospect of diminution of horror. "The basic fact that
the mothers held the lives of their children *above all else*
. . . laid the foundations of an ordered society." Reasoned,
wistful, ironic! It was this sort of thing that the newspapers (some of them) called "rushing in where even the
Hull House 'angel' should fear to tread, in an endeavor
to secure personal publicity by the discussion of matters
she does not know anything about," and that the acidu-
lous essayist Agnes Repplier described as "the ruthless
sentimentality of Jane Addams." One wonders just how
proud Miss Repplier is to-day of her reiterated story of
the "Boston gentleman of my acquaintance who told me
that he was sick to death of three words, efficiency, reform, and Jane Addams." It was at this time that Jane
Addams herself defined the "freedom of the press" as "the
freedom to misinterpret any statement they do not like,
and to suppress any statement they do not understand."

On December 18, 1916, a week after he had sent
flowers to Jane Addams, Wilson sent a bouquet of identical notes to all the belligerents. He had "long had it in
mind" to suggest that "an early occasion be sought to call
out from all the nations now at war an avowal of their
respective views as to the terms upon which the war
might be concluded, and the arrangements which would
be deemed satisfactory as a guarantee against the kindling
of any similar conflict in future." Jane Addams read this
note with satisfaction mingled with wonderment. This
was precisely along the lines she and the Women's League
had indicated; but it did not go far enough. This was an
offer of mediation, but not of "continuous mediation," nor
of mediation by *all* the neutrals. Mr. Wilson preferred to
act alone? Better that than passive neutrality. She wrote

him on Christmas Day, thanking him; he answered the day he received her note; first regretting that Ida Tarbell was not well enough to be able to serve, as Jane Addams had suggested, on the Tariff Commission, and then adding: "Thank you very warmly for your word about the note to the belligerent powers. I knew that you would sympathize and am happy to think of your sympathy."

Germany said that a speedy assembly, on neutral ground, of delegates of the warring states would be welcome. The Allies said No! Wilson's proposal was too late; the Kaiser's acceptance was "empty and insincere." On January 22nd Wilson replied with his famous demand for "peace without victory," and the assertion that the United States "would add their authority and power to the authority and force of other nations to guarantee peace and justice throughout the world," through a "League of Peace"; accompanied by a statement of several of what became later the "Fourteen Points." Jane Addams wrote again, and this time received no reply. For on January 31st, Germany announced that the next day it would undertake unrestricted submarine warfare. Four days later Wilson told Congress that "all diplomatic relations between United States and Germany are severed."

From Jane Addams's point of view the worst had happened. The worst was not that the United States would now probably enter the war. She did not think it was much worse for the United States to enter the war than for England, France, Germany and the rest to be at war. The worst was that now the war would go on to the bitter end. She did not cease her efforts for peace. But immediately she added such efforts as she was capable of to minimize slaughter and "moralize" warfare. As one of a committee of five she went at once to Washington and had an interview with Wilson. She came away "in deep dejection." She felt, for the first time, that as a "pacifist" she was "officially outlawed." She had telegraphed on the news of Germany's submarine announcement:

> Many of us hope that you may find it possible to meet present international situation in league with other neutral nations in Europe and South America, whose interests are involved. Such an alliance might prove to be the beginning of a league standing for international rights and would at least offer a method of approach likely to involve any one nation in war.

She believed that the Fourteen Points could be consummated "only in an atmosphere free from the rancors of war." Wilson insisted that with Germany sinking neutral ships, there could be no such atmosphere discoverable. At the time, Wilson was right. Where Jane Addams had been right and Wilson had been wrong, was in the time when such standing for international rights could have been insisted on, eighteen months earlier, a year earlier. Now it was too late.

Jane Addams protested against conscription; quite in vain. Then she turned to the defense of the rights of "conscientious objectors"; not quite in vain, this time. Was was declared; the Women's Peace Party, adopting a "program during war time," appealed that "those of opposed opinions be loyal to the highest that they know, and let each understand that the other may be equally patriotic"; and the problem of the behavior of a pacifist in wartime became acutely personal to the best-known woman pacifist in the world.

The position of Hull House in the war might first be

stated. Most of the men residents were for the war. Eight of them who were under thirty volunteered, and six went overseas. Jane Addams's oldest nephew, an Episcopalian minister, forty-six years old in 1917, after being rejected for defective eyesight, managed to be made a chaplain with an artillery unit, spent four months at the front, and was killed in the Argonne a month before the Armistice while distributing chocolate to the men of the battery, moving from gun to gun under heavy fire. Her youngest nephew, thirty-four and married, served as a Y. M. C. A. helper in France for more than a year. Both had lived at Hull House at intervals. Doctor James A. Britton served in the Medical Corps in Washington; George Hooker, now the oldest of Hull House residents, was head of the draft board of the Hull House district, with a corps of volunteers from among the residents helping in the service. The women residents were much divided in opinion, but according to the recollection of older residents, more of them were outside the ranks of the pacifists than in them. Two women were working in France and Russia. Of the neighbors many had already been called to the armies of the countries in which they had been born; few of the others objected to conscription, except on the somewhat confused assumption that they had come, or their parents had come, to America because it was a country of peace. Eleven of the Hull House Boys' Band, with their bandmaster, enlisted as a group and were sent to France, and later into occupied territory. All soldiers from the district were given their last meal "at home" by Hull House, and said their farewells in the Hull House courtyard.

On the other hand, the House was a center of opposition to attacks on "aliens" as aliens. Most of the neighbors who had been born in Europe were under suspicion, especially the Central Europeans, the position of whose former governments in the war was not always clearly understood; as when a group of Rumanians were reported as conspiring against the Government, and it had to be pointed out to the ardent patriot who reported them that Rumania was on the side of the Allies. He could never, he admitted gloomily, "get them little countries straight." The activities against the "Reds"—a generic name for all suspected of affiliation with either Communism or Socialism—were also constant in Chicago as elsewhere:

> Organizations whose headquarters were constantly being raided brought us their "libraries"—pitiful little collections of battered books, to keep for them until the war was over. I always said that we would not hide them, but if they wanted to put the books in our open reading-room we would be glad to lend them the use of our shelves. There would be an occasional copy of Karl Marx or Bakunin, more often Herbert Spencer, but almost always Shakespeare's complete works and a Library of American Literature.

Throughout the war, and after the war, no one was ever arrested at Hull House, though various suspicious groups were watched there. The House was often thought to be "harboring conscientious objectors," but the transparent honesty and sincerity of Jane Addams herself was personally too well-known both to the President, and to Newton D. Baker the Secretary of War—who like Jane Addams had been an ardent advocate of peace in 1916— to be subject to investigation, and her view was that all matters of "conscientious objection" must be openly considered. By March of 1918 the Government had come definitely to accept the theory that even objectors who were not members of religious sects opposed to violence had a right to their scruples, and arranged for them to engage in non-combatant service; which was the only right Jane Addams ever claimed for them.

"Of course," said the Birmingham *Age-Herald*, expressing the general opinion, "the war department never will entertain her plea for the broad sweep of individual exemptions.... If Miss Addams's plea prevailed thousands of men who never had a conviction about any moral issue would get busy and have a conviction against fighting, and thus shirk a true man's duty.... Jane Addams, when it comes to war, is about as convincing as Congresswoman Rankin." Just about. And the war department finally "entertained her plea."

In fact, so far as the Government itself was concerned, Jane Addams remained herself *persona grata* throughout the war. In January of 1918 President Wilson wrote: "It gives me peculiar gratification that you and your associates should feel as you do about my recent address to the Congress and I thank you most warmly for your kindness...."

Secretary Baker never wavered in his view that she was a true patriot. Baker objected vigorously to the compilation of "suspect lists" in general, and to the inclusion of Jane Addams in them in particular: "I have no sympathy with such a general designation as 'pacifist,' which may mean any one of a dozen things, some of them quite consistent with the finest loyalty to the country and some of them inconsistent with such loyalty.... Miss Jane

Addams, for instance, lends dignity and greatness to any list in which her name appears."

Herbert Hoover, whom she had known in Belgium when in 1915 he was in charge of feeding ten million starving Europeans a month, and who had been called back to the United States as Food Administrator, requested her services in promoting the idea of food conservation, and she gave them eagerly. She was sent to speak on the subject in many states. In a few places she was considered "too pacifistic" to be allowed to talk; but in most she was greeted with courtesy, in some even with enthusiasm. Only the women's clubs refused to stand by. Her remarks to the Chicago Woman's Club in Chicago, on April 17, 1917, when she said: "That the United States has entered the war has not changed my views of the invalidity of war as a method of settlement of social problems a particle, and I can see no reason why one should not say what one believes in time of war as in time of peace ..." were greeted with gloomy silence. When she left the club, she said to Mary Smith, "I do not suppose I shall ever be applauded in Chicago again."

But among social workers generally she lost caste. On April 2, 1917, Mrs. Mary Kingsbury Simkhovitch of New York, president of the National Federation of Settlements —Hull House having grown into 170 groups by this time —had announced to the country that

it has been very painful to many of us who hold Miss Addams in deep affection and wholly respect her, to find that we cannot think or act in unison with her. . . . It is imperative for us to hesitate no longer. America cannot hold aloof ... it cannot stand apart, but must rather die that the world may live. . . . I have a personal certainty that the position I have outlined is that which a very large proportion of our group shares.

With a sweep of settlement skirts her social-worker friends thus drew aside from the mistaken woman; presumably also from Miss Lillian Wald of the House on Henry Street, though only Miss Addams is mentioned by name in the letter. By June the Chicago Woman's Club had notified her that the "peace committee" of the Club might meet no longer in the clubrooms.

Early in June she was asked by Catherine Waugh McCulloch, her old Rockford and "suffrage" co-worker, to speak at a Congregational church in Evanston on "Pacifism and Patriotism in Time of War." She said

the pacifist is making a venture into a new international ethics. He is afforded an opportunity to cultivate a fine valor ... for new ethics are unpopular ethics.... The pacifist must serve his country by forcing definitions if possible. If it seems to him that the multitude of German subjects who have settled and developed certain parts of the United States had every right to be considered as an important factor in the situation before war was declared, he should say so. He should insist that the United States declare its refusal to regard the deliberate starvation of the women and children of any nation as a proper war measure. Since war was declared, some of us have had a feeling that we are shirking moral service.

Judge Orrin Carter of the Superior Court, an old friend in the work of foundation of the Juvenile Court, rose in the blank silence that followed her remarks:

"I have always been a friend of Miss Addams," he said, "but—" He paused.

"The 'but' sounds ominous," she laughed.

"I think anything that may tend to cast doubt on the

justice of our cause in the present war is very unfortunate. In my opinion no pacifist measures should be taken until the war is over."

"Perhaps my subject was undesirable for discussion at this time," she said, "but surely that question is one to be referred to the committee that asked me to speak." Mrs. McCulloch closed the meeting quickly. Almost as quickly Judge Carter found himself a national figure. He had been quite right, the eager editors declared all over the country. He had been sincere and brave. No doubt the Judge felt a little bewildered. Miss Addams had given her view, he had given his; and after all she had been asked to speak and he had not. But for the second time in a fortnight Jane Addams was brought up sharply against the realization that she stood alone.

What really saddened her in 1917 and 1918 was this consciousness of isolation. As we have seen, the members of her immediate family went with the stream of "national" feeling, and most of the actual residents even of the settlement she had founded doubted the social value of her stand. She could not but recognize, too, the eccentricity of judgment of some who agreed with her in her pacificism, and the bald wish to avoid "service" of any sort of some who sought her intermediation as "conscientious objectors." But it was not these things which mainly depressed her, but the sense of being apart from her fellows *in the mass.* Hard names she did not mind; misunderstanding and even misstatement she did not mind —much. But this high hard black wall of thought and feeling that shut her off from the rest of her democracy, from the rest of her world, a wall she could not climb or penetrate, a wall on the other side of which stood even

men like Wilson and Newton Baker and even women like
her beloved Mrs. Bowen and her neighbors and friends
of the Hull House ward, and all or nearly all the people of
the city her presence had made more fragrant, and of the
country she loved, all or nearly all of the "common
people" that Lincoln had so praised and believed in—that
wall she minded. She had spent her life in seeking identifi-
cation of her own spirit with the spirit of democracy. If
that fact has not become obvious by this time, then this
book has been written obscurely indeed. She was not made
for a "leader," any more than she was made for a "follower." She was made for a comrade and an interpreter.
Her profoundest conviction had been of the worth and
sanctity of the opinions of others. And now suddenly she
found fellowship with the majority refused, and her interpretation mocked. At times she wondered whether it was
possible that she could be right in a point of view so contrary to the public determination. Yet in her worst times
her strong common sense came to her relief. She had taken
her first steps upon this path of preservation of the human
life and the human spirit so long before, she had taken
them so reasonably, so open mindedly, so inevitably in the
maintenance of that "integrity" her father had urged upon
her when she was a child, she had walked that path so
straightly for so many years, she wore so many proud
medals of remembrance and proud scars of battle, that she
could not turn round now. What was the being spied upon
by others like a criminal, compared to her own discovery
in herself of faint-heartedness, if she yielded her judgment
to her fear of loneliness? It was at this time too that her
"sense of humor" as many call it, her sense of human
values, helped her most. She was never more vivid in

ordinary talk, never more amusing in her flow of "stories" and of reminiscence, than during these gloomy years. If there was a "funny side" to anything, she perceived it more quickly and emphasized it more surely, than in the prewar years. And her good sense and her spirit pulled her through. She never broke. She never blenched. She never despised. "Our unpopularity," she could write of the pacifists, "was not all the aftermath of hatred. Some of it was due to the noblest emotions many of our contemporaries had ever known." Jane Addams was no saint. But in the power of divine understanding revealed in that phrase, there *is* a touch of saintliness.

CHAPTER XVII

THE CONGRESS OF WOMEN

IN THE latter part of the year 1917, and all through 1918, Jane Addams busied herself not only with the innumerable details of administration of a large institution for social service in wartime, but also in work for the government department of Food Administration. She chose this particular service because it fitted precisely into her own philosophy. She was not in sympathy with the departmental slogan, "Food Will Win the War." She was not interested in winning the war, any more than she was in losing it. She was concerned with Mr. Hoover's statement that "the situation was more than one of victory, it was a problem of the survival of human beings." It appeared to her at moments "as if civilization, having failed to make a community of nations along political lines, was tragically driven to the beginnings of one along the old primitive folkways." Wilson was working, *he* thought, to "make the world safe for democracy." Hoover was working, *she* thought, to make the world safe from starvation. So she did what she could "not only to induce my fellow countrymen to produce and conserve food, but so far as possible to point out that only through such a (civilian) effort could the civilian population throughout a large portion of the globe survive." Her appeal was not for peace—that matter was out of her jurisdiction now—but for "bread in time of war." The quotation is from the title of her book, published in 1922, on the activities of women pacifists, *Peace and Bread in Time of War*. And that appeal was chiefly to women, and followed a groove of thought she had cut years earlier. She develops it in her chapter in "Peace and Bread" called "a review of bread rations and woman's traditions." She not only believed that women would produce more food and conserve it more determinedly if they understood what more food meant in the world-crisis, but she also believed that she might make women understand how particularly feminine was the instinct to give food to the hungry. She thought

there was something as primitive and real about feeding the helpless as there was about the fighting, and indeed in the race history the tribal feeding of children *antedated mass fighting* by perhaps a million years. . . . And the gradual change from the wasteful manner of nomadic life to a settled and much more economic mode of existence may be fairly attributed to . . . women. Mothers in order to keep their children alive had transplanted roots from the forest or wild grains from the plains, into patches of rudely cultivated ground. We can easily imagine that when the hunting was poor or when the flocks needed a new pasture, the men of the tribe would be for moving on, but the women might insist they could not possibly go until their tiny crops were garnered . . . and even timidly hope that they could use the same fields next year, and thus avert the loss of their children sure to result from the alternation of gorging when the hunt was good and of starving when it was poor. The desire to grow food for the children led to a fixed abode and to the beginning of a home, from which our domestic morality and customs are supposed to have originated. . . . It seemed to me that women might . . . so enlarge their conception of duty that *the consciousness of the world's need for food* should become the actual impulse of their daily activities. . . . Further, the difficulty for women has always been in connecting our ambitions to cure the ills of the world on the one hand,

and the need of conforming to household requirements on the other. It was significant therefore that in this crisis the two had become absolutely essential to one another. No great world purpose could be achieved without woman's participation, founded on understanding and sympathy; while at the same time the demand could be met only if it were attached to woman's domestic routine, its very success depending on a conscious change and modification of her daily habits.

In her talks she put that into a phrase. "It is said that 'woman's place is in the home.' But now what she does in the home may determine the salvation of the world." The fire of her imagination stirred flames of pity and understanding. Here and there they cheered her as the country had cheered Daniel Webster when he spoke of "Liberty *and* Union, one and indivisible!" Here and there too they not only were moved by her sincerity, but understood the implications of her philosophy. She was putting women in her place in the conduct of world affairs. Her talks were for the "advancement of woman" as well as for the preservation of human existence: "As I had felt the young immigrant conscripts caught up into a great world movement which sent them out to fight, so it seemed to me the millions of American women might be caught up into a great world purpose, that of conservation of life."

In these months of talking to the country about food, she herself fed largely on her memories. She remembered that it was not commercialism but humanitarianism which for the last three years had determined the political relations of Belgium and the United States. In the midst of the Russian revolution, she remembered Kropotkin's statement that "never was land so energetically cultivated as by French peasants in 1792." She remembered Tolstoy's prediction to her at Yasnaya Polyana that "the

Russian peasants in their permanent patience, their insatiable hunger for bread labor, may at last make war impossible to an entire agricultural people." She remembered stories of Russian soldiers on the Austrian front in 1915 who gave themselves up to capture because they had heard that war prisoners in Austria were working on the land, and they wanted to "put seed into the ground somewhere more than they wanted to fight." The allies, the United States at any rate, were fighting for an abstract conception of democracy. Jane Addams's conception of democracy was not abstract. Her democracy was one of equal opportunity for health, labor, service and understanding. Might this democracy not come more surely through a determination to feed the peoples than through a determination to kill them; through an eagerness to preserve life rather than through an eagerness to destroy it? Toward this end she strove; while the newspapers varied between asking the smart question: "What has become of Jane Addams? In trying to hog the limelight she seems to have stepped out of it altogether," and the reiteration of the silliness of her ideas and the falsity of her statements. Why had Hoover fed the Belgians? Because the Germans had cut the hands off Belgian children. And now "Jane wants us to feed the German children too. The German children at least have hands to put their food into their mouths."

One newspaper said: "Jane Addams says that Russia quit the war because the Russian peasants love their enemies, and won't fight because they would rather work on their farms. Jane forgets that if the Allies did not fight, the Russians would have no farms to work on. The Germans would have them all."

One other sort of memory she fed upon, and it was ashes in her mouth. For years she had been telling her neighbors around Hull House that this America they had come to was a free country, a peaceful country, a country of opportunity, to the advancement of which they had much to contribute; she had urged citizenship upon them. A room at Hull House was used to register men for the draft:

In they came heavily, one man after another.... I knew most of them.... I said nothing beyond the morning's greeting, but one of them stopped to speak to me. He had been in the Hull House citizenship classes.... He spoke from the bitterness of his heart:

"I have you to thank if I am sent over to Europe to fight. I went into the citizenship class because you asked me to. If I hadn't my papers now I would be exempted."

At last came the news of the Armistice, three weeks after the news to Jane Addams personally of her oldest nephew's being blown to pieces by a shell in the Argonne. Her first duty was to carry out the orders of the Congress of Women which had met at The Hague in 1915, three and a half years before. That Congress, it will be remembered, had made plans for a conference of women to be held "at the same place and time as the Peace Conference" which they had then anticipated at the end of the war. The women had naturally supposed that this Peace Conference would be held in a neutral country, and that both sides would be represented. When the place (Paris) of the Conference, and its composition (of representatives of the Allies only) were announced, it was obvious that the plans of the women must be changed. Women from Germany and Austria and the smaller countries allied with them could not go to Paris. The American delegation headed by Jane Addams went over at Easter, and finally arrangements were made to hold the women's Congress at Zurich in Switzerland. Even to Switzerland the French delegates were refused permission to go. The others convened on May 12, 1919, in the same week, as it happened, that the representatives of the Central Powers were admitted to the Peace Conference at Paris. Between the time of her own arrival at Paris, and the Zurich meeting, Jane Addams spent five days on a visit to the war-devastated regions of France, under the auspices of the Red Cross. She looked for her nephew's grave, and with the help of a representative of the Friends' Service Committee found it finally after a twenty-four hours' search, "the third in one of three long rows." His mother had brought Jane Addams up as a child. His birthday and Jane's were three days apart, she was only twelve years older. All the preceding summer he had written to her twice a week; he was the censor of the letters of the artillery company to which he was attached. "I shall never come back," he had written. "I shall probably be killed, but if I am not I shall not come back. There will be too much to do over here that is worth while, and I should not like the thought of having come to Europe only for uselessness."

She went to Zurich wondering how she would feel at meeting women who had officially been her "enemies" for two years:

Walking the streets of Zurich the day we arrived I turned a corner and suddenly met one of the Austrian women who had been a delegate to The Hague congress and had afterward shown us every courtesy in Vienna when we presented our

Neutral Conference plan. She was so shrunken and changed I had much difficulty in identifying her with the beautiful woman I had seen four years before. She was not only emaciated as by a wasting illness, looking as if she needed immediate hospital care—she did in fact die three months after her return to Vienna—but her face and artist's hands were covered with rough red blotches due to the long use of soap substitutes, giving her a cruelly scalded appearance. . . . I felt the same sort of indignation that had welled up in the presence of the starving children in France. What were we all about that such things were allowed to happen in a so-called civilized world? . . . At the evening meeting preceding the opening of the Congress this dying woman told us that many Austrian women had resented not so much the starvation itself as the fact that day after day they had been obliged to keep their minds steadily on the subject of procuring food until all other subjects for living were absolutely excluded.

Sixteen countries were represented at this Congress,— Austria, the Argentine, Australia, Denmark, France, Germany, Great Britain, Holland, Hungary, Ireland, Italy, Norway, Roumania, Sweden, Switzerland, and the United States. The "Who's Who" of the delegates included the names of many of the best-known women in Europe. From the United States had come twenty-two women as delegates, and various others as visitors; the delegates included Emily Balch, Kate Barrett, Alice Hamilton, Florence Holbrook, Florence Kelley, Lucia Ames Mead, Congressman Jeannette Rankin, Mary Terrell (representing the colored women), Lillian Wald, Carolena Wood, among others. Jane Addams presided, and the character of her presiding may be illustrated by one typical remark made on the first day: "The president called attention to the short time left for the many who wished to speak, and said that a discussion of the ideal as compared with the practical might lead nowhere. She would beg the speakers to keep to the concrete question before the Congress."

Jane Addams was in Zurich on business. But so were most of the members of the group. The first resolution proposed was passed unanimously. The Congress urged the governments of all the Powers assembled at the Peace Conference that for the relief of the peoples of all countries from famine and pestilence

immediate action be taken
   (1) to raise the blockade; and
   (2) if there is insufficiency of food for transport
      (a) to prohibit the use of transport from one country to another for the conveyance of luxuries until the necessaries of life are supplied to all peoples;
      (b) to ration the people of every country so that the starving may be fed.

The Congress believes that only immediate international action on these lines can save humanity and bring about the permanent reconciliation and union of the peoples.

This resolution was telegraphed to Paris. Wilson replied at once: "Your message appeals both to my head and to my heart, and I hope most sincerely that ways may be found, though the present outlook is extremely unpromising, because of infinite practical difficulties."

When Jane Addams read his reply to the Congress, amidst "a hush, a tension impossible to describe," there arose from all the women "a sigh of religious resignation, as if a good man were doing his best, and in the end must succeed." But they were soon to be disillusioned regarding his success. While they were in session they received a copy of the treaty. They were the first public body to discuss it. They resolved that

this International Congress of Women expresses its deep regret that the terms of peace proposed at Versailles should so seriously violate the principles upon which alone a just and lasting peace can be secured and which the democracies of the world had come to accept.... The terms of peace deny the principles of self-determination, recognize the right of the victors to the spoils of war, and create all over Europe discords and animosities which can only lead to future wars.... The principle of justice is violated and the rule of force continued.... A hundred million people of this generation in the heart of Europe are condemned to poverty, disease and despair which must result in the spread of hatred and anarchy within each nation. With a deep sense of responsibility this Congress strongly urges the Allied and Associated Governments to accept such amendments of the terms, as shall bring the peace into harmony with those principles first enumerated by President Wilson.

First "enumerated" by Wilson, yes, in the Fourteen Points. First suggested however by the previous Women's Congress, at The Hague. And Wilson himself thought he had got more or less what he went to Paris to secure! Poor Wilson. Not for almost a year after the women had exposed the true inwardness of the peace terms did John Maynard Keynes disturb the business world with his fuller exposure along similar lines of thought. Not until the second celebration of Armistice Day in London was a British ex-officer found to say: "For every man who a year ago knew and said that the Peace Treaty was immoral in conception and would be disastrous, there are thousands now." The women had been more quickly comprehending.

They voted to form an organization to be called the

Women's International League for Peace and Freedom—
the name suggested by a congress of a League for Peace
and Freedom held at Geneva, Switzerland, in 1867, which
Garibaldi had sponsored and at which Victor Hugo had
presided. They adopted a constitution; they passed resolutions; they voted that Jane Addams "and four other
members" should go as a delegation to present seven resolutions to the International Peace Conference, and one to
the Conference of the Allied and Associated Powers. The
"other members," subsequently selected after a spirited
discussion, were from Great Britain, France, Switzerland
and Italy respectively. All the resolutions were elaborate,
specific and most carefully drawn; there were plenty of
lawyers among the delegates. They concerned peace terms,
a League of Nations, a Women's Charter to be presented
for the consideration of such a League, women's votes in
all plebiscites, military action specifically in connection
with Russia and Hungary, and amnesty for war prisoners
and conscientious objectors. After four days of intense
and intelligent discussion, Jane Addams closed the conference with a brief speech at a huge banquet in the
Zurich Town Hall. She said in part:

In Paris I took dinner one night at the house of Mr. Herbert
Hoover. He told me a very touching tale of all the difficult
things he had had to do during the war and since the war.
None had been more difficult than the requirement to pass
through a starving country with trainloads of food, and enter
another country, of course also hungry. For instance, at one
of the docks to which a shipload of food came, the men who
had to unload it were hungry and their wives and children were
hungry, and their work was to see that the food got into an
enemy country. They said, "We cannot do it." It was found

necessary to appeal to their good-will, and to use "moral suasion." Then they did it. When the great test was put upon them to go hungry that their enemies might be fed, nothing but a moral appeal could meet the situation. So we shall have to believe in spiritual power. We shall have to learn to use moral energy, to put a new sort of force into the world *and believe that it is a vital thing*—the only thing, in this moment of sorrow and death and destruction, that will heal the world.

So ever since the W.I.L. has worked to put on a new sort of force in the world and believe that it is a vital thing.

Jane Addams and her delegation went to Paris, duly presented the resolutions of the Congress, found "Mr. Hoover's office apparently the one reasonable spot in the midst of the widespread confusion"; and then accompanied by Mary Rozet Smith and that pitiless and life-giving inevitable aide Dr. Alice Hamilton, Jane Addams went, at the invitation of the American Friends' Service Committee, into Germany. They traveled through Holland, crossing the border on the first civilian passports issued there since the signing of the peace, and reached Berlin. They had seen the starving children at Lille, 40 per cent tubercular, almost all the rest suspect, "just a line of moving skeletons." They had seen 600 starving Austrian children at Zurich, just arriving to be "guests" in private homes, with winged shoulder blades and wobbling pipe-stem legs. Now in Berlin, Frankfort, Leipzig, and in scores of villages they saw them again, at Leipzig each swallowing the pint of "war-soup" which was his noon meal, wheat or rye flour, and sawdust, stirred into a pint of hot water; no "bread" till supper, so that they did not whimper with hunger so long before getting off to sleep. Sir George Paish said that 100,000,000 people in Europe were facing starvation.

In Berlin a group of dough-boys of the American army of occupation asked Jane Addams to a reception. She went, and made them a little talk. When she returned to her hotel she was rebuked by one of the English women present.

"You would eat with soldiers in uniform?"

"Certainly. Why not?"

"If I found a wounded soldier in uniform at my very door, I would not take him in."

"Oh, I think you would," she said. "You would take him in, and feed him, and take off his uniform. Isn't that what we are working for—to feed the world at our doorstep, and take off its uniform?"

She returned to the United States in August, disappointed in the sort of League of Nations that had been formed, but eager for the United States to enter it, and still more eager to get food to Europe. When she had returned, a pacifist from a war-torn Europe, four years before, she had found herself comparatively acceptable. Now, peace having been declared, she discovered somewhat to her surprise that she was in her country's bad books. She was accused of being pro-German! She promptly appealed to, among others, Americans of German descent for food for the German children. When she arranged a meeting in Chicago to present the children's case, no word of it appeared in any Chicago newspaper printed in English. Even the "German-Americans" were a trifle suspicious of her. She spoke of the work of the Friends' Service Committee in France, and in the smaller Allied Central European countries, and was listened to politely; but when she talked of its work in Germany, auditors shrugged their shoulders and left the hall. She did not call attention to the fact that Wilson had appealed to the German people to rid themselves of the Hohenzollern régime if they wished peace, and that the German people had done just that. Such a statement would have been "political," and might have provoked a riot. She merely went everywhere she had a chance to go, or could make a chance to go, telling what she had seen and what needed to be done. She thought herself that she spoke more effectively than she had ever spoken, even in the days when they had called her the best woman speaker in the country; but her very effectiveness was against her. She was stirring up sympathy for Germany, and in behalf of the work of an organization, the Friends, whose members were conscientious objectors. That was enough. She found herself again under actual espionage. The war was over, but evidently, in the minds of many people, the danger was not, and certainly the enmity was not. This was the time when educators like Professor Robert Herrick of the University of Chicago, writing in the newspapers, could say that "for a hundred years the slightest trace of German blood in the veins of any man would be held as a reproach." And it is interesting to observe how long this unpopularity of pacifists lasted. Doctor Maude Royden says:

In America in 1912 I learned that it was unsafe to mention Jane Addams's name in public speech unless you were prepared for an interruption, because the mere reference to her provoked such a storm of applause. They told me that Jane Addams's mere promise of support to Mr. Theodore Roosevelt was worth a million votes to him. . . . And I was in America again after the war, and I realized with a shock how complete was the eclipse of her fame ... her popularity had swiftly and completely vanished.... How well I remember, when I spoke in America in 1922 and 1923, the silence that greeted the name of Jane Addams! The few faithful who tried to applaud only made the silence more depressing. What she must have suffered! It was the characteristic of Jane Addams that she could not put on armor, not even defensive armor. This is the very soul of peacemaking, when a person's very heart is not defended, and in this sense Jane Addams was the most completely defenseless person in the world. She was defenseless in the profound sense in which Christ was defenseless.

It was not quite so bad as that. She could still smile. When as late as 1924, at the fourth International Congress of the W.I.L., when in her presidential address she was forced to apologize for "certain currents of intolerance never before encountered at our previous Congresses," she could say:

I beg of you not to take this situation too seriously. The American delegation does not, for it knows how easily newspaper attacks are manufactured and how ephemeral is the consequence of such attacks.... In London in 1915 I saw the business portion everywhere placarded by huge posters which shouted to the passerby, "To the Tower with Ramsay Mac-Donald," "The Pacifist to the Tower." These placards had been put up by one Horatio Bottomley, an editor, who is at present in jail, in "the Tower" so to speak, while Ramsay MacDonald is Prime Minister of England. It proves once more, does it not, that this old world of ours, though it does not always progress, certainly always turns around, and that night and day alternate with fair regularity.

In these years of "unpopularity," in fact, laughter was a "defensive armor" she assumed pretty constantly. No one who was much in her company can forget the flow of "stories" in these years, some reminiscential but more spontaneously applicable to whatever subject was up for discussion: "A pacifist," she admitted, "is never surprised when he is called a traitor and a coward. He is not even astonished—unlike Noah Webster's wife when she caught the dictionary-maker kissing the cook. 'Mr. Webster,' she said, 'I am surprised!' 'My dear,' he answered, 'it is we who are surprised; *you* are astonished.' But we pacifists are not even astonished."

After she died, there was considerable discussion over her "favorite poem," that it might be read at memorial meetings. Arnold's *Rugby Chapel* seemed to be generally agreed upon. One can only say that he heard her cite oftenest in the years after the war Arthur Clough's *Say not the Struggle not Availeth*, with its famous close:

> And not by eastern windows only,
>   When daylight comes, comes in the light,
> In front, the sun climbs slow, how slowly,
>   But westward, look, the land is bright.

As a "teacher" of English poetry, one was compelled to suggest that although the theme was inspiring, the verse itself was a bit clumsy and rough.

"You mean," she said, "clough."

And too it was in these years after the war that the D.A.R. published their "blacklists," and finally brought out their "Spiderweb Chart," showing the "radical" connections of Jane Addams and fifty others. As president of the W.I.L. Jane Addams was declared to be "a factor in a movement to destroy civilization and Christianity" and "aiming to destroy the government of the United States." With his hand upon his heart this biographer testifies that to his knowledge the animosity of the D.A.R. against her personally never gave Jane Addams anything but amusement. Recollecting her original membership in early Hull House days, and the honorary membership given her after as a juror in the Paris Exposition of 1900 she was able to secure a Grand Prix for its exhibit, she positively chuckled. She said: "The spirit of the D.A.R. is like our early American humor, distinguished more for robustness than for subtlety." Inclusion of her name in the earlier "Lusk Report" had been inevitable, though it had considerably annoyed Mr. Newton Baker and Mr. Hoover, who thought her services valuable to the country. Attacks upon her from time to time by the American Legion she took much more seriously. She did not favor the Reserve Officers' Training Corps even in the colleges, and military drill in the high-schools she vigorously opposed. As the Legion was officially in favor of these things, she not only expected but welcomed argument from them. What disturbed her was the frequent misrepresentation of her point of view, and the recrudescence of the old lie about her charging that soldiers were cowards. "I have of course never thought so or said so before," she remarked, "but it seems to me a little cowardly for officers to use poisoned weapons." The real cause of war, she thought, was misunderstanding, and she disliked to see soldiers, in particular, rely upon misunderstanding and false statements for the promotion of a point of view, however admirable their conception of their own purpose and patriotism might be.

Meanwhile through the years the W.I.L. expanded. Its third Congress was held in Vienna in 1921, its fourth in Washington in 1924, its fifth in Dublin in 1926, its sixth in Prague in 1929. At each of these Jane Addams presided. Finally forcing through her resignation as President in 1929, after a tenure of fourteen years, she was elected Honorary President for life. No new president was elected; instead, three chairmen to carry on. At the Prague convention twenty-six countries were represented. The old "statement of aims" was reiterated. Here it is:

The W.I.L. aims at uniting women in all countries who are opposed to every kind of war, exploitation and oppression, and who work for universal disarmament and for the solution of conflicts by the recognition of human solidarity, by conciliation and arbitration, by world coöperation, and by the establishment of social, political and economic justice for all, without distinction of sex, race, class or creed.

Hull House and the W.I.L. were the two great "organizations" through which Jane Addams worked. She founded Hull House, she did not found but personified the Women's International League. Her influence was wider than any organization influence, her work lay in many fields, her power was not an organized but a personal power. Nevertheless the little headstone that hides in the shadow of the tall family monument in the Cedarville cemetery bears these words only:

JANE ADDAMS

OF

HULL HOUSE

AND

THE WOMEN'S INTERNATIONAL LEAGUE

FOR

PEACE AND FREEDOM

CHAPTER XVIII

POST-WAR REFLECTIONS

THE old-time friends of Jane Addams and of Hull House, though not many of them were in sympathy with the W.I.L., did not join in the "pacifist-hunt" and "red-hunt" that many newspapers, the militarists, and the more ignorant sort of politicians carried on during and after the World War. Contributions to the work of Hull House held up well. After 1913, no new buildings were added at Halsted and Polk Streets, but there was really no special need for them; building went on briskly at the Bowen "Country Club" at Waukegan, and the activities of the House were not guillotined or even mangled by any sharp drop in funds. In 1917 Hull House had an income of $60,000; in 1922, $70,000 and in 1929, when it celebrated its fortieth birthday, $95,000. For current expenses, in addition to the building funds and the funds for endowment, Jane Addams had personally collected or contributed about $25,000 a year. Her own income from owned property had sunk to below $100 a month, but from magazine articles, royalties, and fees when she lectured for pay she made enough to live on, and to give away to various members of her "family," to Hull House, and to many individuals and individual "causes," more than half of what she earned. A "suite" of two rooms and a bath had been fitted up for her at Hull House in 1902, but she insisted that the architect should so connect the bathroom that other residents might reach it from their hallway, saying that she "didn't like to be selfish with luxuries" and there she made her home most of the year when she was not "on the road" or in Europe. Summers, both before and after the war, when she was not abroad, she went to Bar Harbor, staying with Mrs. Bowen or, later, in a house in Hull's Cove (the name has no connection with Hull House). Mary Rozet Smith had bought the place and fitted it up, but Jane Addams had purchased a small share in it and they were assumed to own it jointly. Bar Harbor is full of memories of Jane Addams. She went there first in 1905, and except in the years she was away from the United States, spent a part of every summer there for twenty-seven years. She loved flowers, and Mrs. Bowen's gardens were as beautiful as any in that city of beautiful gardens. "I cared more about her criticism in taking her through my gardens," Mrs. Bowen says, "than I ever did for that of any one else. She was full of judgment and full of appreciation, especially of the loveliness of trees. Whatever we looked at, she had almost always some apt little verse to apply to it, whether it was a scene or a single flower."

Jane Addams could really rest at Bar Harbor. The one objection to it from her point of view was the fact that for many years automobiles were barred from the island of Mount Desert. Driving behind horses frequently gave her something too much like asthma to be disregarded. But when motor-cars were permitted, she found Mount Desert quite perfect. She celebrated her fiftieth and sixtieth birthdays there quietly with members of her family invited by Mrs. Bowen, and her seventieth birthday with a magnificent dinner in her honor given by what she called "innumerable potentates." The story of that dinner will have to be told in its place, but here may be slipped in a personal experience which immediately preceded it. This biographer and his Bryn Mawr-graduated daughter were spending two weeks at North Haven, a hundred miles or so down the coast of Maine from Bar Harbor, and as a reward for the daughter's tender care of her scholarship and of him, he arranged for a plane to fly them up and "see Aunt Jane." Jane Addams was on the pier waiting for them when they arrived at eleven o'clock in the morning.

"We'll drive around the island before lunch," she announced. "I feel very flattered; no one ever called on me in an airplane before so far as I remember." So we drove round the island, and when we got back to the cottage for luncheon Mary Smith was a little reproving.

"I told you to come straight back," she said.

"I know you did," Jane Addams answered guiltily, "and I meant to, but I was too excited at seeing my family to remember."

"You go and lie down," said Miss Smith.

"Indeed I shall do nothing of the sort," said Miss Addams. "I never felt better in my life."

"Do you know," said Miss Smith, turning to us, "what your aunt has been doing? She went to New York five days ago, to see about one of her books, have her picture painted, and visit Ellen Starr in the hospital. She ran all around New York alone for three days, and last night she hurried back to meet you. She had to take an upper, it was all she could get, got off at Calais at four in the morning, managed to get here at half-past nine, had her breakfast and went right down to the pier for fear you should come in earlier than you said."

"And you should have seen me," remarked Miss Addams placidly, "getting in and out of that upper. I said to the porter, 'Don't you think I'm pretty smart on a ladder?' and he said, 'Lady, I never saw anybody as stout as you that was so agile.' "

In her long lifetime Jane Addams made twelve journeys abroad, spending a total of a little more than one-tenth of her seventy years out of the United States. Often she went as a delegate, as in 1900 to the Paris Exposition; in 1913 to the International Suffrage Alliance at Budapest; in 1915 to The Hague; in 1919 to Zurich; in 1921 to Vienna; in 1922 at The Hague again; in 1926 to Dublin; in 1928 to Honolulu, as president of the Pan-Pacific Women's Union; in 1929 to Prague. In January, 1923, after the second Hague convention, she started from Paris with Mary Smith on a trip around the world, which occupied her almost nine months. She was always "a bad sailor," and on various trips she was overtaken by most serious illness. In Japan in 1923 she was operated on again for the kidney trouble which had bothered her from 1915 to 1918. In Dublin in 1926 she had a first attack of angina pectoris, which left her with the "bad heart" from the weakness of which it had been subsequently assumed she would die; though it was not her heart which finally betrayed her. But in spite of sea-sickness and in spite of far more serious ailments, she always enjoyed these journeys. "I don't think I am adventurous," she once remarked, "but I have always liked to get about." The journey round the world was something like General Grant's, except that he was welcomed by kings and she was welcomed by peoples. Everywhere she was received triumphantly. The contrast between her treatment by the newspapers abroad and in her own city interested her. "To some," she said, "it almost seems as if an internationally-minded person should be defined as a friend of every country except his own." She visited India, the Philippine Islands and Japan, and spoke on many occasions in Manchuria, Korea and China. Landing in Japan at Shimonoseki, she was asked by the provincial government to address "the people of the city," which she did. The next day the government officials of Osaka offered her "the freedom of the city," and she talked on "Women and Peace" to all the thousands who could get in to the largest public hall. Many of the Japanese newspapers carried a translation of this speech in detail. The governor of the province gave a great dinner for her, and again her speech was reported in full throughout Japan. That night she was taken ill, and the next morning she was transported to Tokyo, where she was once more operated on for the old kidney trouble which had dogged her since childhood, and which had been aggravated by an accident in China. She was in the hospital at Tokyo for three weeks. Messages were received from the Imperial Court, at which it was reported a reception in her honor had been planned. A month later she was able to sail for Honolulu, and so home.

She brought back many personal gifts of considerable value, which in accordance with her invariable custom she gave away to others as soon as she returned to America. An old friend once gave her a "lorgnette" set with diamonds. "J.A.," the friend said severely, in presenting the gift, "I make only one condition; you are *not* to give this to anybody else before I have got out of the room." "I never did such a thing in my life," exclaimed Miss

Addams indignantly; whereupon a chorus of "boos" went up from all her other friends who were present.

On this round-the-world journey she found herself particularly interested in Japan and India. She thought the interest of the educated Japanese and Indian women in the "terribly poor of the Orient" and in other women was astounding. The customs of the countries were ironclad, had been ironclad for centuries; the conventions governing women were often almost as rigid as death, and yet these women of opportunity took on the responsibility of others who were opportunity-less, with an alertness and a determination that "shamed me," she said, "when I remembered the freedom I had had as a young person, and how slowly I had realized what my own freedom was for." She thought that it was because these Oriental women "still retained so much of their basic occupation, their basic interest in agriculture," still connected their duty with the great duty of providing food for the hungry, that they could easily turn to other occupations. She was keenly interested also in the women of Burma:

In the good old days of suffrage speeches, we had always quoted the women of Burma as perhaps the freest in the world. They have lived up to expectations and it is not strange that England allowed them to vote at the age of eighteen, although the women of India could not vote till they were twenty-one and the women of England, at that moment, not until they were thirty.... Perhaps the women of France are the only women comparable to the Burmese women in business acumen. ...It is only in variety of occupations that the women of America surpass Burmese women.

On her return from this journey round the world, Jane Addams was asked by the women of many countries to issue a "Christmas Message" to the women of the world, which she did. She said:

We know the world is not at peace nor is there enough active goodwill in it to accomplish the healing of the nations.... We stand shamefaced in the midst of the Christmas rejoicing. ... The divided nations of Europe are in a panic of fear and apprehension.... It is as if He whose birthday we celebrate had never uttered the words "Love alone can cast out fear," as if he had never given a basic command to His followers, "Be just and fear not."... The United States of America, caught in a traditional dislike of "foreign entanglements," abandons the solemn covenants made in her name, restricts her immigration, increases her tariffs, and refuses to consider her war loans as part of the international responsibility she assumed in 1917. ... Those nations in the Orient which have so recently entered into world-relationships that they could not escape a share in the World War, have unhappily acquired a new consciousness of the part military preparedness may play in the attainment of the national ambitions of statesmen. May China and Japan with their agelong veneration for the teachings of sage and saint ... realize that that nation is already "perishing by the sword" when military authority dominates civil life, when talk of foreign interference is substituted for discussion of internal reforms, when the fear of warlike neighbors is deliberately utilized to postpone the day of disarmament. In Africa, in India, in the Philippines,... may the millions who are "being prepared for citizenship" renew their resolution to continue the policies of a great teacher who more than any other is steadfastly committed to the typical Christian adventure, as yet untried, of "non-resistance." May at least one nation of Oriental peoples actually fulfil that essential doctrine preached by Him who was born on Christmas Day on Eastern soil.

It is a sober, unsentimental message, "shadowed by a compunction and a curious sense of futility," as she herself said. She thought it a time to stir, as one might, not the hearts of women but their intelligences to realization.

Soberly and unsentimentally it was received; there was a sharp increase in the membership of the W.I.L. everywhere.

It was natural that during the years from 1920 on, however, the human interests of Jane Addams, so far as they were grouped, should shift to a considerable extent from immigrants, and even from women, to youth. Of course it was a shift back, so far as it was a shift at all. It was young people in whom she had been primarily interested when she went to live at Hull House; young people to whom she had primarily appealed in that first fine speech at Plymouth in 1892, "The Subjective Necessity of Social Settlements"; young people about whom she had written the book nearest her heart, *The Spirit of Youth and the City Streets,* in 1909; child-labor legislation for which she had most strenuously tried for the first twenty years of her Hull House residence. But after 1909, she had been most concerned with the position and advancement of women, and with peace through international understanding, which was merely an extraordinary extension of her concern with the aliens who were her Hull House neighbors. By 1920, however, the "freedom of women" was practically won—the only cause for which Jane Addams ever did battle, perhaps, in which she positively felt that any sort of final victory had been gained. The battle for immigrant opportunity in Chicago she had turned over to the Immigrant's Protective League. The battle for internationalism of spirit she kept on with undauntedly, but she grew, not discouraged, but a little bit disgusted, with the struggle. She could not help recalling that although in 1917, the only woman member of Congress had interrupted the roll-call on the declaration of war to say, "I want to stand by my country, but I cannot vote for war," in 1929 the eight women in Congress were said to "disagree on the tariff, prohibition, and farm relief, but to be united for 'national defense.' "

Finally, by 1920 Jane Addams was beginning to grow old in years. She was sixty. She had many grandnephews and grandnieces, one in each family named for her as a matter of course, and she began looking backward. She began, as it were, to grow younger as she grew older. About a year before she died, one of her nephews, himself verging on sixty, remarked:

"At what age does one begin to feel that he is over that famous crest, and on that famous downhill slope of life, one reads so much of?"

"I don't know," she said. "Apparently not at seventy-three. At that age one still has the odd sensation of being in the front line trenches, if you don't mind my using a non-pacifist figure of speech."

But because she was getting on in years, no doubt youth began especially to appeal to her. Her chapter on "Contrasts in a Post-War Generation," in *The Second Twenty Years at Hull House,* is one of the wisest things she penned. But not one of the warmest. It has to be admitted that she was not quite satisfied with the "post-war generation" in the 1920's.

She saw a good deal of it. She was, in spite of her pacifism, in demand as a speaker at colleges and universities, at commencements and on other occasions; honorary degrees were frequently offered her—fourteen in all, in her life, more than twice as many as any other American woman—some of which she accepted, and some of which she declined. (In a spirit of freakish sorrow, this biog-

JANE ADDAMS AT SIXTY

Her days were as full of labor at sixty-five as at thirty-five.

rapher got out the trunk which at the moment contains, closely packed, her thirteen vari-colored "hoods," the Mount Holyoke hood not there as yet, opened the trunk and again looked over those parchment certificates of honor, dating from 1904 to 1935, wondering whether any other "unofficial" person in the world would ever be so scholastically honored; and glanced once more over the little half-sheet of note-paper which is with them, containing Jane Addams's list of them, in type, in pen-writing, and in pencil. "This is all, I think," she wrote, but she forgot one. *Lacrhymæ rerum.*)

She saw a good deal of youth, too, round Hull House; the "post-war generation" crowded in there in even greater numbers than ever before. And she was inclined to feel that they were letting themselves be controlled and even standardized by the desire to be "successful."

She credited them with courage in the rejection of inhibitions. She credited them further, and if they will not think the term sentimental, she credited them lovingly, with a great eagerness to accept responsibility, and to make responsibilities for themselves. But she was inclined to feel that they were not strikingly unselfish in their definition of what those responsibilities should be. She saw in them a greater desire than she herself had ever felt, or yet felt, to "play safe and let well enough alone"; a dread of change. The inevitable burden of youth, his fear, or her fear of not "making good," his consciousness of a weakness in himself that he has not had experience enough to know is in all men, plus his dubiety of the wisdom of change—was the combination, she speculated, "overwhelming their nascent strength and forcing them into an undue conformity?" Or perhaps, she added in her

gentleness, "are we all equally afraid of what will happen
to us if we do not carefully conform, and do the young
simply conform more obviously in their anxiety to do it
'properly,' just as they are more meticulous as to their
hats and shoes?"

She had seen young people without opportunity, without recreation, without healthful surroundings; and as
the years had passed she had seen conditions change in
some degree, she could even feel without arrogance that
she herself had done something to advance the change,
until the four-year olds no longer pulled out basting-
threads all day for what amounted to three cents in wages,
and died like flies, communicating their own contagious
diseases to the garments they struggled with, but instead
went to kindergartens or played in swings in the open
air. Until the fourteen-year olds no longer tended machinery ten hours a day, often losing their fingers, sometimes
their lives, out of the inattention of bored or exhausted
childhood, but instead were keen or light-heartedly mis-
chievous in the school-room, she did not much care which,
and shouted valorously about the playgrounds; until the
very children of the thread-pullers were able to make
their way into and through college. Until the death-rates
had dropped, and the I.Q.'s had risen, beyond comparison
with those of the "bad old days." She had seen the barred
gates of opportunity open and the young come pouring
through. But then she had also seen, largely she thought
on account of the war and its effects, the rates of juvenile
delinquency rise. And the young of her own "class" she
saw no longer going into the settlements, answering the
call of "subjective necessity," but holding aloof from
sharing and seeking; hiding their hopes and their own

formulations of the secrets of success in their own clever and calculating hearts, polite, intelligent, evasive, and—perhaps—selfish. She watched them eagerly. She was too optimistic to be fearful, and she was very little disturbed by what used to be called in those days "flaming youth," but she was doubtful of what seemed to her a mere smoulder of the spirit. Was the fire low, and was each one inclined to hug his own fire without consideration of whether his neighbor had coals or not? In Calcutta she had found young Hindus bewildered because "no protest came from the student body of the United States against the Supreme Court decision that a Hindu might not become an American citizen. They thought our young people should be defending the basic doctrines upon which the new nations, including the United States, had been founded. They believed that the young throughout the world were united in upholding these doctrines, and they could not understand indifference when this breach of principle had been made."

In her study of youth she reached no final conclusion. It was possible, she thought, that her generation had been "too exclusively concerned for the masses, too intent upon the removal of what seemed unfair restrictions for the man at the bottom of society. Have these young people inevitably gone back to liberty (particularly sex liberty) for the individual? Does the pendulum have to swing back and forth from individual to collective effort, and does it always seem inconsistent *as the two advocates pass one another?*"

Suddenly and sharply, more suddenly and sharply than ever before in any time of peace, the "depression" in 1929 was to swing back the pendulum in the United States to "collective effort" again. But this of course she could not guess. Meanwhile, she comforted herself with the observation that among the new generation there was

a marked increase of interest in world affairs. There is a new awareness of other people, a lively interest in foreign matters and at least the stirrings of a will to organize this politically chaotic world. . . . In approaching life by a new synthesis they evince a fine sense of social adventure and of course utilize the tireless energy of discovery which belongs so preëminently to youth. . . . The next generation will never know what its own world would have been, had the millions of young men killed in the war survived and been able to bring to tangled affairs their experience and understanding. . . . There may be a poetic justice in the fact that our generation will be crippled forevermore by the effects of the war which we failed to avert, so that we must humbly depend upon the untrammeled hopes of the young. . . . After all it is not so much that different generations are hostile to each other as that they find each other irrelevant. This son shrugs his shoulders at the watchwords which thrilled his father, but out of his own more fragmentary experience searches desperately for new ones to meet his own need.

And she concludes her analysis of the "post-war generation" with one of those many hopeful, unhurried, put-yourself-in-the-other-fellow's-place comments that so distinguish her writing and characterize her personality:

If we continue to unite our unremitting efforts to organize for a more reasonable life upon the earth's surface, we will gradually make possible the utilization of a new dynamic. We will almost inevitably begin to grope our way toward what our generation calls human brotherhood, but which the post-war generation would, I am sure, rather designate as a wider participation in life.

It was in these years of the 1920s that the United States was undertaking the long-urged effort of prohibition by Federal law of the sale of intoxicating liquor of every sort. If the chapter on youth in *The Second Twenty Years at Hull House* is the wisest, the chapter on "A Decade of Prohibition" is the weakest. So far as it is a presentation of facts from personal experience, it is interesting.

She was aware of many strange and dramatic situations among the Hull House neighbors, families ruined by liquor and groups made contented by saloons, the comedies and tragedies of bootlegging, the confusion between old habits and a new lawlessness, and her specific instances are often variously exciting. But she was either unwilling or unable to set forth any such definite conclusions forcing her to action as had made her a resident at Hull House, a worker for labor legislation and for woman suffrage, a thoroughgoing pacifist and an ardent internationalist. She had said, and she remembered that she had said, as far back as 1897, that "I have no faith in the denunciations of saloons and of drinking; it is my conclusion that drinking is largely the indulgence not of appetite but in the social instincts common to the human race."

She knew that she had tried in her own neighborhood not to "get rid of the saloon" by direct action, but to substitute some place in which the social instincts could be developed without the unpleasantnesses that often accompany the consumption of alcoholic drinks. She herself never drank even beer or wine, but most of her friends did. No record is available of any speech she ever made on behalf of the eighteenth amendment. On the other hand, she had been more or less in the thick of the fight for state action for women's suffrage, and she could not forget that the great opposition in all those fights had come from the brewers and the distillers, who believed that if women could vote they would vote liquor down. She had been for a long time in almost absolute despair over the Chicago dance-halls in the days when they were run chiefly to sell liquor, and when in consequence instead of providing recreation they provided ruin for the young girls, and in many cases for the young men as well. And she had faced many a terrible tragedy that liquor had caused. So on the whole her hopes were with national prohibition. But as she watched the experiment she was unable quite to make up her mind that it was working.

It enormously improved the condition of the dance-halls. That she could see, and that was almost a decisive factor. That young people could be brought together for enjoyment, without such risks as they had been made to run in the past, was of immense importance to her. It advanced, too, the economic prosperity of her neighborhood. More men brought home their pay undiminished to their families; and as the pay increased through the "golden years," the former poverty of the district advanced almost to prosperity. And the "stock arguments" against prohibition, the repetition of conventional phrases about "personal liberty," and its contradiction that "more people are drinking than ever"; the assertion that the amendment was "unfair to the soldiers who had had no chance to vote"; even the contention that "disregard for the prohibition law is lessening the respect for all laws," she put aside. They did not seem to her to go to the root of the matter. She thought she could trace such phrases to the liquor propagandists. If there had been nothing else to be considered, she would have been wholeheartedly for the amendment. But—it seemed to have increased violence. There was less disorder, but there was more murder. And much of the lawlessness it seemed to provoke was the kind of lawlessness and violence she hated worst —the lawlessness and violence *of the authorities.* Individual crime was bad enough, but what amounted to legalized crime, the development of the principle of protection, and the slaughter by the police of even the people who paid them for protection, seemed to her pretty nearly the depths of horror. It was organized, authorized spiritual debauchery. Was the amendment responsible for it? If so, did the unquestionable values of the amendment outweigh the evil of this debauchery?

On the whole, she thought they did. Then rose another question. What was the amendment itself but force? It was impossible to make people righteous. You had to get them to hunger for righteousness. This was the old problem of the ethical value of processes as opposed to the actualities of accomplishment. On the whole, here too, she concluded, the amendment was justifiable. There had been a ripening process of thought and experience of which it might fairly be called the fruit. She reviewed historically the previous attempts on the part of the Federal Government "to interfere with the drink situation." She reviewed the long struggle between the women and the liquor-interests. She developed in her own mind an analogy between the amendment prohibiting slavery and the amendment prohibiting the sale of alcoholic liquors. She considered the international aspects of the matter— naturally. And she concluded just this: "to give up the experiment now [1929] or even seriously to modify the amendment, would mean that we never could be clear as to the real effect of national prohibition." In fact, she concluded, though no doubt by processes of reasoning somewhat different from Mr. Hoover's, that it was "a noble experiment," worth carrying on to see what might result. She ultimately voted against repeal. However, this biographer, at least, never heard her express the slightest lamentation at the repeal of the amendment. But then, she was not much given to lamentation.

CHAPTER XIX

THEY COME TO PRAISE

IN THE latter part of 1926 a particularly vicious and so far as Jane Addams knew an unprovoked attack was made upon her by certain members of the American Legion, renewing the old charge that she had insulted the British soldiers and that throughout the war she had been "pro-German." To some of her friends she showed what she had never showed before, irritation. "You know," she said, "I am really getting old. I find it is not as easy to love my enemies as it used to be."

On her, as on many of her way of thinking, a certain sense of depression had fallen. Charles E. Merriam, professor of politics in the University of Chicago, put it: "I do not know that we can correctly say that liberty is dead, but there is a heavy hand of intolerance resting on the modern world." We of America, according to William Allen White of Kansas, were going about "in a cramped and ill-conditioned world, rattling our little tin bank in one hand and our big steel sword in the other." The old word liberalism had been replaced by the new barbarism "normalcy." The Jeshuruns of business waxed fat and kicked not; nor did they wish any one else to kick. Confidence rose, prices, stocks, and finally wages followed, and the last thing the people of the United States desired was complaint of materialism. The bubble swelled in brilliant colors, and whoever attempted to comment on its fragility became unpopular. Europe was becoming a chaos as a result of the war and the treaty—as the women had told the Peace Conference it must; but the United States was rich beyond the dreams of avarice. Therefore internationalism like spirituality was at its lowest discount. We were so "prosperous" that we could even regard as an asset the money we had given to other nations to destroy in war. That money had disappeared, but we were, most of us, unaware of that fact. We thought not only that we held four kings, but that with the "war debts" we had an ace in the hole. Naturally, people like Jane Addams (look back over her Christmas Message) were unpopular.

For the restatement of the theories of social progress and liberalism, a dinner was planned in Chicago in January of 1927. At the first meeting of the committee the plan turned out to be for a demonstration in honor of Jane Addams. It was organized by a "citizens' committee" of one hundred and fifty, a committee which for both distinction and variety had never been equaled in Chicago. There were on it, besides many of her best friends among the "social workers," the great group of her admirers among university presidents, bank presidents, manufacturers, judges, lawyers, doctors, ministers, meat-packers, authors, and even editors and generals. They secured the "Furniture Mart," which had the largest floor space in the city, fifteen hundred sat down to dinner, and many hundreds were turned away because they had not got their tickets in time. A woman "toastmistress" being demanded, Mrs. Bowen was to have presided, but she fell ill and Miss Julia Lathrop took her place. The speakers included Mayor Dever, William Allen White—the only imported talent, as Miss Lathrop whimsically pointed out

—Judge Hugo Pam, and Professor Charles E. Merriam. Jane Addams had urged that "nothing be said about her," that the dinner remain "philosophic," but nobody paid attention to her urging. A few of the innumerable letters and telegrams from all over the country were read, including a warm and genuine tribute from President Coolidge. Of the messages Jane Addams perhaps enjoyed most a word from her old companion in disarmament, Doctor Aletta Jacobs of The Hague, and the reminiscential, fiery letter from William Kent, the rich young man whom in the 1890's she had "converted."

Her idea of *mutual* benefit from democratic associations took a long time to percolate through my mind. But my admiration of her made me think diligently, and so in the end I blundered onto the basis of her theory and practice.... She holds the leadership of the whole world, of those who are intelligently striving for practical idealism ... although from the beginning she has been subject to misjudgment and persecution, partly out of innate human cussedness, which makes some of us regret the demise of the devil, on whom we would like to heap the blame, but more largely from the human weakness described by the chorus in some old Greek tragedy as "dark ignorance and hurrying unsure thought." But when I see the simplicity of Jane Addams's formula, I positively believe in the possibility of a better and kindlier world.

There was eloquence of the old hell-roaring and tear-raising type; one very old-timer insisted that there had been no such dinner in Chicago since Robert Ingersoll and Mark Twain had praised General Grant at the Army of the Cumberland reunion in 1879. But there was also wise and uplifting philosophy.

William Allen White, after a long and brilliant analysis of democracy, concluded:

Prosperity, if it is to be also progress, must be only a means of promoting self-respect. Justice is not merely a by-product of prosperity. ... If we have nothing to give ourselves but money, and nothing to give the world but guns, we are poor indeed. ... Jane Addams is one who knows that life in the main and in the end is a manifestation of some vast inscrutable purpose; that when life moves forward it is following in the age-long quest for self-respect. Let us gather faith to-night that the vision of self-respect, the vision of mankind groping toward brotherhood, has come deeply into million of lives. That vision still lives. That dream shall survive our sleep. Miss Addams has followed faithfully this great vision through the years. We give her our loving gratitude for her life.

Judge Pam said:

I am the only speaker to-night whose father and mother were immigrants. ... I was born within two blocks of Hull House, the old Hull House which was to be born again when Miss Addams settled there. But little did I think as I trudged past that corner, in the 'seventies, on my way to school, that it was to become the Mecca of every spiritual pilgrim in this great city, the laboratory testing life, out of which was to come the certainty that to devote oneself to the welfare of others is the surest way of achieving one's own welfare.

Professor Merriam said:

More than any other woman in America she has caught the brooding spirit of the mother and understood how to appeal to what Lincoln called the better angels of our nature. If you say it is not possible for any one to be at once a statesman without a portfolio, a professor without a chair, and a guiding woman in a man made world, I answer that it is not possible, but—here she is!

And finally Jane Addams replied:

I suggested that we try to keep this dinner impersonal, make it a discussion of the Liberal in the present situation—the up

and down of the waves of public feeling in regard to various
movements dear to all of us. And I realize that I have merely
been the hook upon which to hang all the fine things that have
been said. I am very grateful for the affection and interest you
have brought here this evening; yet in a way humiliated by
what you say I am, for I know myself to be a very simple
person, not at all sure I am right, and most of the time not
right, though wanting to be; which I am sure we all know of
ourselves. I can only hope that we may go on together, working as we go for the betterment of things, and with thorough
enjoyment and participation in those many things which are
making for righteousness.

Two years later there was an almost equally personal
celebration of her usefulness as a citizen—the celebration
of the fortieth anniversary of the founding of Hull House.
The average number of "residents" at Hull House and
in the apartments adjacent to it had become about
seventy, of whom in 1929 fifteen had been in residence
for more than twenty years, seven for more than thirty
years. Some six hundred people had lived there at one
time or another, including the prime minister of Canada,
the president of the General Electric Company, the president of the American Telegraph and Telephone Company,
the president of the University of California at Los
Angeles, the most distinguished living American philosopher, the first head of the United States Children's
Bureau and her successor, and many others almost as well
known. (Ramsay MacDonald, prime minister of England,
and Professor Masaryk, president of Czechoslovakia,
never lived there, though the son of the one and the
daughter of the other did.) The income of the House,
from endowments and annual contributions, had risen to
approximately ninety-five thousand dollars a year. Its

"activities" had so increased that merely to enumerate and outline them involved a "year book" of fifty large fine-printed pages. More than three hundred thousand men, women and children a year went there; not including "sight-seers," who were innumerable. And yet, it had *not* become "an institution." It had remained a home, in the real sense a "center of life" for the residents and for the neighbors. Dinner there was as much fun as ever. At Thanksgiving Jane Addams's own "family" gathered there as naturally as any New England farmer's family to the "old homestead." When you went in, if you were not neat, you left your hat and coat lying on a chair, and if nobody amiably hung them on a hook somewhere, when you left you found them where you had left them. Even the people who came to enlist the services of the Immigrants' Protective League were not "cases"; they were all individuals, neighbors. As for the innumerable club-members, they regarded Hull House as their own. Many of them were the children of former club-members. Children of immigrants and aliens went out from Hull House clubs into college or business, and came back to "live at the House," or give classes or look after clubs there. Whatever language you spoke, you could find somebody to talk it with you; you could read Dante in Italian or in translation, work in wood or words, begin as a baby in the nursery and go on through the St. George's and the Hull House dramatic club to fame on the national stage, if you had it in you. Singers and pianists who had come up through the music school came back to perform for the children. There were people of the ward who had been to thirty-five of the Christmas parties at Hull House. The neighbors went to Hull House to ask questions, not to be asked questions by "social workers." All this has been called "the result of the spirit of Jane Addams," but one does not think so. She was a born executive as well as a born sympathizer. She was away for months, sometimes for almost a year, at a time. But the spirit of Hull House never altered. Her death will not change it. There is no one there now as famous as she became, but there are none there unlike her in sympathy. Some such apply for residence occasionally, to secure "training in social work," but they are squeezed out by the force of House-opinion before they are fairly in. This biographer, who never lived there except as a small boy, who never shared the residents' impulses or comprehension, but who has watched the "House" for forty-five years, speaks whereof he knows.

So in 1929 a great celebration of the "fortieth anniversary" was decided upon, and a great celebration was held. All the famous ex-residents returned to it; there were days and nights of dining and speechmaking; the bankers and the lawyers and the ministers and the brokers and the businessmen and the newspapermen and the statesmen (men and women) who had lived there returned to oh and ah over the size of the place and the variety of its neighborhood concerns, to wonder at the cleanliness of the ward and note the absence of saloons and drunks (those have returned since), and to congratulate Jane Addams. There was not a great deal said of high sociological value, or even high philosophical value perhaps, though John Dewey was there in a high place, emanating a sort of intellectually complex, divinely quiet wisdom. But the object was of reunion, and a reunion it was. Jane Addams moved about, shifting chairs and rehanging pictures and picking up hats. Was she well? Yes indeed, she was always well. And how were Mary and Lucia? Was Lucia five or six now? Six—she thought so, but she never could quite remember. Lucia would be writing her name on her Christmas card this year, perhaps. A cable from whom— Clara Ragaz in Switzerland? That was nice. There were more programs in the Octagon. Yes, the old nationality maps in the Octagon are very much changed now. The Mexicans are perhaps as interesting as any. Do you remember when the gypsies began coming? This was Angelo—what *was* Angelo's last name? He died not very long after that picture was taken. I shall call my book *The Second Twenty Years*, I think; I am very poor at titles, in spite of all the practice I have had.

Such was the impression the old residents had retained of her, and such it will always remain with them. *The Second Twenty Years* was published in 1930, when Jane Addams was seventy. She had not published a book for eight years, though she had written much; articles, speeches, editorial comments. They had been fighting years. Her country had not been "internationally-minded." The League of Nations, the World Court, her countrymen had shunned. Immigration had been vigorously restricted. Russia had become a specter and "communism" a word for the quarrelsome only among the average men and women. Years after the war there were American citizens still in prison for the expression of their political opinions. Peace was a soiled dove. Yet for international understanding, and for peace which could come, she believed, only through international understanding and coöperation, she had worked as steadily as she had kept on working in the neighbors' interests, and her own inter-

Photograph by Wallace W. Kirkland

REUNION AT HULL HOUSE

Jane Addams and the oldest residents of Hull House on the fortieth anniversary of its founding.

ests round Hull House. *The Second Twenty Years* is largely a record of those efforts. Or rather perhaps an analysis of them. It is less narrative, gives less of her personal experience, than its predecessor, *Twenty Years at Hull House.* And it is a much sadder book. In her recollections of Woodrow Wilson, indeed, there is in it a faint, a very faint shadow of bitterness—the only such shadow that can be distinguished in her dozen volumes. Perhaps indeed it is not there. Perhaps one only sees it as the shadow of a shade—the shade of her undoubted feeling that in refusing to consider the plan of "continuous mediation," Wilson had made a great mistake, a personal mistake. The refusal to try that plan, the three more years of horror and destruction that followed, that might in part have been averted, was the great tragedy of Jane Addams's life; of all her defeats, the only defeat that she could not forget. From that surrender by her leader she rode away as General Wade Hampton from Appomattox, sword in hand, but she never ceased to mourn over a great, lost opportunity.

The next interesting celebration was her own seventieth birthday dinner, already mentioned. Mr. and Mrs. Henry J. Morgenthau (ambassador to Turkey under Wilson) gave the luncheon, inviting seventy guests, at their summer home in Bar Harbor, a few miles from Jane Addams's own cottage. One of her oldest friends spoke, Doctor Francis Peabody of Harvard, who though he had never taught sociology, had had a course in the 'eighties in what the boys called "drunkenness, drainage and divorce"; and one of her newest friends, whom she thought to be "as intelligent as he is amusing, and as spirited as he is young, and that is saying a great deal,"

President Robert Hutchins of the University of Chicago; and Arthur Henderson, son of her admired Arthur Henderson, British Labor Party Minister of Foreign Affairs; and Doctor Richard Cabot of Boston; and Mr. Morgenthau, and John D. Rockefeller, Jr. Doctor Cabot said "she had always loved her neighbor as herself," and Mr. Rockefeller amplified the idea by saying that such had been the admonition of Christ, and Jane Addams was the most Christlike of all living human beings. "But she has moved the world by the strength of her will," declared Doctor Peabody, who may have been right. She replied humorously. If it were true, as Doctor Cabot had said, that she had "an infinite capacity for understanding human failures," then she was in a position to follow out the philosopher's injunction "know thyself." And she told them her old, favorite story—of the occasion when she had been sitting with the dean of an Episcopal Cathedral, "out west," and he had complained bitterly of a bishop who as he said, "associated with radicals."

"Perhaps," she had suggested, "he hopes to do them good."

"Nothing of the sort, I fear," the dean had replied gloomily. "The fact is, he likes those people."

It was a cheerful birthday all round. Mrs. Bowen had begun it with a letter enclosing a gift. "It was a blessed day for me when you came into my life," she wrote. "The enclosed check has no strings attached. You may spend it for candy, or even for sending the dove of peace to the cleaners. You will doubtless want to make some new resolutions on your birthday. I suggest, (a) be careful of spots. (b) watch your step."

The United Press had forced on her a list of eleven

questions, no less, her answers to which were to be printed everywhere. The original draft of her answers is before me, ornamented with strange drawings which she was simultaneously making for one of Mary Smith's grandnieces. Some of her answers in that draft would have amused the public. But she sent off finally an admirable set of replies, beginning "No special wisdom comes at seventy, I find; can be secured only through adaptation to a changing world." She thought women had brought into politics a more careful consideration of both health and humanitarian questions. Of prohibition she thought it had "doubtless secured a higher standard of living for the families of workingmen"—only that and nothing more. She thought the best remedy for unemployment was "widespread measures established by employers and enacted by government for insurance against unemployment and destitute old age." She considered that the greatest sociological improvement during her life had been "conferences and treaties between the governments of the world for reduction of armaments, outlawry of war, and the establishment of the world court." She looked for greatest improvement in the future "along the lines of greater international comity and goodwill." She thought that changing standards among young women, though easily misinterpreted, did not affect basic morality. And some questions, such as her views on the present possibility of "abolishing poverty" and on "birth control," she declined to answer in a few words. It is on these unanswered questions that her first draft is particularly individual, indeed one might say snappy. On the whole, however, she enjoyed the questions. "One goes on answering the same questions in the same way for many years," she said, "and it really seems to me that the public must be either very patient, or very thoughtful."

At this time she was awarded by the Greek Republic the Medal of Military Merit, to recompense her services to the fatherland, because during the World War period "she worked energetically for the Greek Army, having offered precious services to the fatherland." The particular services thus rewarded had been, she discovered, the permission given to the Greeks of the Hull House neighborhood to use Bowen Hall for squad drill of men who were waiting to be sent over to join the Greek Army, of which mention was made in the daily Army Report. She preferred to believe, however, that the medal was actually the expression of the affection for her of her Greek neighbors in general.

In February of the next year, 1931, Jane Addams was pronounced by a committee (of men) assembled by a popular woman's magazine, as first among the "twelve greatest living women of America." She accepted the honor philosophically. "One of the committee," she remarked, "formerly regarded me as a traitor, and I am quite sure that two at least of the others had never heard of me before this 'contest.'" The "jury" was composed of Newton D. Baker, Doctor Henry Van Dyke, Otto Kahn, Booth Tarkington, and Bruce Barton, advertising executive. The other eleven "greatest living women in America" were (in alphabetical order) Grace Abbott, Cecilia Beaux, Martha Berry, Willa Cather, Carrie Chapman Catt, Mrs. Calvin Coolidge, Minnie Maddern Fiske, Helen Keller, Florence Sabin, Ernestine Schumann-Heink, and Mary E. Woolley. In the same month Mark A. DeWolfe Howe of Boston, who had been awarded the

Pulitzer Prize for a biography of Barrett Wendell of
Harvard, picked the "six outstanding present-day Ameri-
cans"—Jane Addams and five men, including Calvin
Coolidge, Thomas A. Edison, Henry Ford, Alfred E.
Smith, and Sergeant Alvin York. The list certainly did
credit to Mark Howe's catholicity of interests; there could
hardly be two people further apart in spirit than Barrett
Wendell and Jane Addams, though both were "cosmopoli-
tan" in their different ways. Other "lists" followed—
Archibald Henderson's "Contemporary Immortals," in-
cluding Jane Addams and Edison, but no others of the
Good Housekeeping or Howe groups; President Dowell's
(of Mercer University), giving the "seven greatest
Americans," also including Jane Addams, Edison, and
Ford, but adding George Washington, Abraham Lincoln,
Woodrow Wilson, and John D. Rockefeller; Mrs. Catt,
leading off with Jane Addams as "the greatest woman,
present or past." Many others; Jane Addams was on all.
"My real achievement," she said, "is to have reached
seventy without having become dependent." Her principal interest that year aside from Hull House and international understanding was in the effect of the growing
"depression" on the very young and the very old. She
wrote and spoke constantly on the necessity for the relief
of the "spiritual needs" of young people:

During these troublous times, particularly, young people must
be helped. To leave school or college full of high hopes and to
find that there is no place in the world where one may be
put to honest work is profoundly discouraging, and may cripple
an ardent young spirit. At such a period young people need to
be able to turn to normal, healthy group activity in neighborhood clubs or settlement houses. . . . In meeting the social diffi-

culties created by the depression, let us remember that all the generosity in the world will not suffice unless we realize that food, shelter and clothing are but a part of our obligation to the needy. Let us at least maintain, let us if possible extend, the institutions that minister to subtler needs. . . . The present moment is in the hands of the mixed lot of us, old and young. The situation requires limitless patience and comprehension, which surely should be supplied more readily by those who have been subjected to life's training.

For the more "material" needs of the old, she vigorously advocated a system of old age pensions. She became chairman of the Illinois Committee for Old Age Security, and campaigned strenuously for pension bills which were introduced that spring before the state legislature. She could not forget the long horror of the "poor-house" her neighbors had felt, nor its comparative expensiveness for the provision of what in the end was not so much individual security as individual despair. Mrs. Catt had given as Jane Addams's special quality the ability to "stick to a project until she made it a success, and then to keep on sticking to the success," and Mrs. Catt was not far wrong. At seventy Jane Addams was sticking to the suggestions she had made at forty, and again at fifty. Some of them she had seen adopted and then discarded. But she was in no way discouraged. "If my ideas are a wreck, as some people say," she remarked, "I can still feel the rudder in my hand and I think I can still steer. I have been asked if I have the courage to begin my work over again. I can only say that it takes more courage to abandon one's principles and habits of life than to keep on with them."

In the same way she kept on with her work for international understanding, for "world peace and freedom." Here she saw light ahead. From heading a small minority, she had come to find herself surrounded by what she felt was a majority. President after President had encouraged the country to join the World Court. The League of Nations, though her own country persistently remained aloof, and though its labors had often been in vain, had continued to function for many years, and that continuance she thought was in itself "the great thing." An international movement for "the outlawry of war" had resulted in the Kellogg Pact, and though Jane Addams herself had no final faith in any enduring peace that depended on the agreement of changing statesmen and changing governments, she greeted the Pact with a cheer, as splendidly educational. And education for peace and mutual international friendliness was beginning to have its effect on the young people particularly. She felt quite sure of that. She saw the schools and the colleges vocal with opposition not only to war, but *to the idea of war*—her own opposition over forty years. In January of 1931 she was a speaker—and as usual when she appeared on any program, the "principal speaker," at a Conference at Washington on the cause and cure of war. Delegates were present from forty-four states. Hoover was heartily in sympathy. The Chief of Naval Operations, the president of the Navy General Board, the commanding general of the 27th Division in the World War, the Secretary of Commerce, stood with her and spoke also. When a self-styled representative of the D.A.R. attempted to "heckle" Miss Addams, there were not hisses but laughs—so far had the Capital, at least, come on since the days seven years before when a similar meeting had been sneered at by the press, and the speakers had been "drummed down" by the heels of young men in uniform who declared themselves to be, "as members of the American Legion, opposed to treachery." Jane Addams, navigating the seas of "peace by understanding," could feel the rudder in her hand more firmly than ever, and perceive the disappearance at last of certain dangerous reefs ahead. There were still plenty of reefs. As Mrs. Bowen had intimated with a smile, the dove might still be sent with advantage to the cleaners. But the green leaf in its beak was greener than before, a spray of hope.

After the Washington Conference Jane Addams went out to Arizona to avoid the worst of the Chicago winter, which her health could not stand any more. She found her old friend, Ida Tarbell, out there, teaching a winter class in biography. (From a phrase in a letter she wrote at that time, "It seems that biography is an Art. I certainly discovered that autobiography was an Art that I did not possess," this book was suggested.) In Arizona she was informed of the magazine award for "greatness," and she gave an interview to the United Press, in which she as usual placidly included hunks of imaginative wisdom.

The more extended freedom from traditions of the women in all countries is building greater forces of idealism than any previous century has ever known. . . .

We must have more action and less theory. The only way to help others is by pushing vigorously but kindly through and beyond all difficulties. . . .

To find a native talent in a man, woman or child, and then see that it is exercised, is one of the greatest objects of all social work. . . .

The Arizonians liked her and admired her. "It isn't so much that you hear she is somebody," a young gentleman who was in newspaper work in those parts informed this biographer, "as that she is such a damned nice old lady you can't help falling for her." They had her buying land in Arizona on which to "spend her declining years." The governor took advantage of her presence in the state to call a state conference on crime and delinquency, for her to address. She told them that prohibition was not responsible for crime, that "the alien element" was not responsible, that increasing the degree of punishment would not stop crime, that the only hope for betterment lay "in greater knowledge of criminals and crime, and particularly individualizing crime, which means having the punishment not 'fit the crime' so much as *fit the criminal.*" She went into details; offered them statistics and personal experiences; solidified each statement with evidence; and ended: "To make progress in this way requires great patience, freedom from any spirit of hate or revenge (strong and normal passions I grant) and the unremitting and never-ending search for the truth."

Few in the audience agreed with her, especially about prohibition and the alien, but they stood and cheered her when she finished; and when the well-meaning chairman of the meeting took her by the arm to escort her to her chair, and she "broke loose," as one spectator reported it, and walked to her chair unassisted, they cheered again, and waved their handkerchiefs. She smiled. She realized that now in her old age, the audiences she had faced so long, the groups she had led, were beginning to feel "protective" of her. She had been so long a protagonist, sometimes of popular ideas, sometimes of unpopular, and the years of her sixties had been so generally illiberal years, that she found it hard to grow used to her own cherishment. She had mothered the country; now the people were

inclined to mother her. But she had no idea of "departing
in peace."

She went back East in time to vote in the Chicago
mayoralty election and was presently notified of her
second award of the year, the M. Carey Thomas Prize of
$5,000 by Bryn Mawr College. This was a very different
matter from a solemn ranking among women by a random
committee of gentlemen. This was a recognition of "eminent achievement" by women whom she herself honored,
and she was deeply touched. One of her grandnieces had
been graduated from Bryn Mawr in 1929, and Jane
Addams insisted that this niece should accompany her
when she went to receive the award. "I'll pay your
expenses out of it," she said. "But you must come down
and see your old college and your old aunt together, two
hearts that beat as one." The Philadelphia surroundings
of Bryn Mawr had long been dear to Jane Addams. Her
father and mother had both been born within a few miles
of Philadelphia, had been married in the neighborhood.
Some of her family, notably "Aunt Elizabeth" Reiff, about
whom she was always full of affectionate, humorous
reminiscence, lived near Philadelphia. And she breathed
freely in the Quaker atmosphere of the place. "Rockford
and Swarthmore have been nearest my heart among the
colleges," she said, "but now I can be a Bryn Mawr girl
too." The ceremonies were graceful and to her delight
chiefly feminine. John Dewey, her old friend, was there to
bear testimony; but all the other speakers were women—
Grace Abbott, Mrs. Catt—"I have fought the wild beasts
at Ephesus beside Mrs. Catt for centuries, it seems to
me," she said, "and she makes me think of Alan Breck
Stuart—'is she no a bonny fighter?' "—and Miss Frances

Perkins, then of the New York State department of labor, formerly a Hull House "resident." Miss Thomas herself, the only person who had previously received the award, one of the stateliest of great ladies, was not only approving but affectionate. "They liked me," Jane Addams reported afterward. "I could feel it." President Park of Bryn Mawr said:

That you are a woman of eminent achievement, that you have made a fuller life possible for women, needs no reiteration from me. But you have achieved a greater thing than this. You have not alone led us into a profession which you half created, into wider opportunities, to more nearly commensurate awards. You have, by walking in it yourself, shown to American women the hard path of democracy. For the helpless, young and old, for the poor, the unlearned, the stranger, the despised, you have urged understanding and then justice.

From Bryn Mawr Jane Addams went, a month later, to her own fiftieth graduation anniversary at Rockford College, the eighty-fourth commencement of the institution. Eight of her sixteen classmates, all who were living, were present. She said to the class of 1931:

No doubt we of 1881 seem to you positively prehistoric. Yet our responsibilities were yours, and yours are what ours were. May I warn you against doing good to people, and trying to make others good by law? One does good, if at all, *with* people, not *to* people. It is easy, for instance, for us to take liquor away from the Negro in the South for his good, and from the immigrant laborer in the North for his good, but the curious result is this—a law passed by people who are quite sure that they themselves do not need the law at all.... Democracy is perhaps not an attainment, but a process—the process according to which we do not force law upon others, but make it for ourselves, and morally binding on ourselves therefore as its makers.

After a quiet summer at Bar Harbor, she went to Washington in October to present to President Hoover a petition in favor of international disarmament, signed by 200,000 American women voters—part of a world-wide petition, which with more than six million signatures was taken before the Disarmament Conference at Geneva in the following February. Again she was enthusiastically received at Washington; foreign diplomats and their wives were invited by President Hoover to be present at the reception of the petition, and the "correspondents" publicized her in positively glowing terms; it was even asserted that she, and she alone, had induced President Coolidge, four years earlier, to back Briand's proposal for a bilateral Franco-American anti-war agreement, and that out of this proposal had come the Kellogg Pact. In Washington it was apparent that Jane Addams had become a sort of "elder statesman." It was well understood that she had declined appointment as an American delegate to the Disarmament Conference itself, on the ground of her ill-health—an appointment that went to President Mary E. Woolley of Mount Holyoke College, to the great satisfaction of Jane Addams.

From Washington she went to New York, to receive another $5,000 prize—this one for being "the outstanding woman of the year," from yet another popular magazine. She was again grateful. "Hull House," she remarked, "certainly needs money as never before." She gave $500 of the prize to the Chicago Community Relief Fund, and the rest of it to the House for current expenses in the promotion of what she had already called "recreational relief" in the depression. This was the third award of the year; but the best-known award of her life was still, in the same year, to come.

In November of that year she caught a cold which developed into a persistent bronchitis. She had been told that a major operation for the removal of a tumor was immediately necessary, because the growth might become malignant at any time; but that she could not be operated on until her cough was better. The doctors watched her constantly—it was something like a race between the bronchitis and the operation. On the day after Thanksgiving this biographer went to see her in her rooms at Mary Smith's home on Walton Place in Chicago, and she said quizzically,

"I have something to tell you, but I'd better not. It is strictly confidential."

"About your operation?"

"Oh, that? No; that will come along presently. This is something nicer."

"What is it?

"I am instructed to tell nobody."

"Then tell me."

"Go over to the bureau and open the second drawer on the left. There is a telegram on top of things. You can read it, but you must be quiet."

It was from the Norwegian Minister at Washington, informing her that "there had been attributed to" her and Doctor Nicholas Murray Butler, the Nobel Peace Prize for 1931; that the award would be made on December 10th at Oslo; that she would be good enough to keep the information "entirely personal."

"Do you think they would regard Mary Smith and you as entirely personal?" she inquired. We thought so.

Ten days later, the bronchitis having to some extent cleared up, Jane Addams was taken down to Baltimore, to Johns Hopkins Hospital, where the surgeons had a new sort of anesthetic that was thought to be safer than any other in cases involving a weak heart. In the hospital, on December 10th, she received the formal notice of the award of the prize. The prize was "officially distributed" that day at the Nobel Institute in Oslo, in the presence of the King and Crown Prince. The American minister at Oslo received the gold medals and the diplomas for both Jane Addams and Dr. Butler, and Professor Halvan Koht made an address in their honor. A fourth of his speech was about America, a fourth of it was about Doctor Butler, and the other half of it was about Jane Addams. Regarding America Professor Koht said, "There is scarcely a nation in the world with such power over war and peace." About Doctor Butler, "If there is a man I can call typically American, it is he, with his great capacity for work and ability for administration." About Jane Addams however he spoke at length:

She is the foremost woman of her nation, not far from being its greatest citizen.... When the need was greatest she made the American woman's desire for peace an international interest.... In Jane Addams there are assembled all the best womanly attributes which shall help us to establish peace in the world.... She clung to her idealism in the difficult period when other demands and interests overshadowed peace.... She was the right spokesman for all the peace-loving women of the world.

Cables of congratulation poured into the hospital from twenty countries; telegrams and letters by the hundred. President Hoover, General Pershing, and the Hull House

Harlequin Club joined in the acclaim. There were a few notes of half-regret: Doctor Maude Royden's word from England, for instance, "Joyful congratulations stop vexed at divided prize stop you are unique." And a distinguished woman statesman wired, "Three cheers this is certainly good news although I wish Nick might have been eliminated." There was in fact, among genuine disbelievers in war as a method of settlement of misunderstandings, the feeling that Doctor Butler had abandoned during the war, when the advocacy of peace was unpopular, the right to be considered a genuine advocate of peace. Said one writer:

When we entered the war, Miss Addams fought with unexampled courage for free speech and although she was pilloried in the ribald press she never flinched before the clamor. She has never changed her opinions or apologized for them, and for that reason America is proud of the honor conferred upon her. But it is very sad to have to relate that Doctor Butler was among the first in our country to surrender his mentality to war hysteria. In his case it was particularly discreditable, as he was a man of culture and university training and was familiar with European political conditions. He condemned Senator La Follette in bitterest terms ... dismissed Professor Cattell and other members of the Columbia staff because they refused to surrender their mental integrity to popular hysteria ... rebuked Wilson for his "hesitancy" in coming to the aid of the Allies. ... He cannot look back on this chapter in his history with honor or with pride ... and he has ever since adopted a policy of silence about it.

The only evidence that Jane Addams shared this view of her co-prizewinner is the fact that several copies of the foregoing article were found in her files after her death, and the further fact that she never, so far as is known, expressed to any friend pleasure at the company in which she found herself. She never minded what flag one fought under, but she disliked desertion of your flag under fire.

The day after she was notified formally of the award, she was operated on, and the new anesthetic worked badly; she was in a state almost of collapse for thirty-six hours. Then she rallied; but after a month in the hospital, she found herself still very weak. Late in January she was taken to Florida to recuperate. By March it was clear that she would not be strong enough to go abroad as she had planned, to the sixth Conference of W.I.L. at Grenoble, and to Oslo to talk on peace. Meanwhile she received the money award which accompanied the prize, approximately $16,000, and promptly gave it to the W.I.L. She wrote to the Executive Committee:

The award is to go to the *International* W.I.L.P.F., $12,000 invested as an endowment, the interest to be used for the expenses of our Headquarters Office. In case the W.I.L. ever comes to an end or is ever given up, I should like the money to revert to the international work of the Foreign Service Committee of the Society of Friends; $3,000 will be put at the disposal of the International Executive Committee to be used at their discretion; it may be necessary to use part of this $3,000 for the Grenoble Congress. I hope there need be no publicity about this use of the award money; it would be unfortunate to give the impression that we are now financially provided for and can spend with less careful consideration.

The rest of the award she used to repay herself for a loan of $500 she had already made to the W.I.L., and for her own traveling expenses if she should be able to go to Grenoble. As she was not, she subsequently gave it to the American section of the League. Her explanation of this disposal of the prize was that it had been given her not for her own work, but for her work in connection with the

League, and therefore the money portion properly reverted to the League. Her gift was, one is informed, the largest ever received by the organization from any one source; an interesting illustration of how much can be accomplished without large endowments.

In January 1933 Miss Addams exercised her right as a Nobel prizewinner to nominate for the Peace Prize of that year Sir Norman Angell. She further organized an American committee of great distinction to support his nomination, and provided the very small funds necessary for secretarial work and postage in connection with the organization of this committee. He had, she wrote, "once more in 1932 perhaps better than any one else stirred the public conscience to a desire for a finer international comity." Sir Norman received the award.

It may be worth noting that though in 1931 Jane Addams was awarded $26,000 in money prizes, she never included those sums in her careful list of "earnings of J.A. for thirty-seven years," which was found in her desk after she died, nor though $26,000 was almost as much as she had earned in the preceding sixteen years altogether, did she keep any of it for her own expenses. It may also be interesting to point out what sacrifice of earning capacity Jane Addams's long campaign for international understanding involved. In the ten years preceding 1915, her average earnings were a little less than four thousand dollars a year. In the next fifteen years, they were less than fifteen hundred a year. In five of those fifteen years, when she was at the peak of her intelligence and power, she earned less than one thousand dollars a year; less than the yearly salary of many a country minister, far less than the wages of many of the girls who were in the Hull House clubs. And finally it may be noted that no member of her family, no resident of Hull House, and so far as is known no friend except Mary Smith, was aware that her pacifism and internationalism involved any financial sacrifice whatever. Jane Addams never much liked Carlyle; but in this matter she followed his advice to "burn your own smoke."

CHAPTER XX

QUIET YEARS

SLOW recovery from the Baltimore operation, and the warnings of a weak heart, kept Jane Addams away from Hull House until April, and made it impossible to carry out her plan to go to Oslo and make her Nobel Prize speech, or to go to the Grenoble Conference. She was at last beginning to realize that she had been a fragile person all her life without knowing it, and that weakness had finally caught up with her. She would have to be careful. She still made speeches and climbed stairs against the doctor's advice, but she did her best to make things easier for her friends who worried about her. She agreed to spend only afternoons and early evenings at Hull House, working quietly in her room at Mary Smith's in the mornings. She was compiling another book—she almost always spoke of her writing as compiling—this one of her ideas on the relation of religion to conduct, of the effect of a belief in a future life on behavior in this. She would include in it a group of the memorial addresses she had made for her friends, old and young, who had died in the preceding years. There had been many such talks. One had been at Altgeld's funeral, thirty years before, when some of her friends had warned her that if she spoke, she would seriously affect the subscriptions to the work of Hull House. Odd, that warning seemed in retrospect! For Altgeld had become a legend of goodness over the years, and besides,

Vachel Lindsay had ennobled his memory in an immortal poem. But she did not include the Altgeld address; perhaps because she had admired him rather than felt affection for him, and these were to be words about those she had loved. Turning back to her old guide, Plato, for a title, she called the little book *The Excellent Becomes the Permanent*. She dedicated it to Alice Hamilton, "whose wisdom and courage have never failed when we have walked together so many times in the very borderland between life and death." Not only the borderland when they were seeking to prevent the death of others, but the borderland between her own life and death, she meant; for time and again "Doctor Alice" had been with Jane Addams when the undiscovered country had lain very near. Doctor Alice had never asked Jane Addams what her attitude toward the future life was, but many others had; she accepted the responsibility, now that she was an old woman, of trying to decide. But the striking negative thing about the book is that in it she does not show herself coming to any decision.

It is not, however, a negative book; it is in thinking as positive, as clear, as she ever showed herself to be in thinking of service in this world. It is so positive, so clear, and beyond all so eloquent, that it evades quotation. It has sold hardly at all, compared with her other books; yet one can hardly imagine how a reader once acquainted with it could dispense with its words.

From the very beginning, the picture of "Jenny Dow," the noble acceptance of uncertainty and the beautiful transformation of uncertainty into a boon, "the paramount interest of life, all that makes it lofty and worthy, all that lifts it above the commonplace, lies in the sense of mystery that constantly surrounds it, in the consciousness that each day as it dawns may bring the end either to ourselves or to our best beloved"—to the very end, the final sentence "no altar at which living men have once devoutly worshiped, no oracle to whom a nation long ago appealed in its moments of dire confusion, no gentle myth in which former generations have found solace, can lose all significance for us, the survivors," there is no page without its high consolation, no phrase from which the sunlight of imagination is withdrawn. Paragraph after paragraph has been copied down in evidence of this, and then laid away again. Now that Jane Addams herself has crossed the borderland, the book must speak for itself, as a whole, or not at all. Perhaps its feeling is too Greek to permit the volume to become a Christian handbook. Perhaps it is as spiritually "international" as Jane Addams's impulses were politically so, and we are bound to the lower criticism of our various creeds. Such phrases as "Lead, kindly Light," or "I hope to meet my Pilot face to face when I have crossed the bar," are acceptable partly because they are vague. Jane Addams's ideas of religion and of immortality are no more vague than her ideas of legislation or arbitration. She makes her possibilities definite. Only, she presents more possibilities than one. Let it go. The book no more lends itself to summary than does a mother's love, or the Book of Revelation.

Julia Lathrop died, and a door closed on one of the longest, gayest and richest of Jane Addams's experiences. She has written of it in *My Friend Julia Lathrop*, a partial biography of which she completed the final draft only the week before she died. "It has been much like writing my autobiography over again from another point of view," she said. Jane Addams included Julia Lathrop, as she did Alice Hamilton and Florence Kelley, in her own brief list of "great women of the twentieth century," or as she called it sometimes "the woman's century." With Julia Lathrop gone, and Florence Kelley gone, Jane Addams felt her own responsibility anew. There were others coming on in her field, many others, but she had depended on those two for so long! She turned almost fiercely to the use of mere men once more for the accomplishment of social legislation.

The Republican and Democratic conventions were both to be held in Chicago. Jane Addams presented to the platform committees of both parties her program of needed legislation, for which she believed the time to be ripening if not ripe. "I have been coming before platform committees for a number of years," she said, "and always to speak for unpopular causes. Sometime I hope to appear for a popular cause. That time hasn't come yet, but perhaps it is on the way." She wanted six things: a reduction of tariffs; recognition of Russia; refusal of governmental protection to commercial investments in other countries, large or small; entrance into the world court; the cancellation of war debts; and government control of munition manufacture. She got none of them, of course, from the Republicans. From time and Roosevelt she subsequently got the recognition of Russia and the *de facto* cancellation of the debts, but it was precisely the blinking *de facto* cancellation that she did not want alone; she wanted an open-eyed acceptance of facts. She did not discuss repeal of the eighteenth amendment, though she had been widely quoted as saying that in her own neighborhood prohibition had reduced the amount of drunkenness and made family life safer and more comfortable. The papers called her suggestions "too big a dose to swallow," but on the whole they spoke well of her. "Perhaps," she said, "they think I am too old to make much trouble for any one any more." She laughed over her inclusion, along with Edison and Ford again, among the twenty-four living persons "certain to be remembered in a hundred years," but she did not laugh at the vote of a thousand inmates of San Quentin Penitentiary, who decided that among the twelve greatest "men" of the century Jane Addams had to be listed—along with Clarence Darrow, Longfellow, Edison and Ford again, Lincoln, the Wright brothers, and—somewhat surprisingly according to chronology—Sir Francis Bacon. "I think," she said, "they must read books more than they do newspapers." She took no active part in the presidential campaign; she found herself unable to decide between her old fondness for Mr. Hoover and the untried eagerness of Mr. Roosevelt. The continuance of the depression, and of its effect on youth, appalled her:

Unless normal times return soon, the United States will be faced with the strange problem of taking care of a demoralized generation. An impoverished generation can be dealt with. But even actual hunger is not as grave a problem as that arising out of the spiritual demoralization of those who in the eagerness of youth seek work and cannot find it anywhere. They will become morally scarred veterans of a conflict as devastating as war. Without the zest of youth, how is progress possible? And to be unable to find work for "thine hand to do," is to die to zeal.

In September her old friend Raymond Robins, who had stood at her right hand against the police and the mob hysteria in the Isaak case when McKinley was murdered, disappeared. A few thought he had been killed, a few that he had been kidnaped. Jane Addams remembered a similar disappearance in her own experience, that of Edmund Waldo thirty years before. Waldo, a brilliant young Harvard graduate, a resident of Hull House, had suddenly dropped out of everybody's knowledge. An intensive and extensive search revealed nothing; it was literally years later that he turned up in Florida, victim of an amnesia so complete that he was never able to tell where he had been or what he had done. This writer, sleeping one night in a room adjoining Waldo's in a Polk Street tenement across the street from Hull House, was wakened by shrieks from down the hall, a man's voice in a sort of dull monotone of cursing, then as he lay trying to realize his whereabouts, the pleasant singsong "Harvard accent" of Ed Waldo, repeating "Put down that knife, please, put down that knife, please." Duty required the writer to get out of bed and join the party, which he did with a still-remembered reluctance, just in time to see Ed, a chair in his hand, facing a man with a knife; a woman lay on the floor in the corner, watching them. The man moved forward, Waldo swung the chair and knocked him out. The woman jumped up and rushed at Waldo. "Keep her away, please," Waldo said, and bent over the man and removed the knife. "Please take her down the hall and lock her in my room and then get some water from the sink," he said. The woman went quietly enough, the water was brought, and Waldo administered first aid to the man on the floor, who came to presently. "They will be all right now, quite all right I think," Waldo said.

"Shall I go for the police?"

"Why the police? This is a family matter. I know these

people. They will be all right. He was just a little drunk of course. You can let her come in now." When the woman was brought back, Waldo talked to her.

"I am sorry. He was not going to hurt you I think but I was not sure. Do you want me to stay here? I thought not. Tell him I will give him the knife in the morning." We went back to Waldo's room, and Ed delivered a short rambling lecture on marriage.

"It brings out the worst in men sometimes. But it always brings out the best in women. I knew she would go for me; that was why I was glad to see you come in."

"You might have called to me."

"My dear fellow, I hadn't time, really." He went to bed again, and so did this biographer, but not to sleep. Readers must pardon this digressive account of the only "dramatic" experience this biographer ever had around Hull House. Jane Addams remembered Waldo's wandering away, and fully believed that Raymond Robins had done the same thing. He had; but the months before he was found were full of anguish to her.

In October Swarthmore College, on the occasion of a joint celebration of Founder's Day and the 250th anniversary of the landing of William Penn, honored Jane Addams with a degree, and she made a fine speech. The degree was in recognition of her "service to human welfare at home and abroad, and for her magnificent work in the cause of international peace," the first of her many university degrees to emphasize her work for peace, and she liked that. Swarthmore was a Quaker college, and hers were Quaker traditions. She was so excited that as she said afterward, "I really believe I said I was a descendant of Penn, or implied as much anyway; I heard myself doing it!" She contrasted Penn's treatment of the Indians with the Puritan treatment, and with the current attitude of the American people toward immigrants and "aliens." Penn was tolerant, fixed in his own principles but acceptant of the ideals of others. The Puritans believed themselves to be a chosen people, and it made them arrogant, intolerant, and self-righteous. The charge of self-righteousness to-day lies against us all in America to some extent, and this characteristic can be traced back to the earliest settlers of New England:

The national self-righteousness is often quite honestly disguised as patriotism. It is really, however, part of that adolescent self-assertion, sometimes crudely expressed in sheer boasting, which the United States has never altogether outgrown. It is also, in another aspect, that complacency which we associate with the elderly who feel justified by their own successes and have completely lost their faculty for self-criticism.

She was seventy-two. She smiled and the audience smiled back at her. She did not believe she had quite lost her own faculty for self-criticism and neither did they, but they enjoyed her gentle irony at her own expense. But she went on with strong feeling:

Such impatience with differing opinion as we see now has never before been evident in the framework of orderly government. It is a stultifying situation. More than ever now in this period of world-wide maladjustment the nation needs all the free and vigorous thinking which is available. We must realize that narrow-mindedness, which includes fanatic nationalism, is suicidal.

The Swarthmore audience agreed that Jane Addams had been "superb," but the press did not like her talk much. In calling the "country" inclined to narrow-mindedness and boastfulness, she meant the newspapers particularly, and they knew it; some of the editors knew too that coming from Jane Addams, even such mild words were hard words. But her scholarship was too much for them. She built up her assertions on a foundation of historical evidence that stood like a rock, and not an editor ventured to assail it. She returned to Chicago and issued a strong statement in behalf of the candidacy of Henry Horner for governor, a statement that ended typically, "Dante's assertion that the wise man is he who has learned of life is most certainly applicable to Judge Horner."

"Who's this Dante?" demanded a Republican politician, and a wiser one answered, "Maybe you don't know, but there are a lot of normally Republican dagoes over where she lives that do know, and they know who she is, too. That'll mean a lot of votes."

Jane Addams voted for Hoover and Horner, but Roosevelt was elected, as the world knows, and she at once began campaigning again for old age pensions, which she knew Roosevelt favored. The poorhouse, "as my old friends always call it, even though we try to give it the more pleasant name of infirmary," was an expensive system. "If aged people had small pensions with which they could pay for their care, neighbors and relatives would often be willing to look after them, without the salaries and overhead expenses of the poor-farms." She was headlined everywhere for a suggestion she made at a dinner given in her honor by "the business and professional women" of Chicago:

A woman should fill a woman's place in the world, not a man's place. There are women's talents and women's energies, as there are men's talents and men's energies. To statesmanship she can contribute sympathy and understanding, to business the feminine instinct for coöperation rather than competition. It is easy to blame a businessman for greed, but historically what have men been but economic fighters for their families and for themselves? If men are greedy, let us not imitate them, we women who have not even the sanction of history for selfish competition.

Jane Addams advises women not to imitate men, said the editors. Not imitate their *greed*, she laughed a little wearily. She was informed that she "led the poll" of the National Council of Women for the "twelve greatest American women" whose portraits when the ladies were selected were to adorn the Hall of Science at the Century of Progress Exposition in Chicago the following summer. But in the end Mary Baker Eddy led the poll with 102,000 votes; Jane Addams was second with 99,000, Clara Barton third with 96,000, Frances Willard fourth with 90,000. Susan B. Anthony, Helen Keller, Harriet Beecher Stowe, Julia Ward Howe, Carrie Chapman Catt, Amelia Earhart Putnam, Mary Lyon, Mary E. Woolley, followed in order. It was at this time that Jane Addams made her own list, omitting Mrs. Eddy, Clara Barton, Helen Keller, Amelia Putnam, Mary Lyon and herself, and for them substituting Lucy Stone Blackwell, Julia Lathrop, Florence Kelley, Alice Hamilton, Florence Sabin, and Lillian Wald. That was just before Christmas, and at the family Christmas dinner we joked with her about it.

"Were you afraid to put yourself on such a list, or don't you think you belong?"

"Do I have to tell my own family," she demanded, "that modesty is my only really strong point?"

She closed the year with what was for her a "fiery"

speech on peace. The distinction between "offensive" and "defensive" wars, between "imperialistic" and "anti-imperialistic" wars, had disappeared. The drive for peace must be made against war as such, against war as an instrument of settling disputes of any kind:

How many millions of people are there in the United States to-day who are still certain, after more than seventy years, that the Civil War was an offensive war waged by the North? How many millions are there who still believe it was an offensive war declared by the South? The terms offensive and defensive in regard to war do not define facts, they define opinion, points of view. . . . Germany was "imperialistic," seeking a place in the sun. France was "imperialistic," seeking a Rhine frontier and colonies, not dominions. . . . Wars are not waged for honor, or for understanding, but for destruction. . . . War cannot be got rid of by outlawry, but only by an increase of understanding of the values of life. Even disarmament will not prevent war, it will serve as the greatest single educational force toward a comprehension of the truth that war is never necessary.

In January Jane Addams's old friends of the Union League Club gave another "testimonial banquet," at which she reviewed her early years at Hull House:

In those days people in Chicago believed firmly that the reward of virtue was success, and that railroads could do no wrong. A great fortune was evidence of long-continued industry and honesty, and only the railroads could "develop" the country. Mr. Yerkes managed to convince a good many that other qualities besides honesty and industry sometimes went to the acquisition of a fortune, and the Pullman strike in 1894 led others to the belief that the railroads were like human beings, and could do wrong. Then the city and the country began to make progress toward social regeneration.

She listed the "Hull House beginnings" of which she was most proud: factory inspection laws; playgrounds and small parks; the establishment of the Juvenile Court, and later of the psychopathic clinic which grew into the Institute of Juvenile Research; workmen's compensation laws. "We started some of these things, and coöperated in all as best we could." She glanced at prohibition, remarked that "you asked me here in friendship but not to talk of peace," and intimated that sound legislation for unemployment insurance and old age pensions was her own principal "national" concern at the time. It was a gentle, humorous speech. She reminded them of the occasion twenty years earlier when she had lost her hat in a crowd which Roosevelt was addressing, and the Union League Club had sent her a check for fifty dollars to buy another. "I had never paid more than ten dollars for a hat up to that time, and I never have since," she declared, "but once or twice I have had more expensive ones given me, I am not sure whether out of generosity or a sort of doubtfulness regarding my customary appearance."

In 1933 she centered most of her public appearances around the Century of Progress, as most Chicagoans did perhaps. She was the honorary President of the World Fellowship of Faiths, which met in a Congress like the Parliament of Religions at the old World's Fair in 1893, in which she had taken a considerable part. The World Fellowship sought "to help mankind to develop a new spiritual dynamic," and religion as a dynamic, not religion as a consolation or for personal salvation was what she had long preached. Governor Horner appointed her Honorary Chairman of Illinois Hostesses at the Century of Progress, and as such she coöperated in arranging programs at the Illinois Host House throughout the summer. It was, however, the "quietest" year she had ever spent, except those actually in bed with one or another illness or operation. In the autumn she went back to Bryn Mawr for a week of lectures and conferences with the girls, and "I only hope," she wrote, "they are getting as much out of it all as I am." As usual in the early winter she developed a bronchitis, and that particular bronchitis was a bad one. Suddenly her heart, which had been "acting splendidly," betrayed her. She was put to bed in her own room at Mary Smith's house, and there she lay for more than four months. She could presently see her secretary two hours a day, dictate occasional paragraphs of an article, and confer with the Hull House residents, and by the end of January move from her bed to her chair once a day; that was all. Mary Smith, also weak with bronchitis, brooded over her constantly, entertaining her with gallant humor. Then came the greatest personal tragedy of Jane Addams's old age, worse because more immediate than even the death of Julia Lathrop and of Florence Kelley. Late in February Mary Smith's bronchitis ran into pneumonia, and in the first week of March, in a room only twenty feet away from Jane Addams but a room which she could not reach, Mary Smith died.

That was a dreadful day.

The funeral services were held in the house. Jane Addams lay in her bed in the upper room, facing the door, and listened to the children from Hull House singing, and Doctor Niver's short, beautiful, broken talk. We took Mary Smith away to Roseland, Alice Hamilton as always remaining within call of Jane Addams. To me while she lived my aunt spoke of those hours, of those days, only once.

"I thought over everything," she said. "I suppose I

could have willed my heart to stop beating, and I longed to relax into doing that, but the thought of what she had been to me for so long kept me from being cowardly."

As soon as she could be moved, Alice Hamilton took her away to her own summer home in Hadlyme, Connecticut, on the bank of the Connecticut River. A small separate suite of rooms had been built for her adjoining the Hamilton cottage. Strength returned. She began working hard on her biography of Julia Lathrop. In August, when her old friend and physician Doctor J. B. Herrick went down to visit her, she insisted on climbing the stairs of the old mill which was a part of the place, to show him the view. She adopted a cane, but with its aid she moved briskly everywhere—rather too briskly as usual, Doctor Herrick thought. In the fall she came back to Chicago, to a suite of rooms at Mrs. Bowen's; Mrs. Bowen had had an automatic elevator built in during the summer. Jane Addams at once began spending her afternoons and evenings again at Hull House, conferring with scores of people, advising constantly on the Government's Chicago housing scheme, resuming her old life. She insisted that she was as well as she had ever been in her life, that "her funny old heart," as she always called it, "was behaving splendidly." She was really being "good," Doctor Herrick said. "One can't tell at all. You might be called on the telephone at any time and told that she was gone. Or she might live for years, still able to work. In any case, she will have to wear herself out. She can't rust out; it isn't her way." At the usual "family Christmas dinner," the first for years that Mary Smith had not served, Jane Addams was hearty.

"But," she said, "if you are really going to write my biography, you had better get to work. You know the

JANE ADDAMS'S SUMMER HOME AT HADLYME,
CONNECTICUT

Photograph by Bradley

JANE ADDAMS'S SUMMER HOME AT BAR HARBOR, MAINE

story about old Mr. Swift? You must know it, it goes back to the horse-and-buggy days." So she told us the story of Mr. Swift, and the biography was begun the next day. We went over to Hull House together, and she showed me the files of her records. There were a truckload of them.

"What you are going to do with them I can't imagine," she said. "Either now or later."

"I shall give them to the Jane Addams School of Social Service at the University of Chicago, when they call it that."

"You will have them on your hands for a long while," she commented. "Some day they will call it the Abbott School, after my two 'good 'abits.' " She meant Edith and Grace Abbott, whom she tremendously admired.

CHAPTER XXI

SHE GOES IN PEACE

WITH Mrs. Bowen, Jane Addams went from Chicago in January to spend ten weeks in Arizona, near Phoenix. There, apparently in better health than for two years, and without any sense of failing strength, she worked steadily on her biography of Miss Lathrop. She was not quite satisfied with it. "I am too near her, and I miss her too much," she said. She felt also that although she had not lost her power of organization, she was unable to "put things" quite as she had been accustomed to putting them. "I think I am growing verbose," she wrote, "but you will tell me about that when I get back to Chicago." She spent some time also reading and making marginal comments on the first draft of the first eight chapters of this biography, which were sent her as they were composed. She did not like the introduction much. "My dear, you mean well, but you exaggerate," she wrote opposite one passage of it, and at the end, "This is all very well, but don't you think the schoolboy who admires his old aunt is just a *little* evident?" The other chapters pleased her better, though she was dissatisfied with certain minor interpretations. She wrote, "You do not do justice to my stepmother. She simply did not quite *fit* in Cedarville, and therefore people said harsh things of her, they still do I know, but you must not let them 'buffalo' you, as they used to say." And of Miss Sill, "I was homesick

410

my first month at Rockford, and a little disappointed at
not being allowed to go to Smith; resentful, I suppose you
might call it. And besides they urged church affiliation on
me, and I was not a Christian at seventeen, but I suppose
a Deist; much worried and confused. That was why I got
off on the wrong foot with Miss Sill, who was a determined as well as a devoted woman, but I came to admire
her very much, though as you say never altogether to
agree with her. I never professed Christianity at Rockford, nor till I was twenty-five. If my father had lived I
might never have joined a church at all, I suppose, but of
course it is all very far back." And later, "Some of us were
determined that Rockford should really be a college, as
the charter provided, and we did rather force Miss Sill's
hand, I think. It seemed to us very important *in the development of the position of women in the West* that
Rockford should be in the full sense a college." And opposite the passage in which her talk at Plymouth, Massachusetts, in the summer of 1892, on "the subjective necessity of social settlements" is compared with Emerson's
"American Scholar," she wrote, "My dear, people will
laugh! But I did like it myself, all but the title, which was
terribly involved. I never seemed to have any gift for
shortening titles, did I?"

In February she was made the recipient of the American Education Award for 1935, an illuminated manuscript
reciting her importance as an educator "by example and
precept. . . . She has taught us that a better understanding
of life comes from a willingness to learn from life, indicated how the joys of fellowship and the inspiration of art
may be added to the tools of knowledge, and in her life
and her philosophy has taught tolerance and peaceful com-

munity living, first at home and then in the world at large."

She was asked to make, and did make, a brief speech on an international broadcast of the National Education Association. The arrangements for her participation from Phoenix were expensive. "For six cents I could have sent my remarks on to the studio to be read there," she remarked. "I hope they were educational; they were certainly not very thrifty." On March 23rd she sent to Berkeley, California, to receive an honorary degree from the University of California on the occasion of the fiftieth anniversary convocation of the university. Herbert Hoover and Miss Frances Perkins, Secretary of Labor, were also recipients of degrees. When Jane Addams returned to Chicago, she was full of stories of this occasion. Miss Perkins after her speech, whispered to Miss Addams, nodding toward Mr. Hoover, "I do hope I didn't say anything to annoy him."

"I saw you were skating on thin ice," Miss Addams whispered back, "but you needn't have worried, he was asleep most of the time." A Miss Ijams had appeared in the newspapers as declining to meet Miss Perkins at an alumni luncheon, and subsequently engaging in a controversy with Mrs. Roosevelt over the reason for this refusal.

"Did you meet Miss Ijams?" this biographer asked Miss Addams. "She seems to be a silly woman."

"Why, not at all silly," Miss Addams replied. "She said what she thought and said it very clearly. I can understand her point of view. What I can't understand in a Californian is her inhospitality." Then she added with a smile, "I mean to a guest. To ideas, I don't suppose Californians are any more hospitable than the rest of us."

After the exercises were over, knowing that an old Rockford College friend was living in Berkeley, Jane Addams looked her up. She found the little house open, but apparently empty. So she went round to the back, and found "what seemed to me a frail old lady," she said, giving orders to a man who was working in the garden. They went back into the house, and seeing a particularly comfortable chair, Jane Addams said, "Now you sit there, and I'll bring this other chair over."

"What do you mean, telling me where I am to sit in my own house?" replied the old lady indignantly. In telling the incident with great delight Jane Addams remarked, "She really felt insulted, and she was of course quite right. I remembered that she was old but I forgot that she was very little older than I."

Returning to Chicago at the beginning of April, Jane Addams at once resumed her daily routine, working in the morning on the revision of Miss Lathrop's biography, and spending every afternoon at Hull House, seeing whoever wished to see her. She made also a sort of "public appearance" at a benefit concert in Orchestra Hall for the Hull House Music School—the first "benefit performance" of any sort in the long history of Hull House. Schumann-Heink sang, prefacing her singing with the whimsical remark, "It is too bad to be oldt!" whereat the whole audience rose and applauded standing. Edith Mason sang, magnificently. The Chicago Women's Orchestra played, and the pianist was a young man from the Hull House Music School. Jane Addams sat peacefully in one of the center boxes, and rejoiced in the success of the occasion. A day later she went down to the University of Chicago to consult Miss Grace Abbott on the Lathrop biography, and to visit the youngest of her great-grandnieces, with proud stories of all of whom it is to be feared she afflicted her friends. The baby had a cold.

"They tell me," Miss Addams said, "that I mustn't catch a cold. My heart won't stand it. But you can't catch a cold from a baby when it is just sitting in your lap, you know."

Then came the meeting of the Women's International League in Washington, the twentieth birthday of the League, which was to be celebrated by a great dinner to its founder and honorary president, Jane Addams. Accompanied only by Mrs. Robert Morss Lovett, Miss Addams arrived in Washington on May 1st, went at once to the Fox Movietone studios for pictures, lunched with Josephine Roche and Doctor Alice Hamilton, saw the newspaper correspondents, and rested. Next day she had a stream of callers, mostly old friends like the Gerard Swopes and Mrs. Harold Ickes. Mrs. Roosevelt gave a reception at the White House, but Miss Addams thought it was wiser to save her strength. In the evening came the dinner in her honor in the Willard Hotel ballroom, twelve hundred present and many turned away—said to have been the largest dinner ever given at the hotel. Speakers were Congressman Caroline O'Day of New York, Mrs. Roosevelt, Secretary Ickes, Doctor Hamilton, Sidney Hillman, president of the Amalgamated Clothing Workers of America, Gerard Swope, president of the General Electric Company, Oswald Garrison Villard, and Miss Addams herself. "It is for being yourself that I thank you to-night," said Mrs. Roosevelt. "When the day comes when difficulties are faced and settled without resorting to the type of waste which war has always meant, we shall look back in this country upon the leadership you have given us, Miss Addams, and be grateful for having had you living with us." Secretary Ickes in closing an eloquent and warm-hearted speech declared:

Jane Addams has dared to believe that the Declaration of Independence and the Constitution of the United States were written in good faith and that the rights declared in them are rights that are available to the humblest of our citizens. She is the truest American that I have ever known, and there has been none braver.... Parents who want to develop the finest in their children will bring them up in the Jane Addams tradition and those so reared will be the best citizens of their generation—steadfast, neighborly, serene and simple, crusaders in the never-ending fight for a finer and better social order that will be firmly grounded upon justice and the determination that others shall not be denied an opportunity equal to ours to enjoy the same fullness and richness of the American way of life that we demand for ourselves.

Gerard Swope said that "all barriers fade into insignificance in our respect and affection for Miss Addams"; Sidney Hillman that "her life has been a beacon in the dark periods of our history, and she has been the center of some of the finest activities of the human spirit"; Oswald Garrison Villard that "we are surely met less to praise Jane Addams than to recite our own rare fortune that she has been and is of us, that it has been our country that gave her to the world."

All the speeches were written out in advance. Jane Addams herself had written out a speech, but when she rose she offered no word of it; her reactions were extemporaneous. In her mind she had reviewed, as she had sat listening, the huge dinner at the Furniture Mart in Chicago, the seventieth birthday dinner at Bar Harbor in 1930, and she began by saying just what she had said on those occasions, "I do not know any such person as you have described here to-night." She went on to admit that "I have never been sure that I was right; I think we all have to feel our way, step by step." But, she said, she felt like the prophet of the single tax, who was asked to speak at a funeral and declared that since so many were present he would utilize the occasion to discuss the single tax. The dinner was a celebration, not a funeral; nevertheless she would speak not of the "alien celebrity" they had described, but of peace:

We don't expect to change human nature, we people of peace, but we do expect to change human behavior. . . . We may be a long way from permanent peace, and we may have a long journey ahead of us in educating the community and public opinion. Ours may not be an inspiring rôle. But it tests our endurance and our moral enterprise, and we must see that we keep on. . . . I perceive a rising tide of revolt against war as an institution, against war as such. Yet, we are suffering still in many ways from a war psychology; the armies have been demobilized, the psychology has not. The worst thing about war is not the poison gas which wipes out lives and destroys cities, but the poison it spreads in the minds of man. . . . In case of any more unfortunate accidents, we must be ready not only with political institutions, the League of Nations and the World Court, but with an educated public opinion which shall fight this poison's spread.

On the next day Miss Addams lunched with a number of the women who had gone with her twenty years before to the first meeting of the Women's International League for Peace at The Hague. After luncheon she went to a broadcasting studio to listen to and participate in the radio "peace program" which had been arranged for that day. There were speakers in London, Paris, Moscow and Tokio; six months had been required to perfect the arrangement, which were reported to have been the most complicated in the history of broadcasting so far. The major assemblage was in McPherson Square, where many men and women of international and national prominence had gathered; but as the day, though warm, was damp, it was thought wisest for Jane Addams to remain indoors. The British Ambassador spoke, introducing Lord Robert Cecil and Arthur Henderson in London; the Japanese Ambassador introduced Prince Tokugawa in Tokio; the Russian Ambassador introduced Krupskaya, widow of Lenin, in Moscow; the French Chargé D'Affaires introduced Paul Boncour in Paris; Norman Davis and Miss Josephine Roche spoke from Washington. Ambassadors and speakers from round the world alike paid their tribute to Miss Addams, and expressed their hopes for peace. Miss Roche, Assistant Secretary of the Treasury said:

Honored and acclaimed to-day by the officials of many nations as she has been for years by their peoples, America's greatest woman, Jane Addams, sees to-day another milestone passed in humanity's slow but ever-forward march toward co-operation and understanding between mankind. Deeply stirring as this unparalleled tribute to a rare human being and leader has been, all of us listening have been equally moved by the determined, common purpose making itself felt through all the messages that have come from across the seas and lands, the purpose to make peace prevail. But peace is born only of justice, justice between men and nations. Because she has lived and given all of herself for the cause of social and economic justice, Jane Addams knows beyond all others the full meaning of peace, and she will now close this international program.

Once more, to the amazement of those in the studio, Miss Addams laid aside her prepared speech, and with a full heart and a clear mind spoke extemporaneously round the world. She briefly and precisely summed up the message of the representatives of each of the five great nations, and concluded:

The Women's International League joins a long procession of those who have endeavored, for hundreds of years, to substitute law for war, political processes for brute force; and we are grateful to our friends from various parts of the world who recognize at least our sincerity in this long effort.

Leaving Washington the next day, she reached Chicago, accompanied by Mrs. Lovett and Doctor Hamilton, on May 5th. Jane Addams was in high spirits, and apparently in better health than even she had been in Arizona.

"You have no idea how kind they were in Washington," she said. "Did you hear what they said about me?"

"Some of it. I liked Ickes particularly."

"I liked *all* of it," she said. "They made me feel as if I were still in the front line trenches. Probably one never gets over that feeling, though. I have always wondered when I should understand that I am an old lady."

Next day she resumed her work on the life of Julia Lathrop, and in the afternoon went to Hull House. At dinner there she told sixty "residents" about the Washington experience. The following week she worked steadily on the book, at Hull House, and with the Chicago Housing Committee, and in addition on May 10th attended a meeting of the Cook County Commissioners called to discuss measures of providing funds for temporary relief. "I

don't know why they wanted me there," she remarked,
"unless it was as a sort of moral influence on the Federal
Administration." After a Sunday at the Bowen Country
Club, she drove down on Wednesday to the South Side to
see an old friend in Billings Hospital, to call on Mrs.
Frank Lillie who was invalided at home, and to visit an
employee of Hull House who was at Mercy Hospital. Mrs.
Lillie, laid up with arthritis, could not come downstairs.
Jane Addams climbed two-thirds of the way upstairs
against Mrs. Lillie's protests, and sat down on the steps.
"Now we can talk comfortably," she said. Returning to
Hull House, she dined as usual with the residents; for the
last time. She never saw Hull House again. She had gone
there to live on September 14, 1889—forty-five years and
eight months before.

Early on the morning of May 15th she had a sudden
and severe attack of pain in the left side, low down, which
lasted until about five. She did not call Mrs. Bowen's
nurse, who found her at seven o'clock cheerful though still
in some pain.

"Why didn't you ring your bell?" the nurse asked.

"I understood I was to ring that if my heart was bad,"
Jane Addams said, "and there was nothing wrong with
my heart."

Doctor Britton came and found signs of some acute infection, but neither he nor Doctor J. B. Herrick could
make a positive diagnosis. Next day she was somewhat
better; but on May 17th the two physicians decided to
call in a surgeon, Doctor Arthur Curtis, in consultation.
He came at half-past five in the afternoon, and after a
short examination advised an operation the next morning.

At half-past eight the next morning Mrs. Bowen went in to see her, and found her reading a novel, *Young Renny,* one of the "Jalna" stories by Mazo de la Roche. She put her finger in the book to keep her place, and remarked,

"Perhaps the patient should say a few last words. How long before the ambulance is supposed to be here?"

"Fifteen minutes," Mrs. Bowen said.

"Then I can finish this novel," she said. "There are only a few pages left, and I'd like to get through them."

Half an hour later she was in her room at the Passavant Hospital, alone on the ninth floor, which the hospital authorities opened for her. The operation was begun at a quarter past eleven. To the complete astonishment of the surgeons, Doctor Curtis and Doctor Charles Elliott, it showed not only the knotted intestines which had been anticipated, but a cancerous condition which was inoperable. She had had a cancer for a long time, probably since soon after the Baltimore operation in 1931, and no one had suspected it.

The real fear of the physicians now was that she would recover from the operation; for if she did, nothing could be in store for her but a few months of agony, and death in pain. She did rally; was conscious and clear-headed the night of the eighteenth, and throughout the nineteenth, suffering only from thirst, and understanding without complaint why the doctors could not let her drink any water. There were still two chances in five, the doctors thought, that she might live. Both her temperature and her blood-pressure remained low, quite contrary to the experience at Johns Hopkins three years before.

"When I was a child," she murmured once to Doctor Britton, "I had an old doctor friend who told me that the hardest thing in the world to kill was an old woman. He seems to have been right." Doctor Hamilton, who with Mrs. Lovett stayed with her at the hospital, would not have her told of her real condition. "If she recovers, she mustn't be told," Doctor Hamilton insisted. "I can go on to the end with her if she doesn't know, but if she does know, I can't." So nobody except one member of her family was told, and Chicago and the country waited in some hope. Messages of course came in from high and low. From two of her friends who were themselves ill the news of the operation was carefully kept, in the fear the shock might overcome them.

On Monday afternoon, May 20th, however, she began to sink. She could be roused only to answer questions by the doctors. Once Doctor Britton asked her if she would like a little water.

"Always," she said. "Always water for me." She managed a smile. But she could not take it, and she never spoke again.

By nine o'clock in the morning of Tuesday, May 21st, word of her condition having been bulletined, those of her family who were in Chicago and many of the residents were waiting in the long empty hall of the ninth floor of the hospital. The doctors thought she could not live till noon, then not until two o'clock. Her temperature rose to 107.6° F., but she still breathed. The weak heart, which it had been thought would give out even if she should have a bad cold, beat indomitably on through the long, long afternoon. But for the cancer, it became clear, she might have gone on working for years. She died at eighteen minutes past six. It was May 21st—a family anniversary. One of her sister Mary's children had been born on that day; the baby had died more than forty years before, but Miss Addams had always remembered the birthday.

It was well understood that the neighbors would insist on the opportunity to say a final good-by to Jane Addams, and so arrangements were made that she should lie at rest in Bowen Hall from two o'clock on Wednesday afternoon until eleven on Thursday morning. A guard of honor during this period was composed of members of the Hull House Dramatic Association, oldest of the Hull House groups, and former members of the Hull House Boys' Club. The procession passed the coffin, sometimes in a thin line, sometimes more than two thousand in an hour, but unbroken. Workmen, coming in at six in the morning, with their lunch-boxes, placed them on a bench at the side of the room, then knelt as at a prie-dieu, and prayed in low voices. One, a Greek, when he discovered that she was not to be buried "by state," as he had supposed, nor after services in a church, nodded in approval. "Her no just one people, her no just one religion," he said. "Her all peoples, all religions." Children, in their best clothes, came and passed silently by hundreds, her own six-year-old great-grandniece among them. She looked about curiously; she had never been at Hull House.

"Are we all Aunt Jane's children?" she whispered.

The funeral service was held at half-past two on Thursday afternoon in the central court of the Hull House buildings. The high brick walls, shutting out the streets, were draped everywhere with flowers; flowers in great cascades hid even the high iron fire-escapes. An hour before the time set for the service, the court was filled with people standing. There was not room for one more. The entrances to the court were closed, Polk Street to the

Photograph by Wallace W. Kirkland

THE FUNERAL SERVICE FOR JANE ADDAMS IN THE COURT AT HULL HOUSE

north of Hull House and the alley to the west were roped off, and there thousands more stood quietly. Halsted Street on the east was closed to all traffic except the street-cars which, horse, cable, or electric, had rumbled on there for all the forty-five years she had lived beside it, and every foot of it except the street-car tracks was packed with her neighbors. The shops, the little restaurants, the saloons, were marked with mourning. Within the court, the young people of the Hull House Music School played a little and sang a little; Doctor Charles W. Gilkey, chaplain of the University of Chicago Chapel, spoke briefly, Doctor Graham Taylor, eighty-one and the oldest of Jane Addams's ministerial friends in Chicago, asked a benediction. Then as quietly as they had assembled and waited, the people stood in the court; there and outside in the streets the neighbors remained a long time.

The body was taken to the Twelfth Street Station the next morning at nine o'clock. In the wish to avoid any demonstration, no announcement of the time of taking it away had been made, and the police escort offered by the City had been declined. At Halsted and Twelfth however, the car stopped. An officer was directing a tangle of traffic. When he saw the hearse coming down from the direction of Hull House, he stopped everything in both directions and came over to the hearse.

"Is it her?" he asked respectfully.

"Yes," said the driver.

"She goes in peace," said the policeman, and when the car had turned left across the traffic, he was still standing, holding up his hand for quiet.

Formal request had been made that Jane Addams might be buried beside Woodrow Wilson in the National Epis-

copal Cathedral at Washington, but just as Hull House
had seemed the inevitable spot for the funeral service, so
Cedarville, where she had been born, and where her
father, mother, brothers and sisters rested, seemed the inevitable spot for her burial. Cedarville is a village off the
railroad, six miles north of the city of Freeport. At Freeport the train was met by a deputation of the city officials.
The shops were closed for the half-hour before and after
the arrival of the train, and while the body of Jane Addams was carried through the streets, the church bells
were tolling everywhere. At Cedarville the coffin was
placed for an hour in the room of her old home in which
she had been born, then in splendid sunlight taken to the
hillside cemetery across the road, below the cliffs on which
her father had planted, ninety years before, the Norway
pine-cones which he had brought with him on his journey
from Pennsylvania. She was carried past the incongruous
World War cannon at the entrance, past the Cedarville
school-children each with a flag held out straightly and
strongly in a proud salute, up the narrow winding road to
the "Addams Lot" on the highest point; and there, while
the oldest friends of her childhood, and their children, and
their grandchildren, and even their great-grandchildren
waited, she was committed to the earth.

The feeling of Chicago, and indeed of the state, during
those last few days after her death was uniquely of pride.
"They seem to think of her triumphantly," said one reporter in the *Chicago Daily News*. The death of no other
citizen of Chicago, perhaps, ever provoked such grief; but
it is quite certain that no other citizen of Chicago inspired
such a sense of glory shared. The immediate resolution of
the City Council, offered by the Mayor and adopted unani-

mously, with its naïve, tremendous final phrase, "the greatest woman who ever lived"; the amazing, brief, broken-hearted words of ex-Governor, ex-Mayor Dunne over the radio, "There was a great woman of the past, the Mother of God, whose name was Mary; and there is a great woman of the present, the Mother of Men, whose name is Jane Addams, and they stand alone in history"; the phrase of Governor Horner, "Her life was dedicated to a self-less service which has few parallels in the history of humanity; no person ever scaled higher peaks"; all carry this note of pride. From the President of the United States and from prime ministers of Europe came messages of condolence, but from Chicago only the one unbroken pæan of praise. It was strange that week at moments for one who had been writing her biography, thinking of her in terms of the popular estimation of thirty years ago, twenty years ago, even ten years ago, when she was so frequently called a "menace," sometimes even a "traitor," to look back upon the indifference, the doubt, even the denunciation, with which her ideas and her service had been received. She who had said of herself that she was "a very simple person, so often wrong," was hailed as the one person who had been always right. She would have smiled. She would have wondered. Had she done good? At least she had done what she could—and unto the "least of these" as unto the greatest. The pæan would soon die away. Would the influence of her understanding endure? Would her interpretation of the splendid possibilities of democracy abide among men? Would her hope for democracy, for a world-democracy of confidence and trust among the nations, be fulfilled? Her city in the end was proud of her, more proud apparently than of any other, far, far prouder of her than she had dreamed or than she imagined she deserved. Was their pride an illusion, or was it a prophecy? For one step farther toward the goal of her efforts, toward goodwill among men, how gladly would she put away the praise and sink into forgetfulness! But perhaps it was a prophecy. Perhaps even these exaggerations meant that the people she had loved, were becoming more understanding one of another. If so—!

So she would have mused if she could have known. And now—to see Mary Smith; and to see her father; and to see Lincoln; and to see God.

No estimate of the ultimate influence of the life of Jane Addams on the city of Chicago as a whole, or on the world at large, is worth attempting. She was not a combatant, never thought of herself as winning or losing in a battle, sought peace without victory. Immediately upon her death, the world began to praise her, as a matter of course. Editorial comment upon her appeared in almost every American newspaper; one, of more than a thousand which this writer saw, remarked that she had meant well no doubt, but had probably done more harm than good. Walter Lippmann in a syndicated article, the *St. Louis Post-Dispatch*, and the *Milwaukee Journal* seemed to many of her friends to come nearest to the expression of what was in their hearts. There was a flood of comparisons of greatness—Jane Addams and Judge Oliver Wendell Holmes, Jane Addams and Abraham Lincoln, Jane Addams and St. Francis, Jane Addams and Mary Magdalene (she would have accepted that comparison with quizzical delight). She was the greatest woman in the United States, she was the greatest woman in the world, she was the greatest woman in history. German and Italian authorities, to the amazement of some, permitted laudatory comments upon her and her work to be printed in those countries. The *Frankfurter Zeitung* gravely explained to its readers that "hull" being the equivalent of shell, Hull House was so called because it was the shell of Jane Addams's humanity. They all stressed her humanity. She had made Hull House a "citadel of compassion." She had deserved much, because she had loved much. She was the "angel of democracy." No doubt, if any legend of Jane Addams develops, it will develop around this conception of her. And that will be a pity. The more one studies her life and her writings, the more clearly one perceives that what counted in her toward the salvation of civilization was her understanding. Her tolerance was wise, her sympathy was perceptive, her sacrifices were planned, her acts were deliberate, her love was reflective. What William James said of her long ago was right, she inhabited reality. She began with the desire to sweep out a little corner "as by God's law," and she went on in that feeling, and therefore she made the action fine. And what she knew, she could express, in words as well as in deeds. It is true that she was humane, it is true that she was affectionate, it is true that she was lovable, it is true that she was brave. But above all she was imaginatively wise. When it was wise, she rose and stood in her own place; when it was wise, she put herself into the place of others. She flew high on the wings of thought, came down squarely upon the landing-fields of action. No doubt she will be most widely remembered for what she was, but she will be remembered longest for what she illuminated. "I think of her," said

Governor Horner of her own state, "as of the evening star, drawing the imagination of man through the clouds to the knowledge of a light that cannot fail."

There will be many memorials of her, of course. The "Jane Addams Memorial Fund," for providing for the work of Hull House at least an annual equivalent of what she was accustomed to raise each year by her own efforts, is well started. Plans are on foot for a park in New York state, for a state park at Cedarville, for a "Jane Addams International Park" on the border between the United States and Mexico, to be kept up by the authorities of both nations. Schools will be named for her; one of the government housing areas in Chicago will be named for her; monuments to her of one sort or another are likely in various countries. These will carry on her name.

The only memorial which those who knew her best hope for is, that by an increase of her sympathy and particularly of her understanding, the democracy of her ward, her city, her country and her world may be advanced.

Then her life will never reach the end.

CHAPTER XXII

IN RETROSPECT

H ISTORY has seldom been interested in moderation. History has sought to record the dramatic in thought and action, and drama is in fact, as it is in definition, a representation of clashes, of rough convictions, of immoderation. They who "only stand and wait," as Milton said, have served, undoubtedly, but they have not shone. The dreamer, the mediator, the man or woman unable to find the right *only* here or *only* there, though eager and able to find it on all sides, has seldom inspired the panegyric of universal remembrance. Force is the buried treasure all men have sought, hidden in the past or hidden in the personalities of their own day. Let one attain victory or martyrdom, and his fame was secure; but the middle road of tolerance, sympathy, compromise has oftenest led into oblivion. Only by crucifixion did Jesus of Nazareth become the Christ of millions. Galileo is remembered not as a scholar but for the conviction of a single phrase, *e pur si muove*. Luther and Loyola are both famous; Erasmus is forgotten though he was "the star of his century." The North triumphed, and Lincoln was assassinated; therefore, and not only because he was Lincoln, is he our Great American.

Having concluded a biography of Lowes Dickinson, E. M. Forster puts to himself the bleak question, "Why should this biography have been written?" He answers by the assertion that Dickinson was "such an unusual creature that no one whom one has met with in the flesh or in all history the least resembles it. He was a very rare being, and on that account alone a book about him is justifiable." So by all means let each of us think about his best friend. But one does not often meet with creatures resemblant of Dickinson in history, chiefly because history has passed them by without much notice.

It may be said of Jane Addams as truly as of any living person, that she was a rare being, and on that account alone a life of her is justifiable. But this book does not seek its justification in that rareness of her being only. It is possible that the times are slowly changing. It is possible that moderation, tolerance, the desire rightly to understand and interpret human society are becoming articles of our American creed. If so, then Jane Addams has been a force; if the national imagination has actually been stirred to an interest in understanding, then history cannot ignore Jane Addams. For it was she who tried hardest, through almost fifty years of ceaseless eagerness, to stir that imagination. The black curtains of ignorance, the velvet drapes of a luxury-embroidered indifference, she tried for almost half a century to push aside.

And whether she moved them or not, her attempts drew attention. Forty years ago the English editor William T. Stead opined that "if Christ came to Chicago," He would stop at Hull House. Thirty-five years ago another Englishman, John Burns, asserted that "Jane Addams was the only saint America had produced." Thirty years ago Theodore Roosevelt, not clearly understanding what she was trying to do, called her "the most useful citizen." If he had really understood her, he must have felt for her, even then, a certain contempt, but perception was not a leading character on the crowded stage of Roosevelt's remarkable personality. Later Jane Addams was, with a sort of comic inevitability, named first on newspaper and magazine lists of "great women" of the United States and of the century. She was the first woman to be awarded an honorary degree by many universities, including the conservative Yale. She was the recipient of half of a Nobel prize for the promotion of peace. When she died the chorus of praise of her rose from all over the world; hundreds of organizations, thousands of editors, called her blessed. Indeed it was the unanimity of this chorus that leads one to suspect a possible alteration in the American attitude toward the sympathetic interpretation of society.

For in her own single purpose of the promotion of that understanding she never changed. Once she declared, "That person is most cultivated who is able to put himself in the place of the greatest number of persons." From the beginning she remained "convinced that nearly all the conflicts arising between men and peoples could be adjusted happily through a little yielding on both sides; that there were hardly any differences of opinion that might not be settled satisfactorily" were the issues once precisely understood. That each side, that every human being, has a right to his own opinions, that independence and integrity of mind are essential, she assumed to be a matter of course; so have all humanists. But she went farther. She very early became convinced not only that "ethics is but another word for righteousness," but also that "many men and women of every generation have hungered and thirsted for it, and found life without it meaningless." And from that conviction too she never wavered. It is that conviction which has been the most powerful magnet to attract to her the intelligence of her time. Just a dream, if you like; indeed, to the genuinely "rugged individualist," perhaps a nightmare. But able men who were pure thought, like William James and Clarence Darrow, or even who were pure act, like Theodore Roosevelt and Herbert Hoover, have alike been thrilled by it, as she has expressed it in word and deed—belief in everybody; belief in the possibilities of good in all people, in all groups, in all nations; belief not only in the possibility of man's moral and social progress through the development of new ideals, but in the desire of man to progress morally and socially. It has been said that whoever does fully and wholeheartedly believe in this possibility becomes the leader of his generation. Certain it is that to whatever extent Jane Addams became the leader of hers, she became so through her fulness of such belief.

It is this very consistency that has made the story of her life difficult to tell well.

It is true that her interests were immensely varied, and her acquaintance was as wide as the world. It is true too that she occasionally mixed impatience with her devotion. She took the pretty general acceptance of her social philosophy for granted rather than with thankful amazement, and sometimes resented the fact that tolerance seems to the fanatic either stupid or a crime. But if only, after the most diligent search, one might hope to find in her that "mixture of motives" which has been thought to define humanity, setting man off from the wolves on the one hand and the angels on the other! It is not discoverable either in what she has written of herself or in what has been ascribed to her in the writings of others. One doubts if it existed in her. The biographer peers about for the vanity which salts self-respect, for the personal ambition which flavors industry, for some unconscious dogma to fix an ultimate boundary of her speculation—upon which he would pounce; but he peers in vain.

Her devotion to the excellent, her sure conviction that Plato was right in his observation that "the excellent becomes the permanent," perhaps to some degree impersonalized her. When in her young womanhood she would stand up to speak at neighborhood meetings, "you could fairly feel the love that radiated toward her from every person in the audience," says an old friend; and it is a law of nature that love runs out only to meet love, not to welcome service. Jane Addams was Friday's child, loving as well as giving. Yet even her closest friends, even the nephews and nieces whom she watched over and "mothered" for many years, sometimes felt her love as a radiation rather than as a direct and individual beam. They adored her, but they felt her sometimes to be a little withdrawn; one for all, rather than all for one. Behind her back, following the custom of the neighbors, her intimates called her "Saint Jane," but to her face such fearless, devoted friends of her own age as Julia Lathrop, Florence Kelley, Alice Hamilton, called her not Jane, but "Sister" Jane or "J.A." If she had married, her husband would have had some reason to be jealous of humanity. Perhaps it was her consciousness of this that kept her from ever marrying. One who loved her with deep devotion said of her whimsically that she had never married because she had never had time. It is the same thing.

There hangs about her something of the romance that

always attaches to the pioneer. She was the first graduate of the first "college for women" to be established in the American West. She founded the first "college settlement" in the United States. She was the first woman in the country to explore what were then called "the slums" in one of our great cities and to bring word to other women, and indeed to men, of the rich possibilities of citizenship that lay in them, like gold in swamps, waiting to be developed. The field has been so criss-crossed with the trails of "social service" in her lifetime that we forget how completely unaware we were of it as anything but swamp a half-century ago.

Not that she ever saw herself in a romantic light, or her work either. What pioneer does? She was an intensely practical idealist, seeing ends to be reached, and trying to find ways and means to reach them; doing the next thing to hand, and "doing it now," like any good business man. As when in 1912 she agreed to second the nomination of T. R. as the candidate of the Progressive Party, not because she was in sympathy with the past of that militarist and political opportunist, but because she hoped to be able to some extent to direct his future; was able to secure at least for the platform of the party a statement of causes and aims that fitted more closely her own program than anything which had ever before appeared in a party document.

In this failure to perceive her own life as romantic, she only reflects the spirit of all pioneers. They seek, as she did, a new home amid new surroundings in which their longings can find a more complete satisfaction, but to establish it they must work hard and long every day. For years her routine was, as she has admitted, "blurred with fatigue," and there is not much that is romantic in being tired all the time. The Hull House records of the 1890's show some three thousand people coming every week for clubs or classes, performances in the theater, dances, or advice and help. Says Mrs. Joseph Bowen, "Miss Addams saw most of these people." She listened to their stories, conferred, suggested, and put them in the way of assistance. At the same time, outside Hull House, she was constantly speaking, writing, raising money as she could, investigating, cleaning up the streets and alleys of the district, lobbying for the passage of regulatory legislation, working fourteen, sixteen, and for one period eighteen hours a day. And a similar routine continued for many years. Her days were as full of labor at sixty-five as at thirty-five, and much the same sort of labor. Not much romance in that!

There is further, however, something romantic in the "inner light" (if one may use a phrase of her Quakerish ancestors) by which she seems to have been guided. She was of course "the receptacle into which all the troubles of the women of the district were poured" (and later the troubles of the women of all the world ardent for peace). And by the illumination of the inner light she perceived all too clearly the steady falling of *lachrymae rerum.* Mrs. Bowen, speaking of early days at Hull House, says: "She impressed me then as always being very sad, as if the sorrows of the neighborhood were pressing upon her, which indeed they were." But the light within was always clear. A great though now little known American, Alexander Stephens, wrote long after he had become both famous and beloved, "Sometimes I have thought of all men I was most miserable; that I was especially doomed to misfortune, to melancholy, to grief.... The misery, the deep agony of spirit I have suffered, no mortal knows. ... The torture of body is severe; I have had my share of that.... But this is slight when compared with the pangs of an offended or wounded spirit. The heart alone knoweth its own sorrow. I have borne it these many years; I have borne it all my life." Nothing of that feeling ever troubled Jane Addams. She too knew the "torture of the body," from spinal abscesses in babyhood which left her with a crooked back till she was twenty-five, on through illness after illness, major operation after major operation; but she never knew the pangs of a wounded spirit. She was often misunderstood, frequently despised, occasionally hated, but nothing except misunderstanding ever affected her spirit and not even misunderstanding offended it. It was this clarity of the inner light, the consistency of her purpose, that pulled her through. Certainly, though she was almost morbidly self-conscious as a child, and even as a young woman, she came by the time she was thirty to realize that consistency, and never lost the comfort of that realization. She relaxed upon it. At the dinner in her honor in Chicago in 1927, when she listened to many speeches of terrifying eulogy, she replied peacefully. "I sat here wondering what kind of person I was that you should be seeing not me, but this mirage you have described. I assure you it is not there. I am a very simple person; most of the time not right, which I am sure we all know of ourselves, but—wanting to be."

Was she a simple person? There can be no doubt of her belief that she was. But surely if she were simple she would be also representative. And she was not representative. She was unique.

She was the first real adventurer in the unexplored country of social amelioration in America. She spoke from thousands of platforms, and her books have been read by hundreds of thousands. She has been sought as an adviser by Presidents and Prime Ministers, but she has never been a member of any political party or elected to any public office. Socialists like John Burns have called her "a saint," but remained gloomily aware that she was not of their way of political thinking. When certain leaders of the Woman's Suffrage group in 1912 announced her as their candidate for President, she merely remarked that women could take a joke, but men could not. Though as a young woman of twenty-five she "joined the church," churchmen of various denominations have from time to time spoken with fierce disapprobation of her lack of interest in religious activities at Hull House. On occasion she helped to organize labor unions, and on other occasions excited the hearty animadversions of labor-unionists. All this variation of interests, all this unwillingness to align herself with any special group, contradicts the assertion that she was simple and makes untenable any supposition that she was representative.

Hull House was not, nor did it ever become, a representative settlement. It has remained the expression of an unrepresentative personality. She planted a flower; it grew great, but remained flower-like. Many others, even of her generation, had deep social sympathy, but hers was deepest. Many others had a passion for social understanding, but not her singleness of passion. It was not the common longing for peace on earth, but the individual splendor of her longing, that set her apart. By that which many others have shared in, she only seems to have been completely possessed. To tell the story of the founder of Christianity and omit the individuality of his conviction of righteousness which made crucifixion seem an episode would be utterly to misrepresent the truth. So to call Jane Addams representative would be to misinterpret her time.

And so in spite of her bright aura of impersonality, her distinction seems to those who knew her best utterly individual, unclassifiable, not comparable with that of any one else in her day, man or woman—though, of course, Tolstoy and Gandhi come to mind. She had reverence for both. But she was too practical to be a follower of the great Russian, and too universal in her sympathies to limit her interests to anything nationalistic. Her distinction cannot be defined by a phrase, nor made plain by any recital of accomplishments. Indeed, she has no long list of achievements to her credit. She did what she could; but if historians shall assert for her, as her contemporaries have so constantly asserted, a claim to greatness, it must lie not in what she did but in what she was.

Simple? Of all well-known Americans since Lincoln, perhaps, she was the most tolerant, yet she was quite willing to be what Newman said no man had ever been, a martyr for a conclusion. She was rooted in principle, yet deft in adaptation; ready, and in small things even impatient, to direct, yet eager to serve; open in attack sometimes, yet so subtle in analysis that that true philosopher William James could write, "You utter instinctively the truth we others vainly seek." She was an imaginative worker; an executive who was at heart a mystic; saddened by life but never frightened by it; aware of risks yet never hesitant to take them; and never forgetful of the great fact that it is as necessary to be understood as to understand. George E. Vincent wrote of "her tolerant and even defensive attitude in behalf of people who opposed her," and it is quite true that she was in the habit of defending her opponents—but why? Because she felt the compulsion to understand them; she merely thought aloud, as it were, seeking the reason for their opposition, like a good general, that she might meet attacks most intelligently.

If she is long remembered, it will be for the quality of her thinking, for her rightness as an interpreter of individuals to themselves and of social groups one to another. In the story of her life there is not the drama of the conqueror, but in her character there is poetry. For half a century she trailed clouds of glory, and about her memory intimations of immortality cling. Representative? If Jane Addams were truly representative, we should now be living in the millennium.

INDEX

Abbott, Grace, 211, 380, 386, 414
Abolitionists, 183
Adams, family, 2
Adams, Henry, 277, 281
Adams, Richard, 2
Adams, Robert, 1
Adams, Walter, 1
Adams, William, 2
Adamstown, 2
Addams, Abraham, 2
Addams, Alice, 28, 40; marries Harry Haldeman, 31
Addams homestead, 9
Addams, Isaac, 2
Addams, Jane, 1, 11, 17, 129, 185, 380, 381, 404, 426, 430, 431 432
Addams, Jane: father dominant influence in life of, 1; association with father as a child, 10; and her father, 17; and father's Civil War attitude, 19; father, character of, 20; remembrance of mother, 22; childhood appearance, 24; character as child, 24; and her sisters and brothers, 24; as guardian of nephew, 25; adoration of father, 25; imitates father, 26; early reading, 26; first idea for house which developed into Hull

House, 27; childhood, 28; and her stepmother, 31; first operation, 32; first proposal of marriage, 32; childhood games and interests, 35, 36, 37; appearance on entering Rockford, 40-41; at Rockford College, 40-64; portrait, 41; description of, 47; and religion, 49; toast to, 52; as debater, 53; editor-in-chief of *Rockford Seminary Magazine*, 54; early writing, 35; reads Darwin, 60; determined to secure degree from Rockford, 61; Junior Exhibition Speech at Rockford, 62; gets A.B., 62; Rockford class president and "valedictorian," 63; gift of $1,000 to Rockford Library, 64; and assassination of President McKinley, 67-68; criticized re McKinley attitude, 68; and assassination of President Garfield, 67; and press, 68; as story teller, 69; operation on spine, 69; first European tour, 1883, 70-74, 76-78; quote re Mile End Road market, 72-73; hate of oppression, 75; first European tour, countries visited, 76-77; and Whitechapel auction, 78;

Addams, Jane (*continued*)
and Johns Hopkins University
society, 79-80; joins Presbyterian church, 80; membership in Congregational church,
81; and finance, 82-83, 88-90,
91; developed "social service," 86; on executive committee of Chicago Housing
Commission, 98; Chicago's
early attitude toward, 103;
philosophy, 106; newspaper
quote, 111, 114-115; preparation of speeches, 116; as
speaker, 116, 117-118; breaks
arm, 120; refused bribe, 121;
talked for pay, 121; gifts of
money carefully considered,
125; and Tolstoy, 127; honorary degree, California, 159;
and Pullman strike, 166;
member of Civic Federation,
168; appointed garbage inspector, 169; authority on
child labor, 184; and delinquency, 185-186; as a personality, 194; and religion,
201-208; attitude toward
saloons, 205; newspaper, association, and individual, attacks, 214-223; visits Isaak,
217; offers of help, 218, 219;
letters of attack, 218; attitude
in Auerbrech Case, 219-221;
attitude toward Rudowitz,
222; attitude toward Gorki
case, 222-223; member Chicago school board, 224; and
Teachers, 225-229; and school
system, 230-237; receives degrees, 238, 239; "second citizen," 238; Yale offers honorary degree to, 238; founds
Chicago Woman's City Club,
239; urged for senator, 239;
"first citizen," 240; intervention in garment-workers'
strike, 240-241; called "the
angel of Hull House," "lady
of God," "a saint," 259; publications, quotes and sum-
maries, 242-261; member of
Jury of International Awards
at Paris Exposition, 265;
chairman Suffrage Committee,
268; and Theodore Roose-
velt, 272-273; 276-277; and
Peace, 279; and "party efforts," 281-283; contracts typhoid fever, 289; poem to
Mary Smith, 289-290; visits
Tolstoy at Yasnaya Polyana,
291; given Wisconsin LL.D.,
degree, 293; speaks on pacifism, 293; speaks at New
York on Peace, 295; presides
over National Peace Federation, 298; speaks on peace at
Carnegie Hall, 296; presides
at Congress of Women at the
Hague, 299; peace efforts and
public support, 312; interview with Wilson, 312; criticism of, 314; kidney operation, 317; contracts pleuro-
pneumonia, 317; to White
House state dinner, 321; letter from Woodrow Wilson,
321; protests against conscription, 326; conscious of
isolation, 332; presides at second Congress of Women, 341;

travels through Europe after second Congress, 345; distressed at condition of European children, 345; abroad after the World War, 346-347; interest in youth, 350; and Daughters of the American Revolution, 350; made president for life of W.I.L., 351; headstone, in Cedarville cemetery, words on, 351; at Bar Harbor, 353; seventieth birthday dinner, 353-354; operated on in Japan, 355; speeches abroad, 356-357; made twelve trips abroad, 355; "Christmas message," quote, 358; and saloons, 365-366; attacks on, 367; dinner in honor of, 370; honors to, 380-381; goes to Arizona, 384; receives money awards, 386; fiftieth Rockford Anniversary, 387; at Bar Harbor, 388; awarded Nobel Peace Prize, 389; operation, 389; newspaper quote re, 391; unable to go to Grenoble, 392, 395; income and prize money, use of, 393; speaks at Republican and Democratic Conventions, 398; honors, 399; degree from Swarthmore College, 401; voted for Hoover, 403; list of "greatest American Women," 404; chairman of Illinois Hostesses, Century of Progress, 406; honorary President World Fellowship of Faiths, 406; at Phoenix, Arizona, 410; degree from University of California, 412; dinner in honor of Washington, 414; spoke on radio, 417, 418; eulogies, 424-425

Addams, Jane, quotes from writings, 10, 14, 19, 32-33, 39, 56, 57, 63, 66, 72, 80, 91, 96, 97, 104-105, 107, 126, 135, 165-160, 169-170, 174-175, 179, 180, 201, 202, 205, 206, 207, 208, 234, 236, 263-264, 265-266, 267-268, 270-271, 275, 277-279, 292, 305, 307, 313-314, 319-320, 322, 323, 326, 331, 336-337, 339, 340-341, 344-345, 348, 351, 357, 364, 372-373, 381, 384, 387, 392, 402, 403-404, 405, 416

"Addams, Jane, Memorial Fund," 428

Addams, Jane, publications, 164, 171, 178, 184, 198, 207, 241

Addams, John Huy, 2, 3, 4, 5, 7, 10, 11, 12, 13, 14, 16, 17, 18, 19, 20, 23, 29, 38, 40, 64-65, 66, 81, 262

Addams, Jane, Professorship of Social Service, The, 1930, at Rockford, 64

Addams, Martha, 24

Addams, Mary, 25, 31, 40

Addams, Mrs. John, second, 29-30

Addams, Samuel, 2, 6

Addams, Sarah Weber, 4, 20, 22

Addams, the, homestead, 15

Adler, Felix, 295

Advance, quote, 114, 204

Alcott, Bronson, 52

Alden, Percy, 191

Altgeld, Governor, 102, 137, 153, 154, 156, 157, 158, 162, 163, 166, 186, 194, 215
American Legion, 214, 350, 367
American Federation of Labor, 282
American Railway Union, 166
Anderson, Sarah, 85
Angell, Sir Norman, 393
Anthony, Susan B., 262, 404
Anti-Saloon League, 282
Armours, 100
Arnold, Judge, 143
Arnold, Matthew, 148
Asquith (Lord), 191, 306
Alkins, Brigadier-General Smith D., 18, 287
Atlantic Monthly, The, 242
Auditorium Building, 98
Averbuch Case, 219-221, 259
Award to Jane Addams, 380, 386, 388, 393, 404

Baker, Newton D., 323, 328, 329, 350, 380
Balch, Emily, 308, 317, 341
Barnett, Canon, Samuel, 89, 106, 159
Barnetts, of Toynbee Hall, 290
Barrett, Kate, 341
Bartelme, Judge Mary, 143
Bartlets, 100
Barton, Bruce, 380
Barton, Clara, 404
Battle Hymn of the Republic, The, 239
Beaux, Cecilia, 380
Beaver, James Addams, Governor of Pennsylvania, 2
Beloit College, 32, 49

Benedict, Enella, 129, 211
Berry, Martha, 380
Besant, Walter, 106
Besant's, Walter, People's Palace, 90
Birmingham Age-Herald, 329
Blackwell, Lucy Stone, 404
Blaine, Mrs. Emmons, 227, 228
Blaisdell of Beloit College, 61
Blaisdell, Sarah, 50, 61
Blake, Mrs. Tiffany, 293
Blarney Castle, 71
Boncour, Paul, 417
Booth, Charles, 195
Bowen, Mrs. Joseph T. (Louise DeKoven), 129, 140-146, 157, 187, 192, 258, 319, 333, 370, 378, 408, 422
Bowen, Mrs. J., 435
Boys' Club and Gymnasium, 191
Boy Scouts, in Bowen Hall, 272
Brandeis, Justice, 138
Britton, Doctor, James A., 327, 419, 421
Britton, Gertrude Howe, 211
Brown, Charlotte Emerson, 61
Browne, W. R., *Altgeld of Illinois*, 166
Bruce, Alexander, 157
Bryan, William Jennings, 53, 115, 295
Bryn Mawr College, 386
Bull-fight in Spain, A, 88
Burns, John, 86, 188-189, 290, 430, 437
Burroughs, John, 239
Busse, Mayor, 232, 237
Butler, Doctor Nicholas Murray, 295, 389
Butler Art Gallery, 122, 191, 209
Butler, Edward, 122

Cabot, Doctor Richard, 378
California, University of, 159
California, University of, confers honorary degree on Jane Addams, 412
Carlyle, 193, 246
Carpenter, Mrs., County Superintendent of Schools, 41
Carter, Judge Orrin, 331, 332
Cather, Willa, 244, 380
Catt, Mrs. Carrie Chapman, 283, 380, 381, 382, 386, 404
Cecil, Lord Robert, 417
Cedar Creek (River), 11, 16
Cedarville, 21, 31, 34, 50, 79, 203, 424, 428
Century of Progress Exhibition, 404, 406
Central Christian Advocate, quote, 218
Chicago, 7, 8, 99
Chicago, Aldermanic System, 173-177
Chicago and Northwestern, 14
Chicago Art Institute, 122
Chicago Association of Commerce, 237
Chicago Board of Education, 215, 233
Chicago Bureau of Charities, 142
Chicago Chronicle, 215
Chicago City Club, 319
Chicago Civic Federation, 162, 163, 186
Chicago Club, 259
Chicago Commons, 205
Chicago Commons, of Graham Taylor, 190
Chicago Daily News, 298, 300, 424

Chicago, families, 100
Chicago Federation of Labor, 185
Chicago, Haymarket riot, 101
Chicago Heart Association, 211
Chicago, history, 100-102
Chicago Housing Commission, 98
Chicago Housing Committee, 418
Chicago, interest in art, 123
Chicago, Juvenile Court, 143
Chicago, Juvenile Protective Association, 143
Chicago, labor unions, 101
Chicago, milk supply, 128
Chicago, Nineteenth Ward, 168
Chicago, Peace Congress, 296
Chicago, population, 1889, 96
Chicago Record-Herald, 239
Chicago School Board, 224
Chicago, School Management Committee, 228
Chicago, School System, 230-237
Chicago Theological Seminary, 190
Chicago Tribune, 158, 231, 259, 319
Chicago, University of, 120, 121, 160, 190
Chicago Woman's Club, 239, 330, 331
Child Labor Amendment, 138
Child-labor laws, Illinois, 183
Child-labor legislation, 115, 151, 185, 259
Children's Bureau, 136, 211
Chronicle, the, 259
Civic Federation, 259
Civil War, 18, 287

Cleveland, President, 166
Clough, Arthur, 349
Colby, Bainbridge, 308
Colvins, the, 209
Commercial Club, 227, 269
Comte, August, 77
Conference of Charities and Correction, 275
Congregational church, 81
Congress of Women, The, 335-351
Congresses of Women's International League for Peace and Freedom, 350-351
"Continuous Mediation," 300-311
Cook County Juvenile Court, 135
Coolidge, Calvin, 239, 371, 381
Coolidge, Mrs. Calvin, 380
Coonley, Mrs., 104
Cornell, Ezra, 252
Cornell University, 252
"Country Club" of Hull House, at Waukegan, 142
Crane, Reverend Frank, 158
Crane, Mary, Nursery, 209
Cranes, 100
Crerar Library, Chicago, 99
Culver, Helen, 94, 95, 192
Curtis, Doctor Arthur, 419, 420
Czolgolz, assassination of President McKinley, 67, 217

Daily News, 221
Darrow, Clarence, 158, 194, 218, 399, 431
Darwin's Origin of Species and The Descent of Man, 60

Daughters of the American Revolution, 214
Davidson, Thomas, 103
Davis, Norman, 417
Davis, Richard Harding, 314
DeBey, Doctor Cornelia, 227, 228, 229
Debs, Eugene, 166, 167
de la Roche, Mazo, 420
Delcassé, 306, 307
Democracy and Social Ethics, 243, 244, 248
Democratic Party, 215
de Nancrede, Edith, 211
Denison, Edward, 89
Dependent Children, Theodore Roosevelt calls conference on, 275-276
Dever, Mayor, 370
Dewey, Gordon, 178
Dewey, John, 178, 235, 254, 375, 386
Dexter, Wirt, 101
Diary of first European trip kept by Jane Addams, quotes from, 72-74
Diary of John H. Addams, 8-9, 10
Dickinson, Lowes, 429, 430
Dorcas Federal Labor Union, at Hull House, 197
Douglas, Corinne Williams, quote re Jane Addams, 47, 51-52
Dow, Jenny, 115, 147, 396
Dowell, President of Mercer University, 381
Dunne, Judge Edward F., 226
Dunne, Mayor, 223, 232, 424
Eddy, Mary Baker, 404

INDEX

Edison, Thomas A., 381, 399
Eliot, President, of Harvard, 295
Elliott, Doctor Charles, 420
Emerson, 105
Emerson, Charlotte, 60
Engel, 101
Epley, Conrad, Illinois pioneer, 11
Erasmus, 429
Ethical Culture Societies, summer school, Jane Addams speaks at, 104
Ethical Survivals in City Politics, by Jane Addams, quote, 171-172
Ethics in Politics, 151-177
European trip, third, 289
Evening Journal, Chicago, 103
Every Day Club, the, 187
Evidences of Christianity, 52
Excellent Becomes the Permanent, The, 207, 244, 396

Fairbairn, Principal, 191
Fairbanks, 100
Federated Women's Clubs of Illinois, 185
Field, Marshall, 100, 162
Fielden, 101
Fields, the, 100
First factory-act, 137
First European tour, 70-74, 76-78
Fischer, 101
Fiske, Minnie Maddern, 380
Flourmill, 4
Flower, Mrs. James (Lucy M.), 186
Ford, Henry, 304, 317, 381

Ford, "peace ship," 316
Forster, E. M., 429
Forum, The, 242
Fox, Charles James, 116
Frankfurter Zeitung, 427
Freeport, 8, 18, 21, 423

Gage, Lyman J., 102
Gale, Stephen, 13
Galena and Chicago Union, Railroad, 13, 14, 23
Galileo, 429
Galsworthy, John, 273
Galt, Mrs., 315
Gandhi, 438
Gardiner, Julia, 64
Garfield, President, assassinated, 67
Garrison, 276
Gary, Judge Joseph E., 102, 156
General Federation of Women's Clubs of the United States, 61
George, Henry, 228
Gerard, Ambassador, 306, 310
Gerner, Maude, 212
Ghent, W. J., 184, 253
Giles, Rose, 129
Gilkey, Doctor Charles W., 210, 423
Ginn, Edwin, 295
Glenwood Manual Training School, 186
Gompers, Samuel, 295
Goodwill, 5
Gorki, Maxim, 222-223
Gorst, Sir John, 290
Grant, General, 355, 371
Great Fire, The, 95, 122
Great Lakes, 12

Green, Thomas H. H., 191
Grey, Lord, 306, 308 (quote)
Grindley, Professor H. S., 128
Grotius, 301
Growing Up with a City, by Mrs. Joseph Bowen, 140
Guild of St. George, 75
Guiteau, Julius, assassinates President Garfield, 67, 217

Hackett, Francis, 210-211 (quote), 212
Hague Congress of Women, 300-306
Hague resolutions, handed to Wilson by Jane Addams, 312
Haldeman, Alice, 256
Haldeman, George, 31, 34, 49, 79
Haldeman, Harry, 31-32, 82, 178
Haldeman, Mrs. William, second Mrs. John Addams, 29-31
Hale, Edward Everett, 295
Haley, Margaret ("Maggie"), 227, 231
Hamilton, Doctor Alice, 144-146, 306, 309, 341, 396, 404, 407, 414, 418, 421, 432
Hamilton, Norah, 211
Hard, William, 228
Hardie, Kier, 290
Harlan, John Maynard, 226
Harper, President William Rainey, 120, 225, 230
"Doctor Harper's Bazaar" (Chicago University), 160
Harrison, Frederick, 88
Harrison, Mayor Carter, 100, 225, 227, 229

Hart, Harry, 241
Harvard Medical School, 146
Haworth, Eleanor Frothingham, quote, 40, 48
Hazenplug (Hazen), Frank, 211-212
Headstone in Cedarville Cemetery, words on, 351
Hearst, paper, 226, 294
Henderson, Archibald, 381
Henderson, Arthur, 378, 417
Henrotin, Mrs. Charles, 158, 187, 295
Herrick, Doctor, James B., 317, 408, 419
Hicksite Quaker, 20
Higinbotham, Harlow, 162
Hill, James T., 239
Hill, Octavia, 290
Hillman, Sidney, 414, 415
Hinman, George, 259
Hirsch, Emil G., 163
History of Trades Unionism, 193
Hobson, John, 290
Holbrook, Florence, 341
Holmes, Justice Oliver Wendell, 138, 244, 426
Honors for Jane Addams, 377-385
Hood, Daniel N., 44
Hooker, George, 212, 327
Hoover, Herbert, 159, 283, 330, 335, 338, 345, 350, 368, 388, 399, 403, 412, 431
Hopkins, Mark, author, *Evidences of Christianity*, 52
Horner, Judge, 403
Horner, Governor, 406, 428
House, Colonel, 307, 308, 309, 313, 315

House on Henry Street, The, 331

Howe, Mark A. DeWolfe, 380, 381

Howe, Julia Ward, 239, 404

Hughes, Governor Charles, 295, 319

Hull, Charles J., 192

Hull House, 14, 50

Hull House: Summer School, 64; and assassination of President McKinley, 67-68; Music School, 75, 423; Picture Gallery, 75; Dramatic Association, 76, 149, 211, 422; history, 93-97; description, 98-99; life at, 108, 112, 114; Begins, 110-128; incorporated, 110; original purpose, 111; hard work at, 115; neighbors' opinions, 113; newspaper opposition to, 115; finance, 120, 373-374, 388; never had deficit, 121; art activity, 122; Public Kitchen, 123-124; Jane Club, 124; Club-house, 125; Public School Art Society, 126; Rockford Summer School, 126; playground, 127; and Chicago milk supply, 128; Woman's Club, 141, 169, 209; Association, 142; Boy's Club, 142, 252, 422; Country Club at Waukegan, 142; and "careers," 148; and child labor, 151-153; and trades-unions, 153; residents, "lobby," 153; called "radical," 155, 159, 160-161; gifts of money, 158; Men's Club, 170, 209; craftsmanship, 181; growth, 190, 208; after ten years, 192; associates, 192; Coffee House, 205, 209; apartments, 209; covers city block, 209; Mary Crane Nursery, 209; Second Decade, 211; Playground, 253; Players, 273; and the World War, 327-328, 339; and draft, 339; post-war activities, 352, 361-364; fortieth anniversary celebration, 373, 375-377; reunion, 378-379; Country Club, 419; records, 1890, 435

Hull, Charles J., 93

Hull Court, University of Chicago, 94

Hull House Maps and Papers, by Julia Lathrop, 135, 168

Hutchins, President Robert, 378

Hutchinsons, 100

Huy, Catherine, 2

Ickes (Secretary), Harold, 220, 415, 418

Ickes, Mrs. Harold, 414

Ijams, Miss, 412

Illinois, 4, 6, 8

Illinois Committee for Old Age Security, 382

Illinois College, 53

Illinois Equal Suffrage Association, 239

Illinois Federation of Labor, 185

Illinois, pioneer settlers, 10-11

Illinois Suffragist, 264

Illinois, Univ. of, College of Agriculture, Experiment Station, 128

Illinois, University of, 34
Immigrant's Protective League, 359, 374
Influences, father, 1
Ingersoll, Robert, 371
Ingram, Canon, Oxford House, 290
International Journal of Ethics, 243
International School of Peace, 295
International Suffrage Alliance at Budapest, 355
Inter-Ocean, the, 233, 259
Interstate Oratorical Contest, 53
Ireland, Archbishop, 295
Isaak, Abraham, 217
Isaak incident, 259

Jacobs, Doctor Aletta, 305, 371
James, Henry, 71
James, William, 117, 243, 293, 427, 431, 439
Jane Club, 124, 157, 191, 209
Jefferson, Thomas, 246
Jeffries, Hon. James J., 238
Johns Hopkins University, 32, 79, 144
Johnson, Amanda, 170
Journal of Education, Boston, quote, 184
Journals contributed to by Jane Addams: (*See* under titles.)
Atlantic Monthly, The; International Journal of Ethics; The Forum; The North American Review; American Journal of Sociology.

Jowett, Doctor, of Balliol, 191
Justice, by John Galsworthy, 273
Justin, Henry, quote, 300-301
Juvenile Court of Chicago, 143, 187
Juvenile Protective Association, 143

Kahn, Otto, 380
Keeley, James, 223
Keiths, the, 100
Keller, Helen, 380, 404
Kelley, Mrs. Florence, 80, 129, 136-140, 152, 153, 154, 183, 228, 315, 398, 404, 432
Kellogg Pact, 286, 383
Kenny, Mary, 157
Keynes, John Maynard, 343
Kent, William, 126-127, 253, 371
Keyser, Frank, "oldest inhabitant" of Hull House, 96
Keyser, Mary, 96, 115
Kilpatrick, 18
Kimballs, the, 100
Kirks, the, 100
Koht, Professor Halvan, quote, 390
Kreidersville, Pennsylvania, 4, 6
Kronprinzessin Cecelie, at Bar Harbor, 296
Kropotkin, Prince, 217, 259, 337
Krupskaya, 417

Lafayette, 222
Lafayette College, 5
LaFollette, 283
Lake Mohonk, Conference at, 295

Landsberg, Clara, 211
Lathrop, Julia, 43, 80, 113, 129, 133-136, 139, 140, 186, 187, 263, 370, 397, 404, 413, 432
Lathrop, Mrs. William, 263
Laughlin, Professor J. Laurence, 292
League of Nations, 282, 286, 346, 376, 383
Leiters, the, 100
Lenin, 417
Libbys, the, 100
Lillie, Mrs. Frank, 419
Lincoln, Abraham, 17, 38, 121, 276, 399, 426, 429, 438
Lincoln, Abraham, letters, 38
Lincoln, "Tad," 38
Linden, Carl, 211
Lingg, 101
Linn, Reverend John M., 50
Lippmann, Walter, 86, 426
Lloyd, Henry D., 152, 191, 292
London Times, quote, 194
Long Road of Woman's Memory, The, 244, 317, 321, 322
Longfellow, 399
Loop, the, 231
Lovett, Mrs. Robert Morss, 414, 418, 421
Loyola, 429
Lusitania, 315
Luther, 429
Lyon, Mary, 404
Lyons, the, 100

Mack, Judge, 143
Madison, Wisconsin, 38
Mandels, the, 100
Mary Magdalene, 426

Mason, Edith, 413
Maude, Aylmer, 291
Mayflower, 1
Mazzini, Joseph, 19-20
McCormick, Anita, 115
McCormick, Cyrus, 162
McCormicks, 100
McCulloch, Mrs. Catherine Waugh, 203, 267, 331, 332
McDowell, Mary, "back of the yards" home, 190
McKinley, President, assassination, 217, 259
McNallys, 100
McVeagh, Franklin, 162
Mead, Edwin D., 295
Mead, Professor George Herbert, 160
Mead, Lucia Ames, 341
Medills, the, 100
Medill, Joseph, 226
Men's Club, Hull House, 170
Merriam, Professor Charles E., 189, 367, 371
Merriam, Charles E., quote, 372
Mile End Road, London, 72-73
Millerstown, Pennsylvania, 2, 4
Mills, Wiley W., 227, 228
Milwaukee Journal, 426
Missionary spirit, at Rockford, 42
Mississippi River, 8, 11, 12, 23
Modern King Lear, A, 164, 175
Moody, William Vaughn, 244, 292
Morgan, J. Pierpont, 226
Morgan, Thomas, 197
Morgenthau, Mr. and Mrs. Henry J., 377
Morris, Nelson, 100

Morris, William, 88
Mount Holyoke College, 40, 43, 388
Mount Morris, Illinois, 45
Municipal Voters' League, 259
My Four Years in Germany, 306
My Friend Julia Lathrop, 397
My Religion, 288

National Conference of Charities and Correction, 238
Natural Consumers' League, 138
National Education Association, 412
National Federation of Settlements, 330
National Federation of Women's Clubs, 158
National Peace Congress, First, 295
National Peace Federation, 298
National Peace Societies, convention in Boston, Jane Addams principal speaker, 293
Neebe, 101
Neighborhood Kitchen, 191
Newberry Library, Chicago, 99
Newberry, Walter L., 13
New Conscience and an Ancient Evil, A, 269
Newer Ideals of Peace, 243, 249, 294
Newman, 438
New York, 42, 67
New York City, 7
New York Times, 314
Niagara Falls, 7
Nineteenth Ward, Chicago, 168, 171, 174
Niver, Doctor, 407

Nobel Peace Prize, 272, 279, 284
Nobel Peace Prize, to Jane Addams, 389-392
Noordam, the, 300
North American Review, The, 242

Occupational Standards, 275
"Octagon" room, 95, 191, 376
O'Day, Congresswoman, Caroline, 414
Ogden, William B., 13-14
Ogdens, the, 100
Oglesby, Richard, 38
"Old Abe," Eagle of Eighth Wisconsin, 38, 39
Olivier, Sidney, 195
O'Leary's cow, Mrs., 95
O'Ryan, P. Shelley, 228
Oskar II, 317
Our Benevolent Feudalism, by W. J. Ghent, 184
Our Herald, 264
Our Penal Machinery and Its Victims, 185
Over Here: Over Here, by Mark Sullivan, 310
Oxford Township, Philadelphia County, 1

Pacifism, 284-299
Page, Ambassador, 310
Paish, Sir George, 346
Palmer, Mrs. Potter, 197, 219, 265
Palthe, Frau, 306
Pam, Judge Hugo, 371, 372
Pankhurst, Sylvia, quote, 238

Parker, Colonel, 253
Parr, Samuel, 34
Passavant Hospital, 420
Patterson, Joseph Medill, 226
Peabody, Doctor Francis, 377
Peace and Bread in Time of War, 299, 336
Peace Conference, 339
Peattie, Mrs. Ella, quote, 84
Pelham, Mrs. (Laura Dainty), 211
Penn, William, 1
Perkins, Secretary, 159, 387, 412
Perrin, Professor Bernadotte, 239
Philadelphia, 4, 5, 6
Pinckney, Judge, 143
Pittsburgh Survey, 274
Plymouth, 1
Pond, Allen, 92, 104, 191
Pond brothers, 122, 210
Pond, Irving, 191
Positivism, 77
Positivists, 88
Post, Louis F., 227, 228
Post, the, 221
Potter, Adeline, of Rockford, mother of Julia Lathrop, 43
Potter, Caroline (Mrs. Brazee), 61
Powers, Alderman John, 168, 170, 173-174, 176-177; (quote), 188, 215, 269
Presbyterian Church, 80-81
President McKinley, assassinated by Czolgolz, 67
Progressive Party, Jane Addams on Platform Committee, 276
Progressive Party, 434
Prohibitionists, 183
Public, The, 228

Public School Art Society, 126
Publications of Jane Addams (*See* under separate titles): *Democracy and Social Ethics; Excellent Becomes the Permanent, The; Long Road of Woman's Memory, The; Modern King Lear, A; New Conscience and an Ancient Evil, A; Newer Ideals of Peace; Peace and Bread in Time of War; Second Twenty Years at Hull House, The; Spirit of Youth and the City Streets, The; Twenty Years at Hull House*
Pullman, Geo. M., 164, 188
Pullmans, the, 100
Pullman Strike, 164, 165, 166, 199
Putnam, Amelia Earhart, 404

Quaker, Hicksite, 3, 20

Ragaz, Clara, 376
Railway, 13
Rankin, Congresswoman Jeannette, 329, 341
Reiff, "Aunt Elizabeth," 386
Reiff, Enos, 4
Religion, 2, 49
Religion, and Jane Addams, 80-82
Religion in Social Action, 208
Repplier, Agnes, 324
Republic and Democratic Conventions, 398
Republican Party, 16, 136
Revolutionary War, 2

Review of Hull House activities, 406
Rice, Wallace, 218
Ridpath, author, "Popular History of the World," 98
Riis, 243
Robins, Raymond, 67, 227, 399
Roche, Josephine, 414, 417
Rock River, 8, 11, 12, 23
Rockefeller, John D., 100, 381, 378
Rockford 4, 11, 52
Rockford, Fiftieth Graduation at, 387
Rockford Library, $1,000 gift from Jane Addams, 64
Rockford Seminary (College), 32, 34, 40-64, 42, 60-61
Rockford Seminary Magazine, Jane Addams, editor-in-chief of, 54-55
Rockford Summer School, 126
Rogers, Bernard F., 230
Roosevelt, President Franklin Delano, 309
Roosevelt, Mrs. F. D., 412, 414, 415 (quote)
Roosevelt-Progressive movement, 1912, 271
Roosevelt, Colonel Theodore, 121, 183, 238, 260, 271, 293 (quote), 296; 300, 319, 430, 431, 434
Root, Elihu, 295
Rosenwald Industrial Museum, 182
Rosenwald, Julius, 182, 240
Rosenwalds, the, 100
Ross, 243
Royden, Doctor Maude, quotes, 283, 347-348, 391

Rublee, Mrs. George, 300
Rudowitz, 222
Rush laboratories, 145
Ruskin, John, 75, 89 (quote), 106, 191, 246

Sabin, Florence, 380, 404
Salisbury, Rollin, 49-50, 53
San Quentin Penitentiary, 399
Savanna, 14
Scannon, John Y., 13
School Management Committee, 234, 235, 280
Schumann-Heink, Ernestine, 380, 413
Schurz, Carl, 222
Schwab, 101
Schwimmer, Madam Rosika, 298, 304, 306, 316
Search for house, 92
Second European tour, 85-90
Second Twenty Years at Hull House, The, 299, 360, 365, 376, 377
Seventieth birthday dinner at Bar Harbor, 377-378
Shaw, Bernard, 88, 195
"She Goes in Peace," 410-428
Sherman's, march to the sea, 18
Shuey, John, Illinois pioneer, 11
Sidwell, Annie, 53
Sill, Miss, 41-44, 61, 63, 64
Sill, Miss, portrait of, 41
Simkhovitch, Mrs. Mary Kingsbury, 330
Six Women, 129-150
Skinner, Mark, 13
Small, Professor Albion W., 160, 163, 190, 191, 243
Smith, Alfred E., 381

Smith, Charles Mather, 158
Smith College, gives Jane Addams degree, 239
Smith College, Northampton, 40
Smith, Henry Justin, quote, 99
Smith, Mary Rozet, 80, 115, 129, 146-147, 192, 209, 289, 330 (quote); 345, 353, 354, 389, 467
Socialism, Fabian, 195
Socalism, Marxian, 195
Sociology, American Journal of, 198, 199, 243
Social workers, unknown in 1889, 112
Sonsteby, John J., 228
Southworth, May, 60
Spargo, 243
Spies, 101
Spirit of Youth in the City Streets, The, 178, 241, 243, 249, 253, 254, 255, 258, 321, 359
Stamford, Senator, 23
Starr, Eliza Allen, 45
Starr, Ellen Gates, 45, 46, 52, 55, 66, 76, 84, 86, 88, 96, 103, 110, 113, 122, 129, 130, 132, 206, 243, 354
Starr, Ellen Gates, writes for school magazine, 45
Stead, William T., 188 (quote), 219, 430
Steffens, Lincoln, quote, 188
Stephens, Alexander, 436
Stephenson County, 8
Stevens, Mrs. Alzina P., 157, 187
Stevenson, Sarah Hackett, 163
St. Francis, 426
"St. Louis," 7
St. Louis Post-Dispatch, 426

Stone, Reverend James S., 219
Stowe, Harriet Beecher, 404
Strikes in Chicago: Garment-workers, 240-241; Haymarket Riot, 1886, 156; International Harvester, 1886, 156; Pullman, 164, 165, 166; stockyards, 1880, 156; street-car, 1885, 156
Stuart, Alan Breck, 386
Stuergkh, 307
Suffrage and Progressivism, 202-283
Sullivan, Mark, 306, 310, 311
Sullivan, Mark, quotes from *Our Times,* 316, 318
Sullivan, Timothy, 187
Sumner, Charles, 183
Swifts, the, 100
Swing, Doctor David, 103, 114
Swope, Gerard, quote, 414, 415

Taft, 238
Tanner, Governor, 154
Tarbell, Ida, 325, 384, 385
Tarkington, Booth, 380
Taylor, Doctor Graham, 163, 190, 191 (quotes); 204, 208, 221, 423
Teachers at Rockford College, 60-61
Teachers' Federation, 225, 227, 231, 233, 269
Teachers, fight for better pay, 225-229
Teller, Charlotte, quote, 181-182
Terrell, Mary, 341
Thomas, Doctor Hiram W., 207
Thomas, M. Carey, Prize, 386
Thomas, Theodore, 71

Thompson, Reverend John, 219
Thompson, William Hale, 237
Tillet, Ben, 290
Times, Chicago, 4
Tokugawa, Prince, 417
Tolstoy, 127, 288, 289, 438
Tolstoy, Yasnaya Polyana, visit
    of Jane Addams to, 291
Toynbee, Arnold, 89, 106
Toynbee Hall, 89, 195
Trades-unionism, 196
Trades-unionism for women, in
    London, Jane Addams studies,
    88
Tribune, 223, 226, 233
Trumbull, Representative Ly-
    man, 38
Tuthill, Judge, 143
Twain, Mark, 319, 371
Twenty Years at Hull House, 14
    (quote); 211, 241, 243, 255,
    256, 258, 377
Twose, George Mortimer Ren-
    dell, 212-214

Union League Club, 259, 274
Union League Club, "testimonial
    dinner" to Jane Addams, 465
United Italy movement, 79
Universal Suffrage Association,
    263

Van Dyke, Doctor Henry, 380
Van Valzah, Doctor Thomas, 11
Villard, Oswald Garrison, 414,
    415
Vincent, George, 191, 439
von Bethmann-Hollweg, 306
von Jagow, 306

Waite, Ella, 129
Wald, Lillian D., 331, 341, 404
Waldo, Edmund, 400-401
Wales, Julia G., 298
Wallas, Graham, 195
Walsh, John R., 215, 259
Wards, the, 100
Warner, Maude, 115
Washington, Booker T., 216,
    275
Washington, George, 381
Waugh, Catherine, 60, 61, 263.
    See also McCulloch.
Webbs, the, 88, 194, 290
Webb, Beatrice, quote, 200
Webbs, Beatrice and Sidney,
    193
Webb, Sidney, 195
Weber, Appolonia, 4
Weber, Christian, 4, 5
Weber, Colonel George, 4, 5, 6,
    23
Weber family, 4-5, 23-24
Weber, Harry, 23
Weber, John, 5
Weber, Sarah, 5, 6, 23
Webster, Daniel, 120, 337
Weir Mitchell's Hospital, 69
Welcome, 1
Wells, Harriet, 64
Wendell, Barrett, 381
Wentworths, 100
"What Shall She Do?" 65-90
Whig, 6, 8
White, William Allen, 367, 370,
    372
Whitlock, Brand, 156
Willard, Frances, 205, 404
Willett, Professor Herbert, 207
Wilmarth, Mrs. Mary, 104, 192,
    220

Wilson, Woodrow, 121, 209, 298, 304 (quote), 310, 312, 315, 319, 321, 333, 381, 423
Winslow, 10
Wisconsin, University of, Madison, 39
Withers, Elsie, 2
Woman's Christian Temperance Union, 205, 263
Woman's Club, Hull House, 170
"Woman's Special," 268
Women at the Hague, 299, 309
Women's Catholic League, 185
Women's International League for Peace and Freedom, 214, 344, 414
Women's Medical College, Philadelphia, 34, 68

Women's Peace Party, 298, 317, 326
Wood, Carolena, 341
Woolley, Mary E., 380, 388, 404
Work for children, 178-189
"The Working People's Social Science Club," 161, 162
World War, 178
World Court, 376, 383
Wright Brothers, 399

Yale, University of, 430
Yeomans, Charles, 212
Yeomans, Ned, 212
Yerkes, 226
York, Sergeant Alvin, 381
Young Renny, 420

University of Illinois Press
1325 South Oak Street
Champaign, IL 61820-6903
WWW.PRESS.UILLINOIS.EDU